# UNDERSTANDING
# NEW MEDIA

# UNDERSTANDING NEW MEDIA

## Trends and Issues in Electronic Distribution of Information

*edited by*

**Benjamin M. Compaine**

BALLINGER PUBLISHING COMPANY
Cambridge, Massachusetts
A Subsidiary of Harper & Row, Publishers, Inc.

International Standard Book Number: 0–88410–977–1

Library of Congress Catalog Card Number: 83–25855

Printed in the United States of America

**Library of Congress Cataloging in Publication Data**
Main entry under title:

Understanding new media.

"Research reports and incidental papers previously published by the Program on Information Resources Policy at Harvard University"—Pref.
Bibliography: p.
Includes index.
1. Telecommunication—United States—Addresses, essays, lectures. 2. Mass media—United States—Addresses, essays, lectures. I. Comppaine, Benjamin M.
HE7775.U53     1984          384.'0973          83–25855
ISBN 0–88410–977–1

For Claire Bishop, the calm in the
midst of a perpetual storm

# CONTENTS

# LIST OF FIGURES

# LIST OF TABLES

# FOREWORD

The age of information has enormous significance not only for business, government, and higher education, but for almost everything else as well. What has happened over roughly the last fifty years is that the range and the versatility of information products and services have broadened tremendously. Since the 1930s the computer and other electronic devices have been at the heart of the phenomenon of decreasing capital costs in information businesses. But along with sharp changes in labor and capital costs have come some rather nasty movements and conflicts in functional regulation.

The regulatory bodies now in place reflect an older, calmer time when people knew, for example, what the U.S. mail was or could tell financial services from telecommunication services. Over the last two decades, however, agencies have come into conflict as the turf boundaries of their "regulatees" have blurred and their own missions have become uncertain. One sees such spectacles as the Federal Communications Commission and the Postal Rate Commission suing each other in federal court concerning which has jurisdiction over what in those peculiar areas where electronic movement of information and physical movement of information run into each other.

Like the consequences introduced by canals, railroads, jet aircraft, and so on, the consequences of the information explosion on the shape of the nation, indeed of the world—in response to a combination of technical, political, and social changes even of this magnitude—may not be immediately evident. Meanwhile the consequences of evolution in the information and communications industries are commanding continual attention from numerous congressional committees and federal and state regulatory commissions.

We already know about some massive geopolitical changes brought on by the changes in the last forty years in information technologies. One manifestation is the change in proportion of occupations in the United States. Agricultural occupations peaked around 1880 and have been declining ever since. Industrial occupations peaked during the two world wars. Service occupations have held their own. The slack in the work force left by agricultural and industrial workers has been taken up by information occupations—by teachers, accountants, computer programmers, newspaper reporters, managers—people who do not turn out a sheaf of wheat or a nut or bolt, but sell advice or write books or give orders or otherwise manipulate information.

This phenomenon is by no means limited to the United States. The Organization for Economic Cooperation and Development (OECD) recently studied the advanced industrialized nations. While the United States leads with, as of about 1970, 40 percent of the labor force in information occupations, Canada is not far behind, then the United Kingdom, Sweden, France, Japan, and so on. This trend is common to all the industrialized nations and is not some kind of fluke.

The consequences of the shift in occupations are profound in almost any dimension of life that one might mention. Everybody continues to be fascinated by newspapers and the television media. To do so is resolutely to look backward. Not that these media are unimportant. The newspapers and broadcast television will be with us for a long time. Paper has certain irreducible advantages for which no amount of electronics can substitute. But it is no longer the sole rooster in the barnyard. The Iranian revolution provides an excellent example.

In the olden days we knew a revolution had taken place when an insurrectionist took over the local radio station and announced, "We're in charge." In Iran the revolutionaries did not bother taking over the radio station. They did not bother taking over the television station. The Shah stayed in control of all the traditional media. But that did not matter any more. Why? Khomeini and his people sat in Paris and used direct distance dialing to telephone their friends throughout Iran, using facilities installed in large measure by means of U.S. technology.

What did not travel by telephone was sent by cassettes—cheap little cassettes of a type anybody can buy at Radio Shack—that went by mail or messenger. And the cassettes were duplicated and circulated. What did not go by cassette was transcribed and then Xeroxed. And what did not get Xeroxed got read by the imams in the mosques. One of my friends, an Iranian who was with National Iranian Radio and Television, said to me, "Our movement was for democracy against autocracy by means of Xerocracy."

And the moral is that our intelligence agencies, our media, and so on have still, by and large, not awakened to the fact that there are now "retail media" like Xerox machines, like audiocassettes, like videocassettes. Remember the big hassle when the Saudis tried to get a ban on the showing of "Death of a Princess" in the United States? This documentary has an enormous circulation in Saudi Arabia—an underground circulation—through cassettes. It is viewed there over and over again, and the Saudis can do very little about it; it is hard to control traffic in cassettes. Bootlegged videocassettes likewise spread images of Benigno Aquino's assassination throughout the Philippines. So retail information technologies—from imams in mosques through cassettes through high-technology direct distance telephone dialing—have altered the shape of political insurgency.

Finally, there has been a shift in our conception of literacy, which follows from combined technological and social change. In Western civilization this point can be made by examining the transition in England from the use of memory as the principal form of administrative, judicial, and business record to the use of written records. The definition of literacy changed drastically from something that was the sole province of clerks in monasteries and perhaps of the king and his court. In 1066, Domesday Book was indeed a written record, but it was only for show; it did not serve as a working inventory of King William's resources. By 1307 there were working written inventories of the king's resources, and even serfs were making contracts with one another in writing, not orally: a profound transformation.

Not much happened really for another few hundred years. The next development usually pointed to as a milestone in communications is Gutenberg's invention of movable type. It did have some effects, but they were less profound politically than the invention of the rotary press in the nineteenth century. That invention and, in general, the industrial revolution—the development of the railroads—again transformed our notions of literacy. The impetus for literacy in the nineteenth century came when education, the three Rs, was regarded as not a matter only for the elite, but as a way of increasing the productivity of the masses. This was done, as observers noted, at the risk of considerable social unrest, often attributed to the rise in literacy. The parallel between the hand wringing over television today and the hand wringing over the penny dreadfuls, the mass press, and even novels in the nineteenth century is fascinating but often overlooked.

What, in modern terms, is a reasonable definition of literacy? A letter from a friend who at one time was a member of Harvard's Board of Overseers says he took every opportunity to insist that it was now as much of a sin to graduate a person from college without at least elementary knowledge of computers as it was to send him out in the world without an adequate knowledge of English. That is a bit too narrowly put, but if computers are thought of as a metaphor for all modern information resources, it is on mark.

The development of these alternate technologies likely will not kill off today's familiar media, but rather transform them to some other shape. The precedent is the radio industry today. In the 1950s, when television finally took off, everybody predicted that the radio industry would die. It is alive and well and stronger than ever today, at least in name. But what lies behind the name is something profoundly different from what it was in the 1940s. The industry has survived; the stockholders have felt no pain; the management is fat and happy. But where radio once was the mass medium of choice, radio is today a specialized medium—fragmented, addressing particular audiences—but profitable doing that. The print media and distribution of information in other forms, such as theatrical film, will experience discomfort—they cannot help doing so—if some significant portion of their revenue base is eroded. They will be transformed in some way, but they will survive.

Anthony G. Oettinger
Chairman, Program on Information
Resources Policy
Harvard University

# PREFACE

## THE PROGRAM ON INFORMATION RESOURCES POLICY

This book is a collection of research reports and incidental papers previously published by the Program on Information Resources Policy at Harvard University. This Program has a unique method of operation, aimed at providing research for policymakers that is different from other, similar-sounding research efforts. For that reason, a short description of the goals and methods of the Program will help put this work in context.

To accomplish its research mission, the Program was established in 1972 with a unique funding mechanism. Because it would be dealing in areas of high stakes and corporate and political self-interest, it set out to establish a broad base of financial support. (A list of contributors current to publication of this book is provided in Appendix A.) The Program made a conscious effort to have participants from all segments of the information business, as well as organizations that are consumers of information. Competing industries and competitors within industries are represented. The Program does no proprietary research for these contributors nor for anyone else. All the research in this book, as well as the Program's other publications, was undertaken on its own initiative and on its own terms. None was paid for exclusively by any vested interest in the issues.

To ensure the accuracy of the facts, most of the studies in this book have undergone the Program's review process. This involves sending drafts of works in progress to knowledgeable reviewers at the organizations who contribute to the Program as well as to others who can lend some specific expertise. The Program asks these reviewers if the paper has the facts right, if it is asking the right questions, if it has identified issues, and if it has correctly represented the interest of the contending parties. This process is intended to ensure accuracy as well as objectivity. It also means that even papers written by authors who work for an organization with a stake in the outcome of some issue can be reviewed by opposing stakeholders. The result is typically a report to which all parties can stipulate to the facts, though ultimately with varying interpretation of what the facts mean. Some of the chapters in this volume are "incidental papers." In this case, they were not reviewed externally, but are included because of their general interest and applicability. These chapters are identified, as are those which are reviewed research papers.

## Information as a Resource

The Program's premise at its inception was the early observation that the traditional telephone business was becoming increasingly intertwined with the computer world. As the former was a highly regulated industry and the latter was young, entrepreneurial and quite unregulated, there was going to be a period of confusion and destabilization both in corporate executive suites and in public policy. Moreover, the Program foresaw that the stakes in the outcome of this merging of computer and telecommunications (or "compunications") technologies were greater than for each of those two industries alone. Compunications was part of an infrastructure that included physical delivery of goods, via the U.S. Postal Service and other private carriers. In addition, numerous other industries, the media among them, had a stake in the outcome of the regulatory battles that could present these industries with new opportunities as well as threats to their existing franchises.

At an even more global level, the Program's underlying theology is that the stakes in the broadly described information business touch on nearly all business and government organizations. Information has always been a resource, but only recently have we seen the first glimmers of understanding of information in the same context as economists describe materials or energy as resources. Information is a resource of similar magnitude. Increasingly, information is being substituted for these other resources. Today microprocessors in automobile engines improve fuel efficiency, thus, exchanging information for energy. Financial institutions are becoming more conscious that information—on interest rates, gold prices, crop size, political instability around the world—is their real raw material. Information resources include expenditures on capital equipment, such as a word processor, or labor, such as a researcher.

In translating information as a resource into a working agenda, the Program has started by looking at the issues facing those who are in the information business. *Understanding New Media* is a piece of that agenda.

An exhaustive list of acknowledgments for those who have aided with this book would include the dozens of reviewers of the individual chapters as well as the many who have provided guidance and insights. They will therefore go unnamed here, but their assistance over the years has been crucial to the Program's goal of accuracy and objectivity. I also want to thank Carol Franco, senior editor at Ballinger, for her encouragement and patience in moving this project along.

Benjamin M. Compaine
Cambridge, Massachusetts
October 1983

# 1 INTRODUCTION

*Benjamin M. Compaine*

As all the various industries that provide information services use more and more of the same communications and computer technology, the traditional distinctions among the communications media are lessening. W. Bradford Wiley, chairman of book publishers John Wiley & Sons, has observed that the real enterprise of publishing is ideas and information.

This notion is at the center of understanding the new media. All media are in the business of ideas, information, and entertainment. The media have relied on available technology to supply those services. Each of today's media was at one time each new: the book did not spring full blown with Gutenberg's press. Rather, it evolved from scrolls and folios. The newspaper as we now know it came into being centuries after Gutenberg. For a considerable period in the early days of broadcast radio, that technology suffered through an identity crisis because it was uncertain what sort of content was best suited for radio. Indeed, today's radio programming bears little resemblance to the radio programming in the days before television.

The research in this book was designed to help public policymakers and corporate planners concerned with the media better understand the arena, jungle environment (pick your metaphor) in which they operate.

1

This book seeks to identify the questions, problems, and most of all the issues[1] that face strategic planners and policymakers through the end of the 1980s and beyond. It identifies the participants and the stakes involved. This is crucial because the universe of players in the media has expanded from the traditional publishing and broadcasting companies to others, such as financial service businesses, retailers, and telecommunications carriers. The heart of this volume is a discussion of the forces and trends relevant to policymakers. It is in fulfilling this objective that technological, political, economic, and other factors are introduced. Finally, in broad strokes this volume describes many of the policy options available and their potential consequences, for example, in Robert Pepper's work on cable and telephone competition for nonvideo business.

Neither remedies nor solutions are provided herein. Nor are there forecasts or predictions of market share, penetration of some technology or another (except where an author is citing someone else's predictions), or advocacy of one policy option over another. There is speculation on what might happen in response to some event or policy as a means of stimulating discussion or providing examples, rather than as a blueprint for the future.

This book, then, is intended to help students, policymakers, planners, and others improve their understanding of what is going on out there in the world of traditional and evolving media.

## WHAT *IS* HAPPENING TO THE MEDIA?

What makes understanding media today more difficult than in the past is the rapidly blurring distinction, not in the content, but among the technologies that convey the content. Today an image on a television screen may be there because it was sent over the air. And it may have been sent into the air by any number of means—from a broadcast tower using very high frequency (VHF), ultra high frequency (UHF), microwave frequencies, or directly from an earth-circling satellite using heretofore more exotic frequencies. Or the picture may be appearing via a cable into the set, not unlike the cable that used to come down from the antenna on the roof, but now from a master antenna that serves hundreds or thousands of homes. The cable operator in turn gets the signals from the same sources available to the household: over the air, including from satellites. The TV picture could also be created by a magnetic tape or videodisc, being played in an appropriate machine in the consumer's home. It all looks the same to the viewer.

The blurring of distinctions gets more involved. The picture on the TV set may not be a conventional video image at all. Instead it might consist of colored dots in the shape of letters, numbers, or aggregated into pictures. It would then be something to read or study, instead of simply to watch. And these images could get onto the television set not only via any of the means just noted, but also via a rather conventional telephone line. They may also have been stored on a magnetic disk or etched into an integrated circuit for retrieval by a home computer.

All of this—and perhaps more—is displayed on a familiar television set. Thus the format of all these different types of transmission is identical: video. But there is more to this complexity. There are some very different formats that use the same transmission mechanisms. Several newspapers, including *The Wall Street Journal, USA Today,* and *The New York Times,* use the same satellites as the cable television programmers to send facsimiles of their pages to plants around the country for use in making up plates for printing national editions of these newspapers. While the end product, the printed newspaper, may look familiar to customers, it is in fact as much a product of new technology as is the more glamorous and heralded video and computer gadgetry.

The newspaper, and indeed magazines and books, have substantially incorporated electronic technology in every production step, including controls on some printing presses. Only the press itself and ultimate physical distribution involve mechanical processes. The content of these print products is largely created using computer terminals in all but the final production stages. This chapter, for example, was written using an Apple II + computer and a word processing program. It was possible (though not done in this case) for the words stored magnetically on a floppy disk to have been transmitted via telephone lines to the computer of the publisher, where it could be edited on a video screen and then stored until time for typesetting. At many magazines and virtually all daily newspapers, the entire production process, from creation of an article or advertisement to the final printing plate, is handled electronically. Even page design and makeup increasingly use computers. There is no paper in the process until the final, fully composed magazine or newspaper pages are created by computer-driven typesetting machines.

The fuzzy boundaries among heretofore distinct media so far have meant more to the suppliers of content than to the consumers. And among consumers, this merging has probably been less visible to at-home users than to business and institutional users. Publishers have a large stake in technology that will help lower their production costs and enable them to reach new audiences. Film studies have a major interest in how their productions can be distributed and at what prices. On the other hand, the customer who plunks down 25 cents for the daily newspaper does not really care about the production process per se. While the economics and even regulation of the product may in fact be reflected in its prices or content, they are invisible to most end users.

There are numerous analogies. With the exception of automobile buffs, the typical motorist is largely unconcerned with what is under the hood, so long as it works reasonably well. Similarly, when most people pick up the telephone to call across the country, they are unaware of the mechanisms for completing that call. It may have gone through an electromechanical switch or a digital switch; it may be transmitted by land lines, microwave, or via satellite. In both of these examples, the technology and other factors do bear on performance, costs, and price, but they are not nearly as salient for the user as for the supplier. (Large, institutional users do pay more attention to these details, whether in making automobile fleet purchases or in evaluating telephone services.)

## THE INFORMATION REVOLUTION?

All the preceding comments are in fact a prologue to the subject of the so-called information revolution. The topic has moved from the academic literature to the trade press and now to popular culture. It is raised as an issue in prophecies of the benefits of the wired nation and the nightmares of Big Brother. It is seen in expectations for 104 channels of cable to every home and a microcomputer in every bedroom. Depending on what day it is, the information revolution threatens the end of individual privacy or could be the salvation from an energy crunch.

Is there anything *revolutionary* in all of this? If there is, what is it? When did the revolution start? When will it be over? What will be the impact on culture and society? The questions roll smoothly off the tongue. They are amenable to neither easy nor definitive answers, although much ink has been and will be spread on paper trying to answer them.

In the sense it is applied to information, according to dictionary definition *revolution* means "a sudden, radical, or complete change." A literal interpretation of this description of revolution would make it an inappropriate label for the phenomenon we are experiencing. The application of computer, satellite, and other technology is not sudden ("happening or coming unexpectedly"), or radical (the ink still rubs off the newsprint and "I Love Lucy" reruns look the same whether transmitted via cable or broadcast), or complete (mail volume continues to increase by billions of pieces annually). Moreover, if something revolutionary were happening, we could not be leisurely writing books about it.

To be sure, there are aspects of the information business that are or seem to be changing rapidly. The price of microcomputers is falling so quickly that price lists arc out of date as fast as they are printed (perhaps they should be computer-generated). In their frenzy to take advantage of potential business opportunities or protect their established franchises, companies are scrambling to start new ventures or team up with others, thus presenting the appearance of ferment and activity. And in fits and starts, some of these changes have been creeping into the mainstream. The number of households that have access to cable television has passed 60 percent, with 35 percent subscribing in 1983. Getting to this level took about thirty years, however, so the development is hardly revolutionary. The first truly residential electronic text retrieval service was rolled out for a few thousand households in southern Florida in 1983, at a cost to users of more than $300 annually, after an investment of at least $600 and perhaps twice that. (A similar service in England was offered in 1980 and had barely reached 10,000 residential users three years later.) Perhaps that is progress, but it is hardly revolutionary.

The other word in "information revolution" is also used as part of another label, the "information age." Information means many things to different people. Information could include all raw data and even electronic bits in computer jargon. It could be restricted only to data that is organized in some usable fashion for humans, as opposed to computers or other machines. While most observers would probably agree that information includes a sales report or a news report, the term gets progressively more slippery if applied to a novel, an advertisement, to a crossword puzzle, to "The Dukes of Hazzard" television show, to a rock record, and to body language. Furthermore, to what extent is it necessary to make the distinction between information and knowledge?

Depending on where one draws the line on what is included as information, the technology that permits immediate access to an electronic data base of legal records might qualify as part of someone's information revolution, while a similar technology that gave users access to video games would not. Should earth satellites that allow corporations to bypass AT&T long-distance facilities for their computer-to-computer data exchange be evaluated differently from similar satellite technology that permits Home Box Office to send "Rocky III" to cable systems around the United States?

Thus it seems that although a case can be made for labels such as "information revolution," such terms alone turn out to be glib shorthand, convenient for attention-getting headlines. This is reinforced by the notion that *information*—substance or content in general—is not really what the changing technology is all about. If anything, we should be using more cumbersome labels such as the "information-*processing* revolution." Content is not changing. The way in which it is stored, processed, and transmitted is undergoing modification. In some cases this means the ability to use this content in new ways, such as when a spread-sheet computer program allows manipulation of numbers that was not feasible previously, or when a lawyer is able to research a vast data base of cases in a fraction of the time it would have taken before cheap computers and associated telecommunications. In other cases it means greater accessibility to content, such as renting a videocassette of a motion picture for viewing at one's own convenience at home instead of going out to the movie theater. These are significant developments. They are changes, however, in process as opposed to content or substance.

## TECHNOLOGY AND OTHER FORCES

In his book *Forecasting the Telephone,* Ithiel de Sola Pool looked at the many predictions by the contemporaries of the fledgling telephone business about how telephony would be used.[2] His thesis is that the least accurate predictions were made by those prognosticators who focused solely on the technology itself. Conversely, those who turned out to be most accurate were those who placed the technology in a context of market analysis, comparing the cost and demand for the telephone to the alternatives. Technology, after all, not only has consequences, but its adoption is often a function of other factors. Sometimes the good or service made possible by some technology does not get produced or adopted because it requires first the development of other technologies. Other times, political or institutional barriers are in the way. In some cases there is social or cultural resistance to the change the technology makes possible. Often several of these factors are acting simultaneously. Some examples follow:

• The development and adoption of the steam-driven rotary press is often given credit as the technological force that led to the penny newspaper in the United States. This was only part of the picture. As early as 1804, the U.S. Congress helped create the economic climate for a popular press by repealing the import duty on rags. Rags were the primary raw material for paper and the United States imported large quantities. Knowledge of the possibility of the manufacture of paper from wood pulp existed, but the existence of cheaper rag paper meant there was no incentive to work on the wood pulp process.

Just about the time the steam-driven press provided new economies of scale in newspaper printing, a seemingly unrelated event in England threatened to stunt the potential of this improved technology. In 1836 the British government greatly reduced, then later eliminated, its tax on paper. As a result mass-circulation newspapers surged in England, driving up the demand for paper and hence for rags. Soon the price of newspapers was escalating, reversing the trend made possible by the steam-driven press.[3] At this point there were economic incentives to develop the technology for wood-pulp-based paper. Once in place, the new, cheaper paper helped launch a second era of newspaper circulation growth, as newspaper prices fell while the number of pages printed doubled.

• There are pitfalls in making a straight-line projection based solely on the implication of some technology. For example, imagine the automobile at the turn of the century. The roads it ran on were mostly rutted paths used by horse-drawn carriages. Mechanics were few. Gasoline was relatively expensive and not widely available. The future of the automobile would look limited indeed if its use was projected on the infrastructure of the time. The widespread use of the automobile, generally credited to Ford's innovative mass-production line, was also made possible by technological developments in road building and oil refining and in government policies leading to the construction of highways designed for automobiles.

• A more recent example has been the long gestation period of the cable television business. Cable was initiated in the late 1940s as a means of providing television signals to communities that could otherwise get no, or only poor off-the-air signals. But the growth of cable proceeded far slower than the prediction of some of its early boosters, in large measure because the Federal Communications Commission (FCC), charged by law with regulating broadcasting and telecommunications common carriers, stepped in in 1962 with the first of a series of rulings that handcuffed cable operators to the advantage of established broadcasting industry interests.[4] Then in the mid-1970s a confluence of regulatory and technological factors spurred the moribund industry. First the courts and then the FCC began undoing many of the regulations that had limited the activities of cable operators. In 1975 Time Inc., owner of the Home Box Office pay-television channel, began transmitting its movies via a communications satellite, instead of by more expensive land-based conduits, including postal delivery of videocassettes to cable operators. Another FCC decision, deregulating the requirements for the antennas needed to receive satellite-transmitted programs, helped cut the cost of installing such an antenna from $100,000 to $5,000. This added to the incentives of cable operators to have antennas to receive programming from more than one satellite.

The printing press and paper, the automobile, and cable television are all among historical examples of the relationship between a product or service made possible by a particularly visible piece of technology on the one hand, and other technologies, as well as political, economic, and cultural factors, on the other hand.

In the 1980s another set of products and services may affect the traditional media industry. They are collectively referred to as the "new media" and are sometimes called the "new information technology." But the viability of an actual service in the marketplace is not determined by the technology itself. Regardless of the bells and whistles of some technology, the adoption of a product or service depends on whether there is a large enough group of customers willing to pay the price. And this in turn depends on their needs and the existing offerings in the marketplace.

## Marketing the "New Media"

Thus while new services such as videotex for the home (see Chapter 11), have been slow to catch on in Great Britain and are barely entering the marketplace in the United States and Canada, electronic text services for segments of the business community are more solidly entrenched. One of the apparently more successful is the Lexis data base of Mead Data Central, paradoxically a subsidiary of a large paper manufacturer. Lexis has on record all decisions of the federal and state courts, as well as countless codes and other material that lawyers need as they prepare briefs or engage in other legal digging. A library of legal tomes can be largely, or totally, replaced by a computer terminal and telephone line. The service is easy to use for those who are not information specialists. But the success of Lexis is due as much to the billing system in the legal profession as to the technology that makes it possible. Lawyers typically bill clients directly for their time and out-of-pocket expenses. Thus the $100 per hour or so that Lexis costs to use can be passed on to the client. Moreover, it might be saving the client money, because its use can save hours or days of research by lawyers or researchers.

Consumers at home, on the other hand, pay for information out of their own pockets. Based on cost to the user alone, an electronic information service that hopes to replace the daily newspaper would have to cost the consumer just 25 cents for unlimited time, including the cost of the phone call or cable hook-up. This means that advertisers must foot much of the bill, just as they do with newspapers, magazines, and television. Alternately, electronic information services could justify a higher price if they provide substantially greater perceived *value* to users.

The media company that wants to engage in services using newly arriving technology also may find itself in unfamiliar territory. A newspaper company knows well the intricacies of selling advertising, delivering newspapers, adjusting newsprint supply, and dealing with various unions. Publishers of all sorts are less familiar with the arcane areas of electronic delivery technology and the regulation of industries in this area. Publishers, and broadcasters as well, understand the components of price setting: Price is a function of cost plus value and the nature of competition. Once they start using the telephone network, they leave behind much familiar territory for the world of tariffed prices, which may or may not bear much relationship to either true cost or demand.[5] Their ability to offer services may depend on convincing politically motivated state public utility commissioners that the local telephone companies should be permitted to offer some needed service (a billing service or multiplexed lines to households, say) at a rate that makes it worthwhile for the telephone company to expend capital to provide this service. And having succeeded in one state, they might have to repeat the process in forty-nine others, with varying results. Cable regulation, with some state and general local jurisdiction, has similar, though less established, pitfalls.

One of the most difficult areas to figure out in attempts to understand the market for new products involving newer technologies is the sociocultural dynamic. That is, what barriers—or proclivities—exist in society to the adoption of the technologically driven offerings? Will bank customers give up live tellers for machines? Will shoppers abandon the shopping mall for the electronic mall? Will office workers exchange their commuting for at-home computing? Can a video display terminal (VDT) substitute for the feel of ink on paper? And for each of these wills, there is also a when and an under-what-circumstance.

Some early anecdotal evidence suggests variations both economic and generational variance to how these questions can be answered. Automatic teller machines (ATMs) have proliferated in the 1980s, after a hesitant start. For the most part banks have given customers the option of using the ATMs or seeing a live teller. One segment of the population seems to find doing business with a machine abhorrent, insisting that it is dehumanizing and refusing to use ATMs. The rest of the universe finds the machines functional and often an improvement.

But the cost of providing bricks-and-mortar banks and live tellers has convinced many in the banking business that the live teller available for routine transactions may be going the way of the milkman. Consumers who wish to persist in the luxury will have to pay for it, either in the form of a charge for each transaction or by keeping a large balance in an account. In 1983 the largest bank in the United States, Citibank, required a minimum balance of $5,000 to qualify for a real teller without a surcharge at some branches. Suddenly many customers who would never use an ATM started queuing up the machine rather than pay the price. Citibank rescinded the policy under competitive pressure and some unfavorable media coverage. However, even competing bankers agreed that Citibank acted prematurely and undiplomatically, not irrationally. But the point was made: Behavioral patterns can be changed when economic stakes are involved.

In the future we may see similar behavior relating to the substitution of electronic print for newspapers or books. At about $6.00 monthly for the daily newspaper, consumers get unlimited time with this vast "data base." An electronic version of the newspaper, at the $26.00 monthly that Knight-Ridder says a customer is likely to spend on its Viewtron service, seems quite expensive in relation. Just as in banking, however, the day may soon dawn when the continuing drop in computer costs and improvements in telecommunications speed will intersect with the trend of more expensive newsprint and physical delivery of the newspaper. At that point the price of the printed product may be greater than the electronically delivered version. Economic self-interest may result in behavioral change.

Video games and widespread use of microcomputers by children in schools and at home may hasten the cultural change that will take place in society's attitude toward print. Today's children are likely to be a generation at ease with the computer keyboard or joystick, who will use the computer daily for both entertainment and more serious pursuit of information, just as adults today buy a newspaper for both news and entertainment.

## STRUCTURE OF THE BOOK

Part I of *Understanding New Media* provides an overview of the information industry in general and the media arena in particular. The map of the information business, presented in Chapter 2, is the result of the collaboration of many but the brain child of John McLaughlin and it has proven to be a useful tool. It provides a workable context for the many pieces of the information business, helping to find a place for apples (e.g., the postal service) and oranges (e.g., newspapers), as well as for other fruits, vegetables, fish, fowl, and meat in the information supermarket. The map can be used for drawing regulatory boundaries and for looking at corporate strategy, as well as for identifying areas of threats to existing business.

The blurring of boundaries among the traditional media suggested a need to rethink the labels such as newspaper, television, or magazine we use for the media. Chapter 3, "Content, Process, and Format," suggests an alternate framework for characterizing the media.

"Shifting Boundaries in the Information Marketplace," Chapter 4, was prepared for the American Library Association's colloquium, "An Information Agenda for the '80s." It describes the need for each of the traditional pieces of this business to redefine its role in view of fundamental policy questions raised, including: Who will pay? Who will have access? Who will profit? How will conflicts be resolved?

Part II looks at forces and trends in the distribution of information. Chapter 5, "Electronic Distribution of Information to the Consumer and Low-Volume Institutional Market," looks at alternatives to physical distribution of information (via the U.S. Postal Service, for example) or to electronic processes in which the supplier controls speed or access time (as in conventional broadcasting). Numerous firms are experimenting with a variety of nontraditional information services, some under the label of videotex (note no final "t") or teletext. What many of these ventures have in common is their ability to deliver information electronically, relying on compunications bypassing conventional channels of distribution for this information.

Although cable television has been implemented initially as an alternative to broadcast transmission, it is being considered increasingly as an alternative method for transmitting data and even voice. In long-distance services, AT&T is facing increased competition from newer carriers. At the local level of the operating telephone companies, several technologies are emerging that may compete for tying telecommunications customers together in the local loop as well as into the long-distance network. Cable television is one of these emerging technologies. In Chapter 6, Robert Pepper looks at the regulatory pressures both encouraging and restraining cable companies interested in expanding into the nontelevision sector of information-transmission services.

Richard Rosenbloom, of the Harvard Business School, asks, "Will the day soon come when the broadcasting transmitter and its tall tower are found only in the Smithsonian Institution?" In Chapter 7, "The Continuing Revolution in Communication Technology: Implications for the Broadcasting Business," he suggests that two general strategies may help broadcasters who are faced with technological change: first, to maintain a "customer-orientation" and second, "to maintain an awareness of impending technological developments."

The section ends with an assessment by Christine Urban of "Factors Influencing Media Consumption." She reviews the literature on consumer behavior toward traditional mass media, such as uses and gratifications, with an eye toward the questions that will have to be addressed to understand consumer attitude in a new media environment. She asks what values the new media will bring to consumers. Who will buy the new media and for what purpose? Are the new media to be added to or substituted for existing media processes? Finally, she summarizes the behavioral responses to traditional media that could be applied to newer media formats.

Part III includes three chapters that look at some of the strategic implications of the change in media processes and formats. John Le-Gates's chapter, "Changes in the Information Industries: Strategic Implications for Newspapers," grew out of a presentation he made to the directors of the American Newspaper Publishers Association in 1980. This was during a period when that group undertook an active lobbying effort in Congress, aimed not at a bill focused on the newspaper industry but at one whose intended thrust was telephone industry deregulation. LeGates suggests that in planning for the changes facing them, newspapers can capitalize on their real strength as providers of content, while contracting out their relative weaknesses in delivery.

In "The First Amendment Meets the Second Revolution," William Read examines the need to reassess the two legal decisions that form the basis of contemporary case law regarding broadcast and print media (the *Miami Herald* and *Red Lion* cases). The issue arises because the Gutenberg revolution, which created the foundation for the "press clause" of the First Amendment, is giving way to a different foundation of mass communication. Moreover the boundaries are blurring not only between print and broadcasting, but also between the institutional media and other modern communicators, in particular corporations not specifically in the media business. For example, the spreading use of computerized mailing lists by corporations illustrates the ability to engage in mass public communication by businesses other than those typically thought of as being media companies.

The section concludes with a short article that originally appeared in *Adweek,* a magazine for the advertising trade. "Newspapers and Videotex: Threats or Opportunities?" briefly summarizes the current state of videotex in the United States and the extent of involvement by traditional newspaper firms. It also notes some of the potential regulatory, political, technological, and sociological problems that stand between the present and a mass-audience videotex business.

The final part of the book includes a chapter on "The New Literacy." Originally published as an article in the journal *Daedalus,* this chapter deals with the notion that all this technological change in information processing makes it likely that society is on the verge of a new step in the evolution of its concept of literacy. Early indicators of the change are the 7 million people in the work force who use video display screens attached to computers for reading and interacting with information; the rapid proliferation and use of video games at home and in arcades, and the growing application of personal computers at home and in the schools; and the trend of higher costs for paper and physical delivery contrasted to growing availability and lower costs for electronic delivery of information. Thus the skills required to store, retrieve, and manipulate information using a computer are becoming increasingly requisite proficiencies to be added to the existing bundle of skills we call literacy.

The "Final Thoughts" of the last chapter of the book raise some of the many questions that remain unanswered about the changing shape of the media and the media business. Suggested there are some of the issues that will be faced by public policymakers as well as by corporate strategists, by those who work in media businesses, and indeed by all consumers of information products and services, as individuals or as institutions.

## NOTES

1.    The terms *question, problem,* and *issue* are often used glibly and interchangeably. For those who set research priorities, however, questions alone are the least worthwhile, because it makes no sense to investigate questions if no one really cares about the answers. A question in which there is some stake assumes the higher status of a problem. The question "Is the moon made of green cheese?" is not of much research concern until it becomes important for an impending landing on the moon. It becomes an issue only when there are conflicting positions. If all parties agree that indeed the moon is made of green cheese and that makes a landing impossible, there is no issue. As soon as an involved party demurs—"We agree it is cheese, but we are confident we can land anyway"—there is an issue.

2.    Ithiel de Sola Pool, *Forecasting the Telephone: A Retrospective Technology Assessment of the Telephone,* (Norwood, N.J.: Ablex, 1983).

3.   Ithiel de Sola Pool, *Technologies of Freedom* (Cambridge, Mass: Belknap Press of Harvard University Press, 1983), p. 19, n. 27.

4.   Christopher H. Sterling, "Cable and Pay Television," in Benjamin M. Compaine et al. *Who Owns the Media? Concentration of Ownership in the Mass Communications Industry,* 2nd ed. (White Plains, N.Y.: Knowledge Industry Publications, 1982), pp. 374–377.

5.   Anthony G. Oettinger and Carol L. Weinhaus, *The Telecommunications Industry: An Eye to the Future,* Program on Information Resources Policy, Harvard University, Cambridge, Mass., 1983. Draft.

# CREATING A FRAMEWORK

# 2 MAPPING THE INFORMATION BUSINESS

*John F. McLaughlin,* with
*Anne E. Birinyi*

Since its inception in 1972, the Program on Information Resources Policy at Harvard University has been monitoring and analyzing developments in a variety of fields that can be called, loosely, the "information industries." Many of the Program's research projects have focused upon developments within a specific traditional information industry (broadcasting, telephone, cable TV), yet we have continually emphasized the interactions among the different information technologies, markets, and types of government intervention. We speak frequently, therefore, about merging technologies ("compuni cations" and "videotex"), and new conflicts among traditional industries. Is "electronic mail" something that "belongs" to the U.S. Postal Service, the electronics industry, telecommunications common carriers, or someone else? Is it regulated by the Federal Communications Commission (FCC), the Postal Rate Commission, both, or neither?

Defining the nature and scope of the information industries, a field marked by fuzziness and turmoil, has been a continuing problem for our Program, as for policymakers and the information industries themselves. This chapter presents a framework for viewing the evolving structure of the information business.

## DRAWING THE INFORMATION
## BUSINESS MAP

Information comes in many forms. It includes news, historical statistics, financial transactions, reference materials, advertising, entertainment, and corporate operating data. Different groups define "information" differently, but for our purposes we have chosen to define it in the broadest sense.

The companies and government agencies that constitute the information business are diverse, with information as their common denominator. Some may exist to acquire information, others to package, store, process, transmit, or distribute it. Some information companies handle information as a service, while others produce and market products to allow companies or individuals to collect, process, or distribute their own information. Many companies are involved in a wide mix of these functions.

Figure 2–1 is our basic map of the information business. On it we have noted more than eighty products and services. These products and services constitute the information business.

The axes of the map are *services* and *products* (top and bottom, or north-south) and *content* and *conduit* (right and left, or east-west). The products-services axis was chosen largely because companies and economists traditionally have viewed industrial activity in this manner. Displaying corporate activities along this axis helps highlight some facets of vertical integration. It also facilitates display of the fact that traditional notions of "product" and "service" may be blurring into a middle ground of "systems," whereby customers mix and match products and services in order to achieve a desired end. Progress along this axis from the product end to the service end also may be viewed as increasing customer dependence upon supplying institutions.

The conduit-content axis was chosen because it helps distinguish between companies that traditionally have viewed themselves as producers of information, such as publishers, and those that provide means for recording information and transmitting it (recognizing, of course, the problem involved in trying to differentiate between "processing," "transmitting," etc.). Progressing along the axis from the conduit end means increasing information value-added—or, in Marshall McLuhan's terms, from moving from medium to message.

## Figure 2-1.   A Map of the Information Business.

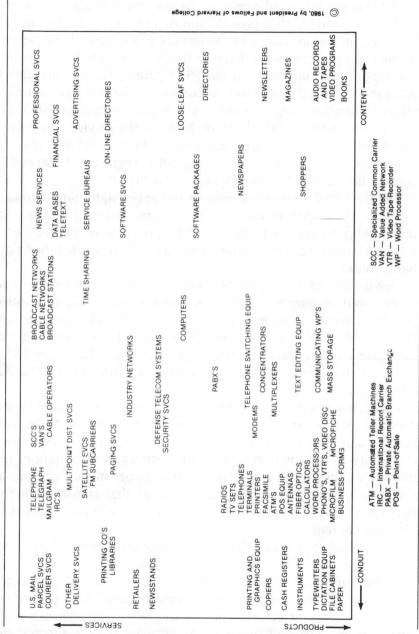

In the upper left-hand corner of the map are activities such as mail and parcel delivery that provide almost pure conduit services. The telecommunications common carriers are placed slightly to the right of mail and parcel services. Because of the nature of the systems that telecommunications common carriers operate, the carriers may be more involved in the information content of the message, at least in terms of duration, entry protocols, and urgency of transmission. Farther to the right are broadcasters, high on the service axis because they have no physical product and midway between content and conduit because of their role of providing both program material and the system that distributes the program material.

"Professional services" appear in the upper right-hand corner of the map. The services are sold by writers, artists, scientists, and others who generate information. The products of their efforts—books, records, television programs—are shown in the lower right-hand corner.

Newspapers and shoppers are shown to the left of books, newsletters, and magazines. Their placement is based on the notion, perhaps arbitrary, that *most* newspapers traditionally have operated their own distribution system (conduit), while the publishers of *most* newsletters and magazines have relied upon the U.S. Postal Service or other middlemen (jobbers, retailers, newsstands) to distribute their product.

In the lower left-hand corner we have simple stand-alone (dumb) products such as typewriters, paper, and filing cabinets. As information value is added to these products, by adding either intelligence or the ability to communicate with other sources of information, they migrate rightward. Thus a blank piece of paper might be dumb but the addition of lines and column headings that transform it to a business form represents an addition of information that shapes the ultimate content.

This mapping scheme exhibits some shortcomings:

1. The products-services approach introduces a substantial measure of subjectivity into the mapping process. As a general rule we have tried to place items on the map from the viewpoint of a customer, but different customers could place the same item differently on a products-services axis. Likewise providers and customers might place things differently. This may indeed be a shortcoming of the mapping technique. It accurately represents some of the structural ambiguities of the information business, however.

2. Like geographical maps, this map suffers from its two-dimensional nature. For visual clarity some items have been inserted above, below or next to other items where conceptually they probably should be overlapping each other vertically and/or horizontally. Similarly the amount of information that can be conveyed is limited. Using the analogy to geographical maps again, we conceivably could display terms such as "Computers," "Mail," or "Telephone" in large, heavy type and "FM Sub-carriers" and "Newsletters" in small type in order to differentiate the relative annual sales of such products and services.

3. Numerous technologies or components are integral parts of the information business but not amenable to our concept. Semiconductors, optical character recognition devices, and electric power, for example, are integral to many of the items shown. We excluded these items from the map but included paper and fiber optics. Frequently it is difficult to determine whether something is a component, a technology, or an end product.

4. Inclusion and placement of a particular item may depend upon the level of aggregation chosen. For simplicity, for example, we handled "financial services" as a single entry on the basic map (Figure 2–2). As suggested by Figure 2–3, further disaggregation of financial services by specific products or services might cause substantial relocations in any direction. Similarly, while we displayed "newspapers" as a single item in the southeast quadrant (product content), this placement is based upon some notions of newspapers as we have known them in the 1900s. If we think of newspapers as packages of information products and services, we might place some pieces of those packages closer to books, some closer to professional services. Despite the foregoing limitations, the map of the information business appears to be a useful tool for looking at some selected aspects of the subject.

## THE EVOLUTION OF THE INFORMATION BUSINESS

In recent years increasing attention has been devoted to the information business. Academics have written of the "information economy," the "postindustrial society," and the "information age."[1] In their advertisements corporations proclaim themselves as

**Figure 2-2.   Financial Services.**

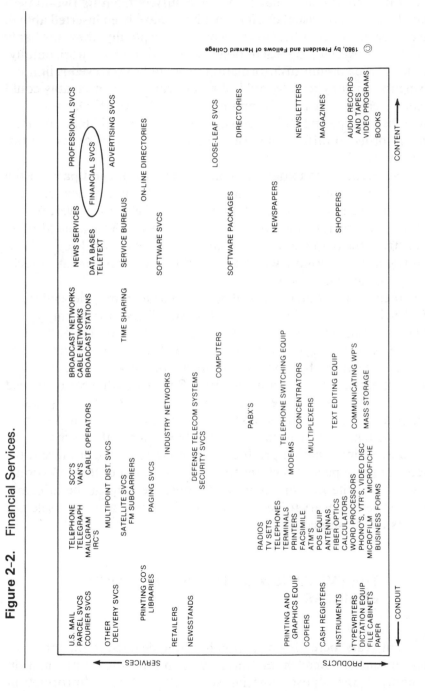

**Figure 2-3.**   Specific Financial Services.

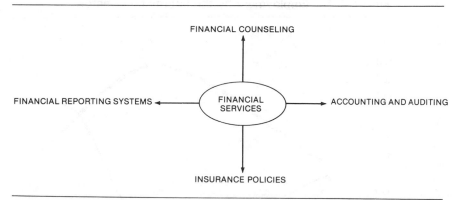

the "knowledge business," "the informationist," or even "The Source."[2] National governments debate "national information policies," and international organizations debate "the free flow of information" and "the new world information order."[3]

The growing importance of the information business is suggested by Figure 2-4, which shows the changing nature of U.S. employment since 1860. In Figure 2-5, we have used our mapping scheme to suggest the nature of the information business in 1780. Some important institutions might be missing from this version (the town crier, the coffeehouse, or tavern), but the overall impression is that information activities once occupied the corners of our map. The term *newsletters*, depicted in Figure 2-5, is used to denote a group of publications that might also be categorized as newspapers, magazines, shoppers, and directories. Some individuals or companies engaged in both vertical and horizontal integration of economic enterprises during this period. Thus Benjamin Franklin worked as a writer, produced books, newspapers, and magazines, developed printing equipment, and sold printing services while serving as postmaster general of the colonies. Perhaps Franklin would have placed himself in the middle of our map and labeled himself "printer."

Figure 2-6, the information business in 1880, shows the establishment of telegraphy, the arrival of telephone and the evolution of newspapers and magazines, but few other changes.[4]

By 1930 (Figure 2-7), the information world looks more cluttered and more familiar, although rudimentary compared to 1980. The most significant changes in our map between 1880 and 1930 probably

**Figure 2-4.**    Employment by the Information Sector.

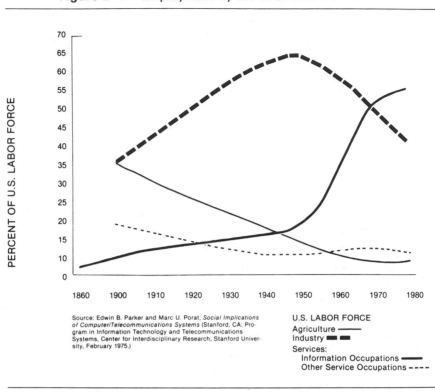

Source: Edwin B. Parker and Marc U. Porat, *Social Implications of Computer/Telecommunications Systems* (Stanford, CA: Program in Information Technology and Telecommunications Systems, Center for Interdisciplinary Research, Stanford University, February 1975.)

U.S. LABOR FORCE
Agriculture ———
Industry ▬▬ ▬▬
Services:
    Information Occupations ▬▬▬
    Other Service Occupations - - - -

were caused by the growth of telephony, the arrival of wireless technology, and the growing appreciation of and demand for information by increasingly sophisticated business and individuals.[5]

Figure 2–8 displays the products and services that entered the information business (in common use) during the 1930–1980 period. None of these products and services occupy the corners of the maps. Each represents an attempt to provide a salable something that bridges the area between information content and conduit. Moreover, as suggested by the shading in Figure 2–9, practically all of these new products and services are dependent upon the computing and memory power of computers or the miniaturization and economies of the integrated circuitry underlying computers as known in 1980. The explosion of *systems* of products and services (noncorner activities) and its impact upon public policy is explored in the next section in terms of public regulation.

**Figure 2-5.** The Information Business in 1780.

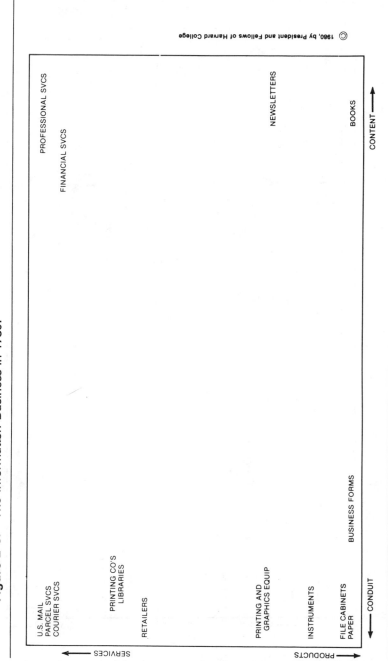

# Figure 2-6.    The Information Business in 1880.

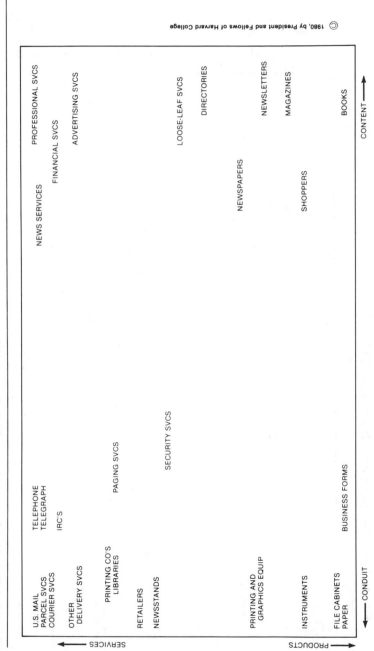

Figure 2-7. The Information Business in 1980.

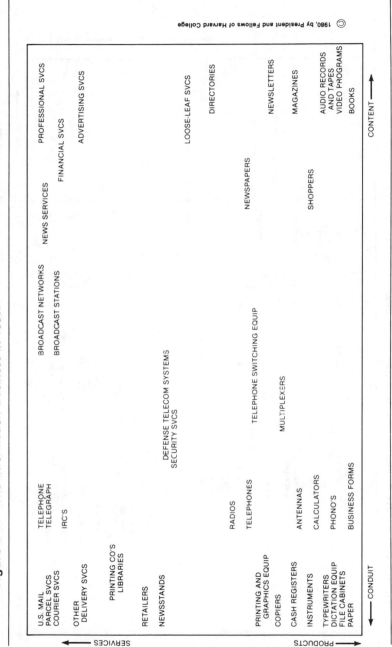

**Figure 2-8.** New Products and Services, 1930–1980.

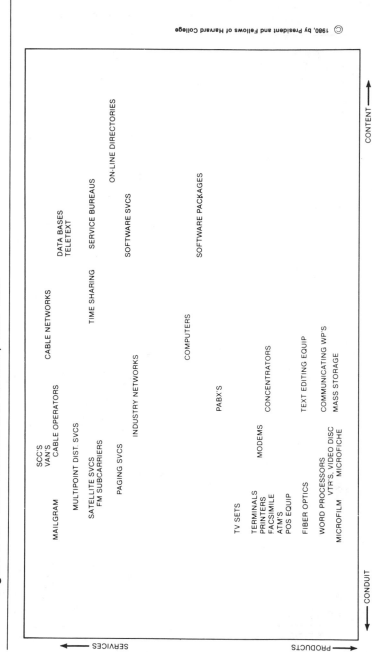

**Figure 2-9.** New Products and Services, 1930–1980: Increasing Dependence upon Computer Technology.

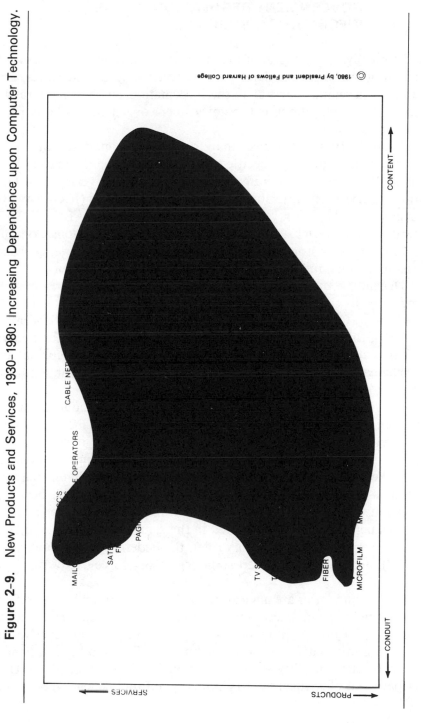

## GOVERNMENT REGULATION OF THE INFORMATION BUSINESS

Historically, many facets of the information business have been subject to government regulation or control. In the United States, government attempts to regulate the information business have ranged from censorship of content to government ownership and control of the postal conduit.

Figure 2–10 uses our basic map to show the boundaries of federal government regulation specific to functions of the information business. Thus the Postal Rate Commission (PRC) oversees the U.S. Postal Service, the Interstate Commerce Commission (ICC) regulates United Parcel Service (UPS), and the Civil Aeronautics Board (CAB) regulates air courier services. The Federal Communications Commission (FCC) monitors telecommunications common carriers, broadcasting, cable, and a number of other products and services.

Depending upon the specific activity, financial services may be regulated by the Federal Reserve Board (Fed), the Comptroller of the Currency (C. of C.), the Federal Deposit Insurance Corporation (FDIC), the Federal Home Loan Bank Board (FHLBB), the Federal Savings and Loan Insurance Corporation (FSLIC), the Securities and Exchange Commission (SEC), and a host of state government agencies.

As suggested by Figure 2–11, these regulatory boundaries are neither fixed nor neat in practice. The PRC and the FCC have conflicting jurisdiction over the regulation of electronic mail. The Federal Reserve Board gets involved in information systems by operating the "Fed Wire" payments system and determining if banks may offer data-processing services. The FCC tells newspaper publishers that they must divest themselves of radio and TV stations if broadcast and newspaper operations are located in the same community. The U.S. Postal Service (in its regulatory role), the Federal Trade Commission (FTC), and the FCC all exert some regulatory force over advertising services.

Some boundaries are unclear or changing over time. Recent efforts to deregulate some telecommunications products and services made the FCC's regulatory boundaries less definitive in a number of areas.

Organizations in the information business, like all other companies, are subject to other types of regulation, including that of the U.S. Department of Justice, the FTC, the Equal Employment Opportunity

Figure 2-10.    Functional Regulation of the Information Business.

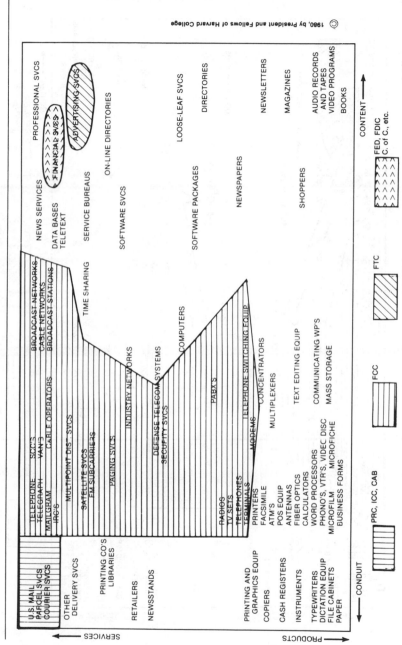

# Figure 2–11.    Movement and Conflict in Functional Regulation.

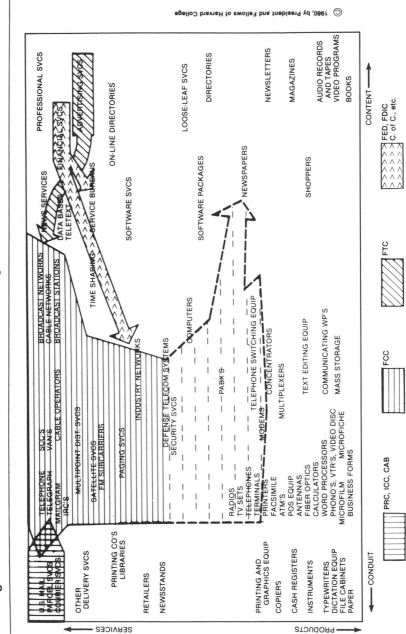

(EEO) Commission, the Occupational Safety and Health Administration (OSHA), the Environmental Protection Agency (EPA), and a variety of other federal and state bodies. In recent years for example, there have been major antitrust actions in the copier, computer, and telephone industries, occasional antitrust forays into the mail and parcel area and official speculation concerning concentration of ownership in the media (see Figure 2-12).

Figure 2-13 (which combines Figures 2-11 and 2-12) suggests the continuing complexities of regulation of the information business. While some of these regulatory complexities may be the product of political philosophy, others stem from the changes in the technologies of the information business. Figure 2-14 shows the regulatory boundaries of 1940. The absence of hybrid products and services may have made the process of drawing boundaries somewhat easier then—relative to 1980.

## CORPORATE POSITIONING IN THE INFORMATION BUSINESS

Our map of the information business appears to be a useful tool for looking at the strategic positioning of individual corporations. In order to apply this technique to specific companies, however, it has been necessary to establish some specific criteria as to whether a corporation should be shown as being in a particular business:

1. Some companies provide a given product or service for their own use but do not offer it for sale. Most large newspapers, for example, operate a "non-postal delivery service" but few market the service to other companies. To deal with such a case we have tried to show companies as engaged in a particular business only when they market the product or service to others.

2. Some companies offer specific products or services in international markets but do not sell them in the United States. Unless noted otherwise, we have attempted to display only a corporation's domestic business activities.

3. Many corporations lease office equipment, computers, and other products and systems to customers. While such leasing does constitute a financial service (and may have a significant impact upon a company's profits), we deemed leasing alone to be an inadequate

**Figure 2-12.** Antitrust Activities.

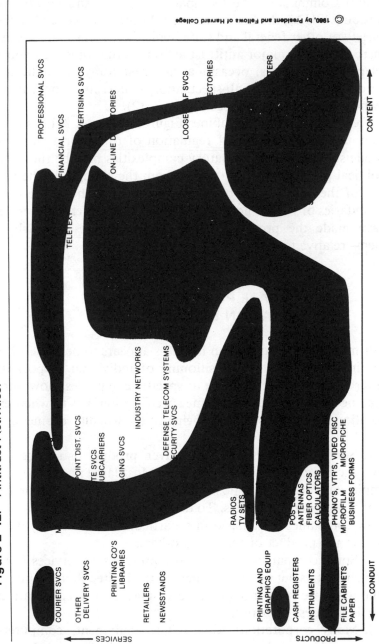

Figure 2-13.  Functional Regulation and Antitrust Activities.

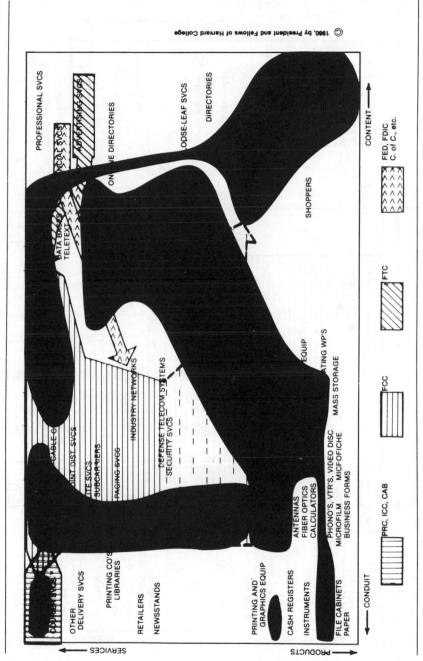

# Figure 2-14.   Regulation in 1940.

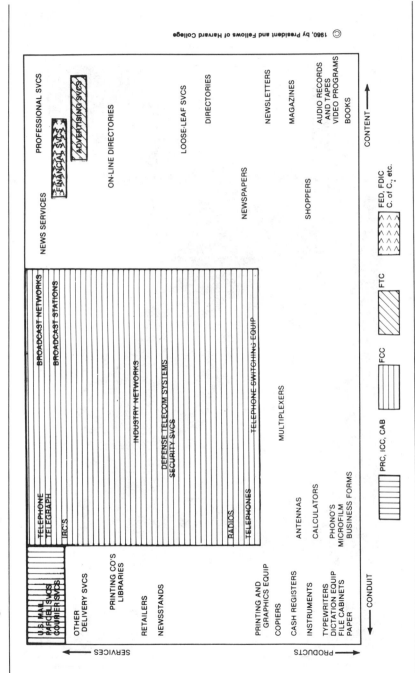

criterion for showing financial services to be part of a company's activities.

Even using these criteria, a company's position on the map can be subject to extensive debate. The following maps, therefore, should be viewed as suggestive, not definitive.

### Information Services and Systems Companies

Much of the current turmoil in the information business is attributable to the growth and changing nature of companies that traditionally provided electronically based information services and systems. These include telephone companies and a variety of corporations involved in manufacturing and marketing computers, office equipment, and consumer products.

Figure 2-15 shows American Telephone & Telegraph's (AT&T) territory on the map. While most of the map seems self-evident, a few items merit explanation. "News Services" and "Data Bases" were included to reflect content-oriented services such as "Dial-a-Joke," "New York Today," and "Sports-Line." "Phone-power" training and marketing seemed to qualify as "Advertising Services." On the other hand we did not include "Professional Services" because Bell Laboratories' research normally is not marketed to others and American Bell International does not market its services in the United States.

Government regulation has exercised a strong influence upon the shape of AT&T's business. Figure 2-16 compares AT&T's business area to the regulatory boundary of the FCC as shown earlier in Figure 2-10. The areas of incongruence reflect decades of legislative, regulatory, and judicial debate.

Efforts during the 1970s to redefine the regulation of the telecommunications industry have resulted in widespread speculation as to AT&T's potential role in a deregulated world. Figure 2-17 depicts the potential expansion of a deregulated AT&T as described by some current policymakers and a variety of potential competitors.

Deregulation can be expected to have some similar effects upon the business activities of the larger independent telephone companies. General Telephone and Electric, United Telecommunications, and Continental Telephone have all acquired companies or launched new ventures aimed at winning a share of the market for enhanced telecommunications services.

## Figure 2-15.    AT&T, 1979.

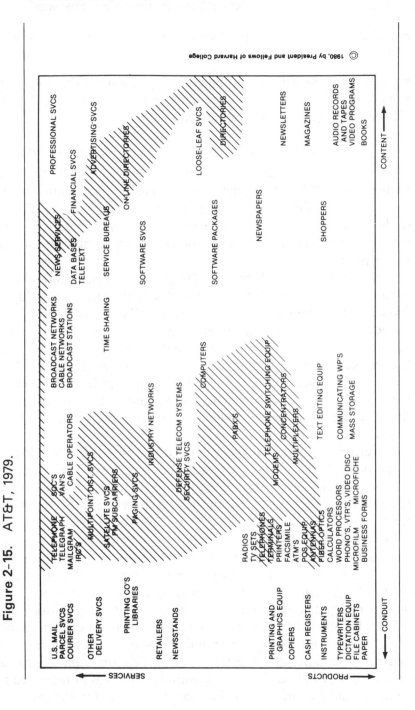

Figure 2-16.  AT&T and FCC Regulation.

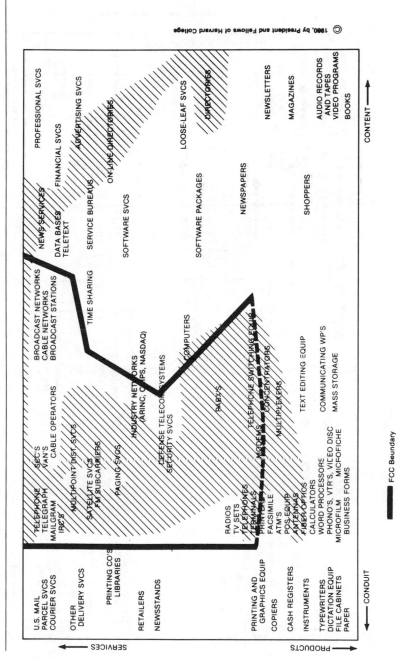

## Figure 2-17.   A Deregulated AT&T?

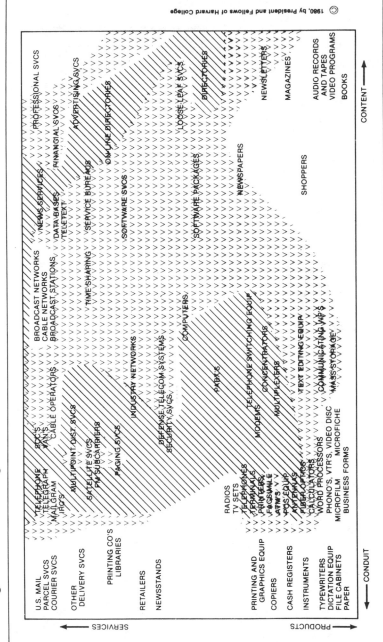

The 1979 U.S. operations of International Business Machines (IBM) are illustrated by Figure 2–18. If we overlay the FCC's regulatory boundary (from Figure 2–10) on the map of IBM's domestic operations, the resultant illustration suggests that IBM has avoided direct entry into regulated sectors in the United States (Figure 2–19).

A different picture of IBM is shown in Figure 2–20. This map includes products and services that IBM offers outside the United States. (Private Automatic Branch Exchanges—PABXs, time sharing, and service bureaus), some of IBM's internal technological capabilities, and the company's joint ventures with Aetna and Comsat (Satellite Business Systems [SBS]) and with MCA (Discovision Associates).

In recent years there has been much speculation in the trade press about a face-off between IBM and AT&T. The speculation is understandable, given the picture of a deregulated AT&T and of IBM with its foreign operations, its technological capabilities, SBS, and Discovision in Figure 2–21.

Figure 2–22 shows Xerox's basic territory as of 1978. Xerox's attempts to expand (or perhaps to integrate some of their businesses) are shown in Figure 2–23, which portrays the 1979 acquisition of Western Union International, the 1979 XTEN proposal and the 1980 announcement of the Ethernet joint venture with Intel and Digital Equipment Corporation. Combining Figure 2–23 with Figure 2–21 (AT&T and IBM) or overlaying these maps with those showing regulatory activities (Figures 2–12 to 2–14) suggests the complexities of industry structure and regulation in the information business.

While some changes in corporate positioning on the map may be responses to changing regulatory patterns, others appear to be reactions to new technologies or internal corporate strategies. Figure 2–24 shows Harris Corporation at three points in its development. Until 1957 printing press equipment represented Harris's primary business. Over the succeeding twenty years, Harris's growth through acquisitions and new ventures resulted in the donut-shaped area shown in the figure. The company's acquisition of Farinon in 1980 appears to fill the previous gap in its territory, while the acquisition of an 18 percent interest in Quotron in 1978 suggests exploration of new, but related, turf.

Movement out of a line of business can be as significant as new ventures. RCA as shown in Figure 2–25 is represented in many sectors of the information business, including financial services with the

**Figure 2-18.** IBM: U.S. Operations, 1979.

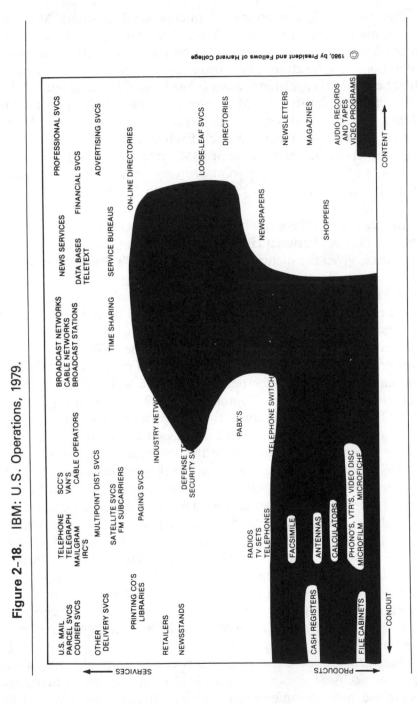

**Figure 2-19.** IBM: U.S. Operations, 1979, and FCC Regulation.

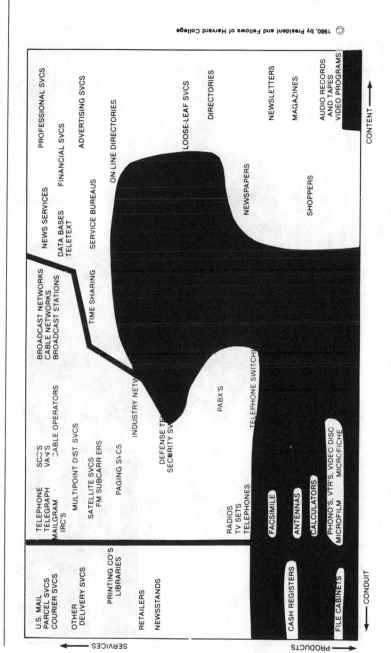

**Figure 2-20.** IBM: Foreign and Domestic Operations, Technological Capabilities, and Joint Ventures.

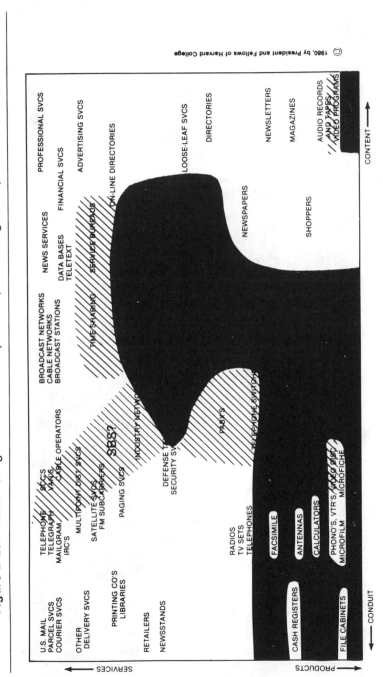

**Figure 2-21.** A Deregulated AT&T and IBM.

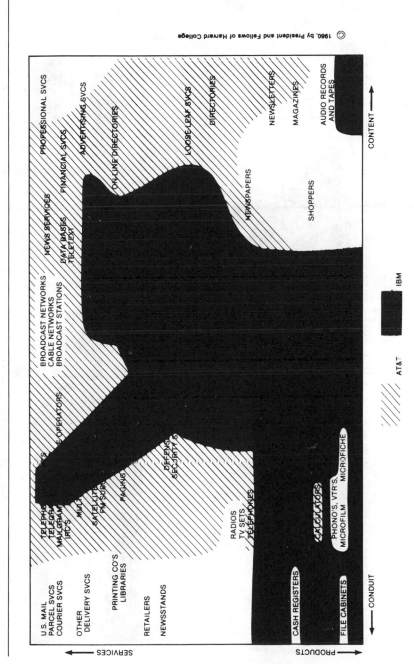

**Figure 2-22.** Xerox, 1978.

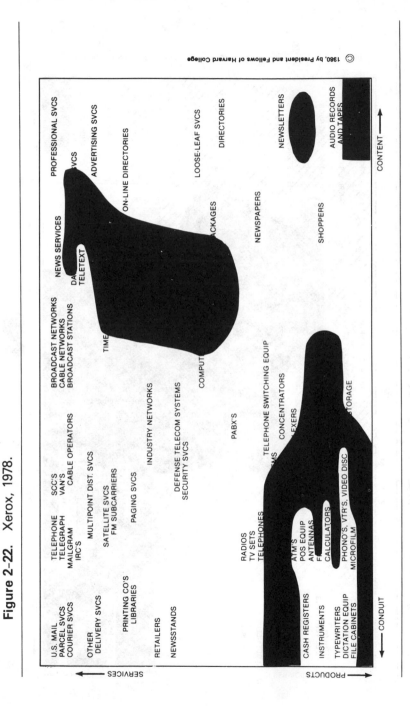

**Figure 2-23.** Xerox with Western Union International, XTEN, and Ethernet.

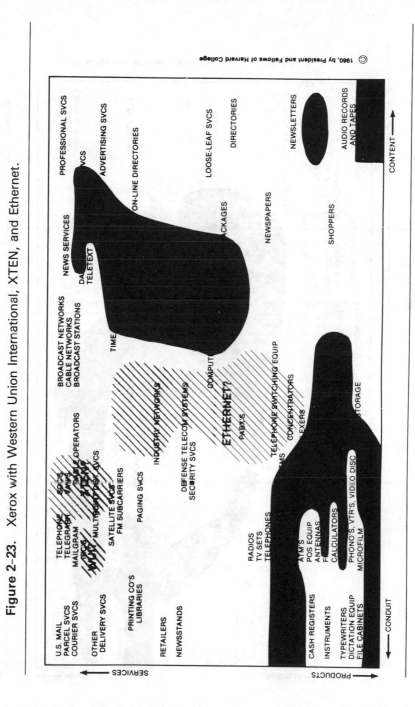

## Figure 2-24. Harris Corporation.

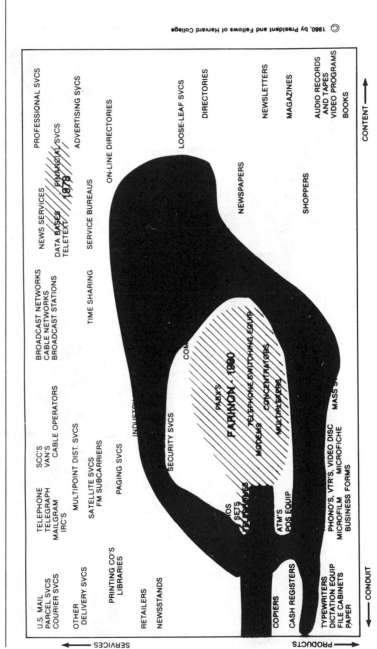

Figure 2-25. RCA, 1979.

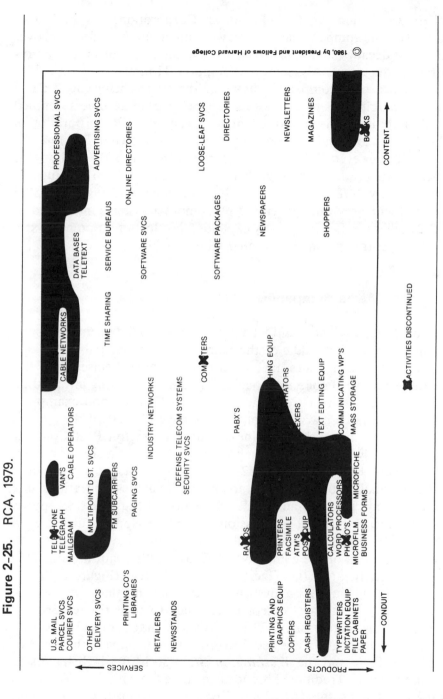

CONTENT →

← CONDUIT

SERVICES ←

PRODUCTS ↔

PROFESSIONAL SVCS

ADVERTISING SVCS

ONLINE DIRECTORIES

LOOSE-LEAF SVCS

DIRECTORIES

NEWSLETTERS

MAGAZINES

BOOKS

DATA BASES
TELETEXT

SERVICE BUREAUS

SOFTWARE SVCS

SOFTWARE PACKAGES

NEWSPAPERS

SHOPPERS

CABLE NETWORKS

TIME SHARING

COMPUTERS

TELEPHONE
TELEGRAPH
MAILGRAM

VAN'S
CABLE OPERATORS

MULTIPOINT D ST. SVCS

FM SUBCARRIERS

PAGING SVCS

INDUSTRY NETWORKS

DEFENSE TELECOM SYSTEMS
SECURITY SVCS

PABX S

TEXT EDITING EQUIP

COMMUNICATING WP'S

MASS STORAGE

U.S. MAIL
PARCEL SVCS
COURIER SVCS

OTHER
DELIVERY SVCS

PRINTING CO'S
LIBRARIES

RETAILERS

NEWSSTANDS

PRINTING AND
GRAPHICS EQUIP

COPIERS

CASH REGISTERS

TYPEWRITERS
DICTATION EQUIP
FILE CABINETS
PAPER

CALCULATORS
WORD PROCESSORS
PHOTO'S,
MICROFILM
BUSINESS FORMS

MICROFICHE

PRINTERS
FACSIMILE
ATM'S
POS EQUIP

RADIOS

ACTIVITIES DISCONTINUED

1979 acquisition of CIT Financial Corporation. As indicated, however, the company has withdrawn from a number of sectors over the past decade (computers, consumer home audio products, point-of-sale equipment, Alascom, and Random House).

The fact that a company is shown on the map as being engaged in a given combination of businesses can be misleading unless coupled with other information. For example, a map of NCR Corporation in 1972 would look quite similar to the 1979 map shown in Figure 2-26. In 1972 however, NCR's revenue mix included $600 million for mechanical products and slightly more than $200 million in computer systems. By 1978 mechanical products revenues had fallen to $52.6 million while revenues generated by computer systems multiplied to $2.24 billion, reflecting greatly expanded production of point-of-sale systems, software, and automated teller machines.

### Media Companies

Growth, turmoil, and conflict are not limited to the electronics-based companies in the middle of the map. Broadcasters, publishers, and other media companies have been repositioning themselves to deal with new ways of collecting, packaging, and distributing information.

The Times Mirror Company (Figure 2-27) is a good example of how some large newspaper publishers have diversified their operations in the information business. The Washington Post Company and the New York Times Company would present a similar picture.

Dun and Bradstreet (Figure 2-28) has been an active participant in the information business for years, primarily in the publications area. On the map, Dun & Bradstreet's acquisition of National CSS appears to be part of a logical progression toward developing further capabilities in processing and distributing the information acquired in other portions of the company. McGraw-Hill's acquisition of Data Resources, Inc. (DRI), suggests a similar strategy (Figure 2-29).

Compiling maps for a multitude of media companies suggests little uniformity of strategy except a tendency to redistribute corporate eggs among more baskets. Thus traditional magazine publishers like Charter Media and Time Inc. buy big city newspapers (the *Philadelphia Bulletin* and the *Washington Star*, both of which have since closed down). Traditional broadcasters like the American Broadcasting Companies, Inc. (ABC) and CBS, Inc. start magazine publishing

**Figure 2-26.** NCR, 1979.

SERVICES

PRODUCTS

CONTENT

CONDUIT

U.S. MAIL
PARCEL SVCS
COURIER SVCS

OTHER
DELIVERY SVCS

PRINTING CO'S
LIBRARIES

RETAILERS

NEWSSTANDS

PRINTING AND
GRAPHICS EQUIP

COPIERS

INSTRUMENTS

TYPEWRITERS
DICTATION EQUIP
FILE CABINETS
PAPER

TELEPHONE
TELEGRAPH
MAILGRAM
IRC'S

MULTIPOINT DIST. SVCS

SATELLITE SVCS
FM SUBCARRIERS

PAGING SVCS

RADIOS
TV SETS
TELEPHONES

FACSIMILE

ANTENNAS
FIBER OPTICS
CALCULATORS
WORD PROCESSORS
PHONO'S, VTR'S, VIDEO DISC

SCC'S
VAN'S
CABLE OPERATORS

INDUSTRY NETWORKS

DEFENSE TELECOM SYSTEMS
SECURITY

PABX'S

TEXT EDITING EQUIP

COMMUNICATING WP'S

BROADCAST NETWORKS
CABLE NETWORKS
BROADCAST STATIONS

TIME SHARING

SWITCHING EQUIP

NEWS SERVICES

DATA BASES
TELETEXT

NEWSPAPERS

SHOPPERS

FINANCIAL SVCS

ADVERTISING SVCS

ON-LINE DIRECTORIES

LOOSE-LEAF SVCS

DIRECTORIES

NEWSLETTERS

MAGAZINES

AUDIO RECORDS
AND TAPES
VIDEO PROGRAMS

**Figure 2-27.** Times Mirror Company.

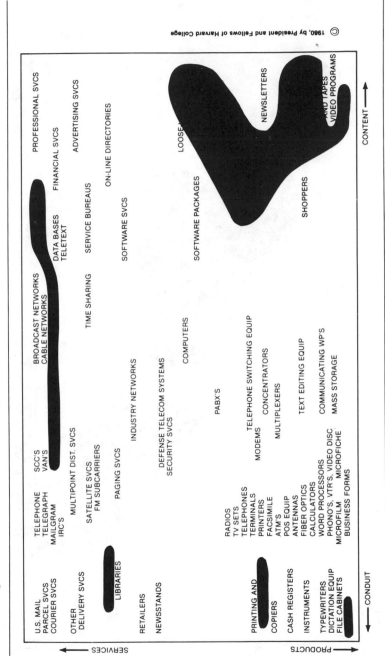

## Figure 2-28. Dun and Bradstreet with National CSS.

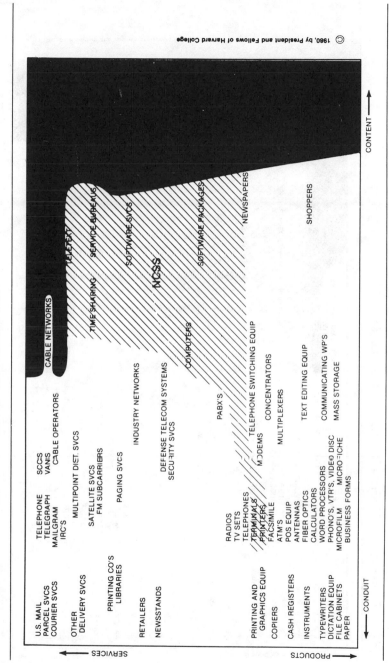

Figure 2-29.   McGraw-Hill with Data Resources, Inc.

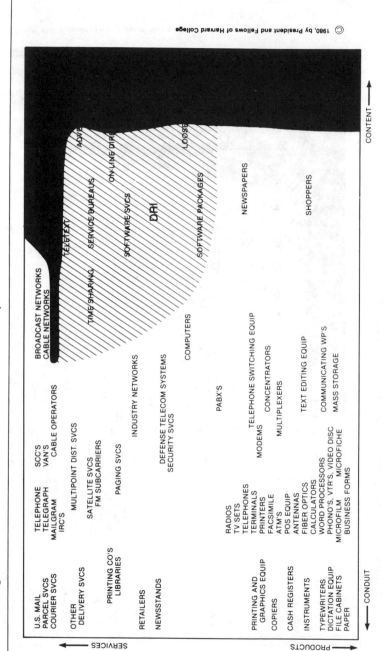

## Figure 2-30. Newspaper Diversification.

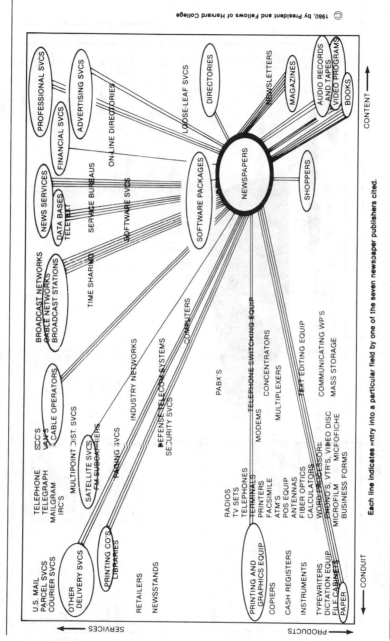

Each line indicates entry into a particular field by one of the seven newspaper publishers cited.

**Figure 2-31.    Chase Manhattan.**

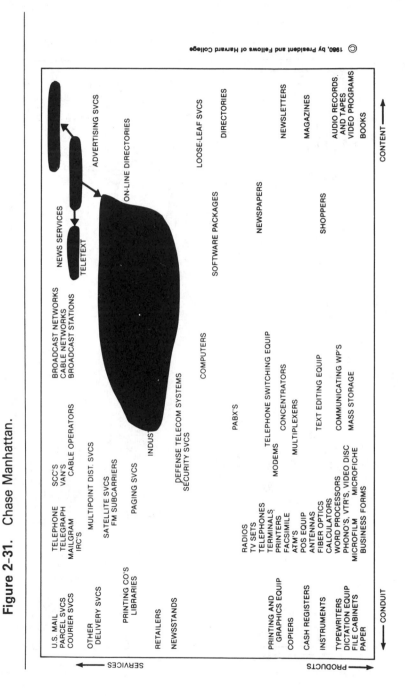

# Figure 2-32. Exxon Enterprises.

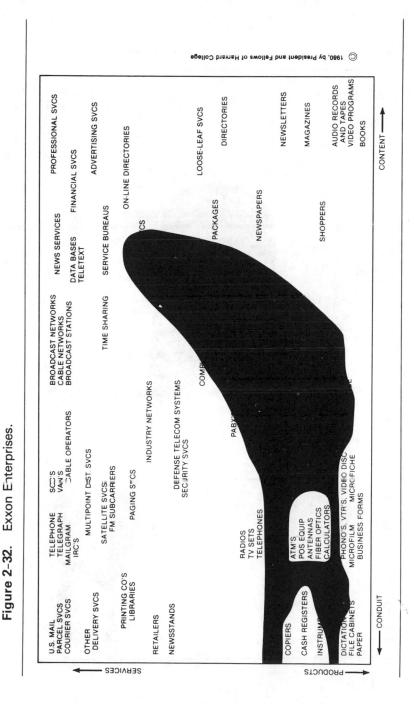

**Figure 2-33.    Volkswagen with Triumph Adler.**

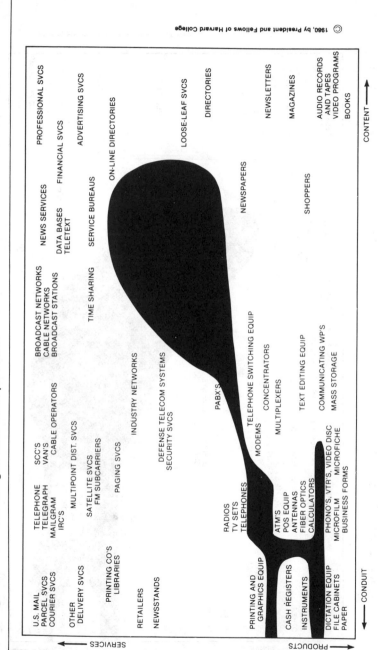

groups. If there is any central focus of interest among such companies, it appears to be the emerging market for cable/pay TV services, but this is far from certain.

The variety of diversification strategies is suggested by Figure 2–30. This map represents the business activities of seven companies generally classified as newspaper publishers.[6]

### New Roles and New Players

The growing market for information products and services has attracted the attention of many companies not previously considered factors in this field. Some financial institutions like Chase Manhattan (Figure 2–31) appear to be making a conscious effort to exploit their expertise and information networks by offering time-sharing, service bureau, data base, and consulting services. Citibank presents a similar configuration.

Figure 2–32 illustrates the territory now occupied by Exxon Enterprises by virtue of acquisitions and new ventures since 1971. While there has been considerable speculation about Exxon's ultimate goals in this field, the company's financial resources make it a potentially important player, even in a game including such giants as AT&T, Xerox, and IBM.

Volkswagen (VW) is another newcomer to the field by virtue of its acquisition of Triumph Adler (Figure 2–33). Considering Volkswagen's earlier attempt to acquire Nixdorf, the Triumph Adler purchase probably should be viewed as part of a conscious strategy to move VW into the information business.

### CONCLUSIONS, SPECULATIONS, AND SUGGESTIONS FOR FURTHER RESEARCH

The mapping technique described in this report appears to be useful for illustrating the evolution of the information business, including the increasingly central role of integrated systems of products and services. The maps graphically display the manner in which the evolution of hybrid products and services based upon new technologies have complicated the regulatory process. Plotting the historical activities of a given company and comparing it to maps of regulatory agencies or to those of actual or potential competitors may provide a quick and simple means for gaining insights regarding a company's strategic direction.

The corporate maps presented represent a small sample of companies examined in the research for this chapter and a much smaller sample of companies in the information business. The examples chosen illustrate applications of the mapping technique and display particular developments in the information business. While dozens of other companies would have to be mapped in order to draw meaningful conclusions on the future of the information business, this research suggested some trends and developments that invite further exploration.

During the 1978–1983 period the information business seemed to exhibit a feeding frenzy in terms of joint ventures, mergers, acquisitions, and new ventures. All of this activity might stem from macroeconomic conditions, or it might reflect particular developments within the information business. Comparison of recent activity within the information business to that in other industries and information industries historically deserves additional attention.

While our mapping efforts focused primarily upon the U.S. scene, our research suggested that the acquisition and joint venture activity on the international level was equally, if not more hectic. N.V. Philips, Siemens, Bell Canada (and its subsidiary, Northern Telecom), L.M. Ericsson, Nippon Electric Company (NEC), Fujitsu, Elsevier, the Thompson Organisation, and other foreign corporations announced acquisitions or joint ventures to enter the U.S. market in 1978–1980. Simultaneously Harris Corporation, National Semiconductor, Xerox, Dow Jones, and a host of other U.S. companies have launched joint ventures aimed at penetrating international markets. The mapping technique might be useful in plotting regulatory boundaries and corporate positioning in other countries and on a transnational basis.

While we did not attempt to indicate it on all of the individual company maps, our research suggests that many companies in the information business have a heightened concern for distributing their products and services to their ultimate customer. All of the major telephone companies are marketing equipment through company-owned retail stores. Xerox, Digital Equipment, Data General, Texas Instruments, and IBM are experimenting with retail outlets for office equipment. Some magazine and newspaper publishers are experimenting with new electronic mechanisms for delivering their information products (Knight-Ridder, Dow Jones, Dun & Bradstreet, McGraw-Hill, and others). Harte-Hanks, Reader's Digest Association, Time Inc., Lee Enterprises, Meredith Publishing, and more are developing or encouraging alternative (nonpostal) delivery systems. Additional research might determine whether these developments simply represent responses to individual industry problems (telephone deregulation, declining unit prices for office systems, increased postal rates) or if they signal some basic reorganization of industry distribution systems.

Many of the corporations shown on the maps are involved in the development of products and services that are sometimes termed "the office of the future." Figure 2–34 uses the information business map to indicate the cluster of products and services most frequently mentioned in discussions of the office of the future. These products and services constitute something of a southwest-to-northeast diagonal on the map. If we consider that diagonal from end to end, we see a combination of dumb (informationless) products and professional services that might be considered the office of the past and present. The introduction of the computer in the middle of the diagonal might be viewed as a factor in reducing dumb products at one extreme of the diagonal and professional services at the other extreme, much as "electronic publishing" might be a diagonal from the northwest to southeast that could reduce the importance of books at one end and mail or parcel services at the other. These concepts merit further investigation.

Conceivably these speculations reflect flaws in the mapping scheme rather than structural traits of the information business. Efforts to eliminate such flaws and improve the basic mapping scheme might be pursued along three lines:

1. Use of different axes. We experimented unsuccessfully with a market axis ("Original Equipment" to "Mass Consumer") and an axis based upon basic resources (paper, semiconductors, energy). Other approaches might be more profitable.

2. Separate maps for different business sectors. In the course of our work we experimented with maps designed to reflect narrower segments of the information business by purposes of the information (news, entertainment) or by information activities (acquisition, processing, storage). These experiments created a host of definitional problems; further efforts along these lines might provide some useful insights.

**Figure 2-34.** Office of the Future.

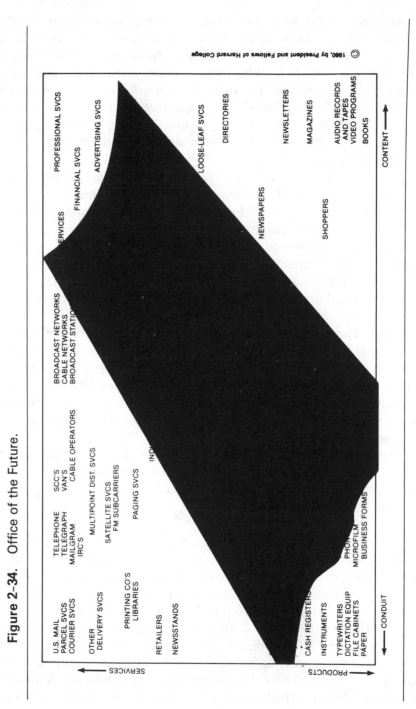

SERVICES

PRODUCTS

CONTENT

CONDUIT

PROFESSIONAL SVCS
FINANCIAL SVCS
ADVERTISING SVCS
DATABASES AND VIDEOTEX NEWS SVCS
TELETEXT
ON-LINE DIRECTORIES
SOFTWARE SVCS
SYNDICATORS AND PROGRAM PACKAGERS
LOOSE-LEAF SVCS
TIME SHARING SERVICE BUREAUS

DIRECTORIES
NEWSPAPERS
NEWSLETTERS
MAGAZINES
SHOPPERS
AUDIO RECORDS AND TAPES
FILMS AND VIDEO PROGRAMS
BOOKS
SOFTWARE PACKAGES

BROADCAST NETWORKS
BROADCAST STATIONS
CABLE NETWORKS

TELEPHONE
TELEGRAPH
VAN's
BROADCAST
CABLE OPERATORS
OCC's
IRC's
MULTIPOINT DISTRIBUTION SVCS
DIGITAL TERMINATION SVCS
SATELLITE SVCS
FM SUBCARRIERS
MOBILE SVCS
PAGING SVCS
BILLING AND METERING SVCS
MULTIPLEXING SVCS
INDUSTRY NETWORKS
DEFENSE TELECOM SYSTEMS
SECURITY SVCS

MAILGRAM
E-COM
EMS

GOVT MAIL
PARCEL SVCS
COURIER SVCS
OTHER DELIVERY SVCS
PRINTING COS
LIBRARIES
RETAILERS
NEWSSTANDS

COMPUTERS
PABX's
TELEPHONE SWITCHING EQUIP
CONCENTRATORS
MULTIPLEXERS

RAD OS
TV SETS
TELEPHONES MODEMS
TERMINALS
PRINTERS
FACSIMILE
ATM's
POS EQUIP
BROADCAST AND TRANSMISSION EQUIP
CALCULATORS
WORD PROCESSORS
PHONOS, VIDEO DISC PLAYERS
VIDEO TAPE RECORDERS
MASS STORAGE
GREETING CARDS

PRINTING AND GRAPHICS EQUIP
COPIERS
CASH REGISTERS
INSTRUMENTS
TYPEWRITERS
DICTATION EQUIP
FILE CABINETS
BLANK TAPE AND FILM
MICROFILM MICROFICHE
BUSINESS FORMS
PAPER

ATM—Automated Teller Machine; E-COM—Electronic Computer Originated Mail; EMS—Electronic Message Service; IRC—International Record Carrier
OCC—Other Common Carrier; PABX—Private Automatic Branch Exchange; POS—Point-of-State; VAN—Value Added Network

3. Quantification. As suggested by the discussion of NCR, coupling sales, investment, or other data to the basic map can make a substantial difference to one's perceptions of the game and the players. Computer mapping techniques can be used to display such data as a third dimension on the present map. Unfortunately the lack of uniform definitions for products and services and the highly aggregated nature of line-of-business accounting elevates such an effort beyond the scope of this project.

## THE INFORMATION BUSINESS MAP, 1983

In 1983 the Program published an updated version of the information business map (Figure 2–35). Although it adheres to the principles of the earlier map, it has been modified to reflect some of the changes in the industry in the brief period since 1980. For example, it shows more detail in the telecommunications sector, identifying separately such services as digital termination services and multiplexing services. It has added greeting cards along the bottom of the conduit-content axis, reflecting another intermediate position between blank paper and a book. On the right-hand side of the map, some products and services were slightly repositioned. Syndicators and program packagers were added, as was viewdata (as distinct from teletext).

The Program also completed research on a study applying the mapping tool to the international structure of the information businesses ("Mapping the Information Business in Europe, Canada and Japan"). European countries include France, the United Kingdom, Italy, the Federal Republic of Germany (West Germany), the Netherlands, and Sweden.

### NOTES

1. Marc U. Porat, *The Information Economy: Reports 77-12 (1–9)* (Washington, D.C.: U.S. Department of Commerce, Office of Telecommunications, May 1977); Daniel Bell, *The Coming of Post-Industrial Society* (New York: Basic Books, 1973). Peter F. Drucker, "Managing the Information Explosion," *Wall Street Journal*, April 10, 1980.
2. See, for example, some 1980 advertisements of American Telephone and Telegraph, AM International, and Telecomputing Corporation of America.

3. Simon Nora and Alain Minc, *L'Informatisation de la Société* (Paris: La Documentation Française, 1978) (English translation, *The Computerization of Society* [Cambridge, Mass.: MIT Press, 1980]); Oswald H. Ganley, *The United States-Canadian Communications and Information Resources Relationship and Its Possible Significance for Worldwide Diplomacy* (Cambridge, Mass.: Harvard University Program on Information Resources Policy, 1979); U.S. Congress, Senate Committee on Foreign Relations, Subcommittee on International Operations, Hearings on International Communications and Information, June 8–10, 1977. See also Chapter 10 of this book.

4. Independent delivery services, or private express companies evolved rapidly along with the railroads during the 1840s and 1850s, but by 1880 many were absorbed or eliminated by postal authorities through enactment of private express statutes. Security services in 1880 included district telegraphs that could summon police or the fire brigade to homes and businesses simply by cranking a handle. Phonographs, typewriters, and cash registers did not come into common use until the late 1880s and early 1890s.

5. Some aspects of the increasing importance of corporate communications and information systems during this period are discussed by Alfred D. Chandler, Jr., *The Visible Hand: The Managerial Revolution in American Business* (Cambridge, Mass.: Harvard University Press, 1977), pp. 120–121, 490.

6. Dow Jones and Company, Gannett Company, Harte-Hanks Communications, Lee Enterprises, New York Times Company, the Times Mirror Company, and the Washington Post Company.

# 3 CONTENT, PROCESS, AND FORMAT: A NEW FRAMEWORK FOR THE MEDIA ARENA

*Benjamin M. Compaine*

There was, not too long ago, a simpler era for the media industries, when a newspaper was a newspaper and television meant whatever the home receiver was able to pick up from one of three commercial networks. Cable operators merely brought a piece of wire into a home so the video image of what the networks were broadcasting might come in sharp, or come in at all, for many users.

By contrast, in the 1980s, participants in the media and allied areas are faced by a rapid change in technology and by what Robert Marbut of Harte-Hanks Communications refers to as the blurring of the distinction that has characterized the individual media. For instance, the television set at home is being used for private showing of theatrical films or for displaying output from a distant computer; homes with cable service are able to view programming that is not available on the old-line networks or, for that matter, anywhere off the air. The talk today is of "narrowcasting," special interest programming for identifiable market segments rather than the broadcasting, which tried to appeal to the greatest mass of recipients.

Today newspaper publishers watch nervously as newsprint costs skyrocket while the cost for computer storage diminishes even faster. Magazine publishers, like their newspaper counterparts, have been reaping healthy profits, yet worry about postal rates and paper costs. Many of those in the print media business are looking at the newer media forms, but are often unsure how to cope with the change. They see videotex and teletext technology, videodiscs, electronic data bases for business, electronic games, personal computers, but are unsure of what it all means to them. In addition, government policymakers at all levels are having to determine how existing laws and regulations should or can be applied to media and technology that did not exist when these rules were promulgated. They also must decide if, where, and when new policies are required.

The purpose of this chapter is to help articulate the meaning of the changes in the media environment and to specify new opportunities as well as areas for policy consideration by governmental bodies. The final section of the chapter suggests directions for research.

## NEED FOR A NEW DESCRIPTION OF THE MEDIA

Mass communiation has frequently been characterized as the process of delivering a single identical message to a large, heterogeneous, and unseen audience in different locations at the same time. The conduits for conveying these messages are termed the mass media.

This description reflects a traditional distinction between *mass* communication and media and other types of communication and media, such as point-to-point communication via telephone and telegraph or individually addressed letters sent through the mail. Today this distinction can serve only as a starting point, for the information dissemination process is changing. Computers and connected terminals in the office or in homes now permit individuals to *select* the information they wish to receive, although they may draw on a large common data base. There are devices that can call thousands of phone numbers and play identical recorded messages for the "recipients." Videocassette and audiocassette recording devices allow individuals to record broadcast programs and play them back at their leisure and however frequently they want. Mass mailings, often addressed only to "occupant," are not new, but electronic mail may provide an added dimension to the mass nature of this point-to-point medium.

Thus the media, which until the 1980s meant just newspapers, magazines, books, movies, radio, and television, today must recognize a new boundary for the term *mass* and, even more crucially, the blurring of the boundaries between the traditional media. Television, for example, today can refer to something that displays signals that are broadcast, as well as signals retransmitted by a cable or originated for cable, signals from videocassettes or videodiscs, and even news and other information sent via telephone lines from a computer.

Even describing the older media is not always as easy as it might first appear. What is a magazine? It usually has a paper cover, but not always: *Horizon*, like many books, had a hard cover for a time. A magazine is usually printed on glossy coated paper, but some, such as *Rolling Stone*, are printed on newsprint. Most magazines carry advertising, but they need not to qualify: *Reader's Digest* did not accept advertising until 1955. Magazines are usually thought of as being published regularly during the year, but there are many publications that look like magazines that only appear one time or just annually. At what point does a newsletter become a magazine? Why is the tabloid weekly *National Enquirer*, treated in most compilations of periodicals and by advertisers as a magazine, even though it is identical in physical format to many newspapers?

When asked to categorize a particular medium, many people respond, "Show me and I'll tell you what it is." But that approach does not give the answer. When a purchased prerecorded videocassette of "The Sound of Music" is played on a television set, is the relevant medium film or television? Is the person who watches the movie on a television set watching a broadcast, a cablecast, a cassette, or a videodisc?

For simplicity this analysis uses the conventional media terms such as newspaper, television, and books, accepting for the time being the implicit characterizations as they are commonly perceived. This is done with the expectation that we will not be bound to rely on the conventional terms and will in fact be seeking to explore our own, perhaps broader boundary for the media arena and its components.

The changing environment that makes defining the media difficult creates new opportunities. It also should alert members of the media companies to possible entry by new competitors, such as computer firms and telephone companies, which have not been traditionally viewed as being in the media business. Their entry may lead to new areas of conflict, not only in the marketplace, but among government regulators seeking to identify their territories and the new media forms and participants. The nature of the opportunities and threats is illustrated in Figure 3–1. This map of the information business shows the juxtaposition of its traditional segments.

**Figure 3-1.** The Information Business Map Showing the Media Arena.

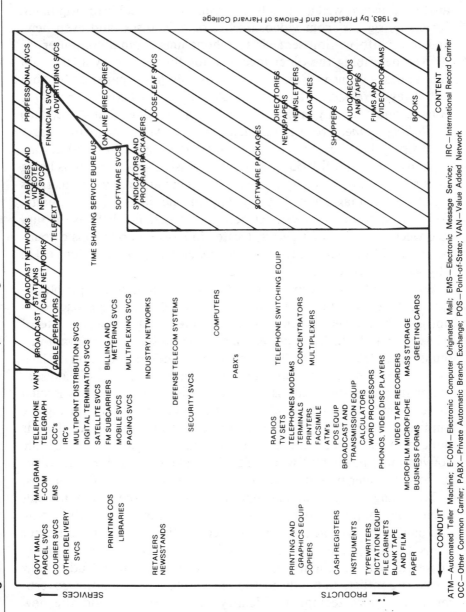

ATM—Automated Teller Machine; E-COM—Electronic Computer Originated Mail; EMS—Electronic Message Service; IRC—International Record Carrier
OCC—Other Common Carrier; PABX—Private Automatic Branch Exchange; POS—Point-of-State; VAN—Value Added Network

## AN ALTERNATIVE SCHEME FOR
## DESCRIBING THE MEDIA

Because terms that describe the media today—"television," "magazine," etc.—have connotations that may inhibit conceptualizing about the future media environment, the Program on Information Resources Policy has experimented with other classification schemes that may be usefully substituted. The goal was to find a simple yet comprehensive framework for classifying the various roles and functions of traditional as well as newer technologies now called the media. As one example, *television* commonly refers to broadcasting to a receiver and video dispay terminals (VDTs), while *cable* has meant sending programming to the VDT by a coaxial wire. However, a different scheme might simply refer to broadcasting and cable as two of many transmission modes for sending programming to VDTs. Program producers thus can look at the alternative conduits, while users of the programming can pick and choose the most effective method for reception of some sought-after information.

A framework that combines pragmatic simplicity with reasonable inclusiveness is outlined in Table 3-1. Its three primary components are *content, process*, and *format*. Organizations engaged in the mass media or communications business are usually enaged in creating, transmitting, or processing information for display via one or more of several possible formats.

The *content* is the information that is provided by the supplier and received by the user. *Information*, as used here, is broadly defined to encompass news, entertainment, music, commentary, advertising, numerical data, narration, and anything else that is transmitted by the design of a sender or at the request of a receiver. (Information has other meanings growing out of a variety of disciplines, but here the broadest possible description is used.)

The components of content are words, notes (as in music), paragraphs, stories, pictures, and so forth. The descriptive characteristics of content include but are not limited to such factors as breadth of the audience (mass, specialized, or individual), market segmentation (business or residential users and demographics), the intent of the message (to inform, educate, persuade, or entertain), and the manner of financing (by users, advertisers, government, and others).

Examples of types of content include news stories, entertainment programs and stories, education or cultural presentations, advertise-

**Table 3-1.** Terms for Describing the New Media.

| Content | Process | Format |
|---|---|---|
| Components | Functions | Functions include |
| Paragraphs | Gathering | Display content |
| Issues | Creating | Implicit message conveyance |
| Words | Storing information | |
| Stories | Handling | |
| | Transmitting | |
| | | |
| Characteristics | Characteristics | Characteristics |
| Breadth of audience | Rate of transmission | Electronic or mechanical |
| (e.g., mass/special interest) | Method of transmission | Degree of permanence |
| Market segment | Cost | Hardware needed for user |
| (e.g., end user, demographics) | Extent of coverage | Source of control over |
| Manner of financing | Type of carrier | rate of content display |
| | (common, dedicated) | Method of user accessibility |
| | Difficulty of use | (random entry, sequential) |
| | Direction of flow | |
| | | |
| Content | Processes | Formats |
| News | Broadcasting | Video on screen |
| Entertainment | Coaxial or other cable | Ink on paper |
| Education | Mail | Electronic or mechanical sound |
| Culture | Private carriers | Optical/Mechanical light |
| Persuasion | Microwave | projection |
| Data | Computer | |
| | Printing | |
| | Disk or cassette | |

ments, statistical data, and legal notices. Certain media formats tend to specialize in presenting specific types of content, but most media have some of each. Newspapers, for example, along with their hard news provide personality profiles as features, crossword puzzles for entertainment, and a listing of polling places as notices. Books, which tend to be either literature or general information, may also be news oriented, as in the case of the "instant" books that Bantam and others publish shortly after an important event. Televised programming is largely entertainment, but there is an important news and informational component. Most theatrical films are also devoted to entertainment, but some have information as their theme.

*Process* refers to both the handling and transmitting of the information. Among the processing functions are gathering, creating, and storing information. This would include a newspaper reporter researching and writing an article, storing it on a floppy disk for editing, hyphenation, and justification by a computer for typesetting and make-up. Another example would be the activities leading to filming a movie, videotaping a tennis match, or creating and providing access to a computerized data base.

The descriptive characteristics for process include, but again are far from limited to, the rate and method of transmission (in baud, bits, pieces, or characters, by broadcast radio waves, coaxial cable, microwave, through the U.S. mail, by trucks, through retailers), the extent of coverage (to many receivers at once, addressed to a single individual, national, local), the type of carrier (common, private, contracted), difficulty of use (technologically simple as in transporting magazines by truck, for example; more sophisticated for key strokes translated for transmittal to a computer), the direction of the flow (one-way, two-way, interactive), and so forth.

Examples of processing components are the transmission conduits, such as broadcasting, coaxial cable, mail and private parcel delivery, microwave, telephone, and the storage/handling modes that include computers, printing presses, and paper.

*Format* refers to the form in which the content is made available to the user or is handled by a processor. This may be as hard copy, such as printed words or pictures on paper. It may be an electronic visual representation, such as that created on a video display tube, and could be as words as well as pictures. It may be a mechanical visual representation such as that created by projecting movie film or micromaterials. It may be an aural representation, such as the sounds created normally associated with the ink-on-glossy-paper periodical that is actually one of several formats available to producers of this information. Thus, for example, magazine publishers, in the traditional sense, do not view themselves as video producers. But in understanding the special *content* expertise that is the basis of a printed magazine, the publisher may more readily accept a more generalized view of business that leads naturally to video productions that are congruent with the existing editorial product. This reasoning can be used for newspaper publishers, broadcasters, book publishers, or record producers.

The blurring of these arbitrary format distinctions is suggested when the CBS television network's "60 Minutes" refers to itself as a "video magazine" or in the title of Westinghouse Broadcasting's prime-time access program "Evening Magazine." Time Inc. tried to translate the fast pace and airy content of its print *People* directly to a video presentation using the same concept.

Even in the absence of an explicit formulation, the importance of this concept of content/process/format rather than television/cable/newspaper has not been lost on some of the strategic planners in the media industry. Some newspapers are experimenting with providing news services for cable channels or viewdata systems. At least one broadcaster is starting to repackage existing news reports for videocassette sales, and movie distributors are already accustomed to expanded channels of distribution for their theatrical productions via broadcast, pay cable videocassettes, and videodiscs. These are just a few of the many possibilities for creative use of content/process/format to expand markets, reduce costs, and increase profit margins. It is the optimizing of this new media menu that provides the real challenge and opportunity for those in the media arena.

Changing information technologies have been providing new formats over the years. The printing press led to mass-produced books, newspapers, and magazines. The wireless led to radio and television. Other discoveries brought about motion pictures, records, and tape recordings. These have expanded the variety of ways in which information—content—can be received by users. Only to a limited degree have new formats created new types of information. Rather, new formats and processes have greatly expanded *accessibility* of information. Film helped move vaudeville, for example, from the immediate experience of only those in the theater at the moment of the show to a much broader audience, all of whom could see the same show at different times and in varying places. Television took this one step further, making such entertainment even more convenient. Televised and radio broadcast news shows are essentially a presentation of the information that was traditionally published by newspapers and before that by personal letter or word of mouth. The form of presentation is changed, but not the *type* of information. Audio tapes are primarily a variant of the record format.

The media arena today is therefore a continuation of this process, with additional conduits and new technology, such as computers, providing an even greater array of formats and hence access to more information (such as being able to share, via television, the astronauts' view of the earth from a space shuttle).

Figure 3-2 provides some examples of the relationship of the media segments along a continuum of producers of content, and processors, by format. It shows that in addition to the conventionally recognized mass media, there are various components that provide

**Figure 3-2.**    A Continuum of Media Participants.

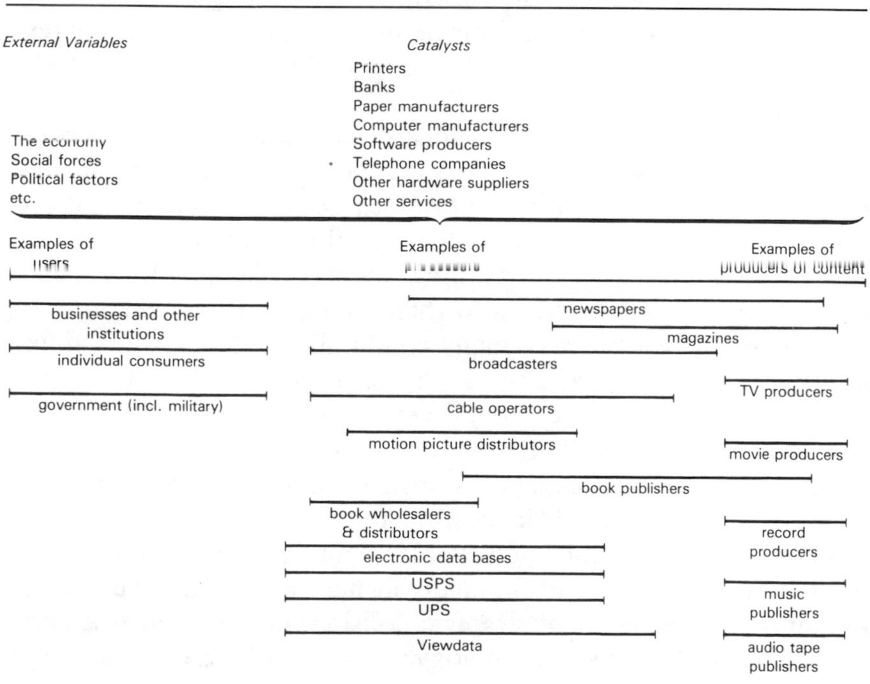

specific services, such as producers of programming for the video format (content) or wholesalers for books and magazines (process).

In addition, Figure 3-2 insists that the media require the services of an infrastructure, here termed "catalysts" because of their crucial role in providing the means for media activity without directly being part of these functions. They include printers, the U.S. Postal Service, telephone companies, banks, computer manufacturers and programmers, paper manufacturers, and other suppliers of equipment and services. It is from within this infrastructure that likely competitors for media organizations may appear, thus creating the possibility of some unexpected conflicts. Figure 3-2 also recognizes that the participants in the media arena help shape, as well as function within, the total economy, politics, and government, social values, and attitudes.

Finally, Figure 3-1 places the media within the context of the larger information business. The relationship between content and process is again highlighted. As a segment of the information business, the media can be viewed as service, as opposed to product, oriented. (This, again, is a matter of perception. A newspaper, for example, could be considered a manufactured product, and thus the U.S. Census Bureau includes newspaper publishing as a manufacturing industry. But from an information viewpoint, it is the content and not the physical product that is key—hence the service designation.)

On the other hand some segments of the media industry have less concern with content. Cable operators today, for the most part, are primarily processors, picking up broadcast signals of others and distributing them. Cable operators have until recently had little or no concern with creating or determining content, although this is changing as programming offerings to them multiply. Broadcasters, particularly the networks, have many conduitlike features, since unlike newspaper, magazine, and book publishers they produce little content of their own. However, they do exert considerable influence over what independent producers decide to offer.

Businesses currently engaged in media activities or those that may be interested in using their existing resources to enter the media business, as well as public policymakers, all have a vital stake in understanding the nuances of the changing nature of media boundaries. For firms, it is a matter of strategic decisions in areas for expansion or even survival as newer technology changes the basis on which their existing enterprise is built. For example, a newspaper publishing company that persists in restricting itself to printing its product in the conventional method and distributing via traditional conduits may find both advertising and readership eroded by competition from other firms providing similar services but utilizing a more efficient or consumer-acceptable technology, such as cable, TV, viewdata, or some hybrid.

In essence what is happening in the media arena is that the previously discrete and readily identifiable segments are merging into a more fluid industry, leading to dissolution of old groupings and crystallizing of new. Increasingly they are using the computer for information storage and retrieval. They are using telephone lines, cable, and satellites for transmitting information, either to the end user (as in the case of broadcasters) or as part of the manufacturing process (as with newspapers). All types of publishers have VDTs in the editorial or composing rooms. Broadcasters, such as ABC, are packaging programs for other forms of distribution, while publishers, such as Playboy Enterprises, are moving toward a similar end. In the middle, the common carriers, such as General Telephone and Electronics (GTE) and American Telephone and Telegraph (AT&T) are looking increasingly like providers of information, either as videotex system operators or as direct information (such as the weather, stock market data, sports scores obtained by calling a special telephone number). As all types of firms that provide information service increasingly use the same technology, there will be a lessening of the differentiation among the traditional media forms in the minds of information consumers.

Through understanding and exploiting the fluid nature of the content/process/format mix, media firms have the opportunity to break out of their traditional mold and broaden their businesses, which should translate into increased revenue and profits. They can reevaluate their customers not as newspaper readers or magazine subscribers, but as *information consumers*, whose interest is in the unique utility of the *content*. These customers will prove less loyal to any particular format or process, given the greater choices and the strengths of different formats and processes to optimize the utility of a specific type of information (an interactive video display via telephone lines and computers for classified advertising, pay cable process for an opera, a printed book format for a description of macroeconomic theory).

Government policymakers are faced with a similar challenge to long-standing practices. Decisions on how direct satellite-to-home-television transmission might be regulated, or whether an electronic-

**Table 3-2.   Examples of Operations among Traditional Firms in the Media, 1979.[a]**

| | Newspapers | Magazines | Broadcasting | Cable System Operators | Books | Theatrical and Nontheatrical Programming | Retail or Wholesale Distribution | Survey Research | Information Services | Paper, Wood, and Forest Products | News Services | Directory Printing | Records and/or Music Publishing |
|---|---|---|---|---|---|---|---|---|---|---|---|---|---|
| American Broadcasting Companies | | | • | | | | | | | | | | • |
| CBS | | • | • | | | | | | | | | | • |
| Doubleday | | | | | • | | | | | | | | |
| Dow Jones | • | • | • | • | • | | | | | | | | |
| Dun & Bradstreet | | | | | • | | | • | • | | • | • | |
| Encyclopaedia Brittanica | | | | | • | | | | | | | | |
| Gannett | | | • | | • | | | | | | | | |
| Harte-Hanks Communications | • | | • | | • | | | • | | | | | |
| Hearst | • | • | • | | • | | | | | | | | |
| Knight-Ridder | • | • | • | | • | | | | • | | • | | |
| Lee Enterprises | • | • | • | | | | | | | | | | |
| McGraw-Hill Inc. | | • | | | • | | | | • | | | • | • |
| Meredith Corp. | | • | • | | | | • | | | | | | |
| Minneapolis Star and Tribune Co. | • | | | | • | | | • | | | | | |
| Newhouse | • | • | • | • | | | | | | | | | |
| New York Times Company | • | • | • | | • | • | • | | • | • | • | | |
| RCA | | | • | • | | • | | | | | | | • |
| Reader's Digest Association | | • | | | • | | • | | | | | | |
| Time Inc. | | • | • | • | | | • | | • | • | • | • | • |
| Times-Mirror | • | • | • | | • | | | | | | | | |
| Washington Post Co. | • | • | • | | | | | | | | | | |
| Ziff-Davis | | • | | | | | | | | | | | |

Sources: Annual Reports, 10-Ks, *Business Week*.

[a]Between 1979 and 1983 some of these companies entered and left areas of operation. The greatest activity was in cable system ownership and video programming.

ally transmitted newspaper to a video screen in the home should be treated under the existing print newspaper interpretation of the First Amendment or the more regulated broadcast models, will depend in part on how well they understand the distinctions among information creation, processing, dissemination, and format.

The research agenda that follows from this analysis, therefore, relates to (1) the nature and interaction among the traditional and evolving formats, (2) the development and role of the various handling and transmitting processes, and (3) the type of content being displayed by each format. Given information, news, entertainment and other types of content identified in Table 3-2, how are they being adapted or can they be adapted by institutional participants to the widening format and process options? How can they optimize such values as profit, access, some of which are compatible and some of which conflict?

## WHAT IS MEDIA POLICY?

Media policy refers to those factors, both private and public, that help shape the strategic decisions of firms and institutions in the information marketplace. Policy is both an outgrowth of and an input to the operating strategy of individual firms. It is a key ingredient in determining the structure of both industries and firms. Overall public policy, of which media policy is a part, is a fundamental component of the political system. Among the many factors that affect public policy are

- The First Amendment to the Constitution. Much of the character and structure of the media in the United States can be attributed to this basic tenet.
- The Communications Act of 1934, which established the Federal Communications Commission (FCC) and the mechanism to regulate the structure (and indirectly some content) of radio and later television broadcasting. The creation of the FCC, the successor to the Federal Radio Commission, was itself an important policy decision of the government and an important departure from the past. It explicitly recognized that the new technology of radio broadcasting and expanding telecommunications required regulation that had a different approach and demanded creation of an arca of policy that had earlier been unnecessary.

- The sundry rulings of the FCC, including the evolving definition of the Fairness Doctrine, limitations on group ownership of broadcasting stations, television advertising aimed at children, cross media ownership, and cable television.
- Congressional legislation establishing public broadcasting, with its unique structure and funding pattern, copyright, and postal subsidies for certain classes of mail.
- Court rulings, many growing out of FCC proceedings: on the Fairness Doctrine, such as *Red Lion Broadcasting* (1969); in the antitrust area, such as the *Associated Press* (1945); access to print media (*Miami Herald*, 1974); and other rulings covering access of the press to court proceedings, privacy, reporter's rights to conceal sources, and libel.
- Other federal and state regulatory agency actions, including policies of the U.S. Department of Labor, the Internal Revenue Service, and the National Labor Relations Board concerning the status of independent carriers for newspapers; state and local authorities that grant cable franchises; the broad questions of government collection and dissemination of data—whether and at what price it should be sold back to the taxpayers and the extent to which such activities should compete with private business.
- Broad government regulations that apply to all businesses, including the media, such as affirmative action personnel policies, taxation, environmental, and safety and health statutes.

### Private Policy

Private policy—policy of the individual firm—must work within the boundaries established by public policy, yet also helps shape public policy. For example, the FCC has determined that a single firm should not own or control more than seven television stations. On the other hand, plans of Comsat and others to establish direct satellite-to-home receiving station programming have had an impact on the FCC's policymaking. The outcomes of private policy on pricing, location of facilities, even whether or not to offer a product or service, are often a factor of public policy.

Among the areas of concern for private policy are the following:

- Market factors. Opportunities in various business segments, degree of competition, cost and pricing variables, maturity of the market, experience of the firm with either the content or the distribution structure of the markets, influence on and from consumers.

- Technology. The degree of expertise and understanding the firm already has or is willing to acquire, the extent of new technology required, cost and payback for requisite technology. An example would be the decreasing cost and increased flexibility of phototypesetting equipment that makes start-up of a new newspaper more practical than using the older hot type.

- Personnel. Not only do firms have a personnel policy (either explicitly or implied), but other areas of policy are affected by personnel, such as the existence of organized unions and labor contracts, the availability of a qualified labor pool, the ability of the firm to attract and promote workers.

- General company strategy. The outcome of the various policy factors is a corporate strategy. It may encompass several policy decisions. A firm involved in newspaper publishing may decide to continue making newspaper and magazine acquisitions, but not broadcast outlets. It may seek to expand through internal growth and start-ups of new products and services or through mergers and acquisitions. A motion picture distributor may have a policy of producing special programming for cable or home videocassette distribution—or of restricting itself to theatrical films.

- Financial community. There is a noticeable difference in the operating strategy of publicly and privately owned firms. The former are typically far more concerned with keeping up their stock price (making acquisitions for stock much easier) and in showing continual growth in earnings per share. Publicly owned firms must disclose a considerable amount of financial information in filings with the Securities and Exchange Commission. Concern with how the company is evaluated by financial analysts is absent in privately held firms, which need not disclose internal financial data.

- Stockholders. There was a time, of course, when stockholders had considerable input in basic policy and strategy decisions. That was when most firms were smaller and the owners were also the managers. Today that situation still does apply to family-controlled firms, but most of the largest companies have ownership scattered among many institutions and pension funds, as well as individuals, so that most policy decisions are left with operating management. Even those firms that manage to maintain family control while going public have had to resort to a variety of trusts and similar devices that provide only a holding action, as deaths and inheritance taxes eventually undo such schemes.

It should be evident that policy issues and policymaking in the media arena are a function of a multiplicity of interactions. In the public sectors these include legislation at all levels of government, regulatory agencies, and the courts. In the private sector technology, economics, the marketplace and human inputs are involved. And all these mix within an environment shaped by larger social and political factors.

## The Broader Implications of Policy

Although public and private policymakers may understand the need for research in media policy, it may not be so evident why policy should be of more than just passing interest to the greater public. However, in a service-based economy that is increasingly dependent on information, the policies regarding the collection, processing, and dissemination of that information affect all consumers of information. The media are major participants in the information process.

The media—especially the traditional mass media—are highly visible parts of everyday life for most individuals in the United States and indeed in much of the world. The availability of the media determines not just *how* we get our news, but what we get, the content. And beyond the news, there is, of course, the vast body of information ranging from the frivolous to the essential that helps shape a vast array of decisions. These include many marketing, financial, and similar decisions by individuals in business, education, government, and other institutions, as well as mundane personal decisions such as whether and where to go out to the movies, which supermarket is offering the best values this week, whether this is a good time to buy a new car, ad infinitum.

Media policy is evident in what is being shown on television (compare U.S. and most European fare), the price of magazine subscriptions, the availability of cable connections in a community, the delivery of the daily newspaper and, for the future, the speed with which possible new technologies are developed as well as disseminated. Whether or not every home will have its own earth receiving antenna or a low-cost connection with a vast computer data bank will depend on policy decisions that are now being made. The outcome of such policymaking may have a substantial effect on society economically and politically as well as socially. At least some observers of the media future see the possible changes as having a more profound effect on the structure of society than any other single development, including energy. Thus the research for the media arena has implications that go well beyond the immediately involved constituency.

## PARTICIPANTS IN THE MEDIA

The media arena encompass firms and institutions that gather, package, distribute, finance or regulate mass communications. These include newspapers and magazines, radio and television, book publishers, the motion picture industry, nonbroadcast video, newspapers, data bases, and advertisers. As seen by the examples in Table 3-2, many players do business in more than one segment.

*Newspapers.*　There are about 1,700 daily newspapers, as tabulated by *Editor & Publisher*. Most are of general interest in a well-defined geographical area. There are also foreign language dailies and special interest dailies, ranging from *The Wall Street Journal* to *Woman's Wear Daily*. In addition, the *Ayer Directory of Publications* lists about 9,000 less-than-daily newspapers, many of them weekly publications in towns too small to support a daily. Usually included under the newspaper rubric, though subject to varying perceptions, are the many "shoppers," usually distributed free, which may carry some editorial material but are primarily or totally devoted to display and classified advertising. Most newspapers are owned by firms that publish more than one publication.

*Magazines.*　The annual *Ayer Directory* classifies about 9,000 publications as periodicals. These include perhaps 2,000 consumer magazines, as well as business, trade, and professional publications, scholarly journals, and association, alumni, and similar periodicals. Although most such publications accept and depend on advertising, others are supported exclusively by circulation revenues, dues, or other subsidies. As with newspapers, most consumer and business magazines are part of multipublication groups.

*Broadcast television.*   The three major commercial television networks, ABC, CBS, and NBC, feed the bulk of programming to 700 VHF and UHF stations. In addition, there are educational or public stations and a loose network to serve them, financed by government appropriations plus private and corporate donations. The networks themselves each own five VHF stations scattered among the major markets, while other firms also own chains of local stations. Most programming is purchased by the networks from independent film producers and studios. On occasion ad hoc networks have come into being for a particular purpose or series.

*Broadcast radio.*   The rise of television changed the nature of radio from a national, network-programmed medium to a largely local, independently programmed medium. There are seven radio networks and 5,600 commercial AM and FM stations, the latter being the fastest growing segment of the industry. In addition, there is a small cadre of public/educational stations.

*Cable television.*   Unlike the other, more established media, cable has tended to function primarily as a carrier rather than as a provider of original information. The genesis of cable was in providing stronger reception of conventional broadcast signals in remote areas. Today, over 4,000 cable systems rely on broadcast television signals from the network affiliates plus retransmission of some independent stations for the bulk of their fare. They also provide premium pay-TV service that provides theatrical films and some productions specially produced for this form of distribution. There has been little cable operator-originated programming, other than giving news headlines, weather, and sports scores, often using automated display rather than a live announcer. Since 1979, however, cable operators have been offered an increasing variety of original programming from independent networks, such as USA Network and ESPN.

*Books.*   There are 2,000 book publishers enumerated by the U.S. Commerce Department, but this may understate the true number of small but active publishers. R.R. Bowker Company identifies nearly 500,000 titles in print, with 40,000 to 50,000 new titles appearing each year. Books include such diverse segments as trade, college, and elementary-high school textbooks, religious, professional, university press, and mass market paperbacks. Channels of distribution vary significantly for different types of books and require the participation of wholesalers, jobbers, retailers, and postal services.

*Motion pictures.*   There are an estimated 4,900 producers and distributors of films, most of them in the nontheatrical end of the business. Theatrical movies are shown in 11,700 theaters, many of which are part of circuits or chains. Most theatrical films are distributed by six major firms and more than any other segment of the media depend on foreign sales for a major portion of revenue and profit. The nontheatrical film industry includes educational, promotional, and other business films. The federal government is particularly active here, either through its own production or in contracts to independents.

*Nonbroadcast video.*   There is a growing role for video in both the home and business/government/educational organizations. Many large firms have their own networks that serve television outlets in their scattered corporate and divisional offices, using copies of in-house prepared videocassettes or standardized purchased programming. Schools and colleges use closed-circuit and taped programs for instruction. The home market consists largely of recycled theatrical films and a few specially made special interest programs for the 6.3 million home videocassette units and 400,000 videodisc players in homes in mid-1983. At least eighteen firms are supplying half-inch cassette units for the home market, while a handful of firms have entered the licensing and production of programming area. The nonbroadcast use of the television set is the fastest growing (though small) segment of the mass media.

*Newsletters.*   These are a distinctive form of publication generally regarded as being neither magazines nor newspapers. They are periodicals, usually devoted to a highly specialized topic and hence audience. Most often they are sold on a subscription basis at a relatively high price, with little or no advertising. Even newsletters with a very small circulation (some distribute 100 copies or less) may be highly influential within the constituency of their readership.

*Data bases.*   The rapid and continuing reduction in the cost of computer storage has created a new form for data-base storage and retrieval. Vast quantities of data on a broad list of subjects are now available on a real-time basis, mostly to business, government and other institutional users who are willing to bear the charges to get timely information. A subindustry of data-base utilities has also been created to facilitate the dissemination of this information.

*Advertisers.*   Most of the media are supported totally or predominately by income from advertising. Users on the other hand receive the content for free (in the case of broadcast or "shoppers") or for less than the full cost of production (daily newspapers, most magazines). Books and theatrical film are the two major media that are user supported. (Though there may be some question as to whether or not continued postal subsidy for fourth class mail is not in fact subsidizing mail order book publishers.) In 1982, advertisers as varied as the U.S. Army and Frank Perdue spent about $66.6 billion, most of that through the mass media. The largest share went to newspapers, followed by television. Analysis shows that advertising expenditures have remained at a nearly constant 2 percent of Gross National Product since 1940.

*Consumers.*   Users of the media receive information at less than full cost of production. The major expenditure to receive broadcasts is the one-time investment in a television or radio receiver. The price of a daily newspaper covers about 30 percent of its cost (including profit margin), while consumer magazines charge about 35 to 40 percent of cost. Many trade magazines are also provided free. Consumers must cover the total costs of books and films, although many of the latter in the nontheatrical category are sponsored. Cable and premium channel use is supported so far by users, but cable operators do get some sponsored films and may eventually find some support from advertisers. Nonetheless consumers spend less than advertisers on mass media.

### Indirect Participants—The Infrastructure

Besides firms directly involved with supplying information to a mass audience, there are other less obvious participants. The government is not only involved through FCC regulations, antitrust rulings, and labor laws, but also as a competitor through films and publications for sale. Of great concern to the print media are the manufacturers of paper, both newsprint and coated groundwoods, used by newspapers and magazines, respectively. About 90 percent of all newsprint produced in the United States and Canada is consumed by newspapers, while coated stock of the quality used by most magazine publishers is sometimes in such short supply that it has to be imported from West Germany and Finland. Manufacturers of these grades of papers have their fortunes closely allied with the publishing industry.

Ink, a petroleum-based product, has become an increasingly large expense for publishers, especially newspapers. Print media also rely on various transportation forms, especially trucks and trains, for the delivery of raw materials as well as for the distribution of their products. The magazine industry in particular has a great dependence on

**Table 3-3.**  Revenue of Major Segments of the Mass Media, 1981.

|  | Value of Product Shipments or Revenue, 1981 | Percent of Total |
|---|---|---|
| Newspapers | $19.5 billion | 28.4% |
| Broadcasting | 13.5 | 19.7 |
| Periodicals | 9.9 | 14.4 |
| Cable TV | 2.1 | 3.1 |
| Books | 6.9 | 10.0 |
| Theatrical film | 4.4 | 5.4 |
| Newsletters, data bases, spoken word audiocassettes, etc. | 1.4 | 2.0 |
|  | 57.9 | 84.0% |
| Consumer electronics (television and radio receivers, home video recorders, phonograph and hi-fi equipment) | 11.0 | 16.0 |
|  | $68.7 billion | 100.0% |

Sources: U.S. Bureau of Economic Analysis, as published in *U.S. Industrial Outlook 1982*, except for film, newsletters and other, which are estimated by the Program on Information Resources Policy.

the U.S. Postal Service, a relationship that many publishers are questioning in light of greatly increased second class mailing tariffs. All the media, but especially print, are affected by the availability and cost of energy. The paper-manufacturing industry is the fourth largest user of purchased energy, while big city newspaper presses use considerable amounts of electricity. Television and radio broadcasters require electricity to send out their signals, and a vast amount of electricity is consumed by television receivers. Broadcasters also need the hardware such as cameras, editors, and transmitters. Finally, there is the considerable reliance on the telecommunications system of wires, microwave, and satellites provided by AT&T and other telephone companies and a growing cluster of private carriers.

In absolute size the revenues of the traditional segments of the media arena (not including indirect participants) as reported by various trade associations and the U.S. Department of Commerce, were about $58 billion in 1981, or 2.3 percent of Gross National Product (Table 3-3). By way of comparison General Motors (GM) had sales of $60 billion, Exxon $97 billion, and IBM $34 billion. Adding the value of consumer electronics shipments (including imports) adds $11 billion to a more broadly defined industry.

## THE NEED FOR MEDIA POLICY RESEARCH

### The Media and Shifting Boundaries

It has become increasingly difficult to make definitive statements on who are the players in the arena. The U.S. Postal Service for example, is seen in Figure 3-1 as being almost a pure conduit for information. Nonetheless it may be viewed as a competitor for advertising dollars that might otherwise be spent in traditional newspapers, magazines, television, or other media. This is because the degree of competition from direct mail promoters depends in large measure on the policy the Postal Service assumes in pricing bulk mail—used frequently for direct mail promotions—as well as how the advertising portion of newspapers and magazines is treated in second class rates.

This also highlights one of the many policy-related conflicts. In recommending second class rates to the Postal Rate Commission, the Postal Service can influence the costs of magazines, making them more expensive to consumers and as advertising vehicles and thus potentially diverting some business to direct mail.

Boundaries are shifting in other ways as well. Earlier, newspapers, magazines, and books were published by printers. Today only newspaper publishers tend to have their own printing plants, and even then it is the daily newspapers that tend to combine the two functions. For the most part the information-gathering process has been separated from the mechanical reproduction process. Though still considered manufactured products for Census purposes, magazines, books, and many newspapers should be properly categorized as service businesses. Such changes in boundaries are not just of recent vintage. In the early colonial days of this country, many newspapers were also run by the local postmasters, in an era where the post office was the focal point of information exchange.

Boundaries for functions are shifting as well. Filmmakers include in their revenue projections sources such as a pay-TV network like Home Box Office, videocassette, or videodisc duplication in addition to sales to more traditional broadcasters and conventional worldwide theater distribution. With the development of two-way (interactive) cable, or other pay-per-program techniques, the economics of film distribution may change so that the pay-TV market would be the primary income source and get the first showing, with theatrical release and broadcast showing to follow.

The home television set has long been used as a receiver of largely mass-consumption entertainment. From its inception, it has also functioned as an educational tool, receiving broadcasts such as Sunrise Semester as well as being used in closed circuit to show instructional lectures or demonstrations in the school room. Today the television set is also used as a screen for electronic video games. It can also receive, with an adapter, messages sent via airwaves or telephone wires from a computer. It may also serve as the output mechanism for home computers. Thus the television set has multiple functions.

Changing boundaries mean that agencies like the FCC will continue to have to cope with increasingly ambiguous regulatory arenas. For example, Comsat, the private satellite firm, has spent its existence carrying the messages of others at a fixed tariff. With its proposal to provide subscription television directly to millions of homes, it is assuming a new role—and one for which existing regulation does not explicitly have any precedent. Similarly, while FCC policy prohibits new newspaper/television joint ownership in the same city, the

**Table 3-4.**  Summary of Media Participants, Stakes, Forces and Trends.

| Participants | Stakes | Forces | Trends |
|---|---|---|---|
| Firms gathering and packaging information content<br>Newspapr publishers<br>Magazine publishers<br>Radio and TV producers<br>Book publishers<br>Motion picture producers<br>Data-base publishers | Share of the information market<br>Maintaining format identity | New technology<br>Information needs<br>Economics<br>Competiton<br>Politics<br>Regulation | Shifting boundaries<br>Conglomeration and cross-media ownership<br>Threats and opportunities |
| Firms and institutions engaged primarily in distributing media<br>Broadcasters<br>Cable system operators<br>Videocassette duplicators<br>Private delivery services<br>U.S. Postal Service<br>Telephone companies<br>Satellite carriers<br>Pay-TV distributors<br>Data-base brokers<br>Magazine/book wholesalers | Share of conduit market<br>Expanding avenues for distribution | New technology<br>Economics<br>Competition<br>Politics<br>Regulation | New opportunities<br>Possible new regulation<br>Broader competition |

| | | | |
|---|---|---|---|
| Firms and institutions providing raw materials and essential services for media producers<br>Paper manufacturers<br>Film and tape manufacturers<br>Telephone companies<br>Computer hardware and software suppliers<br>Banks | Ability to enter arena as competitor and maintain role as supplier<br>Long-term economic viability of media-related business | New technology<br>Customer needs<br>Regulation | New opportunities<br>Threats to existing business |
| Firms, institutions, and individuals providing economic support<br>Individual consumers<br>Advertisers and their agencies<br>Libraries<br>Other institutional information consumers | Cost for service<br>Quality of information<br>Diversity of sources<br>Ease and availability of information access | User needs<br>Economics<br>Technology<br>Competing formats | Slow to change from traditional patterns<br>Military and business pick up new technology first |
| Legislative and regulatory bodies<br>Federal government<br>State and local governments<br>Trade associations and self-imposed codes | Political credibitliy<br>Social welfare<br>Economic impact | Politics<br>Special interests<br>Economic impact | Uncertainty in applying existing law<br>Conflict between regulation and first amendment<br>Deregulation |

subject of newspaper/cable cross-ownership introduces a new level of complexity and jurisdictional uncertainty.

The boundaries are shifting as firms move into arenas that they previously did not consider part of their business. An early example was when Westinghouse and General Electric moved into the broadcasting business to further sales of the radio receivers they were making in the 1920s. Newspapers were slow to move into radio, but finally did and moved into television as well. Now, new decisions must be made: Is the viewdata/teletext field a natural extension for newspaper publishers, broadcasters, cable operators, telephone companies, or even computer firms? Should special interest magazine publishers be considering getting involved in programming for videocassette, videodisc, or cable special interest programming? Table 3–4 shows the extent of holdings of a sampling of media industry firms.

## SUMMARY

The media industry today is characterized by shifting boundaries and blurred lines of demarcation of what were once plainly identifiable industries. Television today no longer refers to a single broadcast mode and will become increasingly less broadcast dominated. Newspapers are not necessarily restricted to an ink-on-newsprint format.

The limitations of traditional descriptions can be overcome by characterizing media in terms of content, process, and format. Content includes news, entertainment, persuasion, and culture, for example, and covers the information activities of the traditional newspaper, magazine, book publishers' or television programmer's editorial function. The components of content include words, issues, paragraphs, stories, and the like.

Process covers the highways or means of carrying information, as well as the gathering, handling, and storing of information. It is crucial in promoting dissemination of information, through telephone lines, cable systems, satellite and microwave transmission, trucking systems, private carriers, the Postal Service broadcasting, and other conduits.

The format is the physical form in which the information is presented to the user. It may be ink printed on paper, images created electronically on a video display terminal or by projection through a film or slide, sounds recreated by an electronic or electromechanical process, or other possibilities.

The Program's research in the media arena is aimed at furthering an understanding of the changing media environment, with a focus on areas of concern to policymakers in both public and private institutions and firms.

# 4 SHIFTING BOUNDARIES IN THE INFORMATION MARKETPLACE

*Benjamin M. Compaine*

By conventional measures, the content portion of the traditional information industry is relatively small, even in the information-intensive U.S. economy. Measured in terms of revenues of all firms in the media and entertainment industries listed in Table 4–1 the industry represented 3.9 percent of the Gross National Product in 1981. The 106,000 libraries of all types in the United States spent an estimated $1.2 billion on materials acquisitions in 1978, or 2.0 percent of all information products and services sold.[1]

However, conventional measures do not suffice when dealing with the amorphous and inexact concept of the value of information. For example, how can we calculate the value of the information an airline pilot uses to guide a jet to a precise destination? The weather reports, the navigational aids, the on-board computer read-outs, pilot knowledge, intuition and experience are all synthesized in routine decision-making. How could these information inputs be measured in concrete terms?

At the outset, then, it must be clear that describing the information marketplace is a different order of problem from characterizing the marketplace for toothpaste, or even for newspapers. It is with this caveat and in this context that this chapter will attempt to give some perspective on issues and policies for the 1980s and beyond.

**Table 4-1.** Revenues and Expenditures of the Information Industry, 1970–1981, $ Billions. (See Explanatory Notes, Appendix 4A)

| | 1970 | 1971 | 1972 | 1973 | 1974 | 1975 | 1976 | 1977 | 1978 | 1979 | 1980 | 1981 |
|---|---|---|---|---|---|---|---|---|---|---|---|---|
| **Compunications** | | | | | | | | | | | | |
| Computer software and service suppliers | $ 1.6 | $ 1.8 | $ 2.1 | $ 2.6 | $ 3.2 | $ 3.8 | $ 4.5 | $ 5.3 | $ 6.3 | $ 7.5 | $ 12.8 | $ 15.3 |
| Computer systems manufacturers | b | b | 12.2+ | 14.4+ | 16.6+ | 18.8+ | 21.2+ | 23.8+ | 28.0+ | 31.2+ | 37.7+ | 42.6+ |
| Electronic components and accessories | 7.3 | 7.3 | 8.8 | 10.8 | 11.3 | 10.1 | 12.4 | 15.4 | 17.9 | 22.7 | 27.6 | 28.2 |
| Mobile radio systems | 1.9* | 2.2* | 2.4* | 2.6* | 2.9* | 3.2* | 3.5* | 4.2* | 5.0* | a | a | a |
| Satellite carriers | 0.0* | 0.0* | 0.1* | 0.1* | 0.1* | 0.2* | 0.2* | 0.2* | 0.3* | 0.3* | 0.4* | 0.5* |
| Telegraph | 0.4 | 0.4 | 0.4 | 0.5 | 0.5 | 0.5 | 0.5 | 0.6 | 0.6 | 0.6 | 1.2 | 1.4 |
| Telephone | 18.2 | 20.0 | 22.6 | 25.5 | 28.3 | 31.3 | 35.6 | 40.1 | 45.2 | 50.6 | 55.6 | 63.7 |
| Terrestrial common carriers | 0.0 | 0.0 | 0.0 | 0.0 | 0.0 | 0.0 | 0.1* | 0.1 | 0.2 | 0.3 | 0.4 | 0.7 |
| **Media and entertainment** | | | | | | | | | | | | |
| Advertising | 1.4 | 1.4 | 1.6 | 1.7 | 2.0 | 2.1 | 2.5 | 2.8 | 3.5 | 4.0 | 3.7 | 4.6* |
| Broadcasting | | | | | | | | | | | | |
| Radio | 1.1 | 1.3 | 1.4 | 1.5 | 1.6 | 1.7 | 2.0 | 2.3 | 2.6 | 2.9 | 3.3 | 3.7* |
| TV | 2.8 | 2.8 | 3.2 | 3.5 | 3.8 | 4.1 | 5.2 | 5.9 | 6.9 | 7.9 | 8.8 | 9.8 |
| Book publishing | 2.4 | 2.7 | 2.9 | 3.1 | 3.3 | 3.5 | 4.0 | 4.9 | 5.4 | 5.5 | 6.1 | 6.9 |
| Cable TV | 0.3 | 0.3 | 0.4 | 0.5 | 0.5 | 0.9 | 1.0 | 1.2 | 1.5 | 1.8+ | 1.7 | 2.1* |
| News wire services | 0.1+ | 0.1+ | 0.1+ | 0.1+ | 0.1+ | 0.1+ | 0.2+ | 0.2+ | 0.2+ | 0.2+ | 0.3+ | 0.3+ |
| Motion picture distribution and exhibition | 1.2+ | 1.2+ | 1.4+ | 1.8 | 2.3 | 2.5 | 2.4 | 2.7 | 3.4 | 3.5 | 4.1 | 4.4 |
| Newpaper publishing | 7.0 | 7.4 | 8.3 | 8.9 | 9.6 | 10.4 | 11.7 | 13.0 | 14.6 | 16.2 | 18.0 | 19.5* |
| Organized sports admissions | 1.1 | 1.2 | 1.2 | 1.2 | 1.4 | 1.4 | 1.6 | 1.8 | 1.9 | 2.1 | 2.3 | 2.5 |
| Periodical publishing | 3.2 | 3.2 | 3.5 | 3.9 | 4.1 | 4.4 | 5.0 | 6.1 | 7.2 | 8.3 | 9.0 | 9.9* |
| Printing, book and commercial | 8.8 | 9.1 | 10.0 | 11.0 | 12.0 | 12.9 | 14.9 | 16.5 | 16.5 | 18.6 | 20.6 | 22.8* |
| Radio and TV communications equipment | 9.3* | 8.7* | 9.1 | 9.7* | 10.6* | 11.9* | 13.2* | 14.9 | 16.9 | 19.6 | 23.8 | 27.8* |
| Theaters | 0.1 | 0.1 | 0.1 | 0.1 | 0.1 | 0.1 | 0.1 | 0.2 | 0.2 | 0.3 | 0.4 | 0.5 |
| **Postal** | | | | | | | | | | | | |
| U.S. Postal Service | 6.3 | 6.7 | 7.9 | 8.3 | 9.0 | 10.0 | 11.2 | 13.0 | 14.1 | 16.1 | 17.1 | 19.1 |
| Private delivery services | 0.8+ | 1.1+ | 1.3+ | 1.5+ | 1.7+ | 2.1+ | 2.3+ | 3.0+ | 3.5+ | 4.3+ | 5.2+ | 6.1+ |

| | | | | | | | | | | | | |
|---|---|---|---|---|---|---|---|---|---|---|---|---|
| **Financial and legal** | | | | | | | | | | | | |
| Banking and credit | 61.1+ | 68.9+ | 77.6 | 101.3 | 136.2 | 132.7 | 144.7 | 159.4 | 195.3 | 242.7 | [a] | [a] |
| Brokerage industries | 40.6+ | 47.4+ | 55.3 | 61.0 | 64.1 | 69.1 | 80.6 | 59.4 | 68.2 | 92.2 | [a] | [a] |
| Insurance | 92.6+ | 103.5+ | 113.8 | 123.6 | 133.2 | 148.8 | 173.1 | 196.5 | 223.2 | 235.5 | [a] | [a] |
| Legal services | 8.5 | 9.6 | 10.5 | 12.2 | 13.7 | 14.8 | 16.2 | 18.4 | 21.4 | 24.8 | [a] | [a] |
| **Miscellaneous manufacturing** | | | | | | | | | | | | |
| Paper and allied products | 9.5 | 9.8 | 11.0 | 12.9 | 17.0 | 16.2 | 18.9 | 20.2 | 21.9 | 25.4 | 28.7 | 35.2* |
| Photographic equipment and supplies | 4.4 | 4.7 | 5.6 | 6.4 | 7.5 | 7.6 | 8.8 | 9.9 | 11.5 | 13.4 | 15.9 | 18.0* |
| **Miscellaneous services** | | | | | | | | | | | | |
| Business consulting services | 0.9+ | 1.1+ | 1.1 | 1.5 | 1.7 | 1.8 | 2.2 | 2.6+ | 2.9+ | 4.7+ | [a] | [a] |
| Business information services | 0.8* | 0.9* | 1.0* | 1.1* | 1.1* | [b] | [b] | [b] | 2.7* | [b] | [b] | 4.1* |
| Marketing research services | [b] | [b] | [b] | [b] | [b] | 0.3+ | 0.4+ | 0.4+ | 0.5+ | 0.6+ | 0.7+ | 0.8+ |
| **Total revenue** | $293.7 | 324.9 | 376.9 | 433.3 | 499.6 | 527.3 | 600.1 | 645.0 | 749.5 | 863.8 | 305.4 | 350.5 |
| **Government expenditures** | | | | | | | | | | | | |
| Census Bureau | 0.1 | 0.1 | 0.1 | 0.1 | 0.1 | 0.1 | 0.1 | 0.1 | 0.1 | 0.2 | 0.8 | 0.3 |
| County agents | 0.3 | 0.3 | 0.4 | 0.4 | 0.4 | 0.4 | 0.5 | 0.5 | 0.6 | 0.6* | 0.7* | 0.7* |
| Libraries | 2.1 | [b] | [b] | [b] | [b] | [b] | [b] | [b] | 5.7* | [b] | 6.6* | 7.5* |
| National intelligence community | 5.6* | 5.4* | 5.4* | 5.7* | 5.9* | 6.3* | 6.7* | 7.4* | 7.8* | 8.3* | 9.2* | 11.0* |
| National Technical Information Service[c] | 0.0 | 0.0 | 0.0 | 0.0 | 0.0 | 0.0 | 0.0 | 0.0 | 0.0 | 0.0 | 0.0 | 0.0 |
| Research and development | 15.3 | 15.5 | 16.5 | 16.8 | 17.4 | 19.0 | 20.8 | 24.0 | 26.5 | 29.0 | 31.6 | [a] |
| Schooling | 70.4 | 76.3 | 83.3 | 89.7 | 98.0 | 111.1 | 121.8 | 131.0 | 140.4 | 152.1 | 169.6* | 181.3* |
| Social Security Administration | 1.0 | 1.2 | 1.3 | 1.4 | 1.8 | 2.2 | 2.6 | 2.7 | 3.0 | 3.2 | 3.6 | 4.0 |
| **Total expenditures** | $94.8 | 98.8 | 107.0 | 114.1 | 123.6 | 139.1 | 152.5 | 165.7 | 184.1 | 193.4 | 222.1 | 204.8 |

* Estimated.
+ Lower bound.
[a] Not available as of January 1983.
[b] Not available.
[c] Under $50 million annually.

The term *marketplace* seems to presuppose that information is indeed a commodity, like cotton, paper, or chopped sirloin steak. This may be a reasonable assumption, but it must be tested against alternative economic approaches to the nature of information. Information also may be viewed as being merely a theoretical construct, having features unlike other commodities and therefore requiring its own unique treatment. There is an alternative that admits to some commoditylike characteristics on the part of information, but that recognizes other distinctive features as well. For example, typical commodities are tangible. Information may not be. Most commodities lend themselves to exclusivity of possession. Information, however, can be possessed by many individuals at the same time. In addition, there is frequently little or no marginal cost to the provider in reaching a wider audience, as in the case of a broadcast signal. Once out of the transmitter, the signal's cost to the broadcaster is constant whether one or 10,000 households are tuned in.

Without engaging in an economist's discourse on the manner in which information should be treated, let it suffice here to emphasize that whichever of these three (or perhaps additional) approaches to characterizing the understanding of information economics is used will have a fundamental impact on information agenda-setting and policy-making criteria.

### THE CHANGING FACE OF THE INFORMATION BUSINESS

Technology is clearly a driving force behind the need to create an information policy. As John McLaughlin has graphically pointed out in his maps of the information business (in Chapter 2), a simple landscape in 1780, characterized by widely separated and clearly demarcated industry segments, had yielded to an only slightly more complex picture in 1880. But by 1980 much of the open territory had been filled in, highlighting the convergence of what had been easily recognized arenas of either transmitters of information or creators of information. Many of these new industries owe their existence to the emergence of electronic computers in the past thirty years and to the extensive development of the telecommunications infrastructure in the last hundred years. The confluence of these two technological wonders has produced a hybrid "communications" arena that underlies much of the changing structure of the information industry.

The information business maps in Chapter 2 make it possible to see the dynamic movement taking place behind seemingly static labels. Within the information industry players such as the U.S. Postal Service, the Washington Post Company, Dun & Bradstreet, Citicorp, Exxon, Harris Corporation and numerous others of all sizes, public and private, foreign, transnational as well as domestic are having to cope with the changing technology and its impact on their self-perceptions and on their traditional markets. For example, newspaper publishers who once saw classified advertising as being exclusively their turf are now coming to realize that new methods of information distribution, such as cable TV systems, as well as telephone lines, coupled to near or distant computers, broaden the realm of potential competitors for this service. Similarly, mass market retailers and financial institutions are starting to see these channels as providing new opportunities for expanding their traditional lines of business or otherwise redefining their roles.

Thus traditional elements of stability have been lost, as blurring boundaries become the rule in the ever-more-crowded information business. But as is frequently the case during periods of structural upheaval, the same factors are creating opportunities for those individual firms and entrepreneurs that are nimblest in staking out new territory, unhindered by the blinders of the old order's architecture.

## STRUCTURING THE NEW FRAMEWORK

If the territory is in fact changing, then it is necessary to consider modifying the labels that used to be applied to the old world. For example, a newspaper publisher used to be one who transformed certain types of information into a product, a true commodity in the form of ink on newsprint. A book is a familiar print format, and television is a term commonly used to connote that medium that sent programming ranging from "Laverne and Shirley" to "the CBS Evening News" into the home. A library has been a repository for books, and a bank a repository for money.

The breakdown in this method of labeling can be seen in the use of such makeshift terms as "electronic newspaper" or "video publishing." Some libraries have access to "on-line" data bases as well as on-line catalogues. Banks, which for years have sold themselves at the retail level by proclaiming friendly, personal service, are finding profitable consumer response to machines that handle their transactions twenty-four hours a day, perhaps at a distant site. And consumers in the home, who have long been used to thinking of the television set as a passive instrument, are being asked to interact with the video display through video games, two-way cable, personal computers, and on-line data bases that have been called "viewdata." In a *Science* magazine article some years ago, Edwin R. Parker and Donald A. Dunn described the system of the future combining the computer, wires, and the video screen as a "combined library, newspaper, mail-order catalog, post office, classroom, and theater."

Changing information technologies are most important today in expanding *accessbility* to information. Content of messages is not changing so much as the range of alternative conduits by which it can be processed and transmitted and the variety of formats in which they can be displayed.

For much of history, man was limited to symbolic representations by ink on some material for information storage (other than in personal memory), and transmittal was limited to word-of-mouth or limited point-to-point physical delivery by some kind of courier. The printing press helped multiply the available supply of these products and therefore became an inducement to demand via reduced costs and prices. The development of the telegraph and the telephone for the first time permitted messages to be sent bypassing the physical distribution network. Film, then broadcast technologies—first radio and then television—added a new dimension by allowing the sender of the information to reach a mass audience with one common message. Film and television, moreover, released information providers from having to deal exclusively in symbols in the form of written and spoken words by enabling them to show images that presumably could correspond one-to-one with the intended reality.

Perhaps the best way to begin to identify the issues that may be raised by the convergence of new information technologies with existing information needs is to create a scenario that speculates on how the individual family may be getting its information in 1990.

Here is the picture that could be painted by a futurist looking at 1990.

It's a crisp November morning. The ring of an alarm wakes up Mrs. Frost at 7:00 A.M. She turns on the TV set, but instead of tuning to the "Today" show she hits a few buttons on a calculatorlike device and the local weather report fills the screen. Mr. Frost joins her, presses a few more keys and last night's basketball scores appear. Yet another set of instructions bring into view some news headlines. The Frosts get the two kids off to school and prepare for work. After a quick breakfast Mr. Frost, an oil trader for a major energy company, sits down at his desk in a corner of the bedroom and turns on a video display terminal (VDT), which has a typewriterlike keyboard, and types some instructions. Immediately a message appears on the screen, describing a delay in a crude-oil shipment and telling him to call his boss. Frost also asks for other messages and gets a screenful of them. He gets busy on the telephone, calling his boss at home and completing other business tasks, using the telephone and his VDT to send and receive messages.

Meanwhile, Mrs. Frost is working at her desk in the family room. She is an assistant vice president at a major commercial bank. Her routine and methods are similar to those of her husband. At lunchtime the Frosts eat in the kitchen and turn on the television set to call up some information on meat specials at the local supermarkets. Chopped sirloin—at $3.89 a pound—looks pretty good at the A&P. They decide to order some, along with several other items, and confirm the order using their keypad. Delivery is scheduled for between 4 and 5 o'clock that afternoon.

Mrs. Frost has scheduled a meeting at 2 o'clock with the financial VP and controller of a client. At the appointed hour the conference call is made and the three talk, each from their at-home offices. The clients have a new cash flow statement and put it on their facsimile machine to send to Mrs. Frost's machine, and the conversation continues. Mr. Frost, meanwhile, is writing a few memos on his VDT. Since he is a slow typist and an atrocious speller, he transfers the memos to his secretary, whose own terminal notifies her of work waiting. She makes the corrections on her screen and forwards the memos to the electronic mailboxes of the appropriate recipients.

At 3.30 P.M., the kids come home from school. Careful not to disturb Mom and Dad, they go into the recreation room in the basement and keep busy. Jennifer Frost, ten years old, turns to channel 71 on the television to watch an entertaining science program for children. Her four-teen-year-old brother, Buzz, decides to start his homework, a report on the space program that sent an American to the moon in 1969. He goes to his TV set with its full keyboard and types in "manned space program, U.S. 1960–1970." In seconds, forty words appear on the screen, the start of a long article on the subject from the World Book Encyclopedia database service. The text also makes reference to some film clips of the lift-off and moon landing stored on one of the videodiscs that came with the subscription to the World Book. Buzz puts disc 3 into the machine and pushes index 3357; the television set shows the historical sequence of the first step on the moon.

The Frosts by now have signed off their machines. The local and national news shows are on during dinner, but the Frosts like to have family talk while they eat, so their video tape machine records the shows for later viewing. After dinner and the news (which he skimmed through with his fast forward control), Mr. Frost goes back to his desk to clean up some work on his terminal. Mrs. Frost calls her mother in Florida and discovers that she answers the call at a friend's house across town where she is playing mah-jong. Later, while reading the newspaper, Mrs. Frost remembers she had wanted to check the classified ads for painters to give estimates to do their house. Using the TV set and keypad, she queries the newspaper's classified section and finding no one who looks good, calls up the Yellow Pages classifieds, which produces ads from several painters offering off-season specials that week.

While Buzz finishes his report, the rest of the family gathers to watch a live telecast of the Pennsylvania Ballet performing at Lincoln Center in New York. It is being carried by the Sears Satellite Broadcasting Network. Before bed, Buzz and Mr. Frost play a game of electronic Scrabble, using a program that they selected from the cable company's computer. Before retiring herself, Mrs. Frost sits down at the family's personal computer and calls up the Dow Jones data bank to get an update on the performance of the family's securities. Using a purchased program, she uses the current prices to compute automatically the current market value and to determine total appreciation. The computer also reminds her that a few bills are due for payment that day, so despite the late hour she calls the bank and responds to the computer's voice with her account number, to whom the bills are to be paid, and the amount of each. She thinks of how pleasant it is to conduct this transaction by talking rather than using the terminal. As an employee of the bank, she feels that the experimental system using voice recognition has been quite reliable and is pleased to be one of the few hundred to have access to it.

Ready to retire, Mr. Frost winds up the old alarm clock and pulls out the alarm set lever. As he drifts off to sleep he thinks that the loud and familiar tick-tick is a pleasant change from the quiet hum of the electronic terminals all day.

Let us summarize the technology that the Frosts made use of. Everything mentioned is available or could be available today.

First, the Frosts have a viewdata service, such as England's Prestel, or Knight-Ridder's Viewtron. Having memorized certain index numbers, they can get such screens of information as news headlines, weather, and sports. The television set is being used as a video terminal, connected to a small computer in the city by a telephone line. Using an auto dial feature, the computer is dialed whenever the viewdata unit is turned on.

Clearly both Frosts have an office at home. Their employers have provided them each with what is essentially a small computer, complete with some memory, a keyboard, and video display terminal. They are connected to their respective host computers by a telephone line and each Frost has in addition yet another telephone line for normal voice communication.

The videotex system was used by Mr. and Mrs. Frost to do some comparative food shopping and ordering. Mrs. Frost has a facsimile machine by her desk, which transmits a full 8½- by 11-inch typed sheet of paper over the telephone line in under one minute. They also have hard copy printers, so that finished documents that are meant to be kept on paper can be transmitted without resorting to physical mail or messenger delivery.

Jennifer Frost turned to channel 71 on the two-way cable system. The program she watched was put out by Western Publishing Company, a Mattel subsidiary. The cable companies purchased the program and offer it on the pay-per-view premium service, which means that the Frosts will be billed $1.00 for that show. Buzz made use of the World Book's data base connected to the video terminal by telephone lines. The Frosts paid $500 for up to 10 hours per month of connect time over five years. Thereafter, they will have to pay additional, but lower fees. Buzz also made use of the optical scanning videodisc machine the family purchased from Pioneer. World Book also sold an annual videodisc summarizing the year's events incorporating news clips and other special material.

Of course, they have a videocassette tape machine to record off-the-air programming. It may be one of the older ½-inch Beta or VHS machines, or a newer ¼-inch longitudinal video recorder. Mrs. Frost reached her mother because of the call-forwarding service that the local telephone exchange offered. Mrs. Frost's mother had dialed a local computer and told it the number where she could be reached, so her daughter's call automatically was transferred to the mah-jong game location.

In recent years, the Frosts have been able to receive high-quality special interest programs via direct broadcast satellite—the method by which the Pennsylvania Ballet program came into their home. A concave dish, three feet in diameter, sits on the roof of their house. They have access to as many as six channels of high-quality cultural, educational, and other entertainment programming.

The Scrabble game Buzz and his father played is an optional feature of the cable system. By subscribing to the game service, the Frost's can choose from among 100 electronic games stored in the cable operator's computer. Their television set incorporates a small memory capacity and thus all the instructions needed to play were sent down the cable and stored, so playing the game itself required no computer time—it is entirely self-contained in the home.

The Frost's have a personal computer with which they can write their own programs, or they can buy off-the-shelf programs. The computer also can tie in to many of the data-base networks that have been initiated by a variety of firms, including traditional publishers such as CBS and Dow Jones, as well as the banks, mail order merchandisers, government agencies and AT&T. In this case Mrs. Frost has merged current on-line stock closings from Dow Jones with an internal program that has stored the family's holdings. It is the internal program that computes the portfolio's value, saving computer connect time with the on-line network.

While much attention is being paid to the video display terminal as a means of output display and the keyboard or keypad as input, great advances are being made in computer voice recognition and synthesis. Many moviegoers still remember Hal, the all-too-human computer in Stanley Kubrick's movie *2001: A Space Odyssey.* Using a system that may well be ready for mass application by the end of this decade, Mrs. Frost had a "conversation" with the computer, told it what bills she wished paid, with the computer prompting her with appropriate responses at each stage. If such processes become commonplace, the VDT and keyboard may turn out to be merely an intermediate stage for communication with computers as voice-to-voice—the manner in which people are most used to conducting many transactions—becomes possible again.

Thus we have had here a glimpse of much of the new technology: two-way cable, viewdata, electronic mail, word processing, facsimile, videodiscs, videocassettes, microprocessors, direct satellite broadcasting, home computers, on-line data banks for the home, voice synthesis, voice recognition, and so on.

The old-fashioned wind-up alarm clock of the Frosts hints that not all of the older ways are going to be replaced by new technology. Indeed in the history of technology, innovation often coexists with the old. The telephone did not eliminate the need for old-fashioned mail service, nor have radio and television caused the demise of newspapers, magazines, or threatrical films; in each case, though, the older medium has had to adapt to a different environment.

## PROBLEMS AND POLICY

A number of questions arise from the Frost scenario, and others can be gleaned from the changing information industry map:

### Who Will Pay?

Consumers of information do not always pay its full cost, at least not directly. For magazines, the subscription price often accounts for 35 to 40 percent of total revenue, the rest coming from advertising. Many professional and trade magazines are financed completely by advertising sales. Newspaper publishers count on advertising for 70 to 90 percent of revenue. Traditional television and radio broadcasting is paid for exclusively by advertising, with the user having only the cost of the receiver (and of course, the indirect cost paid in purchasing products that have been advertised).

Other information formats are user supported. Books, scholarly journals, newsletters, and most electronic data-base services are totally user supported (with the exception of subsidies professional societies may provide for their publications). Residential telephone service, although paid for by users, nonetheless has traditionally been subsidized indirectly by higher rates business paid for telephone service. Long-distance charges also were set high enough to help subsidize local service. Recent deregulation of telecommunications seems to be pushing prices to reflect costs more directly.

The rate of diffusion of the newer information services may well depend on how they will be financed. The costs of all the hardware alone that the Frosts used, not counting their at-home office equipment, could easily approach $4,000 in 1980 dollars, plus repairs and eventual replacement. In addition, charges for cable, premium programming, and additional telephone services that would be needed to connect the various terminals with the information-laden computers could total $1,200.00 annually. Finally, prerecorded programming for a videodisc player would be discretionary, but at $7.00 to $20.00 per program, each would be equivalent to the price of a hardcover book.

The magnitude of this level of expenditures suggests that not all these devices will achieve equal penetration in the consumer marketplace. It remains to be seen to what extent advertisers will find ways to use these devices in ways that have roughly the same impact as current advertising vehicles.

## Who Will Have Access?

Will the current movement of increased user-supported information undermine efforts by the poorer segments of the community to gain equal access to information? By 1983, the 34 percent of homes that already had cable bringing televised programming had information services that those without cable did not, such as special interest programs in Spanish, topics of interest to the black community, news services, and in some cases shopping information. Some businesses in these wired communities can get financial information that business in noncable areas cannot.

Some critics are already worrying that the new technology will further separate the information haves from the have-nots and—to the extent that information is power—will create a society stratified according to who can afford how much information. Although such an argument flies in the face of the historical evidence that technology *lessens* such gaps, it has given rise to such questions as: Should some government agency (thus the taxpayers) subsidize certain information hardware and programming for the poor? Should public libraries be diverting funds from the purchase of books to video display terminals and data-base subscription for use directly by patrons? Should videodiscs be lent out the way books now are? At what point can teachers give assignments that presuppose placement in the home of the required cable hook-up or computer?

## Who Will Profit?

Today the creators of information share the profit with those who market and deliver it. Remuneration at all levels is often based on agreed percentages of the revenue or gross profit. In the case of a book, sales are relatively simple to measure. In musical recordings it may be by the number of records sold or amount of radio playing time.

Technology has been creating problems, however, because it has become increasingly simple to capture and transmit information without the knowledge of its owner or licensee. The photocopying machine has reduced the sales of some books or journals, as have computers that permit resource-sharing by libraries. Besides the professional pirating of records, audiocassettes have encouraged unmeasured millions of off-the-air radio recordings of music or recording from a borrowed album. Now a U.S. District Court has rejected the argument of two theatrical film distributors that videotape recorders deprive them of legitimate revenues. To what extent, for example, may millions of people recording shows fail to show up in TV ratings surveys, thus affecting advertising rates? In the future, distributors of programming via satellite will have to contend with people who have earth stations that can pick up their signals for free. (Actually most such signals do have or could have some form of encryption, but unauthorized "black box" decoders are likely to appear to unscramble the signals. This would lead to a game between the transmitters and the pirates of increasingly complex—and costly—encryption.) And will there be a mechanism in the computer to keep track of the number of times users have retrieved information created by any given author?

Furthermore, new formulas may have to be worked out to account for the changing roles of wholesalers and transmitters of information. Today's jobbers, independent distributors, and carriers of physically delivered products will have counterparts in the totally electronic processes in the form of information utilities, such as Lockheed's Dialog, enhanced service common carriers such as MCI, and packet-switching networks such as Telenet. The consumer will still depend on the traditional common carrier telephone systems for at least part of the transmission, while larger businesses and institutions may find themselves dealing with specialized services that have their own facilities to completely bypass the telephone network, such as the Satellite Business Systems venture of IBM, Aetna, and Comsat.

### How Will Conflicts Be Resolved?

The information business maps (chapter 2) point out the growing potential for conflicts among players due to the breakdown of clearly defined and understood territories. The line has become virtually indistinguishable between communications and data processing services. The ability of the hypothetical Mrs. Frost to reach her mother at a telephone that ostensibly has a number different from the one called is but one small piece of evidence that the telephone system is already an "intelligent" network. Other potential conflicts include compatibility of equipment from numerous manufacturers with one another as well as the software—or information content—of competing suppliers. There are, for example, at least three incompatible videodisc systems announced for the marketplace. The ability of any given electronic database to communicate with a user's terminal may depend on some form of compatibility being built into the system either by standards or through programming. The very mention of standards sends certain elements of the information community into a tizzy. Compatibility comes only at some expense; it may be in the form of years of negotiation among participants, at the expense of delaying widespread adoption of the technology. It may be in the form of engineering intelligence into the system, at the cost of the research and development as well as the slower processing speeds for such intermediary transformation. Or it may be in the form of a dominant supplier forcing a de facto standard via market domination, at the expense of reduced product differentiation and experimentation.

Although the marketplace is often an adequate method of conflict resolution, it is sometimes not up to the task, or it may take longer than society is willing to tolerate. In such instance the government may have to broker a solution. This was seen in the compromises involved in creation of the Copyright Act of 1976 (recognizing that conflicts still arise). In the past, the federal government has had to resolve conflicts on a resolution standard for television, on the technology for color television, on mandatory incorporation of click dials on television sets for UHF, and in 1980, on a single system for stereo AM radio transmission.

Also in the broadcast area, the federal government has long been in the conflict resolution business in its licensing procedure for multiple contenders for limited broadcast frequencies. Today some of the conflict is occurring at the state and local level, as in the granting of cable franchises among competing interests. As a portent of what may become a recurring issue of cross-media ownership, the state cable commission in Connecticut has banned the firm that owns the only newspaper in Hartford from simultaneous ownership of the two cable systems serving the same area.

The information technology of the 1980s will also be likely to stir up conflicts within the government. In mid-1980, for example, some members of the Congress took issue with the authority of the Federal Communications Commission to undertake what these elected officials perceive to be their task in the (de)regulation of communications. Such is the nature of a dynamic information industry environment.

## Who Will Provide What Services and under What Conditions?

The ultimate roster of players in the information marketplace will affect the outcome of the conflicts. It may well include many of the traditional suppliers of information goods and services, such as Dow Jones, CBS, RCA, the Harris Corporation, AT&T, the U.S. Postal Service, and IBM. But we may also see the participation of firms from industries that only in recent years are beginning to be viewed as entrants into the information business: financial institutions like Citicorp, American Express, and Merrill Lynch; retailers such as J.C. Penney or Sears; paper manufacturers like Mead Corporation; and the federal government, through its vast holdings of public information adaptable to electronic distribution directly to the public.

## What Are the Transnational Implications of Technologies that Recognize No Boundaries?

Canada has long been sensitive to the threat of being an information satellite of the United States because the impact of that status on its people's national identity. Therefore, they have adjusted local laws to limit ownership of communications companies by aliens and have further restricted the "made in the U.S." content of their print and electronic programming.

In Western Europe, public positions supporting free flow of information must be contrasted to stringent restrictions being implemented in Sweden, Germany, and France, among others. Revised regulations from the West German Ministry of Posts and Telecommunications issued in April 1980, for example, ensures that all data transmitted by telephone lines into or out of that country travel on lines controlled by the Ministry.

In addition, the less developed nations are demanding that they have a share of the limited satellite frequencies that Japan and the Western world would like to take for their own expanding military and civilian information transmission needs. Although these nations have neither the hardware nor the information needs for such allocations now, they stood together at the World Administrative Radio Conference in 1979 to establish their right to a piece of the sky.

## IMPLICATIONS FOR LIBRARIES AND
## THE INFORMATION MARKETPLACE

Little of this new technology is changing the *content* of the communication itself. When we talk about cable, computers, and videodisc players we are talking about machines or processes for *distributing* information. But it is still the information itself and how it is to be used that should remain both the starting and ending concern of the information revolution.

Videotex, for example, will succeed as a residential service only if it can provide information in a form that is inherently superior to the information that is already available using traditional formats. In Great Britain, Prestel is offering airline flight schedules. Anyone who has tried to use the Official Airline Guide knows how complicated it is to figure out prices, current service, and connections. It still remains much easier to call a travel agent, who can make use of the new technology, which does not yet seem appropriate for residential use. On the other hand one of the most popular uses of Prestel has been for off-track betting, presumably because it can provide up-to-the-minute odds and track conditions better than a newspaper printed the previous night.

That the emphasis should be content is reinforced by looking at the traditional information formats. A book or magazine publisher today does not own the hardware—the presses—or even the delivery mechanism for its product. Few suppliers of televison programming own a station, let alone a network. The opportunities are in the information *creation*—the programming. Conversely, consumers are going to invest in the new hardware only if they perceive it will provide them with information that is different or in some way better than what they now have. While a few aficionados like to buy new gadgets, faced with the great expense and bewildering array of options, the mass market is likely to develop with less abandon. The rapid growth in cable systems today comes only after nearly twenty years of annual predictions of its imminent take-off. Government regulation had a hand in holding it down, but it also needed the programming support not available until earth satellites made programming distribution inexpensive and universal.

The information future may be analogous to a supermarket. There will be many products and services offered by numerous vendors. A few, such as videodisc players and software, should find a mass market,

as will at least basic cable and accompanying special interest pro-
graming networks and syndicates. Other parts of the package will be
used by relatively small but not necessarily congruent segments of the
population. Rarely have the contemporaries of technological innovation been able to foresee accurately their most popular applications.
Edison expected the phonograph to be a great cultural and educational device. Television was also predicted to be a powerful medium
for education. Several years ago holography was promoted as a mar-
velous technology for industry, art, and defense. Today it is used to
sculpt three dimensional busts.

Thus the eventual application of much of the new technology may
be a coming together of several forces that are required to create a
new product or service. The mass circulation daily newspaper needed
more than Gutenberg's printing press. Technology had to produce
cheap paper and develop the steam engine to attach to a rotary press.
Increased literacy, sufficient disposable personal income, and a political climate favoring mass circulation were among the factors that
stimulated the coming of age of the modern newspaper.

One crucial element in this is an understanding of the capabilities
and limitations of the technology. A typical telephone line can carry
far less data per second than a cable channel, but this may be quite
sufficient for most home or office textual information, since we read
far slower than the transmission and display speeds. Although a cable
channel does have a broadband characteristic, it is difficult to create a
switched network using cable as deployed by CATV companies. Unlike the telephone system, which can connect any telephone terminal
with virtually any other one in the world, for practical purposes the
cable user today cannot go any further than whatever is located at the
base of the local cable transmitter. A major investment would be required to convert today's CATV system into one paralleling the existing telephone network.

### Agenda Items

One specific agenda item that follows from the content, process, and
format framework for the information industry concerns the self-
description of traditional participants. Clearly, the old description
will not serve well in the 1980s for the newspaper publisher, television
broadcaster, or library manager. It will be essential for all institutions
to rethink the economics of the marketplace.

Traditionally, information has been sold in the marketplace, although some of the conduits, such as the U.S. Postal Service, have been subsidized by the government. Libraries, for one, have purchased information of the type that is primarily user supported. Thus few libraries today have viewing rooms for advertiser-supported television, having concentrated more on relatively expensive books and journals. If the age of electronics does indeed shift more information to electronic distribution, then it follows that libraries will have to overcome their long affiliation with a particular format—the printed page—and shift more of their acquisition budgets to new formats, such as electronic data bases. It may also require a change in typical expense categories, as the new technology demands extensive acquisition and maintenance of video hardware and growing reliance on usage-sensitive services, such as "connect time" for patrons instead of one-time investment in books. Expenditures, on data-base subscriptions, telephone lines and computer time on the one hand and expensive video display terminals and perhaps videodisc players and programs on the other hand, may be required to continue providing the same types of information to patrons as they are now doing.

This in turn will heat up the debate on how libraries should continue to be financed. Public, academic, or special libraries have not typically charged users to read or borrow books or micromaterials. However, some libraries do charge for newer electronic services, such as searching a remote data base. In some cases the electronic search may even replace the hard-copy sources that had been available simultaneously. The question has arisen of whether the patron should pay the total cost, including overhead, of supporting this system or only some marginal rate reflecting direct costs associated with the search. The urgency of this issue will likely grow as such services become not only more widespread but routine. Thus the library patron who at one time would have "free" access to reference material may in the future have to pay for the same information, unless assumptions that form the basis of library budgets are modified to account for the shift in information processes and formats.

A second agenda item following from this may be a decision on *where* library services are provided. Today the user generally must come to the physical library facility. This could become less necessary for certain types of searches. Already the movement to on-line catalogues presents the possibility of patrons accessing these data bases for literature searches from terminals in their own homes or offices.

Perhaps a stickier problem will be the propriety of patrons' using a commercial data base to which the library has subscribed, but from the user's personal terminal. Presumably this would be cheaper than direct individual or corporate subscriptions to the data base. That is, a call to the library could conceivably give patrons access to remote computers, with a profound impact on the financial viability for the data-base publishers. Some public libraries, such as the Free Library of Philadelphia, allow users to call up a resource person, who may access a data base such as the *New York Times* Information Bank to answer the question. At issue is the need to assess the effects of bypassing that resource person.

A third item, associated with the other two, is *how* the new technology may be used, particularly the on-line data bases. The two most obvious alternatives are either hands-on or through an intermediary. The latter is now most common, in part because of the special protocols needed to efficiently use many of these services, in part because of the limited number of terminals and the expense of allowing uncontrolled access. Continued adherence to this approach would be analogous to the closed stacks system in many large libraries. On the other hand, improvements in data-base protocols, to make them friendly, will make it easier for nonspecialized users to search out information and increase pressure for direct user interaction with the information source.

Finally, in the immediate future, libraries (particularly public libraries) must prepare for possible political problems. Once library managers themselves come to grips with the new technology, they will have to sell the concepts to those who control the purse strings. Managers will have to explain the need to shift some funds from asset acquisition in the form of books, to expense categories for communications and data-base services. It is at this point that some of the social issues of who has access and at what cost may be resolved. But the transition may not come easily, as traditional methods and approaches tend to continue through momentum.

Although we cannot predict with much certainty the exact make-up of the information marketplace of 1990, we do have the knowledge to foresee what the potential array of gadgets—the hardware—may consist of and what capabilities they will have. They will provide information via a variety of processes using optional formats, ranging from the familiar book to emerging possibilities such as computer-synthesized voice.

Technology will most certainly change the information business map of the 1980s. It will create some upheavals of existing methods and traditions and at the same time provide opportunities to enhance profits, service, and scope. There are policy issues that must be addressed both publicly and privately. Several have been examined here. These include:

1.  The financial and economic realities of the marketplace. Individual firms will be making strategic decisions regarding their roles as information providers or processors. Much will depend on the response of information consumers to the choices and prices of the formats and conduits they are offered.
2.  Information equity in society. This is largely a public policy issue. The degree to which it becomes a high priority will depend on the decisions in the private sector on pricing new information services and the degree to which user-supported information products replace those that are subsidized by advertisers, the government, and other sources.
3.  Freedom of information flow and access. This encompasses national policies on transborder data flow as well as the constant need for fine tuning the balance among often conflicting concerns for personal privacy, proprietary information, ownership, and compensation for information—the need and the right to know.
4.  The role of the library. From the users' viewpoint, the library will remain a constant: a repository of information. From the managers' and suppliers' perspective, maintaining that service will require adjustments and reevaluation on how best to achieve the objective of serving the user.

What must be suppressed is the urge that is sometimes manifest in times of change to set policies based on expectations—that is, anticipating *possible* outcomes and trying to head them off before they occur. This can lead to excessive regulation, unnecessary agonizing, and needless expenditures of already scarce human and monetary resources. It is certainly advisable to be alert to potential policy issues, but rather than trying to predict the future, we might better direct our efforts toward what sociologist Daniel Bell suggests is "the more complicated and subtle art of defining alternatives."

### NOTE

1.  Calculated from estimates in *The Library Market for Publications Systems, 1979–1983* (White Plains, N.Y.: Knowledge Industry Publications, 1978).

## Appendix 4A.
## INFORMATION INDUSTRY
## REVENUES—EXPLANATORY NOTES

### Compunications

*Computer software and service suppliers.* Revenues for services (remote, batch, and professional) and software (independent, and, as of 1980, systems house), from International Data Corporation, Waltham, Mass.

*Computer systems manufacturers.* Revenues for leading manufacturers, from International Data Corporation, Waltham, Mass.

*Electronic components and accessories.* Value of shipments, from *U.S. Industrial Outlook,* annual, based on government statistics.

*Mobil radio systems.* 1970–1978 revenues for common carrier and licensed mobile radio; the latter services are estimates based on data from the FCC Common Carrier Bureau, extrapolated from 1965 data. 1979–1981 figures are for total land-mobile radio common carrier equipment and services, except those counted in traditional telephone and telegraph revenues. *U.S. Industrial Outlook,* annual.

*Satellite carriers.* Total operating revenues for Comsat, from the FCC Common Carrier Bureau, and revenues, from operational domestic satellite companies estimated by International Resources Development, Inc., Norwalk, Conn.

*Telegraph.* Total operating revenues for domestic telegraph, from *FCC Statistics of Common Carriers,* with added data from FCC Common Carrier Bureau, Statistics Division.

*Telephone.* Operating revenues, from *FCC Statistics of Communications Common Carriers,* with added data from the FCC Common Carrier Bureau, Statistics Division.

*Terrestrial Common Carriers.* Total revenues for terrestrial operations, from FCC Common Carrier Bureau.

### Media and Entertainment

*Advertising.* Ad agency gross income, from *U.S. Industrial Outlook,* annual.

*Broadcast radio.* Commercial radio gross revenues (less commissions), from *FCC News* and *U.S. Industrial Outlook* (1979).

*Broadcast TV.* Gross advertising plus all other broadcast revenues (less commissions), from *FCC News* and *U.S. Industrial Outlook,* annual.

*Book publishing.* Value of shipments, from *U.S. Industrial Outlook,* annual.

*Cable TV.* Revenues, from FCC Cable TV Bureau, *FCC News* (1979), and *U.S. Industrial Outlook* (1980 and 1981).

*News wire services.* Estimated gross annual revenues worldwide for Associated Press and United Press International, from *New York Times,* United Press International, and Associated Press, plus PIRP projections.

*Motion picture distribution and exhibition.* Gross domestic box office receipts plus remittals from receipts of overseas film rentals from *U.S. Industrial Outlook,* annual, and Bureau of Industrial Economics.

*Newspaper publishing.* Value of shipments (1970–1971) or receipts (1972–1979) from *U.S. Industrial Outlook,* annual.

*Organized sports, arenas.* The market value of purchased admissions to spectator sports by individuals and nonprofit institutions, from U.S. Department of Commerce, *Statistical Abstracts of the United States,* annual, and Census Bureau.

*Periodical publishing.* Value of shipments, from *U.S. Industrial Outlook,* annual.

*Printing, book and commercial.* Value of shipments, from *U.S. Industrial Outlook,* annual.

*Radio and TV communications equipment.* Value of shipments, from the U.S. Department of Commerce, *Census of Manufactures* (actual figures aggregated every five years, projections published annually), and *U.S. Industrial Outlook,* annual.

*Theaters.* Total box office receipts for Broadway and road theaters from *Variety,* weekly.


### Postal


*U.S. Postal Service.* Operating revenues, from the *Annual Report of the Post Master General.*

*Private information delivery services.* Operating revenues are estimates based on figures reported by largest publicly owned firms.

### Financial and Legal

*Banking and credit.* Total receipts for partnerships and corporations and business receipts for sole proprietorships for banking and credit agencies, from Internal Revenue Service, Statistics Division.

*Brokerage industries.* Total receipts for partnerships and corporations, plus business receipts for sole proprietorships for real estate brokers and security and commodity brokers, dealers, exchanges, and services, from Internal Revenue Service, Statistics Division.

*Insurance.* Total receipts for partnerships and corporations and business receipts from proprietorships for insurance agents and carriers, from Internal Revenue Service, Statistics Division.

*Legal services.* Business receipts from sole proprietorships, partnerships, and corporations, from Internal Revenue Service, Statistics Division.

### Miscellaneous Manufacturing

*Paper and allied products.* Value of shipments, from the *U.S. Industrial Outlook,* annual, based on government statistics.

*Photographic equipment and supplies.* Value of shipments, from *U.S. Industrial Outlook,* annual, based on government statistics.

*Business consulting services.* Business receipts for management and public relations firms for sole proprietorships and partnerships, from Internal Revenue Service, Statistics Division.

### Miscellaneous Services

*Business information services.* Estimated revenues of newsletters, loose-leaf services, data bases, and research services, from Knowledge Industry Publications, White Plains, N.Y.

*Marketing research services.* Research revenues of the ten largest companies, from *Advertising Age,* weekly. (This survey appears annually in May-June).

## Government Expenditures

*U.S. Census Bureau.* Total of federal and trust fund outlays, from U.S. Department of Commerce. (1980 figure is for a decennial year in which extra funds are allocated for redistricting according to Congress.)

*County agents.* Sum of federal, state, local, and nontaxable appropriations, from U.S. Department of Agriculture.

*Libraries.* Total expenditures, from Knowledge Industries Publications, White Plains, N.Y., based on U.S. Department of Education, National Center for Education Statistics figures, plus PIRP projections.

*National intelligence community.* Budgeted expenditures for U.S. defense, military intelligence, and communications (which includes the National Security Agency), and the Central Intelligence Agency, from the *Budget of the U.S. Government,* annual.

*National Technical Information Service.* Sum of appropriations and sales, from NTIS Budget Office.

*Research and development.* Functional outlays in federal (not industrial or educational) research and development, from *Statistical Abstracts of the United States,* annual, and *Science and Government Report,* November 15, 1982, National Science Foundation.

*Schooling.* Expenditures by federal, state, and local public and nonpublic elementary and secondary schools and institutions of higher learning, from *Statistical Abstracts of the United States,* annual, and U.S. Department of Commerce, Bureau of the Census.

*Social Security Administration.* Total administration outlays, from the Social Security Administration.

# TRENDS AND FORCES IN DISTRIBUTION

# 5 ELECTRONIC DISTRIBUTION OF INFORMATION TO THE CONSUMER AND LOW-VOLUME INSTITUTIONAL MARKET

*Benjamin M. Compaine*

On May 27, 1978, in Columbus, Ohio, Warner-Amex Cable Communications' Qube cable television service started operating. For the first time in the United States, a viewing audience had a two-way link with the transmitter of commercial televised programming. To some this was the opening shot in what has since been a salvo of communications offerings to the residential or small business user. Or it may be only one among many of a continuing stream of novel marketing ideas that fail to find widespread consumer acceptance, destined to be a footnote in the future history books of technological progress. ("Residential" and "consumer" are used interchangeably here to refer to nonbusiness or institutional end users.)

Qube is simply the elaboration of particular pieces of technology that themselves are not new. It builds on digital computers, which in 1980 were entering their fourth decade of use and on coaxial cable, which had been around even longer.

For technological innovation to have mass impact requires interaction with a complex set of factors, including economic and social conditions. Thus Qube became feasible in 1978 in part because the cost of using computers had come down significantly, not because the possibility of using them had only then been perceived. In assessing

123

policy research priorities in the electronic delivery of information to consumers and small business, this chapter therefore starts with the premise that it is becoming newly *feasible* to consider applying much of "new media," such as videocassettes, on-line data bases, and interactive cable, for certain low-cost purposes.

The purpose of this chapter is to explain and justify the need to study the broad territory that can be characterized variously as local distribution of information, distribution of information to residential consumers and other relatively low-volume users, new retail channels of information distribution, or electronic distribution of information to the low-volume consumer/institutional market. In effect, it presents the rationale for undertaking a series of specific, well-defined projects. Together, they will sort out the options and their implications created by these so-called new media for traditional information suppliers (publishers and programmers) as well as processors and carriers of the information (broadcasters, telephone companies, cable operators, the U.S. Postal Service, and private couriers).

## WHY EMPHASIS ON LOW-VOLUME USERS

The needs of the market composed of consumers and small institutions differ from the needs of the market composed of large industry and government. The latter are viewed as the cream by many suppliers of communications services. Initiatives such as those coming from Satellite Business Systems (SBS) seek to provide specialized services for high-volume movers of electronic data to high-volume users. The U.S. government, especially the military, has its own needs and suppliers. Consumer and small business users, on the other hand, need relatively low volumes of information from the information supplier to recipient. Suppliers of information, such as data-base publishers or cable operators, are in reality high-volume information processors and may use services similar to those being proposed by SBS and others for their own activities of gathering and storing information. But in reaching the many dispersed end users, they may be best served by a distribution network that can efficiently handle relatively low volumes of information to scattered end points. Thus the systems being developed for the large-volume users will be of unneeded sophistication and probably will be too expensive for the low-volume users. Like the increasing competition in the long-haul, high-volume market, however, local distribution, dominated in the past by a local telephone company, a few local broadcasters, and the U.S. Postal Service, may also be on the verge of a rapid growth in the number of alternative conduits into the home and work place. Moreover the so-called low-volume customers are a large aggregate market.

## A SAMPLER OF NEW MEDIA ACTIVITIES, CIRCA 1981

IBM, best known for its computers and office equipment, for a time was also a partner in a firm that manufactured videodisc players and videodiscs. American Telephone & Telegraph (AT&T) has experimented with electronic delivery of directory information to residential users via telephone lines for text display on a video screen. Newspaper publisher Knight-Ridder was testing a consumer-oriented electronic data-base accessible via telephone lines for display on a common television receiver's video screen. Dow Jones was trying out a method of delivery of its News Retrieval Service via satellite and cable channel. Its Ottaway Newspapers subsidiary, along with United Press International (UPI) and others were providing news to homes via cable. Bell Laboratories and an Exxon Enterprises subsidiary were two of several firms making rapid strides in perfecting voice recognition and synthesis. And the Federal Communications Commission (FCC) had announced a major policy statement that attempts to clarify the long-murky demarcation line between unregulated data processing and regulated communications. Commercial broadcasters ABC, CBS and RCA were all producing plans for either hardware and/or programming for videodiscs, videocassettes, and cable. Brief vignettes of some relevant activities at a sampling of firms are given in Appendix 5A to suggest the breadth of interest.

For the most part these and many similar activities underway at a variety of firms in the traditional media industry as well as in other seemingly unrelated areas, such as banking, were largely prototypes or experimental. While many of the hardware components are proven, such as the computers or terminals, the tentative nature of many of these early ventures is indicative of the unknowns regarding the systems engineering, economics, marketing, regulatory, internal organizational, and human behavior aspects of these new technologies. Indeed, how the various components will perform when pulled together into systems may be a question subordinate to whether and under what conditions the other factors will combine to make such potential systems at all viable.

## THE DYNAMIC ENVIRONMENT OF THE NEW MEDIA ARENA

### Background

The uncertainty of directions and outcomes was succinctly expressed by Albert Gillen, president of Viewdata Corporation of America, a subsidiary of Knight-Ridder Newspapers, Inc., one of the largest newspaper publishers in the United States. He noted that Knight-Ridder's motivation for its Viewtron experiment is a mixture of "fear and hope." The fear is that some of these electronic interactive news, entertainment or advertising services may supplement or replace the conventional newspaper. "The hope," he adds, "is that we may become part of a whole new business, based on complete home information centers that include viewdata, videotape recorder, video disks, computers, and so on."[1]

Like traditional broadcasting and telephony, the so-called new media of viewdata, teletext, videocassettes, and videodiscs, two-way cable, and on-line randomly accessible computer data bases share the characteristic of being able to deliver information electronically. Except in the case of prerecorded videocassettes and videodiscs, which still must be distributed via some transportation network (through retail outlets or a postal service), these conduits use airwaves or land lines to move information from supplier to user. What distinguishes them from the older electronic "mass" media, however, is that they aim to provide, for the first time at the consumer level, a greater access and degree of selectivity on the part of the user with the information source. Thus the user may have access to a specific piece of current information, such as a sports score, a traffic report, a bank balance, the current price of an item at a particular retailer, or the rate for a classified advertisement, as well as to historical/reference data, such as a movie review or a political candidate's position on an issue reported on years previously.

Paradoxically, we can describe a model home information and entertainment product already in common use that provides a broad range of information and entertainment, provides built-in storage, is easily portable, integrates graphics and text, allows user self-pacing and random access to any portion of the data base within five seconds, allows for branching, provides hard copy and is completely updated every twenty-four hours, yet comes at a low price to the consumer— 25 cents per connect hour or less. All of these characteristics describe the traditional ink-on-newsprint daily newspaper. Therefore, what these new services must offer is added values, such as timeliness or memory manipulation. To be considered truly interactive requires the ability of the user not just to *request* information from a data base, but to send data *out* of the home. This might be to order something, respond to a poll, have security monitoring, or conduct financial transactions with a bank. Subscriber-to-subscriber services, such as electronic mail, are another example of a potentially innovative function.

Otherwise these new media are only so much technology, which consumers will greet with a yawn and closed billfold. So far as a TV viewer is concerned, a program that a cable operator has obtained via satellite transmission technology is worth viewing only if the program is attractive, not because its transmission technology is exotic. Similarly, the ability to find out airline flight times by using the home television set hooked up by a telephone line to a computer does not necessarily provide any information (and indeed may provide less) than the consumer would get by phoning a travel agent. And putting a list of important dates in a home computer file is not in itself necessarily a cost-effective improvement over a handwritten list tacked to a cork board. Thus, what must be contrasted with the gee-whiz electronics that the technologists give us is the reality of the marketplace and consumer demand. For unlike computers, radio, or electric calculators, which hindsight shows to have filled real voids, the newer media must still prove that they can perform new, better or less expensive services for those who must finance them, be they users, advertisers, or others.

This is not to say that technological developments that have provoked ambivalent reactions characterized by Knight-Ridder's Gillen are insignificant. In part this is because we do not yet know all the ways in which the new technologies may eventually be *applied* in creating forms of entertainment or information. Nor is it known how consumers as well as businesses will adapt to and adopt innovative formats and processes for their information needs and wants.

But more than the development of some technology is necessary for it to find application as in the case noted earlier in the book, the

Gutenberg printing press. Nearly 400 years elapsed after its invention before the appearance of the mass-circulation newspaper. What was missing was the rest of the infrastructure that would make possible an inexpensive product, such as technology to produce cheap paper from wood pulp, an increase in literacy to help produce a market, and a rise in disposable personal income, not only to provide the funds with which individuals could purchase the paper, but also to create the environment for commercial interests to find it worthwhile to advertise mass consumption products and services. Not the least significant was the coming together of the steam engine with a rotary press, the former a distinct technology, the latter an improvement on the basic press. Combined, they provided the crucial elements in being able to offer an efficient means for producing a mass newspaper. The spread of the railroads and the stringing of the telegraph lines also extended the potential audience and coverage for publishers.

Although dissemination of technology appears to be more rapid in the twentieth century than in the past, it is still dependent on the same factors of demand on the one hand and integration of technology into a system on the other, to produce an infrastructure that is socially, economically, and politically appropriate for the culture.

Indeed it could be further argued that technological advances can be encouraged or impeded by the existence of institutions—either private or public—that are already entrenched or perform similar functions. For example, neither radio, computers, nor calculators met strong institutional barriers, and their dissemination was relatively swift. In some cases the new can help the old, as television has helped create interest for certain types of magazines (e.g., *Sports Illustrated*) or theatrical films for paperback versions of the book. In contrast, telephones, which competed more directly with well-entrenched postal and telegraph services, took nearly a hundred years to become truly universal in Western society, particularly in those European nations where the government postal authority also had control over telephone and telegraph. Even in the United States, it was not until 1946 that 50 percent of residences had their own phones. Economic, social, and cultural barriers may also prevent or delay implementation of technology.

Undoubtedly, more recent media vehicles will eventually have some impact on older forms, just as the development of radio cut substantially into the share of advertising expenditures that had been held by newspapers or the share of personal consumption expenditures devoted to theatrical film was affected by television. But to the extent that new media duplicate services of entrenched old media, it may be decades before the effects are major. Anthony Smith, in his analysis, believes that breaking into the existing audiences of entrenched media will occur "only when [the traditional media] are politically and financially ready for it."[2]

If we step back from the whirlwind of breathless headlines announcing new developments, mergers, and acquisitions in the media business, we realize that the components of the "second revolution" (see Chapter 10)—the television set, a textual display, typewriterlike keyboards, paper printouts, telephone lines, coaxial cable, and computers—have been around for decades.[3]

But something has changed. These devices or techniques are being combined in new ways to create opportunities for information consumers to seek and retrieve information in ways different from the recent past. It is generally accepted that the *economics* of information storage and transmission have changed, lowering costs. This appears to result from

1.  Technological advancements in computers and associated integrated circuits
2.  The addition of earth communications satellites that can be used instead of or in combination with traditional land lines and microwave transmission
3.  Improvements in conventional telephone facilities, including such services as packet-switching and others tied to the application of computers through telecommunications
4.  General advancements in electronics that have produced potentially economical information storage and playback devices such as videodiscs and videocassettes.

Thus it may be argued that the "new media" are not really so new. Components of words, pictures, and sound are the same. The display of textual material, just because it may be "written" on a video screen rather than on paper, is not revolutionary for the user; nor is the production of moving images and accompanying sound on a television set a novelty. What *are* different are the new *alternatives* that information users may have in accessing information—much (or most) of which already exists in some format.

Table 5-1 summarizes the major traditional routes. Although print media today may be using electronic systems internally, the final product

**Table 5-1.** Primary Forms of Distribution Used by Traditional Media.

| Traditional Medium | End-Product Format | Primary Distribution Mechanisms |
|---|---|---|
| Newspapers | Ink-on-paper | Press to paper to<br>  Trucks to carriers for home delivery and newsstands |
| Magazines and newsletters | Ink-on-paper | Press to paper to<br>Postal Service to addressee<br>  Trucks/train/plane to private carrier to addressee<br>  Trucks/train, etc. to wholesalers to retailers to buyer |
| Books | Ink-on-paper | Press to paper to<br>  Trucks/train to wholesaler (sometimes) to retailer to buyer<br>Postal Service to addressee<br>Private carrier to addressee |
| Television and radio | Video/audio | Telephone company or alternative circuits to local broadcast transmitter to user receivers |
| Messages<br>  Written<br>  Oral | <br>Ink-on-paper<br>Audio | <br>Postal Service to addressee<br>Telephone lines, switched to recipient |
| Motion pictures | Visual projection of light through film, with optical audio soundtrack | Common carrier trucks or Postal Service to theaters |

is still produced on a press of a design more than a century old and is distributed by a physical, labor-intensive process that is even older, save for the replacement of horses by trucks.

Advances in technology have enabled the print media to expand their markets or create new ones, however. The *Wall Street Journal* is printed at twelve plants throughout the United States, thanks to a cost-effective facsimile process using satellite transmission, thus shortening the physical delivery route and reducing delivery time. *The New York Times* commenced in August 1980 a similar procedure for transmitting made-up pages from New York for printing in Chicago as a means of eliminating airfreight for papers printed in New York for subsequent midwestern distribution. *Time* and *Newsweek* have long printed copies around the country and abroad to minimize physical transportation. But now they also are turning to satellite transmission to reduce lead times for printing. But in the end, the finished product still must be delivered by mail or private delivery services to newsstands and homes. Videocassettes and videodiscs are examples of hybrid technologies, combining new forms of information storage with reliance on traditional distribution mechanisms of retailers and postal services.

Table 5–2 identifies alternative distribution processes as perceived in the early 1980s. This group of conduits is being discussed at meetings of the American Library Association, the National Cable Television Association, the FCC, and the Senate and House Communications Subcommittees. They are the basis of new magazines such as *Channels of Communication* and of newsletters that include *Information and Data Base Publishing Report* and *Video Print*. And they are the impetus for projects such as Canada's Telidon and Project Ida, ABC Video Enterprises, and CBS Cable, to name a few.[4]

Table 5–3 summarizes some of the services that are in place or are possible using the electronic processes. Clearly it is the process, not the type of content, that is being changed by technology. The table also suggests that a *mix* of distribution methods is available, no one of which may be equally appropriate for bringing all types of content to a variety of end users.

### Questions Raised

A large number of questions has arisen from the new technological possibilities. What is the size of the low-volume residential/institutional market for information relative to the large-volume institutional users? How can the complexity introduced to the heretofore well understood traditional channels for distribution available to both suppliers and users of content be sorted out?

Although many of the private ventures and public policy inquiries are motivated by either technology or a vision of a market, is a market

## Table 5-2
## Some Characteristics of Residential and Small Business Electronic or Video Distribution Channels, 1980.

| Distribution Channel | Technological | Economic/Financial | Market | Regulatory | Human | Uniqueness | Major Limitations | Primary Format |
|---|---|---|---|---|---|---|---|---|
| Cable, including premium service | Two-way potential Broadband outbound, limited bandwidth return Unswitched Almost unlimited channels (12-78 now) | Capital intensive Large cash flow High marginal profits Primarily user supported | Urban/suburban households Nearly universal TV set penetration Nontraditional TV viewers special interests | Byzantine Exclusive franchises State/local regulated Limited and lessened federal control Content controlled by franchisee | Friendly and familiar In two-way, invasion of privacy | Vast capacity Need for new programming No FCC content limitations | Unswitched Regulatory/political barriers for entry Capital needs Where will programming come from? | Video |
| Traditional TV Broadcast via stations (including STV) | Broadband Unswitched Limited spectrum VHF/UHF disparities Capable of encoding | High entry cost for existing frequency Modest equipment costs High sales margins and ROI One-time cost to user in receiver Most programming from third parties | Nearly universal Mass audience Premium TV in noncable areas | FCC licenses Relatively well understood process Renewal almost automatic | Friendly Need decoder for STV | Low marginal costs for additional viewers | Limited channel capacity FCC | Video |
| Multipoint distribution service | Broadband Microwave frequency Low power | Low entry compared to VHF/UHF broadcast Need microwave units | Urban TV households where there is no cable | FCC | Need special decoder Friendly | Alternative to UHF/VHF | Limited power and range Need to provide users with special receivers | Video |
| Direct broadcast satellite TV | Broadband Unswitched Subject to rain, other microwave Unproven | Low capital investment for program supplier Lease transponders Customer-purchased receivers Large cash flow User supported | Rural Apartments and similar complexes | FCC earth station permit (sometimes) Copyright? Challenge from traditional broadcasters | Friendly in principle Unknown new piece of hardware Aiming receiving dish | Low marginal costs for additional viewers | Unknown technology Limited channel capacity | Video |

| | | | | | | | |
|---|---|---|---|---|---|---|---|
| Videodisc | Digital or analog Optical or capacitance Self-contained Relatively large storage per disc especially in optical | Low capital investment (software) Requires substantial user hardware investment Continual software cost to user | All TV households, entertainment, games Educational institutions Business | None | Mostly friendly Interactive may take some learning Several incompatible systems | User controlled Interactive potential | Major hardware costs Continued software costs Competing standards | Video |
| Videocassette | Self-contained Complex mechanics | Low software capital investment Substantial user investment in hardware and software | Upscale TV users and "videophiles" Educational institutions Business and government | None | Friendly Several incompatible systems | User controlled Time shift | Only sequential access (no random access) High cost | Video |
| Telephone network | Analog or digital Narrow band switched | Common carrier Low-cost data transmission alternatives Low capital investment to use Flat rate, timed message rate: toll | Nearly universal household/ institutional | FCC tariffs PUC tariffs Increasing competition in terminals, enhanced services, long distance | Friendly in voice More complex when used as part of data retrieval | In place inexpensive and reliable | Low-speed data transmission Narrow band | Voice Video Print |

**Table 5-3.**    Examples of Services Offered via Electronic
Conduits.

| | One-Way | Interactive |
|---|---|---|
| Cable | Basic<br>  Retransmission of<br>    broadcast signal<br>  New networks<br>    Sports<br>    Demographic<br>    Special interest<br>    News, sports,<br>    Shopping<br>      (telephone order) | Basic<br>  As one way<br>Referenda<br>  Shopping, on-line<br>    ordering<br>Classified ads |
| | Premium—Flat rate<br>  Feature films<br>  High culture<br>  Special sports and<br>    entertainment | Premium—Pay per view<br>  As in one-way<br>  Games<br>  Information services<br>  Security services |
| Broadcast | Traditional commercial and<br>    public television and radio<br>Direct broadcast satellite to<br>    homes<br>  Premium cable offerings<br>Teletext | Abilitiy to capture and hold<br>    desired frame |
| Off-line | Videodiscs<br>  Theatrical films<br>  Special interest<br>    programming<br>Videocassettes<br>  Films<br>  Special interest<br>  Off-air recording<br>  Home movies | Videodiscs<br>  Programmed learning<br>  Random access reference<br>  Sales: catalogs<br>Cassettes?<br>Home computer |
| Telephony | Recorded information services<br>  Weather<br>  Sports scores<br>  Stock reports<br>  Time<br>  Dial-a-Joke | Traditional voice<br>Viewdata/data-base access<br>  Tree structure<br>Full keyboard<br>  Reference<br>  News and information<br>  Shopping<br>Financial transactions (EFT)<br>Home security<br>Electronic mail |

Source: Program on Information Resources Policy, Harvard University.

segment that looks good on paper or a technology in prototype form going to be practical and economical in the field?[5] Recall, for example, the experiments with facsimile newspapers conducted in St. Louis in the 1930s and surfacing periodically since then, all leading to little commercial application.

What do we need to know to better understand the market (particularly the consumer market) for the types of information processes being proposed? Are experiments or ventures by Knight-Ridder, CBS, The Times Mirror Company, AT&T, WETA-TV in Washington, D.C., and Project Ida in Manitoba, Canada going to provide useful insights?[6]

Similarly, little is known about the economics of information. How will or can the newer distribution technology be financed (by users, advertisers, government)? From what pool of disposable personal income (from existing media budgets or as a substitute for other expenditures, such as energy)?

What are the potential social impacts of the technology? What can be or should be done?[7] What has been, should be, and may be the response of government at the various levels to the changes being brought about by information and communication technology? Questions of privacy, competition, regulation, First Amendment rights, and jurisdiction only begin to suggest the policy questions that already have been raised (by FCC and the Congress on telecommunications deregulation) or may be raised.

In what ways might information technology affect the structure or function of *user markets*? These include, for example, possible use by retailers for video catalogs or on-line sales promotion and ordering.

### Areas of Potential Conflict

The change and movement at work in the arena have already suggested the foregoing questions. These, in turn, raise the possibility of conflicts among various players and interests. Among them are the following:

- The technologists, who seek resolution of compatibility among competing systems in agreement on standards, versus the pragmatists, who seek political accommodations in achieving compatibility.
- The vested interests and markets of existing players, who wish to preserve their turf, versus the new players, who see the technology as opening up new avenues for their own entry into information businesses.

- The preservation of legal, moral, or ethical norms, such as First Amendment guarantees of the press versus concerns on the part of individuals for privacy of records, guarantees of copyright.
- Foreign firms eager for a segment of the U.S. market as suppliers of hardware, carriers of content, or providers of information versus a spirit of protectionism for domestic industry and concerns in government and elsewhere of foreign control of communications.
- Congressional jurisdiction over the boundaries of administrative law versus the flexibility and perceived mandate for federal regulatory agencies to oversee their respective industries; state and local governments staking claims to regulating areas that are perceived by the federal government to lie within its territory.

### Policy Issues to Be Addressed

The questions and potential conflicts give rise to the policy issues that will have to be addressed by both the public and private policymakers. Among those that should be most salient in the 1980s are the following:

- To what extent is an organization currently in the information creation business and to what extent in the information distribution business? In what areas does the organization wish to operate?
- Which mix of conduits is most appropriate for disseminating various forms of content to existing markets?
- Which conduits do users want or will they use to receive desired information? Answering this question entails balancing cost versus utility, ease of use versus speed, and so on.
- Who controls or should control the various conduits, and under what set of rules?
- Who has access to these conduits as senders or receivers, and under what conditions?
- What interpretation of the First Amendment right of freedom of the press should apply to various conduits—the broadcast model, the print model, or some new model?
- To what extent should social or economic changes that result from new processes and formats of information distribution be anticipated? By whom and to what end?

## Stakeholders

The obvious players in the market for distribution of information include the telephone companies; other common carriers, such as MCI; the U.S. Postal Service and alternative private delivery services of physical products (United Parcel Service, Federal Express, newspaper distributors); cable system operators; broadcasters; newspaper, book, magazine, and other publishers both traditional and electronic; earth satellite operators; and the providers of programming, such as feature film producers and producers of other types of video or audio programming.

Prominent players in the public sector include the Congress, particularly those legislators and the staffs involved on the House and Senate communications subcommittees, regulatory agencies at both the federal and state levels, especially the FCC and state public utility commissions; executive branch policymakers, such as the National Telecommunications and Information Administration; and local city or town bodies responsible for awarding and overseeing cable franchises.

Other participants in the process are the manufacturers of related hardware components, such as computers, modems, keyboards, television and radio receivers, video display terminals, videocassette and videodisc machines, and other electronic components. Libraries, market research firms, manufacturers of paper and other products, advertising agencies and advertisers all have a direct stake in the media industry in roles as either information producers, processors, or providers of physical display materials (paper, ink, presses). In addition, there may be some new types of services or products that may arise over time, particularly for financial institutions and retailers for numerous types of transactions.

## SUMMARY

Technology is widely viewed as a driving force behind a host of new communications and information products or services. The past indicates that technology alone does not create change. Individual technological developments often must await companion innovations that create *systems* that eventually become widely disseminated. In most cases technology must be combined with economic, sociocultural, and political changes before major dislocations of established institutions or procedures are felt in society at large.

In 1980 there were indications that technological developments in the area of communications conduits and information processing are creating the potential for a radical realignment of traditional mass media institutions. The central element in processes known as cable, viewdata, videodiscs, satellites, is distribution of information to the low-volume user, the consumer or small business.

### APPENDIX 5A.
### SELECTED COMPANY PROFILES[8]

### AT&T and Independent
### Telephone Companies

AT&T has always been interested in encouraging use of its services. Both AT&T Long Lines and the Bell System operating companies promote long-distance interstate calling. Various operating companies, but New York Telephone in particular, have added various message services, such as weather, time, sports scores, and jokes, which add message units to local customer bills.

The existence of AT&T's vast communications network makes it a logical choice for use by those who wish to transfer information electronically. AT&T itself has been investigating opportunities for home data information services through its partnership with Knight-Ridder in the viewdata experiment in Coral Gables, Florida, and a go-it-alone Electronic Information Service it proposed for Austin, Texas in May 1980. In the Florida venture AT&T is providing customer terminals, telephone lines and frame creation terminals (for information providers) to the project. GTE has been involved with similar technology in its participation with Insac, the British marketer to that country's Prestel viewdata service. GTE has purchased U.S. rights to the technology.

AT&T has been exploring another avenue for opportunity in the directory area. In Albany, New York the company gave a small number of homes and businesses access to the entire 518 area code directory assistance file on-line, including Yellow Page listing by name and category. Participants also were able to access Manhattan Yellow Pages. Customers were given full keyboards and video display terminals and a special "dedicated" telephone line that automatically dialed the computer when activated. The objective of the experiment was to find out if customers would use the computer, how useful they found it, and to see if it might cut down on directory assistance traffic. (The French PTT has announced a program to give all telephone subscribers a dedicated directory assistance terminal.) However, some people in the media industry, especially newspaper publishers, see experiments such as those in Albany and Austin as an indication of AT&T's interest providing a daily updated classified directory that could compete with newspaper's strong position in running classified advertising. Although limited until 1990 in its latitude in entering the content end of the business as the result of the Modified Final Judgment it signed in 1983 to end the U.S. Justice Department's antitrust suit against it, AT&T could still become a formidable threat in the future.

## CBS Inc.

CBS Inc. is a media conglomerate with major interests in broadcasting, recorded music, book publishing, consumer magazines, toys, musical instruments, hi-fi retailing, and direct mail sales. In 1979 it earned $200.7 million on $3.7 billion in revenue. Besides running one of the three major commercial television networks and one of the seven radio networks, it owns five television stations and fourteen radio stations within the ten largest markets. Its book publishing divisions include Holt, Rinehart and Winston; W.B. Saunders; and Fawcett and Popular Library paperbacks. Its magazines include *Family Weekly* Sunday newspaper supplement, *Woman's Day,* and *Field & Stream.*

CBS is organized into operating groups according to the traditional media formats; hence, the publishing group, which includes books and magazines; broadcast; records; and the Columbia group (toys, mail order, musical instruments, and retailing). To date, CBS has primarily restricted itself to serving residential consumers. With the exception of textbooks, marketed to schools and universities and the medical and health care fields, CBS has not been a supplier of information to the business or institutional market.

While continuing to pursue its normal business, CBS has been investigating new media opportunities in several of the corporation's divisions. A consumer video group is developing video programming for distribution via cable, videodisc, and videocassette. Significantly, it has been made part of the record division. The broadcast group has experimented with teletext—transmitting information over the air in the invisible vertical blanking of the interval of the television picture. And CBS has proposed the adoption of the French Antiope teletext standards, while other industry segments appear to be more interested in adopting another standard perhaps unique to the United States. CBS broadcast executives are also continuing to search for secondary markets for broadcast television programming, such as through video-cassette or videodisc sales.

Within the publishing group, the interest has been on developing a plan for publishing in a variety of nontraditional formats, including videodisc, videocassette, and on-line data base. CBS is seeking to marry its expertise in publishing with the new electronic distribution channels and the computer.

It sees itself as a leader in this regard, pioneering appropriate marketing, pricing, and distribution strategies. CBS can be viewed as a traditional publisher and distributor of information that is taking seriously the need to find methods to continue to sell information, using the appropriate processes and conduits.

## Citicorp

Citicorp, the nation's second largest bank holding company, has made a major commitment to the consumer segment of banking. It has aggressively marketed its VISA and Master Charge credit cards and has been among the leaders in installing and promoting automated teller stations. It is studying consumer attitudes toward using video display terminals in the home to conduct financial transactions.

## Mead Data Central
## (Subsidiary of the Mead Corporation)

Mead Corporation is known primarily as a forest-products company. But is is responsible for creating the first and perhaps most successful full text machine-readable data base for wide-scale access. Mead Data Central's (MDC's) first venture, Lexis, put virtually all federal court and most state court decisions and statutes into an on-line system designed to be accessible directly to lawyers using video display terminals and keyboards.

Lexis is significant for two reasons. First, it achieved a breakthrough in software that accommodates the vast storage needs of the data base and provides rapid response times to a large number of users—all using an economically feasible level of hardware. Second, it developed the system so that it could be used by lawyers themselves, rather than the specially trained resource specialists that are required to use so many of the other electronic data bases. This meant that the casual user would use the system as the need arose, and this gave rise to placement of several terminals in offices. In some law offices almost every attorney has a terminal.

MDC has now applied its expertise to a second service, called Nexis. It contains the full text of the *Washington Post, American Banker, Newsweek,* the *Economist, Dun's Review, U.S. News & World Report,* the BBC's *Summary of World Broadcasts,* the *Congressional Quarterly,* Associated Press, United Press International, and Reuters wire services, PR Newswire, Kyodo English-language wire service, and Jiji Press English-language wire service. Other general and business news services are being added. As in Lexis, searches are made based on specific words of interest to the user, rather than through a general index or tree structure as used in many other data bases. Searches are performed using simple English. MDC is offering, or will soon offer, other terminal-based text-research services based on similar principles.

### IBM

Noted for its large mainframe and other computers, office equipment, and copying machines, IBM is also involved in communications and media. Through partnership in Satellite Business Systems with Aetna Life and Casualty Company and Comsat General, it has become involved in an ambitious venture to provide communications via dedicated satellites and earth stations for users of large volumes of such intra- and intercorporate communications. SBS operates as an independent company under arm's length relations with the partner organizations. The SBS services will be in direct competition with similar proposed services from Xerox and AT&T. SBS has broadened its initial plans to include services such as dedicated private networks, based on shared use facilities, and intercity voice and message service that would use the existing telephone network to complete the local connection.

IBM is also a 50 percent partner with MCA Corporation in Disco-Vision Associates. This new venture produces disks for use with the MagnaVision optical videodisc unit marketed by the Magnavox operation of North American Philips Corporation, the U.S. branch of N.V. Philips of the Netherlands. However, DiscoVision is in turn a 50 percent partner with Japan's Pioneer Electronic Corp. in the manufacture of an optical videodisc player for sale in the United States by Universal Pioneer Corporation and in the manufacture of an industrial model of a player that is marketed in the United States by DiscoVision Associates. Thus IBM is involved in the consumer video market through manufacturing of both videodiscs and disc players.

## Knight-Ridder Newspapers, Inc.

The largest daily newspaper publisher as measured by circulation, Knight-Ridder has thirty-three daily newspapers, as well as a broadcasting group and an interest in newsprint manufacturing (in a used newsprint recycling plant via a joint venture) and book publishing. It is also the most visible U.S. publisher experimenting with an interactive viewdata system, based on telecommunications, computer, and television set display. The firm's subsidiary, Viewdata Corporation of America, has dubbed its system Viewtron. The plan involved rotating a limited number of keyboards and RCA television sets (minus receivers) to a total of 160 homes starting in July 1980. In January 1981 it decided to extend the experiment. AT&T is a partner, providing equipment and telecommunications services. Viewdata has about thirty firms signed up as information providers, many of which are testing this system as a sales tool.   B. Dalton, the bookstore chain, for example, will provide listings of bestsellers and capsule reviews but will also be trying to sell these books through a direct-order option, using the computer. At this first stage of the experiment, Knight-Ridder tested only for consumer acceptance and performance with the system, rather than for price sensitivity. Moreover, the Viewtron system, unlike Britain's Prestel, provides a full keyboard in addition to the simple numerical keypad used for the tree-structure access mode that both systems rely on.

## Scientific-Atlanta

For the first half of fiscal 1980, Scientific-Atlanta (S-A), the Atlanta-based electronics company reported sales up 50 percent and income up 52 percent from a year earlier. Much of this increase was attributed to satellite receiving equipment.

S-A is selling earth stations at the rate of 100 to 150 each week to cablecasters, broadcasters, homeowners, and hotels. The average price of a unit is between $25,000 and $50,000, but as low as $15,000 and falling. Not only have 2,000 (out of about 4,000) cable systems operators put in a "dish" to receive from RCA Americom's Satcom I, but many (one estimate is 65 percent) will put in a second dish aimed at Comstar D-2.

A new market for S-A and its competitors (including Harris Corporation and Hughes Microwave Products) will soon be found at newspapers, which are now planning to use satellite transmission for receipt of AP, UPI, and advertising data.

## Time Inc.

Time Inc. is the leading magazine publisher in the United States as measured by revenue and second only to Triangle (*TV Guide*) in circulation. The company is a major book publisher and distributor through its trade, mail order series, and book club operations. It also has a sizable forest and wood products division. However, the fastest growing segment is video services. This encompasses Time-Life Films, American Television and Communications Corporation (ATC), which is the second largest cable operator, and Home Box Office, the pioneer and leader in the distribution of premium pay-television programming.

All new cable systems that ATC bids on propose two-way capability. In early 1981 the company made public plans for testing a viewdata system of their own, using one of ATC's franchises. It is looking at opportunities for distribution of programming via off-line video formats, such as videodiscs and videocassettes. The firm has been involved in made-for-television movies and is expanding its production of films that have theatrical release possibility in addition to video distribution channels.

Unlike CBS, where the publishing division is the focus of electronic publishing plans, at Time it appears that the video group has taken the lead. Its reasoning is that any information designed to appear on a video screen, even if "printed," is within the video division's scope of business.

### World Book-Childcraft, Inc.
### (Subsidiary of Scott and
### Fetzer Company)

World Book is one of the leading publishers of encyclopedias. It relies on a well-honed field sales force of teachers, housewives, and many other part-timers to sell the encyclopedias via door-to-door sales.

Since 1979 the entire text of the encyclopedia has been stored on-line in a computer. Each year a revised edition is published, with about 35 percent of the pages revised in some way. Given this vast and frequently updated data base, World Book is seeking both protection for its information-supplying capability in light of new technologies for distribution, and additional opportunities for revenue using the technology. This may be in the form of providing on-line access to the data base for consumers, putting supplementary materials in videodiscs or videocassettes. World Book also would like to make additional use of its experienced field staff as well as a large base of customers who, by their purchase of the encyclopedia have already made a sizable commitment to information seeking.

### NOTES

1.  Scott R. Schmedel, "TV Systems Enabling Viewers to Call Up Printed Data Catch Eye of Media Firms," *The Wall Street Journal*, July 27, 1979, p. 46.
2.  Anthony Smith, *Goodbye Gutenberg* (New York: Oxford University Press, 1980), p. 302.
3.  Anthony Smith (in *Goodbye Gutenberg*) calls it the third revolution.
4.  ABC Video Enterprises is engaged in packaging programming for videocassettes and other nonbroadcast distribution. CBS Cable was formed to create new programs for cable networks, but its service was

closed down at the end of 1982 after a failure to attract advertising support.

5.  FCC Docket No. 20828, (adopted April 1980) gives the telephone common carriers, including AT&T and GTE, the right to enter into enhanced communications services. The agreement between AT&T and the Justice Department, as approved by the federal courts, ended Justice's antitrust suit against AT&T and resulted in, among other things, a separation of the local Bell telephone companies from the AT&T parent. This has further freed business opportunities for AT&T.

6.  As explained above and in Appendix 5A, Knight-Ridder Newspapers, Inc. is in partnership with AT&T in the Viewtron viewdata experiment in Coral Gables, Florida. AT&T has also field tested an on-line white and yellow pages directory assistance system in Albany, New York. CBS's activities are also noted in Appendix 5A. The WETA-TV experiment involves testing an over-the-air teletext system in Washington, D.C., under the sponsorship of several government agencies and the Corporation for Public Broadcasting. Its primary purpose is to find out what type of information users seek most often from a one-way teletext system. Project Ida, sponsored by the Manitoba Telephone Service, consists of using the coaxial cable into the home to supply a broad spectrum of services to 100 households, including conventional television, viewdata, fire and security services, electric and gas meter reading and digital telephone service.

7.  See, for example, "U.S. Seen Ignoring Social Impact of Videotex," *Computer World,* June 2, 1980.

8.  As perceived by the author, with each profile reviewed for factual accuracy by the subject firm. Current in 1981.

# 6 COMPETITION IN LOCAL DISTRIBUTION: THE CABLE TELEVISION INDUSTRY

*Robert Pepper*

The number and diversity of intercity communications services have multiplied substantially since the early 1970s. It was during that period that the Federal Communications Commission (FCC) created general guidelines for specialized common carriers and then, in 1977, was forced by the courts to allow new players into the interexchange (long-distance) dial-up voice business.[1] By the early 1980s American Telephone & Telegraph (AT&T) and Western Union had been joined by competitors such as MCI, Southern Pacific Communications, Satellite Business Systems (SBS), Tymnet, and others in the intercity voice and data communications markets. Virtually all of these services, however, still have to use the existing telephone operating company's local loop for "last mile" connection to reach their customers. Only AT&T had the ability to provide a national end-to-end service. In the future, however, it appears that all interexchange services, including AT&T, will be on a much more equal footing with respect to the local operating telephone companies for access to the local loop.

Because of the traditional rate structure for access to the local loop as well as its current technical limitations for data transport, many users of telecommunication services are starting to investigate ways to bypass the local exchange. Indeed local distribution has been called the weak link and "next frontier" in the development of new communications services.[2] One industry with the potential to develop

147

local distribution services in competition with local telephone operating companies is cable television. This chapter examines the implications arising from cable's potential entry as a competitive force in local telecommunications distribution.

## Telephone as Cable Competitor

As an industry, cable television has viewed the telephone industry, especially AT&T, as a potential competitor. Following the announcement in January 1982 by the U.S. Justice Department that it had tentatively reached a proposed settlement in its seven-year antitrust suit against AT&T, Tom Wheeler, president of the National Cable Television Association (NCTA) was quoted as attacking the "closed door agreement" because "only Congress should make decisions as to whether a company as huge and as pervasive as even the new AT&T, should sit astride the flow of news, information, and entertainment."[3] Several weeks later he characterized the agreement as "the greatest deceptive ploy since Br'er Rabbit begged not to be thrown into the briar patch."[4] Irving Kahn, president of Broadband Communications, has characterized AT&T as *the* competition and the proposed settlement as a "disappointment" and a "disaster."[5] And following the announcement of the proposed settlement, the NCTA board passed a resolution opposing AT&T entry into cable television or other mass media activities.[6]

These and similar attacks on the modification to the 1956 consent decree reflect the cable industry's long-held fear that if permitted to offer traditional cable television services (video entertainment, pay programming), telephone companies, especially AT&T, would quickly dominate the market and eliminate cable television's viability. The cable industry is not alone in this belief. In the Modified Final Judgment (MFJ) entered by Judge Harold Greene in August 1982, AT&T was prohibited from providing information or "electronic publishing over its own transmission facilities."[7] In addition, the separated Bell operating companies were to be restricted to providing regulated services.[8]

Since 1970 the FCC had forbidden cable system ownership and operation by AT&T under any circumstance and by colocated independent telephone companies in most situations.[9] Reflecting Commission practice, these restrictions were formally modified in 1981 to allow telephone-cable cross-ownership in small rural markets in which it is deemed uneconomical for a traditional cable company to provide service.[10]

A FCC Staff Report on Cable Ownership released the same month, in 1981, however, proposed the continuation of all telephone-cable cross-ownership rules except for the rural area exemptions.[11] On November 5, 1982, one day after the FCC declined to eliminate its requirement for telephone operating companies to obtain waivers before building or buying a cable system,[12] the United States Independent Telephone Association (USITA) petitioned the FCC to repeal its telephone-cable cross-ownership rules altogether.[13] Noting that the cable television industry "is no longer an infant, but a multi-billion-dollar industry in which many of the system owners dwarf all but the largest telephone companies,"[14] USITA stated that "the speculative evils" presumed by the FCC's ban did not exist.[15]

Two bills considered by Congress in 1981 would have codified these cross-ownership restrictions. The "Telecommunications Competition and Deregulation Act of 1981" (S. 898), passed by the Senate in October 1981, contained provisions prohibiting AT&T from entering cable as well as "alarm services, mass media service, or mass media product."[16] The House version of the legislation (HR 5158), abandoned after subcommittee approval, would also have prohibited telephone-cable cross-ownership.[17] Such congressional action seems to have been superseded by the prohibitions on AT&T activities contained in the MFJ. A comprehensive "Cable Telecommunications" bill submitted at the beginning of the 98th Congress in 1983 contained no cross-ownership prohibitions.[18]

It is important to note that the cable industry is not concerned exclusively about telephone entry into its traditional domain of providing television and other entertainment services. They are just as concerned, if not more so, that AT&T would "destroy cable's developing local distribution business."[19] Nearly a year before the announcement of the proposed consent decree, NCTA president Wheeler said that cable's future lay with the provision of data and other information services and that a settlement permitting AT&T to enter cable "would destroy the independent cable industry," including the cable alternative to telephone local distribution.[20]

The public debate has reflected cable industry fears and hence the notion that cable television requires protection from unfair competition from the telephone companies, especially AT&T. Very little public debate has focused on the related, but inverse, question of the impact of cable television competition with local operating companies (LOCs) on the local distribution of telecommunications services.

Several forces appear to be converging, however, that raise important questions about such competition. It is the objective of this chapter to identify these forces, the players potentially affected by such competition, and some of the social, political, and economic issues that will confront policymakers.

## CABLE TELEVISION: REGULATORY JURISDICTION AND OVERSIGHT

When cable television first developed in the late 1940s and early 1950s, it was not regulated by the FCC or any other federal agency. It was typically regulated, if at all, through the granting of franchises by local municipalities. In 1955 FCC chairman John Doerfer rejected any notion of FCC jurisdiction over cable operation, then known as community antenna television (CATV). In 1958 the FCC rejected a request to classify CATV as a common carrier[21] and the following year found no basis for asserting jurisdiction over CATV despite the pleas from the broadcasting industry.[22] In 1962, however, the FCC denied the use of a microwave service to import distant television signals for CATV distribution because of economic injury to a local broadcaster.[23] The next year the Commission proposed to regulate all microwave-fed cable systems[24] and in 1965 asserted jurisdiction over CATV microwave service[25] and placed a freeze on microwave importation of distant television signals for CATV distribution in the top 100 markets.[26] In its *Second Report and Order*[27] in FCC Docket Nos. 14895, 15233, and 15971 in 1966, the Commission asserted jurisdiction over all CATV operations, mandated local signal carriage and nonduplication protection and required a hearing before importation of distant signals into the top 100 markets. These rules were challenged, but the U.S. Supreme Court upheld the FCC's jurisdiction over CATV in 1968, approving of regulations "reasonably ancillary" to the Commission's regulation of broadcasting.[28]

By 1968, therefore, the FCC's role of regulating cable as an activity ancillary to broadcasting had been established and upheld by the courts. In the next few years, however, the role of cable began to evolve into more than the retransmission system called CATV. The

Sloan Commission on Cable Communications released a report, *On the Cable: The Television of Abundance*[29] in 1971, which proclaimed the potential of cable television as a broadband telecommunications network capable of not just one-way retransmission of television signals, but of one-way and two-way specialized, wideband and narrowband telecommunications services. The FCC had already required cable systems with more than 3,500 subscribers to provide local-origination cablecasting.[30] In 1972 the FCC issued what was known as its cable *Third Report and Order*, which established comprehensive rules governing cable in all television markets.[31] In addition to rules governing carriage of local television signals, the *Third Report and Order* embraced cable's potential, and required a minimum of twenty channels capacity, two-way capabilities, and channels set aside for access by educational, governmental, and public users. The Commission also proposed a fourth access channel for "leased" access, but did not institute it as a formal requirement until 1976.[32]

The 1972 rules, including the 1976 addition, created a quasi-carrier status for cable systems in which they had to provide part of their capacity for use by third parties over whom they had little control. These requirements, as well as others, were challenged by Midwest Video Corporation on two bases: first, that such requirements were in violation of the plaintiff's constitutional rights including First Amendment rights, and second, that the FCC did not have the jurisdiction to impose such requirements. In affirming the lower court's decision overturning the FCC's access, channel capacity, and two-way rules, the Supreme Court stated that such requirements were not "reasonably ancillary" enough to broadcasting to warrant their imposition. The court did not rule on the Constitutional issues other than to say that they were not "frivolous."[33]

It is ironic that when the FCC denied common carrier status for cable in the *Frontier* case in 1958 and then asserted jurisdiction on the basis that cable was ancillary to broadcasting in 1966, it limited its ability to address cable's common-carrier-like functions. The Communications Act of 1934 separates the FCC's regulatory responsibilities into two titles. Title II sets out the rules governing common carriers while Title III regulates broadcasting. Title III specifically prohibits the FCC from regulating broadcasters as common carriers. Unlike common carriers, who must make their service available to anyone on a nondiscriminatory basis and without any control of content, broadcasters were given the responsibility of content selection as well as transmission. In passing the Act, Congress in 1934 did not foresee the situation in which an enterprise might assume characteristics of both broadcaster and common carrier depending upon its mode of operation.[34] Therefore, to protect and require responsibility from the broadcaster and to protect the potential user of the common carrier, the Act forbids the FCC from imposing both forms of regulation upon an activity.

### Blurring Distinction between State and Federal Jurisdictions

The courts, however, have recognized that Title II and Title III distinctions between carriers and broadcasters are no longer easily made. The majority opinion in *National Association of Regulatory Utility Commissioners v. Federal Communications Commission (NARUC v. FCC)* concluded that the FCC could not preempt state regulation of two-way, nonvideo, data communication on leased cable channels on the basis that such activity constituted intrastate common carrier activity and was not ancillary to broadcast television.[35] In stating that such use of cable systems constituted carrier activity, the court distinguished it from noncarrier cable activities ancillary to broadcasting stating that "since it is clearly possible for a given entity to carry on many types of activities, it is at least logical to conclude that one can be a common carrier with regard to some activities but not to others."[36] The court then went on to rule that such activity could not be preempted by the FCC under the terms of Section 152(b) of the Communication Act,[37] reserving regulation of intrastate carrier communications for the states: "It is uncontroverted that the two-way communications at issue will be intrastate insofar as they are carried on by a cable network entirely encompassed within a single state."[38] Conceivably, however, if such communications became interstate in nature, the FCC might assert jurisdiction and preempt state and local action.

In *General Telephone Company of California et al. v. Federal Communications Commission*[39] the Appeals Court upheld the FCC's jurisdiction to require a certificate of public convenience and necessity for construction of cable facilities by telephone companies. The plaintiffs challenged the FCC's ability to regulate their construction of cable facilities for lease to cable operators on the basis that such activity was free from FCC jurisdiction because of the intrastate reservation of Section 152(b). The court held that cable systems are engaged in interstate communication that cannot be separated into a component local delivery system: "The stream of communication is essentially uninterrupted and properly indivisible. To categorize respondents' activities as intrastate would disregard the character of the television industry."[40] The court also rejected additional claims of exemption from FCC oversight, including the carriers' assertion of exemption under Section 221(b) which exempts "telephone exchange service" from FCC jurisdiction.[41] The court's reasoning here was based upon the Act's definition of "telephone exchange service" as a service "operated to furnish to subscribers intercommunicating service. . . ."[42] The court concluded that, "clearly, CATV channel distribution service does not contemplate furnishing subscribers with 'intercommunicating service' of the type usually identified with a telephone exchange."[43] It is possible therefore, that as cable operators move into new interactive services, the regulation of the local cable distribution activity, to the extent it remains intrastate, might still be exempt from FCC jurisdiction under an extension of the Appeals Court's logic in GTE defining the exemption for "telephone exchange service." Such a preclusion of federal jurisdiction could, however, open the door to potential state intervention or possible federal legislation. Indeed legislation introduced by Senator Barry Goldwater in 1983 would prohibit virtually any regulation of such interactive services.[44] Since the courts overturned the FCC's access rules on the basis of jurisdiction and did not rule on the constitutional issues, states and cities have not, so far, been prevented from imposing their own access, two-way, and channel capacity requirements. It is possible, of course, that in the future such local requirements could be vacated by the courts on constitutional grounds.[45]

## TRENDS

Several trends have converged within this regulatory framework in such a way as to position cable television to become a potential major entrant in the local distribution of telecommunication services. First, there has been a trend toward deregulating the cable industry. Since 1976 the FCC, partially on its own initiative and partially under court pressure, has been steadily relieving cable operators of many of the rules designed to protect broadcasters. The second trend is the creation by many urban cable operators of an infrastructure capable of providing local distribution services.

### Deregulation

Since 1976 the FCC has relieved cable operators of many of the regulations imposed to protect local television stations. In 1976 the FCC eliminated the requirement that local franchising authorities approve subscriber rates[46] although most municipalities still require approval themselves as a major function in their typical ongoing comprehensive franchising and regulation of cable. The same year, the U.S. Court of Appeals for the District of Columbia held in *NARUC v. FCC* that the FCC could not preempt state regulation of intrastate nonvideo two-way communications via cable.[47] In 1977 the FCC eliminated most of the standards for cable franchising including life of the franchise, complaint procedures, franchising procedures, and construction schedules[48] although most cities and eleven states impose significant franchising standards.[49] In 1977 the U.S. Court of Appeals held that the FCC had exceeded its authority in imposing restrictions on pay cable's pay services[50] resulting in a virtual elimination of the rules. In 1977 the FCC relaxed its restrictions on distant signal importation making it easier for a cable operator to obtain a waiver to the 1972 rules.[51] In 1980 the Commission eliminated the restrictions on distant signal importation altogether. It also ended the protection of local broadcasters through its rules on syndicated exclusivity.[52] The rule change was challenged by broadcasters but upheld by the courts in 1981.[53] There have also been recent proposals to eliminate the "must carry" rules requiring cable systems to carry all local and significantly viewed television stations upon request, although it is uncertain that these obligations will be eliminated any time soon.

The result of this trend toward content deregulation of cable is that the FCC has reduced its role as protector of the local broadcaster and has virtually eliminated all rules restricting cable programming. Additionally, because it regulates cable as a broadcast function, the FCC does not regulate other common-carrier-type nonvideo services provided by cable as long as they are intrastate in nature.

In light of federal deregulation of cable, most regulation takes place at the local level with the municipality granting the franchise.

Only eleven states regulate cable on a comprehensive statewide basis[54] although others do provide varying degrees of guidance to municipalities though without specific regulatory mandates and regulate aspects such as privacy of two-way systems. Municipal regulation ranges from the nonexistent to specific and daily oversight.[55] Based on trade press reports, however, only a few cities have indicated any activity in either using or regulating cable's potential for providing various local distribution services. New York City, however, has not only demonstrated an interest in such services, it has begun using them in order to save on its telephone bills.[56] Likewise Boston intends to use the institutional loop under construction as part of its new cable system for municipal data transport.[57] With very few exceptions, even states that regulate cable's traditional video entertainment activities do not currently regulate cable's nonvideo local distribution services, although several are now investigating the possibility (see below). For all practical purposes, therefore, cable's local distribution services, where they exist, rcmain unregulated.[58]

### Local Distribution Infrastructures

Even though the FCC's channel capacity and two-way rules have been eliminated, they had an important long-range impact on the nature of thc cable business. In 1977 Warner Cable (now Warner-Amex Cable Communications) introduced a limited two-way interactive cable system called Qube in its Columbus, Ohio franchise area. While the system was highly experimental and unprofitable, it became a symbol of the new and high-technology possibilities of cable television. It was on the threshold of becoming the "broadband telecommunications network" described in the "blue sky" reports of a decade earlier.

In 1975 Home Box Office (HBO) leased a satellite transponder from RCA in order to demonstrate the feasibility of distributing pay movies to cable systems for redistribution to subscribers. Until that time HBO was primarily a regional operation that was having difficulty attracting cable company affiliates because of national (to the operator) and local (playback) problems. Once the service became available via satellite distribution, however, cable operators began buying the service and increasing their revenues. The advent of satellite-fed pay programming (and later advertiser-supported programming) is significant because it permitted cable operators to generate substantial revenue and become profitable in urban areas where before they had been marginal operations. Therefore, after 1975 what had been predominantly a rural and small town medium began competing for the largest and potentially most profitable markets. Potential pay revenue became an important incentive upon which the cable industry sought urban franchises.

The competitive, land-rush atmosphere created by the competition for urban franchises resulted in the largest cable multiple system operators' (MSOs) competing with one another for the anticipated lucrative franchises.[59] In order to get the best deal from prospective operators, cities have hired consultants, created boards and commissions, and have played the MSOs against one another in a bidding process. The companies have learned that what gets them favorable reviews from the consultants and city commissions includes, among others, many channels (as many as 220 in Denver),[60] two-way interactive systems and institutional loops that provide telecommunications services to public institutions and local businesses,[61] local access channels, and support for local production and cablecasting. These systems are also bidding two-way interactive systems because of the possibility of using them for what is expected to be highly profitable pay-per-view programming. Although having a long way to go, the technology for using coaxial cable for two-way communication, including addressability and switching, has progressed significantly in the past several years.[62] The reliability of addressable converters[63] necessary for pay-per-view programming has increased while the prices have dropped over the past several years, and it has been estimated that 2 million such devices would be shipped in 1982 with an additional 3.5 million in 1983.[64] What was begun by the FCC in 1972, therefore, has become institutionalized by the competitive franchising process even though the FCC's requirements were vacated in Midwest Video II.

A variety of economic and competitive forces are providing additional incentives for cable systems to utilize their two-way capacities to generate revenue. A report conducted for the NCTA concluded that the cable industry should expect to find increasing competition in its primary and traditional entertainment business, especially pay channels and pay-per-view services, from subscription television (STV), multipoint distribution services (MDS), and satellite-fed master-antenna systems (SMATV).[65] Additional competition is expected from proposed services such as direct broadcast [to the home] satellites (DBS) and low-power television (LPTV). The industry is also facing high capital costs in building new systems and upgrading older ones as the result of the high cost of money and extensive promises made in franchising competition and refranchising agreements.[66]

The industry has also expressed concern that if it is unable to fulfill promises (including two-way interactivity) made in the competition for franchises, cities may impose heavy penalties including taking over the systems themselves.[67] Systems are also finding themselves in conflict with municipalities and property owners over such issues as easements and the right to serve tenants over landlord objections.[68] There is also concern that the 1982 "Boulder" decision may lead to overbuilding and unrestricted destructive competition.[69]

One way some cable operators have responded to these concerns and pressures is to buy, sell, and trade systems in order to cluster systems geographically to allow for more economical operation and regional interconnection for information (data) distribution as well as entertainment and advertising.[70] Another response to these forces is to develop new potential sources of revenue, for example, by using cable to provide nonentertainment telecommunications services.[71]

The implications of these events for this study is that the cable television industry has developed the technical ability and the incentive to utilize its rights of way to provide specific services in direct competition with regulated traditional common carriers.[72] The result of the trend of deregulation at the federal level converging with the development of infrastructures for potential use in local distribution is that in many cities cable has an option to become an unregulated competitor of the telephone company for private line, enhanced data, access bypass, and other specialized telecommunications services.


## PLAYERS[73]

### Conduit Institutions

*Cable Television Systems.*    Cable television operators control both conduit (transmission) and content. They see themselves primarily as providers of entertainment and information to consumers/subscribers. Until very recently the industry was (and to a large extent it still is) run by technical operations people whose greatest experience is in system construction and operation. Increasingly, there are more marketing people in management whose experience is in selling subscriptions to residential subscribers. These two traditional orientations have resulted in a cable industry that is, for the most part, geared to cater to residential subscribers with entertainment services. Through the large MSOs and NCTA, the cable industry has taken the offensive to push for regulatory changes that relieve them of many of the restrictions previously imposed to protect local television broadcasters.[74] They are now pushing forward to have cable defined as an electronic version of a publisher with all of the First Amendment protections accorded to print publishers.[75]

Cable operators and NCTA reject out of hand that they are common carriers and have become increasingly careful not to allow program providers to lease channels lest they be construed as common carriers.[76] Rather, the trend is either for the cable operators to buy (lease) the programming or to enter into joint ventures in which they have control over content. Because of their traditional control of both conduit and content, cable operators are looking for joint ventures in the new forms of electronic information such as videotext and home shopping.

Many cable operators have promised loops dedicated to local institutions such as the schools and to businesses for data or other content as part of their franchise bids in urban areas. Few of these loops have been activated to date, but those that have demonstrate an ability to provide satisfactory end-to-end service at lower prices than the tariffed local telephone company.[77] Some cable operators see a potential in using these institutional/business loops for private-line data services bypassing the local operating company, and at least three (Cox Cable, Continental Cablevision, and Warner-Amex) have sought to extend this local distribution activity by applying for digital-termination service (DTS) licenses.[78] Other operators are worried that development of these services will classify their entire operation as common carrier,[79] while still others doubt the viability of such services.[80]

Perhaps the most publicized plan for cable-bypass of the local loop was the announcement in late 1982 that MCI would deliver its interexchange service in Omaha, Nebraska via Cox Cable's two-way cable system instead of Northwestern Bell local lines.[81] MCI Chairman William McGowan, who made the announcement to an audience of cable industry representatives, indicated that the Omaha demonstration, initially involving broadband data, was only the first of a number of pending experiments, including some that would use such a cable-bypass for interconnecting MCI's voice network.[82] McGowan was quoted as saying in his prepared remarks that MCI needs "a local distributor who can get us down the block and into the home at a good price. Our goal is to reach this mass market [small business and residential customers] without the interference of the telephone companies."[83] Almost immediately, however, questions were raised about potential technical problems and regulatory implications,[84] and, in early 1983, the demonstration project was postponed.

Another innovative use of cable television plant for local loop by-pass is planned by the largest independent telephone company, GTE. It proposes to use cable television in markets in which it is not the local carrier to provide termination for a new private line (voice and data) service to be offered by its subsidiary, GTE Satellite Corp.[85]

Other players view cable television primarily as a delivery service for consumer entertainment. Broadcasters see cable as a major competitor in local markets primarily for audience as demonstrated by the Television Ad Bureau's (TvB) attack on cable advertising.[86] It is not surprising that many broadcasters also have entered the cable business (e.g., Westinghouse, Cox, Storer, CBS). Program producers see cable as a new means of distribution, enabling them to bypass the three commercial television networks and the difficult syndication market. Many producers are frustrated by cable, however, in their inability to gain access to the systems. Some have indicated a desire to lease channels but have usually been denied.

Newspaper publishers see cable both as an ally and as a competitor. Many newspaper firms own cable systems and see cable as an alternative means to distribute their traditional products of information and advertising.[87] There have been several joint ventures between publishers and cable operators for videotex information services (including Times Mirror and Dow Jones) and at least one joint venture in which the local newspaper is selling advertising for the cable operator in national cable network programs.[88] Newspapers also see cable as a potential competitor, however, if they are not permitted access to cable channels for their use.

Similarly, the potential large-business users who are aware of cable's local distribution capabilities see cable as one more alternative to the local telephone company in the increasingly varied mix of specialized services. A potential barrier to rapid adoption of cable networks for data transport, however, is the concern of knowledgeable telecommunications managers of potential business users that cable systems are unsophisticated and unreliable. Cable operators which have developed their systems in the past based upon entertainment may not yet be oriented toward the communications needs of business users which are the likely users of two-way cable services. Among business's concerns are cable's traditionally lower design specifications, lack of backup power, and lack of redundancy. This perception is a particular problem in the security and alarm business where, if used at all, cable is usually employed as a secondary backup. While any technical limitations can be readily remedied, the institutional perceptions of reliability problems may impede the adoption of cable networks for critical or sensitive communications.

Local telephone companies are just becoming aware of cable's potential as a local distribution competitor, but where a competitive threat is perceived, the local operating companies have been "very, very concerned" about the threat of bypass.[89]

Responding to heavy criticism after the announcement of the proposed settlemement of the Justice Department's antitrust suit, AT&T denied intentions that it wanted to enter the cable television business. Randall Tobias, AT&T vice president for residence sales and services, told the 1982 NCTA convention that AT&T had no interest in providing traditional cable television services and would "not oppose legislative provisions" prohibiting it from doing so.[90] He went on to say, however, that AT&T plans to extend its two-way home and business communications activities and to become "the most viable way of transmitting videotex." In addition, he spoke of "hybrid" cable-telephone two-way systems and other forms of cable-telephone collaborations as examples of how the two industries can work together in ways "beneficial for both." Tobias did note, however, that "cable's emerging data and information businesses will eventually put it in head-to-head competition with AT&T."[91] Although the final modification of the AT&T–Justice consent decree prohibits AT&T from producing information for distribution over its own transmission lines, the cable industry would like to see the ban extended beyond the seven years stipulated by Judge Greene.[92]

Finally, various government agencies view cable primarily as a consumer entertainment medium and, as such, impose few regulations on its operation. Oversight by the FCC at the federal level has been diminishing through a steady program of deregulation. Only eleven states regulate cable at the state level and many of these have been reducing their involvement through a plan of deregulation (e.g., Massachusetts, New York, and California). Several states, however, have begun to look into cable provision of nonvideo services.[93] The greatest regulation of cable is at the local level with the franchising authority. Once the franchise is granted, however, most municipalities do not provide much oversight or impose very many restrictions; their greatest involvement is usually in overseeing rate increases.

*American Telephone & Telegraph Company (AT&T).*   On August 24, 1982 Judge Harold H. Greene of the United States District Court for the District of Columbia entered the Modification of Final Judgment (MFJ) in the government's antitrust suit against AT&T.[94] Although the consent decree signed by the Department of Justice and AT&T in January 1982 ended the government's 1974 antitrust suit against the company, the agreement was technically entered by the court as a modification of the Final Judgment entered in January 1956 ending the government's 1949 complaint filed against Western Electric and AT&T.

The 1982 MFJ required the separation from AT&T of its twenty-two local operating companies.[95] These separated Bell operating companies (BOCs), with few exceptions, are limited to providing "exchange telecommunications and exchange access functions."[96] They are required to "provide to all interexchange carriers and information service providers" access and other services "equal in type, quality, and price to that provided AT&T. . . ."[97] In addition, former BOCs will be prohibited from providing "any product or service, except exchange telecommunications and exchange access service, that is not a natural monopoly service actually regulated by tariff.[98] While these limitations appear, at least initially, to be extremely constraining, the BOCs still have wide latitude to develop the transport business and related functions (billing, directory services, routing).[99] In addition, Judge Greene permitted the BOCs to sell, but not manufacture, customer premises equipment (CPE)[100] and to publish printed classified directories (Yellow Pages).[101] Further, the restrictions imposed on the BOCs can be "removed upon a showing by the petitioning BOC that there is no substantial possibility that it could use its monopoly power to impede competition in the market it seeks to enter.[102]

Although AT&T is free to engage in virtually any activity after divestiture, it is still restricted in several important ways. Under the provisions of the Computer II decision,[103] AT&T must offer any unregulated service through its separate subsidiary American Bell and, responding in part to fears expressed by the publishing and cable television industries, Judge Greene has prohibited AT&T from "electronic publishing over its own transmission facilities,[104] with the exception of electronic directory services (i.e., electronic "Yellow Pages") and audio services such as time and weather that were offered before the settlement.[105] Recognizing the rapidly changing nature of the market, however, the MFJ states that "this restriction shall be removed after seven years from the date of entry of the decree, unless the Court finds that competitive conditions clearly require its extension."[106]

Following the antitrust settlement and forces previously set in motion by the FCC's Computer Inquiry II decision,[107] AT&T is regarded as a potential entrant in the information-provision business. The restrictions on information provision imposed by Judge Greene will inhibit a direct role as an information provider for at least seven years, but through its unregulated subsidiary, American Bell, AT&T will be able to participate in many information-related services. Although it would be permitted to enter the cable television business purely as a transmission provider, it has denied wanting to do so because it has numerous opportunities in other markets.[108] AT&T's largest business in the immediate postdivestiture environment will be interexchange (long-distance) service provided by its interexchange division (formerly Long Lines) which will also provide intrastate (intra-LATA) toll service.

Some players see AT&T as the "800-pound gorilla" and *the* competition. The cable television industry opposed the settlement because they believed it did not go far enough in restricting AT&T.[109] The American Newspaper Publishers Association (ANPA) voiced similar opposition stating that AT&T entry into the information business could impair the "free flow of electronic information."[110] And NCTA president, Tom Wheeler, called for a coalition of newspapers and cable operators to oppose AT&T's entry into the information and entertainment business.[111]

Speaking at the 1982 ANPA annual convention, AT&T Chairman Charles L. Brown conceded that AT&T could not win a "turf war" with the publishers. Rather, he said that the newspaper industry should view AT&T as the existing "transport system" for delivery of their "electronic information service" and, therefore, not in conflict with the "mainstream" of the publishing business.[112]

Although AT&T will be permitted to enter the local distribution market in competition with its former operating companies, whether or when it would is not likely to be known for some time. Its major competitors in the interexchange market view the consent decree and the postsettlement AT&T with varying degrees of trepidation. The seemingly conflicting positions taken by various players who otherwise would be thought to take similar positions is indicative of the complex tangle of interests that has developed as a result of blurred and sometimes conflicting roles. MCI, for example, as an interexchange carrier, "consistently hailed" the proposal as constructive for both AT&T's competitors and consumers because it guarantees equal access to the local loop for "last mile" connections.[113] ITT, on the other hand, is a much more diversified organization that wants equal access to the local loop for its interexchange carrier but, because of its equipment manufacturing subsidiaries, is displeased that the settlement did not separate Western Electric from AT&T nor prohibit AT&T from remaining in the customer premises equipment market. It called the proposed settlement a "decisive victory for AT&T."[114] AT&T, not surprisingly, supported the consent decree modification and opposed legislation limiting activities permitted by the settlement.

*Local Operating Companies (LOCs).*     Independent telephone companies and Bell operating companies (BOCs), after implementation of the consent decree, will look very similar in their capacities to provide local exchange services. New exchange areas called Local Access and Transport Areas (LATAs) are being created as part of the MFJ reorganization. LOCs are highly regulated by the fifty states and face potential challenges from new competitors operating under varying degrees of regulation and restriction. These firms have traditionally viewed their primary business as providing local switched voice, although they are increasingly providing links for data. Their greatest asset is that they provide virtually universal switched service. Their obligation to provide universal service, however, is also one of their greatest burdens. In addition, they have a possible initial disadvantage compared to some of the new entrants because of the narrowband capacity of the "twisted copper pair" although it appears that the "twisted pair" will be able to serve many, if not most, data transmission needs, especially over short distances, once new digital transmission techniques are perfected.[115] They also see restrictive federal and state regulation as a severe burden and constraint on their development of new services.

For the first time, local operating companies (LOCs) are beginning to see potentially significant competition to their traditional monopoly over local distribution and openly express fear of being bypassed. Indeed, one of the major issues in the FCC's access charge proceeding (FCC Docket No. 78–72) was the bypass threat.[116] The proliferation of microwave technology and the potential of fiber optics in the coming decades coupled with the easing of regulatory barriers to entry of new services has resulted in possible new competition for LOCs.[117] Competition from other carrier services in the traditional transmission business is more understandable to the LOCs than the less-familiar operations of cable companies. Whereas telephone companies have traditionally provided discrete services, the cable industry finds it natural to bundle services, such as transmission and programming.

Local operating companies, especially those that are currently part of the Bell system, are viewed by competitors and potential competitors with distrust and a certain amount of fear. The BOCs are restricted, under the settlement, to providing regulated local exchange and local distribution services,[118] therefore creating a market for new entrants in enhanced services. Yet these new entrants fear that independent LOCs (non-Bell) will unfairly be able to compete in the new unregulated areas, including enhanced services and information provision, limiting opportunities for themselves. Cable television operators are particularly wary of LOC competition, both in the local distribution market and in their traditional domain of entertainment and information programming.

*Other Interexchange Carriers (OICs).*    There has been a proliferation of other interexchange carriers in the past several years. OICs are, for the most part, in the interexchange (long distance) low-volume market (e.g., MCI's Execunet, Southern Pacific's Sprint, GTE's Telenet) including voice and data, or the interexchange high-volume business data market (e.g., SBS, Tymnet). A few of these offer end-to-end services, while most have to use the local operating company for the "last mile." Several new services have begun operation to provide alternative last-mile connections or the equivalent to private line services, using multipoint distribution service (MDS) microwave links. Another newly authorized potentially competitive local distribution service is mobile cellular radio, although local LOCs will be able to participate in at least half of the licenses granted by the FCC.[119] Western Union is an OIC that is not new but is often overlooked as a potential major player in local distribution. In addition to its national distribution network, including communication satellites and national microwave network, Western Union wires reach many buildings in older urban markets.[120]

At the interexchange level, these OICs see opportunities, especially in light of the proposed settlement, which will give them equal access with AT&T interexchange (ATTIX) to the local loop for last-mile distribution. They are becoming increasingly aware of the potential for cable in local distribution, as some of them have used cable industry facilities for last-mile distribution in selected sites and demonstration projects.[121]

AT&T views the OICs as important competitors and will likely compete more aggressively on both price and service if permitted to do so by the FCC. The LOCs are not sure how to view the OICs. As long as the LOCs are in the interexchange business and are generating revenue for last-mile interconnection, the local operating companies see the OICs as users of their service and not as competitors. As the OICs move into local distribution or end-to-end services (e.g., with satellite up and down links or DTS facilities), however, the LOCs will begin to see them as competitors.[122] Cable operators who are even thinking about local distribution see these other carriers as users of their alternative local distribution services. Information providers see the OICs as a less expensive alternative to AT&T in interexchange service but, for the most part, have not exhibited awareness of their local distribution potential. This price differential will likely diminish, however, as the FCC implements the equal-access provisions of the settlement and its recently decided upon access plan.[123]

*Digital Termination Services (DTS).* In 1981 the FCC authorized an additional wideband microwave local distribution service for data communications called Digital Termination Service (DTS). DTS is intended to provide the local connection for long-haul data networks (e.g., SBS or Tymnet) as well as for purely local distribution. An experiment in November 1981 involving SBS, Tymnet, Local Digital Distribution Company, Manhattan Cable Television, and Viacom transmitted data between New York and San Francisco using an SBS satellite channel connected with a local cable television channel in New York and cable and microwave (DTS) channels in San Francisco. Participating users in the experiment included RCA Americom, ITT World Communications, Wells Fargo Bank, and Merrill Lynch Pierce Fenner & Smith. The experimental connection entirely bypassed the local telephone operating companies and reportedly demonstrated that such DTS and cable local distribution can provide greater bandwidth at a lower price than AT&T's existing Dataphone Digital Service (DDS).[124] More than twenty-five companies, including SBS, Tymnet, MCI, Western Union, GTE TeleNet, ITT, Contemporary Communications Corporation, Warner-Amex Cable Communications, and Cox Cable Communications have applied to the FCC for authorization to offer DTS. Cox was the first cable company to apply for DTS licenses, and it intends to use DTS frequencies to supplement its institutional networks in eight cities and to extend, via DTS, such services into areas beyond their cable franchises.[125]

On July 15, 1982, the FCC approved the first group of five applications to build intercity Digital Electronic Message Services (DEMS) utilizing DTS frequencies and facilities for local distribution. Each carrier has proposed building an intercity network connecting forty or more local DTS nodes by satellite or terrestrial intercity channels.[126]

As the list of DTS applicants illustrates, DTS is a service that can be developed and used by a variety of players to supplement their existing local distribution services (e.g., a cable company) or to extend their intercity service to the end user (e.g., SBS, Tymnet, MCI). In either case the service is intended to bypass the local telephone operating company and is being sold to potential customers as providing more than twenty-six times greater bandwidth than the existing local loop (up to 256 Kbps vs. 9.6 Kbps) and at a considerable savings over AT&T's DDS.[127] AT&T has responded to this potential competition by proposing to offer new wideband services and by evaluating its DDS rates to see if they can be lowered.[128] In addition, a number of telephone operating companies have indicated that they may be interested in offering similar services.[129]

*Multipoint Distribution Services (MDS).* Multipoint distribution services are microwave common carrier services originally authorized by the FCC to provide closed-circuit television transmissions to multiple points within urban areas. The FCC's rules, adopted in 1974,[130] allocated two MDS channels in each market to be used by common carrier licensees usually operating on only one channel. When it established MDS, the Commission envisioned many communication services in addition to television, such as transmission of high-speed data, audio, and control signals.[131] Thus, many of the early MDS carriers attempted to develop distribution business services; for the most part, however, these proved to be unprofitable because of the high cost of operation and customers' fragmented use.[132]

When pay-TV networks began distributing programming by communication satellites, local operators began using MDS for local pay-television distribution in markets in which cable did not exist. This use "enabled MDS carriers to reduce their marketing costs, for long-term, large-volume sales became possible."[133] One result of the growth of MDS-distributed pay-TV services was the reduction in price of MDS reception equipment—from over $1,000 to under $100 per unit.[134] Once pay services provided a high-volume base of revenue for MDS, the services could provide data and information services much more economically.

However, since most MDS carriers are limited to one channel per market, the increased use of MDS for pay services has resulted in reduced use by data users. In part to remedy this conflict, Microband Corporation of America (a subsidiary of Tymshare), one MDS carrier, has proposed to the FCC that it modify its rules and increase the number of carriers in each market from two to three and, at the same time, allocate each carrier five channels.[135] The second largest MDS carrier, Contemporary Communications Corporation, has formed a joint venture with CBS and has followed Microband's lead in filing for between four and eight MDS channels in each of the markets where CBS owns and operates television stations. Under the agreement with Contemporary Communications, CBS would program and market the service in competition with cable television.[136]

Microband's proposal calls for a multichannel "wireless cable" service called "Urbanet," which would include multiple video entertainment services (e.g., premium channels, pay-per-view programs, and specialized entertainment services); information services (e.g., teletext, electronic mail, data-base retrieval, directories); transactional services (e.g., banking, stock transactions, bill paying, ticket purchasing, home shopping); and value-added services (e.g., security, word processing, and teleconferencing).[137] It is proposed that Urbanet will achieve its two-way capacity by using existing telephone service from the customer to the microwave operator's computer. In addition, Channel View, an MDS carrier in Salt Lake City, began an eight-channel MDS trial in fall 1982. Initial results indicate that multichannel MDS is both technically feasible and commercially viable.[138]

As common carriers authorized to provide local distribution services, MDS providers have the potential to become important players in this arena. To date, however, their major profit-making activity has been in pay-TV, although some observers believe they may become increasingly important providers of last-mile services to interexchange carriers (ATTIX and OICs), in competition with local telephone companies and cable. The per-unit cost of receiving equipment may decline further. And unlike cable, the systems' basic costs are paid for by up-front user-purchased equipment, reducing the capital needs of the MDS carrier. Moreover, with pay-TV revenues covering much or all of the carriers' fixed plant, they could price data communication services at attractive marginal rates.

Cable system operators are generally concerned about competition from MDS and other over-the-air distribution systems[139] and, as of early 1983, the FCC still had not acted on the Microband and Contemporary Communications Corporation proposals. It is not clear what the LOCs' responses to the proposal will be, particularly in terms of the potential for an MDS bypass to the local loop.

*Broadcasters.*    While broadcasters are generally thought of as providers of mass entertainment and information (news), they are also entering the electronic information arena. First, some have begun experimenting with teletext and videotex services, and second, they have begun to use their spare bandwidth (sideband) for paging services and for local data transmission by second parties, including some experiments with remote sensor control. Many broadcasters are intrigued with teletext, but it is not clear to what extent they are aware of the potential in paging or data markets.

Initially, broadcasters, especially the networks, were slow to recognize the new technologies for delivering entertainment and information and actively opposed the development of cable and subscription television.[140] More recently however, led by two of the networks and large group owners, broadcasters have begun to participate actively in new ventures exploiting the new technologies. ABC, for example, has formed numerous joint ventures for cable networks, ranging from a cultural network to a woman's network to pay-per-view sports offerings.[141] It has also proposed a joint venture with Sony for an off-hours pay-television network using its television affiliates.[142]

CBS created a cultural cable network, which ceased operation after a little more than a year because it failed to attract sufficient advertising,[143] and purchased cable systems.[144] It has also formed a joint venture with AT&T to provide an experimental videotex service.[145]

This is in addition to its rather extensive teletext experiments using several of its owned and operated television stations.[146] As described previously, CBS has formed a joint venture with Contemporary Communications Corporation for a multichannel MDS pay-television service in each city where it owns a television station.[147] Contemporary Communications is the second largest MDS licensee and was among the first group of applicants authorized by the FCC to offer Digital Electronic Message Service using DTS facilities.[148] CBS has also received approval from the FCC to proceed with its plans for developing high-definition television (HDTV) direct-broadcast satellites.[149]

Local broadcasters are also competing more aggressively with new competitors. Many have entered the cable business by purchasing cable systems outside of their markets, and some have begun to program cable channels in their own markets, in effect competing with themselves. One station in Madison, Wisconsin has arranged with the local cable operator to provide local programming for three channels so that audiences do not have to tune to out-of-market, cable-imported stations when they are dissatisfied with network fare.[150] Another station, in Moline, Illinois, has undertaken a similar project with consumer, entertainment, and children's programming.[151] Radio stations have also begun experimenting with leasing cable frequencies for cable radio operations in order to extend their audiences by offering formats that differ from those they broadcast.[152]

In addition to extending their traditional entertainment services more aggressively, broadcasters are beginning to utilize their transmission potential for point-to-point or addressed information and data distribution. In an effort to become more independent of federal funding, National Public Radio (NPR) has entered into a joint venture with Mobile Communications Corporation of America to offer a national paging and data distribution service using its leased satellite channels and the sidebands of local member stations.[153] Four commercial firms—MCI, American Express, Metromedia, and Communications Industries—have announced that they will be establishing a similar service.[154] In addition, the FCC has proposed to modify its rules governing FM broadcasting to permit more specialized point-to-point services utilizing FM sidebands (SCA).[155] One firm, Printer Terminal Communications Corporation, offers a local data communications network it calls Local Area Data Distribution (LADD) in the Los Angeles area. The service has a range of 50 to 150 miles, can accommodate multiple users at rates of up to 9.6 Kbps and is currently in commercial operation.[156] These and other data and "audiotex" services (like Dow Jones's DowAlert) provide a potential opportunity for broadcasters to use portions of their bandwidth for specialized local distribution services, without interfering with their traditional services.

Other players see broadcasters primarily as mass entertainment and information producer/programmers. Traditional competing information providers such as newspapers are wary of broadcast teletext's potential, but several who own broadcast stations have begun experimenting with their own versions. Because the use of broadcast sideband distribution of data is so new, there is little, though growing, awareness as to its potential and, therefore, competitive possibilities. One indication of the growing awareness of the potential for this service is AT&T's opposition to the FCC's proposed rulemaking. In comments filed with the FCC, AT&T objected to authorizing unregulated carrierlike service, noting that the proposed service would be ancillary to broadcast operations; it would not be subject to common carrier regulation. Although not opposed to removing restrictions on FM subchannels, AT&T believes that any carrierlike uses of such channels should be regulated as a common carrier, concluding that, "it is arbitrary and anticompetitive to allow an FM broadcast station to provide a common carrier service on an essentially unregulated basis while applying full common carrier regulation to a non-broadcast competitor offering the same service."[157]

## Content Providers

Content providers can be categorized in at least two ways: (1) by whether they currently use the telephone company for local distribution and (2) by the type of content they provide. The following discussion is organized by *type* of content provided but it notes the dominant existing forms of distribution.

*Entertainment Programmers.* Most mass-media entertainment programming is distributed by broadcasting or cable television for simultaneous consumption or in movie theaters for mass but not necessarily simultaneous viewing and by home video (cassettes and videodiscs) controlled by the viewer. This form comprises the vast bulk of content carried on cable television. Coupled with subscription fees or pay-per-view billing, mass entertainment programming, especially movies and sports, account for a significant portion of a cable system's revenue: $355 million in 1979 (19.6 percent) and an estimated $1.1 billion (31.2 percent) in 1982.[158]

Except for network distribution to broadcast television stations for local broadcast, video programming is not distributed via telephone lines. Even the networks' use of telephone company land lines is being replaced by less expensive satellite distribution. Until recently, satellite distribution of television programming to broadcast stations for local transmission was provided only by non-AT&T carriers (e.g., RCA). The FCC, however, has recently authorized AT&T to distribute such programming to broadcast stations via its Comstar satellites.[159]

Most of the mass entertainment content is produced by production companies in Hollywood, New York, and a few other locations. Some of the producers are very large while others, independents, operate with few, if any, assets. Some producers are also owners and operators of conduits, as in the case of the television networks (who are also broadcast station licensees), and cable operators (who may be owners of cable networks, such as Time Inc.'s ATC cable subsidiary and its HBO network). All of these mass-entertainment producer/providers are increasingly involved in cable distribution, but, because they are dependent upon wideband capacity, they do not use telephone for distribution (except for ordinary business functions).

*Businesses.*   Virtually every business generates information (voice or data) that has to be transmitted to other offices of the firm or to other firms. These businesses are very heavy users of telephone distribution for both voice and, increasingly, data. The largest businesses, generating the largest amounts of information (voice and data) have been the largest users of OICs for interexchange communication. They are also the first users of alternative local distribution services and will likely be very heavy users of these services as they develop. Most of the business information transmitted does not need terribly wide bandwidths, therefore allowing them to use existing or upgraded telephone lines. Data communications can be transmitted between user end points that are "dense" or "nondense," packed together or spread out. Both dense and nondense data flow can be between business and business, business and residence, or residence

and residence. Each of these situations may need a different bandwidth and system capacity. New techniques in digital transmission
will likely permit greater use of existing telephone lines for data transmission, although the need for wideband will exist, especially for
high-speed dense data transmission.

An additional type of business data user that has traditionally used
telephone lines is the security and alarm service (e.g., ADT). Such services connect local businesses and residences with a central office usually by telephone lines and occasionally by their own lines. They could
readily shift to alternative local distribution systems serving the necessary geographic areas. Indeed, security and alarm is one of the services
the cable industry is most excited about for future development on
their own and in joint ventures with security companies.[160] Security
firms have been slow to shift from telephone lines to cable, however,
because of a perception that cable systems are not yet as reliable.

*Electronic Publishers.*   Over the past several years numerous players
in traditional information and dissemination activities have entered
the developing videotex markets. Newspapers, wire services, broadcast stations, and magazine publishers have all begun experimenting
with electronic versions of their traditional content packages. In addition, some direct marketing firms, retailers, airlines, and financial
services have begun developing and offering information as part of
these publicly available data bases. Some data bases are distributed
by broadcast signals (teletext) and are not interactive, while others
are distributed by telephone line or cable (videotex) and have the
potential to be interactive. Few of the videotex systems under development or in use require broad bandwidths, so they can use existing
twisted-pair telephone lines for local distribution. This technology as
now implemented does restrict their development and use of graphics.
Many cable companies, however, want to offer these services and
have begun forming joint ventures to provide the content as well as
the distribution for such services. Both NCTA and ANPA were concerned that an unconstrained AT&T would enter the information
creation as well as transmission business and, therefore, were pleased
by Judge Greene's modifications prohibiting AT&T from providing
information over its own lines for seven years. Under the settlement,
the former Bell operating companies will be permitted to provide
transmission capacity, multiplexing and demultiplexing services, information access services, and metering and billing services for
customers, but not information.

### Regulators

The federal government, through the FCC, has some regulatory jurisdiction over aspects of broadcasting, cable television, and interstate telephone service (including local distribution of interstate service). Over the past decade, however, there has been a trend toward deregulation in broadcasting and especially in cable television at the federal level. The FCC has recently eliminated most content regulations for radio stations[161] and Congress has extended the license periods for both radio and television stations.[162] The FCC has also eliminated almost all restrictions it had placed on cable television, mostly following court rulings; for all practical purposes, it merely keeps track of cable systems.[163]

The traditional telephone arena has been slightly different. Although the FCC is deregulating the telephone equipment market,[164] has allowed for increased competition in the interexchange market,[165] and, through its Computer II Inquiry,[166] allowed AT&T to engage in unregulated activities through a separate subsidiary, the Commission was constrained by the 1956 consent decree in how far it could go in deregulating AT&T.

Congress, for the past several sessions, unsuccessfully attempted to encourage competition in telecommunications through legislation. The most recent attempts were S.898, which passed the Senate in October 1981, and H.R.5158, which died after being passed by a subcommittee.[167] New legislation, now that the consent decree has accomplished the breakup of AT&T, is not likely. Most participants would like to see "short-form" legislation consisting of provisions dealing with national security, FCC ability to forbear, and FCC jurisdiction over intrastate toll service. However, it is unlikely that any legislation will pass Congress at least until there is time to observe the effects of the settlement.[168]

The states regulate intrastate telephone service, both exchange and interexchange services. Only eleven states also regulate cable television in a comprehensive fashion.[169] Although they may be precluded from overseeing intrastate inter-LATA service, the state regulators will oversee intrastate local distribution alternatives to existing exchange services. They will have to weigh the social, economic, and political implications of the issues outlined below. Spurred by the opportunity presented by the court's Tunney Act procedures enabling public comment, state regulators and their representative (NARUC) vigorously protested the proposed consent decree modification and have threatened local vetos of provisions of the proposed settlement and protracted litigation.[170] In their comments to the court, the state regulators indicated that they feared the proposed settlement would weaken LOCs within their jurisdiction and thus the goals of universal end-to-end service and low residential rates. Following Judge Greene's acceptance of a modified decree, several states appealed his decision threatening to undo the settlement.[171]

While it is not clear how all state regulators might react to what they perceived as bypass threats to local distribution services, at least three state utility commissions have begun investigations into whether they can or should assert jurisdiction over cable systems' two-way interactive services and impose common carrierlike requirements. The New York State Public Service Commission (PSC), in October 1976, issued an Order to Show Cause Why Manhattan Cable Television, Inc. (MCTV) should not be required to apply for a Certificate of Public Convenience and Necessity for or, alternatively, terminate its two-way, point-to-point broadband data transmission services.[172] After lying dormant for nearly six years, the case was revived by the PSC in November 1982 when it issued a Notice of Intent to Act. By early 1983 the PSC had not ruled in the proceeding.

In New Jersey the Office of Cable Television, which is part of the State's Department of Energy's Board of Public Utilities, established an inquiry into its jurisdiction over and rate regulation of two-way cable services in 1982.[173] The Office received comments from the cable television industry, the alarm services industry, New Jersey Bell Telephone Company and others in mid-1982 but had not issued a ruling by early 1983.

Finally, in January 1983, the Nebraska Public Service Commission issued a Notice of Public Hearing to gather information about Cox's proposed two-way services in Omaha and "to assess the impact of said operations on telephone rate payers and existing carriers of telecommunications service." In April it issued a Cease and Desist Order against Cox's two-way data service.[174] These actions by New York, New Jersey, and Nebraska indicate state regulators' concern about competitive threats to their regulated local operating companies and may be the beginning of lengthy proceedings in each of the states designed to protect local operating companies from bypass competition.

State regulatory commissions have exhibited concern for the viability of their regulated local operating companies since the announcement of the antitrust settlement in January 1982. Individually and collectively, through their trade associaton, NARUC, these state agencies have intervened in both Court and FCC proceedings implementing the MFJ.[175] They have indicated concern for the viability of their local operating companies postdivestiture as well as for the maintenance of universal service and low residential rates.[176] It is not surprising, therefore, that the states have begun proceedings investigating, in part, the potential impact on their regulated LOCs of unregulated competition by cable operators. Unless preempted by the FCC, the Courts, or Congress, such state activity can be expected to persist as long as cable is perceived as a bypass threat.[177]

Local government usually has jurisdiction only to regulate cable television. It is typically the level of government that grants the initial cable franchise and oversees system construction, operation, and refranchising. The cities' ability to regulate cable has been brought into question, however, by the 1982 *Boulder* decision that held that cities are "not exempt from antitrust scrutiny."[178] Nevertheless there are important policy issues facing municipalities in the area of local distribution by cable companies. Resolution of these issues may call for the cities to forgo their natural tendencies to regulate.

## QUESTIONS AND ISSUES

The foregoing discussion suggests that the cable industry may be poised to enter the local distribution market. Many urban cable systems have some of the necessary technical infrastructure as a result of bidding and building institutional and business loops and by having a two-way addressable capacity (for billing and security services in addition to pay-per-view programming). At this time, there appear to be no federal regulatory barriers to cable entry into the local distribution market, while there appear to be significant opportunities for providing alternative private line service and alternative bypass last-mile interconnection for all types of interexchange carriers. Many policy-related questions remain, however, about cable's entry into this market. The following outline of questions and issues provides a framework for examining the public and private policy questions arising from the competing objectives sought by various stakeholders and the options for addressing these questions.

• What objectives, explicit or implicit, underlie current policy about local distribution of telecommunications services? What alternative objectives are sought by which stakeholders?

- What are the pros and cons of requiring/encouraging/permitting/prohibiting cable system operators from offering local distribution telecommunications services?
- If cable system operators are prohibited from offering local distribution telecommunications services, what are the implications for the objectives of the various stakeholders?
- If cable system operators are at least permitted to offer such local distribution services, what are the pros and cons of regulating or not regulating entry and/or operation?
- If entry and operation are not regulated, what are the implications for the objectives of the various stakeholders?
- If entry and/or operation are regulated, what are the pros and cons of state versus federal regulation?
- If the federal government preempts state regulation, what are the implications for the objectives of the various stakeholders arising from the different regulatory regimes that might be imposed?
- If the federal government does not preempt state action, therefore permitting state regulation, what are the implications, for the stakeholders, arising from the different regulatory regimes available to the states?

Specific implications of the above for stakeholder objectives might include the following:

- Implications for fairness and equity arising from opting for entry of unregulated carriers into competition with highly regulated LOCs.
- Implications for universal end-to-end service if new local distribution competitors are permitted to "creamskim" the most profitable services. For example, will LOCs be seen as another "service of last resort," such as the New York City subway or U.S. Postal Service?
- Implications for efficient development of new services if new entrants are prohibited from or restricted in entering the local distribution market.
- Implications for efficient allocation of resources if development and deployment of new services are based upon uneconomic incentives. For example, will efficiencies expected from competition fail to be realized because regulated carriers—LOCs—will be constrained in responding to competition with new services and/or lower prices?

- Implications for users—for example, banks, information suppliers, security companies—if access to transmission networks is not required.
- Implications for regulators wanting to forbear from regulation as local distribution alternatives create competitive markets. For example, do state regulators have the statutory latitude to not regulate competitive services under their jurisdiction?
- Implications for continuity, connectivity, and coordination in local distribution markets if new entrants are permitted to provide services without oversight or service requirements.
- Implications for cable systems retaining control over their entertainment channels if their nonentertainment services are classified as common carrier: What is the likelihood that such classification might result in common carrier classification for all cable services? Would such a risk be an acceptable cost for entry into local distribution?

## SUMMARY AND CONCLUSIONS

As the number and diversity of interexchange communications services has grown since the mid-1970s, so too has the importance of local distribution. Just as AT&T's virtual monopoly in interexchange services now faces competition from a variety of competitors, competition is developing in the local distribution market. The traditional natural monopoly of the local operating companies is being questioned by current and potential competitors and by potential users concerned about the apparent limitations of the existing network. In part this concern is being driven by the increasing use of telecommunications for computer (data) communications and by the need for access to users of competing interexchange services.

Several technologies are emerging as potential competitors in the local distribution market, with cable television potentially the most powerful among them. Because of its enormous capacity in bandwidth and ubiquity in franchised areas, cable has the opportunity to develop as a major competitor in local telecommunications distribution. In developing its local distribution potential, cable itself will face competition from other technologies vying for part of the local distribution market (see Tables 6-1 and 6-2). Whether cable will develop as a major force in local distribution will depend upon economic, technical, and competitive factors as well as policy decisions

**Table 6-1.** Existing Technical Capabilities of Local Distribution Alternatives.

| Services | High-Speed Data | Low-Speed Data | Voice | Video | Real-Time/Two-Way |
|---|---|---|---|---|---|
| Wired | | | | | |
| Telephone | | | | | |
|   Switched network | o | • | • | | • |
|   Private line | o | • | • | o | • |
|   Cable television | • | • | • | • | o[b] |
| Over-the-air transmission | | | | | |
| Microwave | | | | | |
|   MDS | • | • | • | • | |
|   DTS | • | • | • | • | • |
|   Private microwave | • | • | • | | o |
| Broadcast | | | | | |
|   Television (VBI)[a] | | • | | | |
|   FM subcarrier | | • | | | |
|   AM baseband | | • | | | |
| Cellular mobile radio | | • | • | | • |

Key: • = has major capability; o = has some capability

[a]Television could provide voice and video as part of their standard service but not as part of their data transmission using the vertical blanking interval (VBI).

[b]Few systems currently have activated this capability.

**Table 6-2.** Local Distribution Alternatives.

| Service | Level of Privacy, Universality, and Reliability Available (1 = high; 2 = medium; 3 = low) | | | Primary Regulatory Jurisdiction | | |
| --- | --- | --- | --- | --- | --- | --- |
| | Privacy | Universality | Reliability | Federal | State | Local |
| Wired | | | | | | |
| Telephone | | | | | | |
|   Switched network | 2 | 1 | 1 | | • | |
|   Private line | 2 | 2 | 1 | | • | |
| Cable television | 2 | 2 | 2 | | | • |
| Over-the-air transmission | | | | | | |
| Microwave | | | | | | |
|   MDS | 3 | 1 | 2 | • | | |
|   DTS | 3 | 2 | 2 | • | | |
|   Private microwave | 3 | 3 | 2 | • | | |
| Broadcast | | | | | | |
|   Television (VBI) | 3 | 1 | 2 | • | | |
|   FM subcarrier | 3 | 1 | 2 | • | | |
|   AM baseband | 3 | 1 | 2 | • | | |
| Cellular mobile radio | 3 | 2 | 2 | • | | |

by existing or potential regulators. Unlike other local distribution alternatives, cable television's telecommunications services typically are not regulated at any level of government although there are moves in that direction. It is possible, therefore, that cable's success or failure as a local distribution alternative may depend as much upon regulatory responses by state authorities as upon its ability to compete.

Technological developments and market demands are creating regulatory pressures, on the one hand to encourage competition in local distribution by permitting cable to develop without regulatory constraints, while on the other calling for bypass restrictions to protect local operating companies. Since state regulators cannot affect the entry of potential bypass technologies such as DTS, MDS, and cellular mobile radio, they may focus on cable in their attempts to protect local operating companies from potential bypass. However, since cable television is only one of several potential local distribution competitors, regulators need to recognize that even if cable is constrained in its telecommunications activities, local distribution likely will become more competitive in any case.

The key question confronting regulators, therefore, is how to balance seemingly conflicting traditional economic, political, and social objectives (e.g., universal affordable and reliable service, economic efficiency, adoption of technological advances). If, for example, state regulators permit unregulated entry into local distribution by cable television without also deregulating the LOCs, they may be encouraging uneconomic bypass, which might affect rates and universal service. Alternatively, if they prohibit or regulate such entry, they may be limiting or slowing competition that could achieve desirable goals such as more economical and efficient service. Likewise, prematurely deregulating the LOCs could also have undesirable effects.

The key question facing corporate players is the role of the private sector in the policy process. Each potential corporate player needs to evaluate its needs and goals, both short and long range, in terms of the evolving competitive telecommunications environment. For example, is it in a corporate player's best interest to encourage competition in local distribution including bypass of the local operating company or, rather, to oppose such bypass in order to retain subsidies for residential service and maintain the highest degree of connectivity? The importance of corporate involvement in the evolving policy debate is obvious for communications transporters, who will be affected by whatever policy is followed. Less obvious, but no less important, is involvement by nontransport players such as financial institutions, marketing firms, and information suppliers that might be affected by any change in availability or price of service.

If the long-range goal is to have a competitive local distribution market, regulators and corporate players will have to develop policies to manage the transition from regulated monopoly to full competition without causing dislocations from uneconomic bypass or stifling potential competitors.

## NOTES

1. *MCI Telecommunications Corp. v. FCC (Execunet I)* 561 F.2d 365 (D.C. Cir 1977), cert denied, 434 U.S. 1040 (1978).
2. J.L. Charter, D.N. Hatfield, R.K. Salaman, "Local Distribution—The Next Frontier," National Telecommunications and Information Administration, (NTIA-TM-81-54), April 1981.
3. "Freeing AT&T for 'Information Age'," *Broadcasting*, January 11, 1982, p. 27.
4. L. Huffman, "Wheeler Calls AT&T Pact 'Deceptive'," *Multichannel News*, March 1, 1982, p. 4.
5. "After the Breakup, the Breaking Away," *Broadcasting*, January 18, 1982, p. 31.
6. "NCTA Names John Saeman as Chairman," *Multichannel News*, February 22, 1982, p. 1.
7. *United States v. AT&T Co.*, 552 F. Supp. 131, 231 (1982) (Opinion and Order Modifying Final Judgment), *aff'd mem, sub. nom. Maryland v. United States*, 51 U.S.L.W. 3632 (Feb. 28, 1983) (hereinafter, "MFJ").
8. Ibid., at 227.
9. *Final Report and Order*, 21 FCC 2d 307 (1970). It should be noted that despite these restrictions, independent telephone companies are permitted to operate cable systems in areas they do not otherwise service. Also, any telephone company, including AT&T, is permitted to provide cable plant to cable operators for system operation or may offer broadband video services on a regulated tariffed (common carrier) basis; AT&T provides such a service for national distribution of television signals to television stations and BOC's such as New York Telephone provide it for pay-movie distribution to hotels.
10. *Elimination of the Telephone Company-Cable Television Cross Ownership Rules for Rural Areas*, 88 FCC 2d 564 (1981). It should be

noted, however, that the relaxation of telephone-cable cross-ownership rules will not apply to former BOCs under the terms of the MFJ.

11.    CC Staff Report, *FCC Policy on Cable Ownership*, November 1981.
       A strong case, however, can be made to permit cable/telephone cross-ownership as a means of encouraging competition between the two industries as their services converge. In the most articulate and well-developed discussion of the advantages of such an approach, Noam argues that direct competition between cable and telephone in an integrated telecommunications environment "provides the key to a structural solution to thorny monopoly issues in telecommunications." E. Noam, "Towards an Integrated Communications Market: Overcoming the Local Monopoly of Cable Television," 34 *Fed. Comm. L.J.* 209 at 257 (1982).

12.    *Memorandum Opinion and Order in CC Docket No. 80-767,* _____ FCC 2d _____ (released November 9, 1982); "FCC Approved $5 Billion Capitalization for American Bell's CPE Offering," *Communications Daily*, November 5, 1982, p. 3. In joining Commissioner Fogarty in dissenting, Commissioner Quello criticized the current situation as one in which cable "can compete with the telephone companies, but the telephone companies cannot compete with cable. "FCC, in Turning down Reconsideration Requests, Looks toward CATV Rule Notice Next Year," *Telecommunications Reports* 48:45 (November 8, 1982):32.

13.    "USITA's Petition to Repeal Rules," *Communications Daily*, November 9, 1982, p. 8.

14.    "Wants In," *Broadcasting*, November 15, 1982, p. 8.

15.    "Noting 13 Years of Study, USITA Asks Commission to Repeal CATV Cross-Ownership Rules," *Telecommunications Reports* 48:46 (November 15, 1982):44; "Telco repeal," *CableVision*, November 22, 1982, p. 26.

16.    S. 898 Sec. 299(b)(1)(A).

17.    H.R. 5158 Sec. 264 (b). The original version of this bill was amended on March 22, 1982, and passed by the Subcommittee on Telecommunications, Finance, and Consumer Protection on March 25, 1982, by a vote of 15 to 0. Although the amended version of the bill would speed up the separation of the Bell operating companies from AT&T and further restrict AT&T, Section 264 (b) would keep the telephone-cable cross-ownership prohibitions.

18.    S. 66, "Cable Telecommunications Act of 1983," 98th Cong., 1st Sess., introduced January 26, 1983 (hereinafter, S.66).

19.    "Wheeler Urges Trial of Ma Bell Suit," *Multichannel News*, March 2, 1981, p. 16.

20.    Ibid.

21.  *Frontier Broadcasting Co. v. J.E. Collier*, 24 FCC 251 (1958).
22.  *Inquiry into the Impact of Community Antenna Systems, Docket No. 12443*, 26 FCC 403 (1959).
23.  *Carter Mountain Transmission*, 22 RR 163 (1962), affirmed in *Carter Mountain Transmission v. FCC*, 321 F. 2d 359 (D.C. Cir., 1962), cert. denied, 375 U.S. 951 (1963).
24.  28 F.R. 13789 (1963).
25.  *First Report and Order in Docket Nos. 13895, 15233*, 38 FCC 683 (1965).
26.  1 FCC 2d 453.
27.  *Second Report and Order in Docket Nos. 14895, 15233, 15971*, 2 FCC 2d 725 (1966).
28.  *U.S. v. Southwestern Cable* 392 U.S. 157 (1968).
29.  Sloan Commission on Cable Communications, *On the Cable: Television of Abundance*, (New York: McGraw-Hill), 1971.
30.  *First Report and Order in Docket No. 18397*, 20 FCC 2d 201; upheld by U.S. Supreme Court in *U.S. v. Midwest Video Corp.* 406 U.S. 649 (1972).
31.  Cable Television Report and Order in Docket Nos. 18397, 18397-A, 19373, 18416, 18892, 18894, 36 FCC 2d 143 (1972).
32.  *Report and Order in Docket No. 20508*, 59 FCC 2d 294 (1976).
33.  *FCC v. Midwest Video Corp.*, 440 U.S. 689 (1979).
34.  This situation is not unique to cable television; for example, direct broadcast satellites, multipoint distribution systems, FM radio stations, and broadcast television signals can all be used for point-to-point transmissions as well as for "broadcasting."
35.  *National Association of Regulatory Utility Commissioners v. Federal Communications Commission*, 533 F. 2d 601 (1976).
36.  Ibid.
37.  47 U.S.C. Sec. 152 (b).
38.  533 F. 2d 601, (1976).
39.  *General Telephone Company of California et al. v. Federal Communications Commission*, 413 F. 2d 390, *cert. denied*, 396 U.S. 888 (1969).
40.  413 F. 2d 390.
41.  47 U.S.C. Sec. 221 (b) (1962).
42.  47 U.S.C. Sec. 153 (r) (1964).
43.  413 F. 2d 390.
44.  S. 66, Sec. 607(c). Similar legislation was submitted by Sen. Goldwater in 1982 during the 97th Congress (S. 2172); see also, accompanying Senate Report 97-518.
45.  "New York Cable Operators Challenge Access Rules," *Multichannel News*, August 9, 1982, p. 20.

46.  *Report and Order in Docket No. 20618* (1976).

47.  *National Association of Regulatory Utility Commissioners v. FCC*, 533 F. 2d 601 (1976).

48.  *Report and Order in Docket No. 21002*, 41 RR2d 885.

49.  Philip Hochberg, *The States Regulate Cable: A Legislative Analysis of Substantive Provisions*, University Program on Information Resources Policy, Report 78-4, Harvard University, Cambridge, Mass., July 1978.

50.  *Home Box Office v. Federal Communications Commission*, 567 F. 2d 9 (1977), *cert. denied*, 434 U.S. 829 (1977).

51.  *Report and Order in Docket No. 20496*, 65 FCC 2d 218 (1977).

52.  *Report and Order in Docket No. 20988 (Syndicated Exclusivity) and 21284 (Distant Signal Carriage)*, 79 FCC 2d (Part 2 of 2) (1980).

53.  *Malrite TV of New York v. Federal Communications Commission*, 652 F. 2d 1140 (Second Cir., 1981), *cert. denied sub nom. National Association of Broadcasters, et al. v. FCC* 454 U.S. 1143 (1982).

54.  Hochberg, *The States Regulate Cable.*

55.  See, "New York City Puts the Bite on Cable Ops," *Multichannel News*, March 1, 1982, p. 1.

56.  "Belt-Tightening Gotham to Use Manhattan Cable for Data Sending," *Variety*, July 1982, p. 42.

57.  "Cable Gets Ready for Business," *Business Week*, November 22, 1982, p. 119.

58.  See previous discussion of *NARUC* and *GTE* cases.

59.  See, for example: Stan Crock, "As Jousting for Cable-TV Franchises Gets Cutthroat, Tactics Upset Some Officials," *Wall Street Journal*, October 9, 1979, p. 40; John Bloom, "Invasion of the Cable Snatchers," *Texas Monthly* March 1980, p. 93; Tony Schwartz, "Powerful Groups Clash in Battles to Acquire Cable TV Franchises," *New York Times*, July 27, 1980, pp. 1, 31; David Garino, "Competition for Cable TV Rights Heating Up, as St. Louis Discovers," *Wall Street Journal*, March 2, 1981, p. 17; "Cable TV: The Race to Plug In," *Business Week*, December 8, 1980, p. 62; and William Schmidt, "Millions Spent in Content for 'Showcase' Denver Cable Contract," *New York Times*, February 22, 1982, p. A12.

60.  See, "Daniels & ATC Unit Wins Denver on Vote of 10-3," *Multichannel News*, March 1, 1982, p. 1. The 220-channel original bid has been subsequently modified, however, and the city and operator have renegotiated a 60-channel system in part as a result of pressure brought by a lawsuit. See "Denver Council Reacts Favorably to Mile Hi Plan," *Multichannel News*, January 10, 1983, pp. 1, 12.

61.  Ibid.; also see "Two File Bids for Fairfax," *Multichannel News*, February 22, 1982, p. 1.

62. For an excellent discussion of technical matters affecting data transport by cable systems, see Deborah Lynn Estrin, *Data Communications via Cable Television Networks: Technical and Policy Considerations*, (Cambridge, Mass.: MIT Laboratory for Computer Science, May 1982); see also "Multichannel Industries Aim at Growing Business Data Markets," *Multichannel News, Multichannel Technologies Report*, March 1, 1982, p. II–18.

63. An addressable converter is the "black box" installed by the cable company at the subscriber's television set that allows the cable operator to select which homes will receive a particular signal, just as a telephone call "addresses" a particular telephone.

64. "Experts See Lower Prices for Addressable Converters," *Multichannel News*, April 5, 1982, p. 6; see also "PPV and Enhanced Services: Reality Sets In," *CableVision*, November 22, 1982, pp. 244–260.

65. See, for example, L. Huffman, "NCTA Report Predicts Competition Will Cause Drop in Cable Penetration," *Multichannel News*, April 26, 1982, p. 1; E. Holsendolph, "Tougher Times for Cable TV," *New York Times*, July 11, 1982, Sec. 3, p. 1; and "CTAM Melody: How Ya' Gonna Keep 'Em Hooked on the Wire after They've Sampled Feevee?" *Variety*, July 14, 1982, p. 92.

66. See, for example, M. Roth, "A Cable Fairy Tale in Chi Where Everyone Is Wired and No One Makes Money," *Variety*, May 26, 1982, p. 42; T. Schwartz, "Cable TV: High Risk," *New York Times*, July 15, 1982, p. B1; and, G. Livingston, "Promises of Cheap ($2) Cable, 5% of Profits, 52 Channels Help Cablevision Win Boston Franchise," *Variety*, August 19, 1981, p. 55.

67. See, for example, M. Christopher, "Why Local Officials Rap Cable Systems," *Advertising Age*, November 9, 1981; and M. Roth, "Cable-City Marriage Goes Sour, Both Unfaithful to the Other; Oh, What Might Have Been," *Variety*, July 7, 1982, p. 33.

68. *Loretto v. Teleprompter Manhattan CATV Corp. et al.* _____ U.S. _____ (No. 81-244) 50 U.S.L.W. 4988 (June 30, 1982); Chi's Highland Park Case May Turn on Two Unresolved Issues Left from N.Y. Cable Decision," *Variety*, July 7, 1982, p. 39; D. Narrod, "Court Bans Cable Operator from Digging City Streets," *Multichannel News*, July 26, 1982, p. 1.

69. In its "Boulder decision" the Supreme Court ruled that cities and towns are subject to liability under federal antitrust laws when they regulate economic activity such as in granting cable television franchises unless granted specific powers to do so by the state. [*Community Communications Co., Inc., v. City of Boulder, Colorado*, 455 U.S. 40 (1982).] The decision meant that the city of Boulder, Colorado could be sued by the cable television operator that charged that

the city's franchising policies favored a competing company and restrained trade in violation of antitrust law. The cable industry is concerned that one result of the decision will be more overbuilds in which more than one cable company offers service to the same homes. Although most cable franchises are granted as "nonexclusive," with few exceptions, the practice has been that only one cable operator serves a specified geographic area. It is now feared that in order to avoid antitrust liabilities cities may grant multiple franchises if asked to do so at renewal time. D. Narrod, "Boulder Verdict, Renewals May Increase Overbuilds," *Multichannel News*, May 3, 1982, p. 49.

70.   Narrod, "Cable Executives Look to Trades as Consolidation Move Accelerates," *Multichannel News*, June 14, 1982, p. 1; see also "Clustering by Design: Emerging Trend Being Driven by Basic Economic Needs, Demands," *CableVision*, August 16, 1982, p. 49; "MSO's See Greater Use of 'Cluster' Strategy," *Multichannel News*, October 11, 1982, p. 22; "ATC Trades Systems with Group W Cable," *Multichannel News*, December 6, 1982, p. 19; "Cable Interconnects: Making Big Ones Out of Little Ones," *Broadcasting*, March 1, 1982, p. 59; "250 Gather to Investigate Massachusetts Interconnect," *Multichannel News*, October 11, 1982; and "New Jersey Link," *CableVision*, November 22, 1982, p. 73.

71.   "PPV and enhanced services," p. 247.

72.   The issue of whether cable operators will still be required to provide access capacity and production support if local requirements are ever found to be in violation of the Constitution is the topic for another paper. Likewise the issue of mandatory leased access is a related but separate issue.

73.   The description of players and how they see themselves and others in the emerging local distribution arena is based upon the author's observations of how the players see themselves, their competitors, and others. It is intended to generate comment from players to develop a more accurate description of players' self and other perceptions. This approach is modeled on that taken by Kurt Borchardt in *Actors and Stakes, A Map of the Compunications Arena*, Program on Information Resources Policy, Working Paper W-78-8, Harvard University, Cambridge, Mass., June 1978.

74.   See, *FCC v. Midwest Video Corp.*, 440 U.S. 689 (1979); as well as *Report and Order in Docket No. 20496*, 65 FCC 2d 218 (1977), *Report and Order in Dockets Nos. 20988 and 21284* 79 FCC 2d 663 (1980), and *Malrite TV of New York v. Federal Communications Commission*, 652 F. 2d 1140 (Second Cir. 1981), *Cert denied sub nom. National Association of Broadcasters, et al. v. FCC* 454 U.S. 1143 (1982).

75.  See for example, Robert Ross's *Cable Television and the First Amendment* (Washington, D.C.: NCTA, 1981) and statements by NCTA president Tom Wheeler that cable is really in the business of "publishing information," e.g., in Lucy Huffman, "Wheeler Calls AT&T Pact 'Deceptive'," *Multichannel News*, March 1, 1982, p. 4; see also "Cable, Newspapers Should Define Telepublishing before Gov't Does," *Multichannel News*, October 11, 1982, p. 41 and "NCTA Opposes Geller's Plan," *Multichannel News*, January 10, 1983, p. 7.

76.  Lucy Huffman, "Pressure Grows for Law Requiring Leased Access," *Multichannel News*, March 8, 1982, p. 1; and Gary Witt, "Legal Tightrope: Leased Access Can Raise Cable Operator Revenues but Also Can Trigger Common Carrier Troubles," *CableVision*, November 15, 1982, p. 107.

77.  For a description of recent cable-data transmission demonstrations and ongoing projects see Toni Barnett, "Multichannel Industries Aim at Growing Business Data Markets," *Multichannel News, Multichannel Technologies Report*, March 1, 1982, p. II–18.

78.  L. Huffman, "Cox Asks FCC to Approve New Business Data Service," *Multichannel News*, May 3, 1982, p. 9. See below (p. 23) for description of DTS.

79.  See comments by former director of the House Communications Subcommittee, Harry (Chip) Shooshan, "Shooshan Warns Cable to Avoid Becoming Known as Common Carrier," *Broadcasting*, November 23, 1981; "Pressure Grows for Law Requiring Leased Access," *Multichannel News*, March 8, 1982, p. 1; "Legal Tightrope," p. 107; and "Common Carrier Look-alike?" *CableVision*, February 7, 1983, p. 60.

80.  See, for example, comments of TCI president John Malone in Fred Dawson, "The Hottest Story in Town," *CableVision*, November 22, 1982, pp. 242, 244.

81.  C. Mayer, "MCI Explores Use of Cable TV," *Washington Post*, November 19, 1982, p. C1; "MCI To Test Cable System for Telephone Service," *Wall Street Journal*, November 19, 1982, p. 8; "MCI Plans Test of New Cable Tie," *New York Times*, November 19, 1982; and "McGowan Proposes Cable-Telephone Connection for Long Distance Access," *Communications Daily*, November 22, 1982, p. 1.

82.  Mayer, "MCI Explores Use of Cable TV," and S. Schley, "MCI Chairman Seeks Alliance with Cable," *Multichannel News*, November 29, 1982, p. 1.

83.  Ibid.

84.  "MCI Going for It," *CableVision*, December 6, 1982, p. 72. Also see below.

85. "GTE Plans Voice, Data Services by Satellite," *Multichannel News*, March 29, 1982, and "GTE Challenges AT&T with Private-Line Service," *Computerworld*, April 5, 1982, p. 6.

86. TvB president Roger Rice wrote cable advertisers attacking cable as an advertising medium, saying, in part, "Put your commercials where prospective customers can see them [Broadcast television]." "CAB Wants Retraction of TV Ad Bureau Letter," *Multichannel News*, February 22, 1982. Also see, for example, "Ogilvy Downbeat on Network TC Prospects by '90," *Broadcasting*, January 11, 1982, p. 39; and Paul Klein, "The Networks' Incredible Shrinking Pie," *Variety*, January 13, 1982, p. 158.

87. N.R. Kleinfield, "Newspapers Stalk Cable TV," *New York Times*, June 25, 1981, p. D1.

88. "Madison, WI, Newspapers to Sell Cable Ad Avails," *Multichannel News*, June 28, 1982, p. 8.

89. "Cable Seen as Alternative to Local Telephone Loops," *Multichannel News*, December 6, 1982, p. 20; also see below.

90. L. Huffman, "Bell Exec Says AT&T Not Interested in Cable," *Multichannel News*, May 10, 1982, p. 3.

91. Ibid.; see also Randall L. Tobias, "American Bell . . . and the Cable Industry," *Multichannel Almanac*, December 27, 1982, pp. II-8-13.

92. "NCTA Board Puts Deregulation at Top of '83 List," *Broadcasting*, September 20, 1982, pp. 30-31.

93. See discussion of pending state regulatory actions, below.

94. *MFJ*, see note 7, above.

95. Ibid., at 226.

96. Ibid.

97. Ibid., at 227.

98. Ibid., at 227-228.

99. Ibid., at 228.

100. Ibid., at 231.

101. Ibid.

102. Ibid.

103. *Final Decision in Docket No. 20828 (Second Computer Inquiry)*, 77 FCC 2d 384 (1980), *recon.*, 84 FCC 2d 50 (1980) *(Reconsideration Order) recon.*, 88 FCC 2d 512 (1981) *(Further Reconsideration Order), affid. sub nom. Computer and Communications Industry Association v. FCC*, 693 F. 2d 198 (D.C. Cir. 1982).

104. *MFJ*. The MFJ defines electronic publishing as, "the provision of any information which AT&T or its affiliates has, or has caused to be, originated, authored, compiled, collected, or edited, or in which it has a direct or indirect financial or proprietary interest, and which is dis-

seminated to an unaffiliated person through some electronic means."
[Part VIII(D)] at 231.

105. Ibid.

106. Ibid.

107. *Final Decision in Docket No. 20828 (Second Computer Inquiry)*, 77
FCC 2d 384 (1980).

108. See note 91.

109. "Freeing AT&T for 'information age' "; "Wheeler Calls AT&T Pact
Deceptive"; and "NCTA Names John Saeman as Chairman."

110. Press release, ANPA, January 25, 1982.

111. "Wheeler Calls AT&T Pact 'Deceptive.' "

112. "Brown Seeks to Establish Common Ground with Publishers in
ANPA Convention Talk," *Telecommunications Reports*, 48:18 (May
3, 1982), 21.

113. Testimony of William G. McGowan, Chairman of Board, MCI Communications Corporation before the Subcommittee on Energy and
Commerce, U.S. House of Representatives, March 9, 1982.

114. ITT's Corporate Vice President, George F. Knapp appearing before
the House of Representatives Subcomittee on Telecommunications
Consumer Protection and Finance, February 25, 1982, as quoted in
*Telecommunications Reports*, 48:9 (March 1, 1982), 23.

115. See, for example, the discussion of telecommunications technology in
John S. Mayo, "Evolution of the Intelligent Telecommunications
Network," *Science* 215 (February 12, 1982), 831–837.

116. *MTS and WATS Market Structure*, CC Docket No. 78-72, _____
FCC 2d _____, (1982).

117. See, for example, "New Services Key to Survival Say Local Telco Of-
ficials," *Multichannel News*, March 1, 1982, p. 21; W. Falconer and
C. Skrzypczak, "The Bell System on Its Way to a Digital Network,"
*Bell Lab Record*, 59:5 (May/June 1981), pp. 138–145.

118. Notes 97 and 98. Although the MFJ limits former BOCs to providing
"exchange telecommunications and exchange access service," (at
228) several BOC's have proposed building cable television distribution plant for lease to cable operators. Such a "lease back" ar-
rangement might be permitted under the terms of the MFJ if it is
viewed as an extension of exchange telecommunications. However, it
seems less likely that a BOC would be able to contract with a cable
operator as a construction company. See, for example: "Pennsylvania Bell Seeks to Build Systems in Philly," *Multichannel News*,
December 13, 1982, p. 1; S. Paul, "Michigan Bell Seeks to Build
Cable System in Detroit," *Multichannel News*, January 10, 1983, p.
15; "BOCS Already Aggressively Pursue Business Deals with Cable

Companies," *Cable News*, January 14, 1983, p. 2; "C&P Offers to Build D.C. Cable System; BOCs' Interest in CATV Mounts," *Communications Daily*, March 10, 1983, p. 4.

119. *Cellular Mobile Communications Systems, Report and Order,* 86 FCC 2d 469 (1982).

120  See, for example, Robert Metz, "Western Union Turnaround," *New York Times*, April 8, 1982, p. D8.

121. "GTE Challenges AT&T with Private-Line Service," *Computerworld*, April 5, 1982, p. 6; and Barnett, "Multichannel Industries Aim at Growing Business Data Markets."

122. See, for example, the description of cable proposals that will provide "complete business communiations services designed to compete with the phone company" in L. Huffman, "Montgomery Co. Receives Bids from Eight Firms," *Multichannel News*, February 8, 1982, p. 1.

123. "Access Charges Hashed out at Special FCC Session," *Communications Daily*, November 30, 1982, p. 1; "Complex Compromise System of Access Charges, With Minimum Flat Rate Imposed on Users at Outset and Almost Complete Reliance on That Method for NTS Costs at Conclusion of Seven-Year Transition Period, To Be Acted on in FCC's Most Important, Difficult Case," *Telecommunications Reports*, 48:51 (December 20, 1982), pp. 1–3; "FCC Okays Complex Access Charge Plan Moving toward Flat Rate, Customer-Borne Fees over 7-Year Transition," *Communications Daily*, December 23, 1982, pp. 1–3.

124. P. Hirsch, "SBS, Tymnet Experimental Net Bypasses Bell," *Computerworld*, November 30, 1981, p. 10.

125. L. Huffman, "Cox Asks FCC to Approve New Business Data Service," *Multichannel News*, May 3, 1982, p. 9.

126. P. Hirsch, "FCC Gives Dems Green Light to Five Carriers," *Computerworld*, July 22, 1982, p. 12; see also E. Holsendolph, "High-Speed Data Link Approved," *New York Times*, July 16, 1982, p. D1; and "FCC Clears 5 Concerns to Offer New Service for Transmitting DATA," *Wall Street Journal*, July 19, 1982, p. 10.

127. Ibid.

128. P. Hirsch, "Competition for DTS: Bell Moving to Digital Net by '84," *Computerworld*, November 16, 1981, p. 1; and "AT&T Makes New Offering of 1.544 MBPS Service Designated Terrestrial Digital Service, and with Simplified Rate Structure; New DDS And Supergroup Tariffs Set for Late 1982," *Telecommunication Reports*, 48:27 (July 5, 1982), 11.

129. Hirsch, "FCC Gives Dems Green Light."

130. *Amendments of Parts 1, 2, 21, and 43, of the Commission's Rules and Regulations to Provide for Licensing and Regulation of Common*

*Carrier Radio Stations in the Multipoint Distribution Service, Report and Order*, Docket No. 19493, 45 FCC 2d 616 (1974).

131. Ibid.
132. "Proposal of Microband Corporation of America for the Creation of Urban Over-the-Air "Wireless Cable" Networks Capable of Providing Premium Television and Other Broadband and Narrowband Communication Services," Vol. 1, before the Federal Communications Commission in Docket Nos. 80-112 and 80-113, February 1982, pp. 39–40.
133. Ibid.
134. Ibid., p. 41.
135. Ibid., pp. 30–33.
136. A. Pollack, "CBS Requests Approval for 5 Pay-TV Systems," *New York Times*, August 4, 1982, p. D1; L. Huffman, "CBS Plans Multichannel MDS System, May Buy into Ohio Pay Sports Net," *Multichannel News*, August 9, 1982, p. 1; and J. Loftus, "CBS Double Dipping into Pay-TV Flavor," *Variety*, August 4, 1982, p. 37.
137. "Proposal of Microband Corporation," p. 36.
138. S. Cobb, "Multichannel MDS Declared Success, Awaits FCC Action," *Multichannel News*, March 7, 1983, pp. 1, 19.
139. L. Huffman, "NCTA Report Predicts Competition Will Cause Drop in Cable Penetration," *Multichannel News*, 3:16 (April 26, 1982), p. 1.
140. See, for example, "ABC Execs Peddle Anti-Cable Punch to Lunch Bunch," *Variety*, October 15, 1980; L. Brown, "Cable and Disk Programs Not for NBC," *New York Times*, July 26, 1979, p. C19; P. Funt, "Tomorrow—'A Video Supermarket,'" *New York Times*, July 22, 1979, p. D1; or T. Schwartz, "Have the Networks Responded to Cable?" *New York Times*, June 6, 1982, Sec 2, p. 35.
141. E. Pace, "Networks Ease into Cable TV," *New York Times*, December 20, 1981, p. 35; J. Cooney, "ABC Will Offer Cable TV Programming for Performing and Visual Arts in April," *Wall Street Journal*, December 3, 1980, p. 8; "Three from ABC in 1981," *Multichannel News*, November 24, 1980; A. Levy, "Hearst and ABC Make It Official," *Multichannel News*, February 9, 1981, p. 1; "ABC, Getty Oil Form Cable-TV Service Featuring Sports," *Wall Street Journal*, September 24, 1981, p. 48; J. Loftus, "Affils Have Real Sinkin' Spell as ABC Grows in Cable & Pay, *Variety*, September 30, 1981, p. 61; T. Schwartz, "Cable News Service Is Planned by ABC and Westinghouse," *New York Times*, August 12, 1981, p. A1; F. Beermann, "ABC Cable TV Plans Are Roaring Along," *Variety*, February 4, 1981, p. 131; J. Cooney, "ABC Seeks to Set Up Low-Power Stations in Five Cities on Limited Pay-TV Basis," *Wall Street Journal*, January 28, 1981, p. 14; and T. Bierbaum, "ABC Video's

Herb Granath Maps Big Non-Broadcast Plans, High Hopes for Home View," *Variety*, May 19, 1982, p. 85.

142.  F. Beerman, "ABC Shows Its Hand—Lotsa Surprises," *Variety*, May 5, 1982, p. 115; "ABC, Cox Broadcasting Set Pay-TV Venture in Programs, Hardware," *Wall Street Journal*, May 3, 1982, p. 16.

143.  C. Fraser, "CBS Cable to Produce Arts Programs," *New York Times*, November 27, 1980, p. C26; J. Loftus, "Slam-Bang CBS on Cable-Homevid Bid," *Variety*, December 31, 1980, p. 27; J. Loftus, "Paley's Culture Comes to Cable," *Variety*, October 21, 1981, p. 61; J. Boyle, "CBS Cable Will Cease Operation within 90 Days," *Multichannel News*, September 20, 1982, pp. 1, 54; "CBS Cable to Disband," *CableVision*, September 27, 1982, pp. 13–14; J. Baker, "Conclusion of a Class Act," *CableVision*, October 4, 1982, pp. 4–16; "CBS Exec Outlines CBS Cable Problems," *Multichannel News*, November 22, 1982, p. 17.

144.  "CBS Breaks Back into Cable," *Broadcasting*, March 1, 1982, p. 35.

145.  N. Kleinfield, "CBS and Bell Plan Video-Text Test," *New York Times*, October 9, 1981, p. D1; S, Knoll, "CBS, AT&T Venture One Seen as Videotext Giant: Many Poised to Enter Biz," *Variety*, April 28, 1982, p. 47; "CBS and AT&T in 2d Videotex Test," *New York Times*, February 2, 1983; "American Bell and CBS Launch Home Banking Videotex Experiment," *Communications Daily*, February 2, 1983, p. 3.

146.  N. Kleinfield, "CBS Plans to Test Teletext on Coast," *New York Times*, November 14, 1980, p. D4; D. Kaufman, "CBS & NBC Set Teletext Services Soon," *Variety*, June 30, 1982, p. 38.

147.  L. Landro, "CBS Plans Foray into Pay-TV Services That Vie with Cable," *Wall Street Journal*, August 4, 1982, p. 27; see also note 98.

148.  See note 126.

149.  L. Huffman, "Direct Broadcast Satellites Get the Green Light from FCC," *Multichannel News*, June 28, 1982, p. 1.

150.  "Coming Together: The Differences between Cable and TV Stations Are Narrowing as Mutually Beneficial Programming Arrangements Are Being Invented," *Broadcasting*, March 22, 1982, p. 15.

151.  "Broadcaster Programs Cable Systems' Channels," *Multichannel News*, March 22, 1982, p. 41.

152.  "Cable Offers New Opportunities for Radio Stations," *Broadcasting*, April 12, 1982, pp. 74–75.

153.  D. Shribman, "Public Radio in Venture to Transmit Data Text," *New York Times*, April 20, 1982, p. D1; R. Shaffer, "Public Broadcasting Sees New Technology Producing Revenue," *Wall Street Journal*, June 23, 1982, p. 32; "NPR Announces Joint Venture with Dataspeed Inc. to Form Nationwide, Portable Paging and Information Service," *Communications Daily*, November 10, 1982, p. 3.

154. "4 Establish Venture for Paging Service," *New York Times*, July 29, 1982, p. D4.

155. *Amendment of Parts 2 and 73 of the Commission's Rules Concerning Use of the Subsidiary Communications Authorizations*, BC Docket No. 82-536; see also R. Shaffer, "New Rule May Let FM Radio Offer Paging, Electronic Mail," *Wall Street Journal*, August 6, 1982, p. 17.

156. P. Hirsch, "FM Radio-Based Local Nets Advocated," *Computerworld*, December 7, 1981, p. 67.

157. Comments of American Telephone and Telegraph Company in BC Docket No. 82-536 (filed December 17, 1982) at p. 2.

158. *Cable Television 1981*, (New York: Donaldson, Lufkin and Jenrette, 1981), p. 8; 1979 data from FCC data while 1982 data are an estimate by Donaldson, Lufkin and Jenrette.

159. "AT&T Is Allowed to Send Programs for TV by Satellite," *Wall Street Journal*, September 28, 1981, p. 20.

160. K. Lane, "Cable Security," *CableVision*, August 30 1982, p. 65.

161. *In the Matter of Deregulation of Radio*, 84 FCC 2d 968 (1981).

162. In August 1981 Congress extended the license period for television stations from three to five years and from three to seven years for radio. P.L. 97-35, 95 Stat. 357, Sec. 1241 (a).

163. Notes 46–49.

164. *Carterfone* 13 FCC 2d 420 *recon den.* 14 FCC 2d 571 (1968).

165. The Execunet case forced the FCC to open up interexchange MTS to new players such as MCI *(MCI Telecommunications Corp. v. FCC (Execunet I)* 561 F. 2d 365 (D.C. Cir 1977), *cert denied*, 434 U.S. 1040 (1978); *MCI Telecommunications Corp. v. FCC (Execunet II)*, 580 F. 2d 590 (D.C. Cir. 1978), *cert denied*, 439 U.S. 980 (1978). The case reversed the FCC's decision that MCI was not authorized to offer Execunet because they believed that MCI's authority was limited to private line services (*MCI Telecommunications Inc.* 60 FCC 2d [1976] under the general guidelines created for SCC's (*Specialized Common Carrier Services*, 24 FCC 2d 318 [1970]).

166. *Second Computer Inquiry* 77 FCC 2d 384 (1980).

167. M. Warner, "Rep. Wirth Ends Bid to Revise AT&T Pact, Citing Tactics by Firm's Backers," *Wall Street Journal*, July 21, 1982, p. 2.

168. "Quiet Year Seen for Telecommunications Policy," *Communications Daily*, January 2, 1983, pp. 1–2 and "Access Charge Will Become Hot Political Issue If Rates Skyrocket," *Communications Daily*, December 10, 1982, pp. 4–5.

169. Hochberg, *The States Regulate Cable*.

170. "Top Legal Officers of Nearly Half of States Warn Justice and Court of Near Endless Local Litigation on Justice/AT&T Consent Settlement, Expecting States to Exercise Authority within Their Jurisdictions

to Prevent Divestiture or Make Other Changes," *Telecommunications Reports*, 48:18 (3 May 82), 7–9.

171. "Total of 6 Appeal Notices Filed in AT&T Antitrust Settlement Case," *Communications Daily*, October 27, 1982, p. 1.

172. State of New York Public Service Commission, Case No. 27091. While MCTV argues in its comments that cable television is neither a common carrier nor a monopoly and is appropriately regulated by the State's Cable Television Commission, New York Telephone Company, in arguments echoing AT&T's comments opposing unregulated data transmissions on FM subchannels, argues that MCTV's service and its own are "interchangeable" and should be regulated. (Comments of New York Telephone Company in New York State PSC Case No. 27091 [filed January 7, 1983].)

173. State of New Jersey Department of Energy, Board of Public Utilities, Office of Cable Television Docket No. 8111C-6837 (PRN 1982-2) 14 N.J.R. 198 (1982).

174. Nebraska Public Service Commission, Notice of Public Hearing, Released January 6, 1983, and Nebraska Public Service Commission Order to Cease and Desist, entered, April 19, 1983.

175. "Another Dozen Organizations File Comments with Dist. Court on AT&T's Divestiture Plan," *Communications Daily*, February 17, 1983, pp. 2–3; "Access Plan May Produce 'Civil War' between State & Federal Regulators," *Communications Daily*, November 15, 1982, p. 2; and "States Want 'Provider of Last Resort' Authority for Phones and Wiring," *Communications Daily*, December 20, 1982, p. 3.

176. "Telecommunications Officials Give Views on Future of Local Phone Service," *Communications Daily*, February 4, 1983, pp. 3–4.

177. See, for example, S. 66, Sec. 607(c), note 16 above.

178. *Community Communications Co., Inc. v. City of Boulder, Colorado*, 455 U.S. 40 (1982); see note 70 above.

# 7 THE CONTINUING REVOLUTION IN COMMUNICATIONS TECHNOLOGY: IMPLICATIONS FOR THE BROADCASTING BUSINESS

*Richard S. Rosenbloom*

The shape of the broadcasting industries today displays the consequences of past innovations in information technologies. Similarly, the leaders of the industry twenty-five years hence will see the effects of the myriad innovations now emerging. Unfortunately, technological revolutions are much easier to identify in retrospect than in prospect. Business planners must make their choices now, in the midst of uncertainty, and without the benefit of hindsight.

Broadcasters are familiar with radical technological change. Broadcasting began as the radio business, the first great industry spawned by electronics, the greatest technological force of the twentieth century.[1] Radio broadcasting grew to maturity in the 1930s as a business oriented to the mass market, structured around programs and stars, and dominated by national networks. That industry was destroyed by another technological revolution, the advent of television broadcasting. But a new radio industry emerged from the ashes of the old, made possible by technology introduced at the same time that television became a commercial reality. The solid-state revolution in electronics, of which the transistor was the leading edge, made possible low-cost, reliable, and portable radio receivers, and created the conditions for the kind of industry we now see around us, in which local stations geared to specialized audiences have proliferated and prospered.

The underlying forces that gave rise to these past revolutions are still at work. The continuing advance of technology will make possible new products and services that will create new options for listeners and for advertisers. If those options are attractive—and they probably will be—the consequent changes in behavior will produce significant changes in the broadcasting industries once again.

This chapter examines some of the future possibilities for broadcasting, emphasizing those that may be important for the long term. No single new technology can be identified now as likely to produce sweeping change. The continuing broad advance of information technologies, however, is generating an array of new products and services. These changes, in aggregate, could radically alter the structure of the industries concerned with program production and dissemination. What follows is an examination of some of the emerging new technologies that may affect broadcasting. Some possible future developments in broadcasting are suggested and a few simple guidelines proposed that may be helpful in understanding how change comes about and how to cope with it.

An ancient Oriental adage says that forecasting is a hazardous occupation, especially when it deals with the future. Prediction, in the sense of extrapolating recent changes into the future, is an unreliable guide for anticipating long-term consequences in a period of technological ferment. Certainly the future of the information industries will be very different from the present. In the longer term, it seems likely that we will see both new opportunities for and new alternatives to broadcasting as we now know it. Whether the current participants in the industry will be able to exploit some of those opportunities and to compete with some of the alternatives will depend upon their vision and the quality of their leadership. The chapter begins with two generalizations about the nature of technological change, using a bit of history as illustration.

## A HISTORICAL DIGRESSION

### The Consequences of the Stirrup

In the eighth century, an important new technology for riders of horses, the stirrup, was acquired by the Germanic tribes known as Franks, who inhabited what had earlier been the Roman province of Gaul. The stirrup had come to Europe from India by way of China, and the Franks were nearly the last people to adopt it. But they were the first to sense its possibilities for warfare. Combined with a saddle of the right design, stirrups fused rider and horse into a single entity. With a lance thrust before him, the rider thus mounted could deliver a staggering blow.

This one adaptation of an apparently simple technology greatly enhanced the power of mounted troops and changed the nature of warfare. Its effects were far-reaching. For example, because maintaining a cavalry was costly, the Frankish leader, Charles Martel, grandfather of Charlemagne, confiscated great quantities of Church land, which he gave to his retainers on the condition that they remain ready to mobilize to fight on his behalf. The distinguished historian, Lynn White, Jr., traces the effects of these moves and concludes that "the revolution in military technology brought about by the stirrup was the seed of feudalism and . . . chivalric culture."[2]

There were other consequences that could hardly have been foreseen. A knight going full tilt on a strong horse could wreak great damage to any person unfortunate enough to get in the way of his lance. But having impaled someone, the mounted knight would find it awkward to withdraw the lance. The solution to this, soon discovered, was to tie some cloth to a knot near the tip of the lance. Soon men fighting together came to use the same cloth for this purpose. It was then just a short step to an identifying pennant. The seeds of the idea of national identity, symbolized by a flag, were thus planted.

Professor White calls our attention to two points implicit in this story:

1.  Invention is not the mother of necessity. New technology creates new possibilities, but they remain just possibilities, until someone, in some society, perceives and acts on them.[3] Before Charles Martel, the revolution in warfare that was always inherent in the simple stirrup remained latent.
2.  Once new uses of a technology are introduced into a society, there is no telling where the consequences will stop. Charles Martel not only revolutionized warfare, changing the balance between infantry and cavalry for more than a millenium, but he set in motion forces that reshaped the political fabric of Western society.

These points are still valid. Some technological innovations can lead to such profound social change as to warrant description as a "technological revolution." Revolutions are often easy to identify in retrospect but difficult to spot in prospect. It is not possible to estimate the magnitude of the social consequences of new technology by examining only the intrinsic characteristics of the technology. Apparently simple changes in technology can have profound consequences. And those consequences may flow from applications of the technology that may not have been visualized by its inventors.

## HOW TO SURVIVE A
## TECHNOLOGICAL REVOLUTION

What are the business implications of revolutionary change in technology? More specifically, how can a business that lies in the path of change, survive it?

While there are no simple and sure-fire prescriptions for coping with a technological revolution, a couple of ideas are worth mentioning. They can be illustrated with a cautionary tale from the annals of business history.

Fifty years ago, when the radio industry was still young, America's largest corporations were railroads.[4] Two of the 100 largest industrial companies in 1930 were firms whose principal business was manufacturing steam locomotives for the railroads. It is clear in retrospect that technological change brought about the decline of the railroads and the destruction of the steam locomotive industry. Yet, as so often happens, at the time when action had to be taken, few people in either industry perceived the development of new technologies as events that would alter the future of their companies.

For example in 1938, two years after General Motors had begun deliveries of diesel locomotives, A.W. Dickerman, president of the American Locomotive Company, the industry's leading firm, told an audience: "For a century, as you know, steam has been the principal railroad motive power. It still is, and in my view, will continue to be." He was wrong, of course, and in little more than a decade his company was out of the locomotive business.

This is, unfortunately, a common failing. Twenty years ago Theodore Levitt gave it a name in an article that rapidly became a classic. Its title, "Marketing Myopia," aptly describes the weakness. The remedy, Levitt suggested, could be found in adopting a "customer orientation" toward any business.[5] To this prescription one should add a second ingredient, and that is to maintain an awareness of impending technological change.

## Maintain "Customer Orientation"

The railroads are in the business of transporting people and freight. Their fortunes have declined dramatically in the last thirty years even though the demand for transportation has increased substantially. Levitt argued that they "let others take customers away from them because they assumed themselves to be in the railroad business, rather than in the transportation business. . . . [T]hey were railroad-oriented instead of transportation-oriented; they were product-oriented instead of customer-oriented."

Ask yourself what business you are in. You may answer, "the broadcasting business." But to think about that business in traditional terms is to follow the path of those who believed that their business was running a railroad or making steam locomotives. The danger becomes apparent if we recognize that no one needs "broadcasting." "Broadcasting" is a means that is currently efficient for providing services that are in demand. Thinking of it in those terms also makes clear the possibility that someone offering similar or better services, at lower cost or more conveniently, might just take away your customers.

To sum this up in different words, a business can survive and prosper only by providing something of value. If better ways to provide that something come into use, they will supplant the old ways. When this happens, the established business has essentially only two alternatives to decline: either to embrace the new ways and stay in the old business, or to find new uses for the old ways.

Think about what happened when television came on the scene. Important segments of the broadcasting industry rapidly embraced the new technology, following the first of the two paths just mentioned. The mass-entertainment radio business was rapidly translated into the new medium by the existing national networks. Many station owners won TV channel allocations. Eventually local radio stations also found a way to follow the second path as well. They created the new radio business, with the technology of the old, exploiting opportunities that were themselves products of technological change.

The radio industry's customers, for example, are its advertisers, predominantly local advertisers.[6] Its real product, offered to those customers, is its audience. The growing strength of radio has come from its ability to deliver an audience of specified characteristics at relatively low cost.[7] As formats fragment, the audience profile is etched in ever sharper outlines. The audience is there because radio has succeeded in delivering a service that it values and cannot obtain elsewhere at comparable cost or convenience.

## Maintain an Awareness of New Technologies

The central force powering the many contemporary changes in the information industries is the ongoing revolution in semiconductor technology. Steadily, for twenty-five years, the industry has reduced the size and cost of devices and improved performance at a rate that is truly astonishing. The cost per unit of performance has been falling by 90 percent every five years for the last twenty-five years. If that continues, it means that a solid-state product made now for $1,000 will probably cost only $10 to duplicate (in functional terms) in 1990. The efficiency, power, and versatility of digital solid-state technology will probably lead to its adoption, over time, for all communication and control functions in our society.

The changes in capabilities of information technology will continue to be embodied in dramatically improved and different products for audio, video, and data services, and each of these areas will create new alternatives to radio. In audio, a new standard of music fidelity may become common with the diffusion of products based on digital technology. In video, a proliferation of specialized services will augment and perhaps ultimately replace the current mass-audience network service, as technology massively increases the choices available to viewers. Data services are emerging as a distinct service, as information technology of all sorts becomes more easily and inexpensively accessible.

These changes are not on the horizon; they are happening now. What is uncertain is not whether they will occur, but at what rate, and with what consequences. It is not necessary to predict the path of technology in order to anticipate its possible impacts on an industry. In fact, in the past, firms—and entire industries—that have been destroyed by technological change have suffered that fate not because they failed to anticipate the path of technology, but because they ignored the possible implications of change that were already a reality.

The ongoing revolution in information technology will leave no part of the information industries—and broadcasting is a part of the whole—unchanged for long. The question for managers in radio or television is how to track the progress of this revolution and how to anticipate its specific effects on their operations.

## TRACKING TECHNOLOGICAL CHANGE

How can a manager anticipate the future effects of technological change on a specific business? The only honest answer to this is "with great difficulty, and substantial uncertainty." But that does not mean that the problem should be ignored. Uncertainties can be reduced, if not eliminated, and the nature of potential threats and opportunities defined and made manageable.

It helps to recognize three basic points about technological change:

1.  The impact of any new technology on an existing business comes about through adoption of the technology, and not through its creation.
2.  Technological change takes place through an orderly and predictable sequence of steps.
3.  These steps take time, with the result that major change casts a long shadow before it.

### The Case of the Videodisc

These points can be illustrated in terms of an innovation that is very much in the news these days, the videodisc. It is surely one of the most sophisticated bits of technology now available over the counter in retail stores. The videodisc itself looks simple enough, just another plastic platter, not so different from the familiar LP record. But put it in a player (which, incidentally, embodies the most glamorous bits of current high technology, a laser and microprocessors), and the startling result is a beautiful color video program with hi-fidelity stereo sound.

As is often the case, the idea behind this up-to-date innovation is really an old one. John L. Baird demonstrated a working model of a crude system for recording video on a disc in London in 1927.

For the videodisc, the next important steps came forty years later. In 1970 Teldec (a joint venture of the powerful European firms, Telefunken and Decca) demonstrated a disc and player that would reproduce monochrome video comparable to current broadcast quality. By the end of 1972, both RCA and Philips had demonstrated, in their laboratories, alternative systems that produced color pictures and played for longer than the Teldec disc could hope to achieve.

Creating a laboratory prototype of a commercial product is a major step in innovation, but the product has little business significance until it has been refined for volume production and usage, and manufacturing facilities have been created. This always takes time. The first products based on the Philips system reached the market in December 1978; RCA's disc was introduced nationally in March 1981.

It seems likely that the major consequences of this innovation will be recognizable only in the decade beginning in 1985. Only then will we know whether the videodisc will be a success or a failure. And not until even later will disc players be owned by enough American households to become a significant force on mass behavior. At present, the optimists project penetration of 30 to 40 percent of U.S. households by 1990, while pessimists expect the product to flop. As is so often the case, the realists will only be identifiable in retrospect.

## Lead Time for Technology

It may seem unusual to find a prospective major innovation surrounded by so much uncertainty eight years after its "invention" and two years after its introduction commercially. On the contrary, this is the most common pattern in the history of technological change. To translate a laboratory prototype into a commercial product takes five years or more, and the adoption of that innovative product by half or more of its ultimate population of users takes five to seven years at best, and a decade or two most commonly.

Consequently, we can safely say that any technological innovation that will have major business significance by 1985 is already commercially available. Anything that will be significant by the early 1990s has already been invented.

### Guidelines for Corporate Policymakers

These patterns in technological change suggest certain simple guidelines for corporate policymakers:

1.  Recognize that fundamental changes in technology imply both threats and opportunities for established businesses. The ongoing revolution in information technology is just such a major change. Right now it is beginning to make available to ordinary households an array of new products and services that previously were available only in special situations (like defense) or not at all.
2.  Managers must not limit their views to a few glamorous innovations, like videodiscs, satellite communication, home computers, or fiber optics. Many elements of information technology are changing all at once, and they are likely to interact in unpredictable ways. The broad sweep of technological change will exert the most significant force for change.
3.  Avoid the very human tendency to disregard a phenomenon that is shrouded in uncertainty and potentially very threatening. Ignoring it will not make it go away. Some of the uncertainties can be reduced. And there may be real opportunitites there as well.
4.  Don't overreact. Change takes time. Concentrate on trying to anticipate future development of innovations already visible, and on tracking what is happening, the better to improve projections as time goes on.

New information technologies have already touched the broadcasting industries along numerous fronts. Digital computers control the transmissions of the national television networks. Digital recording for audio and video is likely to become a reality soon. Digital broadcasting is a possibility in the longer term.

The broadcasting industries are in touch with and capably adapting to the technologies that are changing the ways in which broadcasters work. If there is revolutionary change in broadcasting, however, its source will not be these. The potential threat to the established industry lies outside it, in the technological changes that are revolutionizing other information industries.

Anticipating the particular ways in which this stream of new technology will alter the information industries is a task fraught with uncertainty. But it is possible to speak with more confidence about some kinds of predictions than about others. There is not much uncertainty about what new services will become commercially practical in the years ahead. There is some uncertainty about when this will happen in each case, although it is clear that some developments will occur sooner than others. What is most uncertain is the consumer response to each of these opportunities. Unfortunately it is just that—for example, whether large numbers of consumers will adopt products built on digital sound-reproduction technology, and at what rate—which is most important in understanding the future impacts on broadcasting.

Despite the uncertainties, it pays to address those questions, formulating answers in the shape of working hypotheses to guide action. Here is one possible approach:

1.  Keep up to date on what technology is offering in the information industries.
2.  Concentrate on what it offers users, not on technical detail; in other words, keep a customer orientation.
3.  Form the best judgment possible about the likely response that users will have to the new product or service, but be careful to avoid the kind of bias exhibited by the steam locomotive manufacturers.
4.  Most important, monitor what is actually happening with the new technology, continually updating your working hypotheses.

## IMPENDING CHANGES IN
## INFORMATION TECHNOLOGIES

This approach can be illustrated by briefly examining a few specific new technologies. Rather than attempt to predict the changes, I will pose the questions that must be addressed for each.

First, radio. Most local radio stations build their programming around music. The low cost and portability of radio receivers and the quality of FM stereo sound have been major factors building radio audiences. What impact will low-cost, high-fidelity portable cassette players have on some segments of that audience? Small players with high-quality earphones are already available at moderate cost. Their prices are falling and their use proliferating. How many current listeners will prefer to play their favorites—perhaps recorded off the air—rather than take what comes on the radio in the car or elsewhere?

Potentially more significant as an influence on audience behavior is the development of digital sound recording. The improvement in sound quality is striking. Will many people care, or will it turn out to be irrelevant, as quadrophonic sound was? The answer will come only as digital records and players become available at affordable cost in a few years. If large numbers of listeners find that they do prefer the enhanced sound quality, it could mean attrition of the audiences for several, perhaps most, music formats. Existing AM and FM broadcasters cannot transmit sound that will match the quality of digital recording. But cable television operators may begin to use some of their broadband channels to transmit this type of high-fidelity program service, providing another alternative competing for the household segment of the traditional radio audience.

Other technologies are addressing another facet of broadcast services: news and information. A component of most news and information services is the reporting of fairly standard types of data—that is, factual information in simple categories, unadorned by interpretation. Weather, sports, and financial reports are typical examples. Electronic media have a natural advantage over print in storing masses of data that require frequent updating. New systems now in experimental, prototype, or introductory stages offer users the as yet unfulfilled promise of easy and inexpensive access to data more comprehensive and more current than either newspapers or traditional television broadcasters can hope to provide. Among these systems are two-way cable systems, teletext, and viewdata and home computers with a telephone link to central data banks. They all make it possible to gain access to some universe of information on a video screen at the request of the user.[8] It seems likely that large segments of the population will have access to one or more of these systems by the latter part of this decade. What will that do to audiences for news and information transmitted by existing media processes?

In video, as in the other categories of application, the broadcast effect of new technology is to expand the consumer's reach and offer the means for greater selectivity about what appears on the TV screen and when it appears there. Instead of being limited to the offerings of three networks all aiming at the same broad audience segments, viewers in many markets will soon be able to obtain services from fifty-two or more cable channels.

The value of those cable channels is being enhanced steadily by linking cable systems with other information technologies. Satellite distribution of programs revolutionized the cable TV industry in the 1970s. In the home, there are experiments in providing new services made possible by combining personal computers with a cable system. Over the next few years we may also see that video recorders and videodisc players can be used to expand the choices available to cable subscribers. In addition, home video players have the potential to become a major alternative means for selective distribution of video programming.

## The Video Process Alternatives

The commercial introduction of magnetic video recording occurred in November 30, 1956, with the first electronically recorded delayed broadcast to the West Coast of the CBS Evening News. CBS used the then-new Ampex "Quad" recorder, which served as the standard of the industry for more than two decades. Since 1959 a half-dozen Japanese firms have concentrated their efforts on developing technologies for the helical scan format, producing several generations of innovative products for use in schools, in business, and in the home.

A continuing stream of technical advances in the magnetic materials of recording tape and recording heads, and in microelectronic circuitry, coupled with imaginative design of tape formats, tape-handling systems, and video circuits, has yielded dramatic advances in product features and performance. Recording density, probably the single most significant performance characteristic, has increased a hundredfold in two decades. A 2-inch wide tape Quad recorder uses 747 square feet of tape per hour of program. The U-format machines, introduced in 1972 and now in wide use for electronic news gathering (ENG), are 10 times more efficient, using 72 square feet per hour. The VHS and Beta format machines now sold for home use are again 10 times more efficient—using less than 7 square feet per hour in extended-play mode. This affects more than just the cost of tape consumed, because greater density permits smaller cassettes and a much smaller machine overall. Combined with the miniaturization of the electronic components, these advances have made low-cost and truly portable video recorders a reality.

Videotape is replacing photographic film as the medium of television news. Home video has become a major industry in the world, and there is reason to expect that the technical advances of the next decade will be no less dramatic than those of the last two. Some speculate that magnetic recording could replace photographic film in all aspects of TV program production, in home movies, and eventually in all aspects of the cinema and even still photography. Home videocassette recorders (VCRs) are currently being sold, worldwide, at the rate of about 6 million units annually.[9] Five years after introduction of the first successful design, Sony's Betamax, this was a $4 billion industry, of which the Japanese account for about 95 percent.

Electronics specialists say that it is a mistake to think that the home recorder is near the limits of technology. They expect continuing improvements in features, such as program review, indexing, and slow motion. Smaller products permitting more flexible use may well be available, and prices should continue to fall, in constant dollars. One plausible scenario suggests that video recorders could be at least as common in consumer use in the 1990s as audiocassette recorders were in the 1970s.

Consumers have been using VCRs in three ways: (1) as a "time-shift" device, permitting the viewer to record broadcast or cable program for later viewing at the time of the user's choice; (2) to expand the menu of available programs, by using prerecorded cassettes; (3) for home movies, as a direct substitute for photography. Of these three uses, it is the first that could have the most fundamental impact on the structure of the broadcasting industry.[10] A broadcaster addressing an audience equipped with VCRs can consider any time to be "prime time," since viewers can program recorders to capture items of interest whenever they appear on a scheduled basis. If and when VCRs are found in 15 to 20 million American households, there will be incentives for around-the-clock broadcasting, with perhaps early morning hours used to transmit programs of relatively narrow appeal, to be recorded by interested viewers. What we are talking about here is really a form of publishing. The technology is here today. The existence of a market (or markets) is yet to be determined.

If that market materializes, the broadcasters may be the first to tap it, but they face a formidable long-run challenge. The broadcaster, in command of a single channel, will be competing with the cable system operator controlling twenty, thirty, fifty, or more channels to distribute programs. The perishability of video now lessens the value of those many channels. Will video recording shift the balance of power?

## Videodiscs

Another type of video publishing industry is in prospect now with the advent of the videodisc. In comparison to VCRs, all videodisc systems share two important characteristics: they can be used only to play prerecorded programs, but they utilize a medium—the plastic disc—that provides notable economic advantages for that function. Even for quantities as low as 10,000, discs can be made profitably to sell at retail for $15 to $25 per two-hour program, while the same material on tape today sells for $50 or more.[11]

The videodisc may turn out to provide the best medium on which to create a true "video publishing" industry. Those promoting this hypothesis point out that "soft publishing" of programs by transmission to recorders in the home requires a high degree of organization and planning on the part of consumers. This could inhibit large-scale development, especially if discs provide a real alternative. The "hard publishing" of programs on videodiscs fits into well-developed shopping patterns, permitting impulse buying, word-of-mouth recommendation, and so forth.

On the other hand, videodiscs require continued reliance on physical distribution channels, including the U.S. Postal Service, trucking, retailers, and middlemen. One of the supposed attractions of the electronic highways is the ability to bypass their traditional labor- and energy-intensive structures.

When viewed as publishing media, from a user's perspective, the alternative disc technologies do have significant differences. The "optical disc," developed jointly by Philips of Holland and MCA, uses a laser to "read" microscopic markings impressed in a plastic disc. Players produced by Magnavox (a Philips subsidiary) and Pioneer Electronics (of Japan) are now on sale in most areas of the United States, along with discs produced by DiscoVision Associates (DVA), a joint venture of MCA and IBM. RCA introduced an alternative system, called the capacitance electronic disc (CED), on a nationwide basis in 1981. A third, an incompatible capacitance system developed by JVC, has been announced for early 1982 introduction.[12]

The optical system has the ability to address any single frame out of 54,000 on a disc. With stop, slow, and reverse motion features and two audio channels, the product has a high degree of versatility for educational and other uses, limited primarily by the imagination of software producers and users.

The capacitance systems, while lacking some of this versatility, have the advantage of inherently lower cost (based on technologies now available) for both disc and player. The first CED players had limited special features, but the technology can be used to offer two audio channels, slow and fast speed, and indexing to relatively small program segments (though not as precise as a single frame).

The winners and losers in the competition among the technologies may be determined by the ability to manufacture high-quality discs, in volume, at a cost. This is the sine qua non for entry into the business. It is still too early to comment on how convincingly the suppliers have demonstrated the ability to do this.[13] If they can get past this hurdle, the systems have a greater chance of surviving or failing based on their inherent appeal to the market. The capacitance technology, now backed by manufacturers with great marketing clout (collectively they have a majority of the U.S. market for TV receivers), seems to be looking to reach the mass market. The optical system employs technology that has been seen as being particularly applicable to users with more specialized interests, such as home instruction and games. In combination with home computers and other new technology, the optical technology could lead to uses still not thought of.

The next overriding question is, where will all the program material come from? The first batch has been the existing stock of theatrical films. Beyond that, there is the model of thriving industries publishing magazines and books of relatively narrow appeal. Given the fundamental characteristics of the videodisc technology, and particularly its economic characteristics, manufacturers of the machines are not expecting to run into any great obstacle to its growth into a major industry. Again, only a retrospective view will attest to their predictive insights.

## IMPLICATIONS FOR BROADCASTING— AND OTHER TRADITIONAL MEDIA PROCESSES

Will the day soon come when the broadcasting transmitter and its tall tower are found only in the Smithsonian, along with the telegraph key and the vacuum tube? That question is likely to be somewhat unsettling to broadcasters, for those two artifacts—transmitter and tower—are central to the very concept of broadcasting. Yet they are being challenged by other communications technologies. It is, after all, characteristic of our industrial society that its institutions are constantly seeking and producing new and better ways. The resultant stream of technological change nowhere flows more briskly than in communications.

If it is inevitable that there will be changes in the ways in which society's needs are met, then it is dangerous for any institution to define its mission in terms of a particular technology. That is what the manufacturers of steam locomotives did. And that is what can happen to those who persist in calling themselves "radio broadcasters" or "newspaper publishers."

The remedy, already suggested, has two ingredients. First, broadcasters should be encouraged to understand their business from the customer's point of view. They need to identify what it is about their business that creates value for others—for advertisers and for audiences. Focus needs to be on the elements of *value,* not on the machinery now employed to create them.

At the same time, media businesses must try to anticipate the effects of technological change. In a fast-changing world, an organization that depends on being reactive, rather than proactive, runs a greater risk. But note that it is technology's consequences, and not the innovations themselves, that need to be forecast. Timing is the critical variable, since it can be as costly to respond five years too soon as it is to be five years too late.

History tells us that it is risky to focus on any single innovation as the likely cause of future changes in broadcasting. What is significant is the broad array of new products and services being developed from the new information technologies. There is a common thrust to these changes: lower cost, a richer menu of possibilities, and greater control by the user.

These characteristics may create great advantages over the traditional media of mass communications for performing certain old or as yet unrecognized functions. To date, we have experienced only the beginning of change in information technologies. The communications industries in the next decade or two will be characterized by more change—that is, by the appearance of more great opportunities for and more serious threats to the established institutions—than in any previous period.

Yet the change will not come overnight. It will come gradually at first, as it usually does. In 1981, it was taking form in the beginnings of an erosion of the position of the television networks and their local affiliates as the only channel for mass distribution of audiovisual information and entertainment. If this trend continues, it will certainly threaten the primacy of traditional network television. What effects would this have on the operations of the television networks and their program suppliers?

What will be the impact on radio by 1990? Those that specialize in news and information may have to watch the development of teletext and viewdata more carefully to determine their threat. Stations with certain music formats are advised to track the personal audio cassettes and digital recording markets. And, of course, because it has so many ties to television—sharing audiences, advertisers, some ownership, and a single regulatory agency—the radio industry is likely to feel the effects of any radical change in television. There will, no doubt, always be an audience for radio. But it is fair to question whether that audience will remain large enough to sustain broadcasting as a commercial activity.

Those whose careers and businesses are tied to broadcasting have a personal stake in technology that affects communications processes. But those with the foresight to face the inevitability of change and the vision to perceive the many opportunities created by the very developments that appear to threaten broadcasting will at least have the opportunity to create a challenging alternative for themselves.


### NOTES

1. Telephone and telegraph are, of course, much older industries. The inception of radio broadcasting is directly attributable to the invention of the vacuum tube, which launched "electronics."

2. Lynn White, Jr., "Technology in the Middle Ages," in *Technology in Western Civilization,* volume 1, edited by Melvin Kranzberg and Carroll W. Pursell, Jr. (New York: Oxford University Press, 1967), Ch. 9, p. 71.

3. White discusses this point also in *Medieval Technology and Social Change* (New York: Oxford University Press, 1962), p. 28.

4. In 1930 the assets of the Pennsylvania Railroad ($2.2 billion) exceeded those of the largest industrial corporation, Standard Oil Company (New Jersey).

5. Theodore Levitt, "Marketing Myopia," *Harvard Business Review* (1960), reprinted September-October 1975.

6. Eighty percent of 1978 revenues were from local advertising.

7.  Radio broadcasters entered the 1980s riding a modest boom in business fortunes. In 1976, after a half-dozen years of cost increases outrunning revenue gains, aggregate profits for the industry turned up. By 1978 they were more than triple the depressed level of 1975. Prosperity has attracted new entrants, and roughly 30 percent of the stations now on the air signed on for the first time after 1970.

    The aggregate figures mask great diversity. Most stations are small and marginally profitable. Of some 5,600 broadcast entities reporting profits to the FCC for 1978, only some 2,600—or 47 percent—reported revenues of more than $250,000 for the year. Even among the larger operations, profitability is not assured—in 1978, 640 of those stations (one out of four) reported net losses.

8.  See, for example, "Why TV Sets Do More in Columbus, Ohio," *Fortune,* October 6, 1980, p. 67.

9.  By 1983 this rate had increased substantially. About 3 million home VCRs were sold in the United States alone in 1983.

10. The second use might also have a longer term impact, but the current economics of tape duplication make mass-market use unlikely. Home movies, as an alternative leisure-time activity, compete, in a sense, with time spent on TV viewing, but probably not significantly.

11. It is interesting that those price and volume figures correspond closely to the present economics of book publishing. The publication of trade books—a $1 billion business in the U.S.—typically takes place with first printings of 8,000 to 12,000 units to be sold at retail prices ranging from $10 to $20.

12. JVC delayed introduction of its system. It was still not on the market in 1983.

13. This refers to information available to the public. Presumably the suppliers have satisfied themselves that they can meet this test.

# 8 FACTORS INFLUENCING MEDIA CONSUMPTION: A SURVEY OF THE LITERATURE

*Christine D. Urban*

A key component for evaluating the media environment of the future is the understanding of consumer behavior toward media: what is known of how consumers perceive, select, and use media, and become "attached" to the media throughout the various circumstances of their private and social lives. Some work done in recent years has explored the technological capabilities of new media formats, but the technological capabilities of a system are not sufficient data for estimating market acceptance or use. Technology is a necessary, but not sufficient, component of the future media environment—which will involve not only new equipment, but new costs to the consumer, new skills and experiences, new differential advantages and (perhaps) a new importance of the media in his or her life. Technologically based projections tell us only what is possible, not what is probable in a future competitive marketplace.

The strongest and most reliable base for predictions of the structure and character of the new media environment is consumer behavior. Today the consumer's use of the mass media is a relatively patterned and explicable behavior, which permits managers of media properties to track their product's performance in the marketplace and understand consumer choice patterns of content or format. For predicting the new media environment, these consumer data may provide a baseline on which hypotheses about new media formats' marketability and potential market position can be built. In fact, given an increasingly crowded media marketplace, a clear understanding of the structure of consumer media selection and use is essential to anticipating consumer reaction to proposed media products and reducing uncertainty on the part of those firms who intend to participate in this marketplace. To investigate consumer reaction only after the introduction of the new system is almost too late, not only leading to faulty entry strategies for the businesses involved, but also perhaps precluding the later collection of generalizable benchmark data. Research on the probable market reaction to new media formats and processes will reduce the likelihood of corporate policymakers going down paths in the marketplace that lead nowhere except to the draining of financial and human resources. It will help public policy planners better determine the appropriate context for their roles in the dynamic media environment.

This chapter reviews the existing literature on consumer behavior toward the traditional mass media and raises some of the questions about demand that must be addressed as part of an assessment of the possible directions of a new media environment. The chapter integrates a wide range of communications research relevant to this subject, summarizes the major influences on media consumption, and analyzes the state of knowledge now available to help private and public policymakers discern the structure of the future media market(s).

In addition, this chapter provides a theoretical and empirical background for further research on the key market questions that must be explored. In general, these market questions fall into four areas:

1. What values will the new media bring to consumers? (What purposes will they serve, or serve better? Which will be most important?)

2. Who will use the new media? How will they be used? (Is there a specific rate of diffusion that can be expected? What penetration pattern is reasonable?)

3. Are the new media to be "added to" or "substituted for" the existing media processes? (What will be the nature of the competition for consumers' time, money, attention and loyalty?)

4. What are the parameters of the new media environment that are measurable and projectable? (Which of the new processes will

significantly influence demand and behavior? Is content or format the key to predicting use and market success?

This chapter is intended to serve as a base of information for further research and decisionmaking regarding the fit of the new media formats (individually and in aggregate) into the consumer market they are entering.

The survey of the literature is in two sections: the first outlines factors that influence media consumption (the individual, interpersonal, situational and media-related influences on behavior), and the second summarizes research on the uses and gratifications of media for the individual and for society. Organized in ascending order, the least-complex variables are discussed first. This structure leads the reader not only through a reasonable conceptual development of the field, but generally through a historical one as well. The currently held generalizations of media are dependent, in large degree, not only on empirical work of the last ten years, but on the theoretical evolution within the field of communications research itself.

Two caveats are appropriate. First, the research summarized here does not differentiate among media content (the information provided), media processes (the creation, gathering, handling, storing, and transmission of the information), and media formats (the form in which the content is made available to the user or is handled by the processor), as these terms are explained in Chapter 3. When use of these terms does not violate or overstate the intent of the original research being discussed, they will be used.

Second, this is not meant to be an exhaustive review of each of the areas of research discussed—nor is the purpose to catalogue the numerous empirical works measuring levels of usage (by hours, issues read) of the present media. It excludes from analysis the following topics: the use of advertising messages by media consumers, the nonconsumer uses of media in business or art, the uses of point-to-point conduits (such as the telephone and telegraph), and the effects of media content on individual consumers or receivers. This survey of the literature is intended to suggest hypotheses to be tested in further consumer-based research, and to highlight findings that could be extended as projectable hypotheses. Most important, however, the research identifies some of the crucial controllable and uncontrollable dimensions of the potential media environment: the key factors that, in the aggregate, motivate and shape consumers' use of the mass media.

## RESEARCH ON THE FACTORS INFLUENCING MEDIA CONSUMPTION

The media function in varied ways, and each also fits differentially into the lives of the social classes. There are (sometimes sharp) class preferences among the newspapers available in a community, in evaluating magazines, in selecting television shows, in listening to the radio, in how newspapers are read, in receipt and meaning of direct mail . . . in the total volume of materials to which people are exposed to and to which they attend in one or another of the media.[a]

### Perspectives on the Research

Social science is replete with studies that attempt to explain and predict behavior by analyzing an individual's demographic, psychological, or social characteristics. Communications research follows this tradition, and for the past forty years has investigated these hypothetical cause-and-effect relationships between who the individual is and how he or she behaves toward the mass media.

Following are some of the highlights or key findings about factors found to influence the volume and type of media consumption by individuals. Not only are the individual characteristics that have been studied examined, but also research on the interpersonal factors, situational factors, and the characteristics of the media themselves that influence behavior are summarized.

### Individual Influences on Media Behavior

Three general clusters of traits have been isolated and defined as individual influences: demographics, psychological factors, and predispositions. As contrasted with the situational, interpersonal, and media-related influences on media behavior, these factors relate only to one individual and his or her media use, most often are not analyzed singly but in clusters (such as "life-style" or "social class"), and are regularly cast as *predictors* of media use or behavior patterns, rather than seen as interacting with that behavior.

*Demographics.*   Although there are a great number of studies that concentrate on identifying the influences of single demographics (age, income, sex) on media behavior, few succeed in explaining large proportions of behavioral difference using demographic factors alone. Of course, there is a large body of research that validates the obvious: that men tend to read more sports magazines than women, or that nonworking women watch more daytime soap operas than men. Beyond this, a number of general hypotheses appear.

First, most researchers find that greater-than-average readership of newspapers and magazines is associated not only with higher levels of income, education, occupation, and perceived social status, but, more important, with what can be called a "sense of community." Variables defining this sense include length of residence in a community or neighborhood, the degree of urbanization, home ownership, employment, and participation in local social and political affairs.[b]

These studies (228,249,272,108,321,338) are consistent in their findings: the stronger an individual's ties to a local community, the greater is his or her use of media, especially print, that reflect in some way that community of interest. In one sense these findings are as obvious as those that suggest strong sex differences or age differences in content preference. Community ties are after all a type of clearly predictable influence on content preference, whether it is the local news of a geographic community or articles in a magazine designed for individuals in a community of shared interest, such as photography or horse breeding. The media not only hold these groups together, but often function as a leader within the community itself (217).

Studies on the influence of age and race find some explanatory patterns, but not as reliably as have the studies isolating the "sense of community." Some research on age as a predictive variable suggests that TV usage peaks in the adolescent and young adult years and then tails off (16,42,188). One study (10) disagrees with these findings. Print usage is just the opposite: The overall amount of reading increases with age (298, 350), although content preferences may change (older individuals might also have a greater "sense of community" as discussed previously).

The preponderance of data, however, suggests that social class and community ties are the two clusters of variables that show most promise for predicting media behavior. This has stimulated communications researchers to investigate seriously the influence of social class, focusing on social stratification (which measures the relationships between people) rather than isolated demographics (which are measures of individual characteristics).

*Social Class and Stratification.*    Early research on the influence of social class on media behavior outlines the major effects that social class has on media use, including the range of choices, the use of the medium itself, and the ability for the individual to order and implement communication (240). Regarding overall communications style, the research finds that the middle class is most familiar with elements of social structure and is also most facile with explaining its media behavior by social rather than personal reasons.

Among the general effects of social class on media use, one is simply the volume and type of media consumed. Research finds that higher social classes not only read more printed materials than do lower classes (1,71,276,275,272), but are more likely to attach credibility to information from printed sources. Lower socioeconomic classes, especially blacks in that category, are more likely to believe oral communications from people, the radio, or television than written communications (1,276). (It is suggested, however, that these differences may reflect geography and social position rather than an inherent class-motivated behavior [82]. It is also possible that the simple literacy proportions that could affect a racially balanced national sample would tend to produce these results.) One summary of the effect of class differences on the volume and type of media consumed concludes:

> Social stratification in a subtle way defines the degree of control an individual can have over the media of communication. The individual in the various social roles of the lower socioeconomic stratums is relegated to passive role of a media consumer. Although only a small minority of persons from the higher strata have actual control over the mass media, the majority feel an active identification with media content because much of it is created and stated in terms of a middle-class value system and lifestyle.[c]

A second influence of class on media use is in content preferences, in the choice literature, versus political analysis, versus gossip columns, and so on. Because of problems in classifying types of content, studies researching the relationship of class to content preferences are difficult to generalize. A number of studies, however, *do* find similar patterns of preference, albeit general ones.

Studies find that higher socioeconomic classes are more likely than average to read, and more likely to prefer "serious" materials such as literary, travel, news-oriented, and public affairs content. Lower socioeconomic classes are more likely than others to enjoy the comics, soap operas, confessions magazines, and other escapist content (1, 186,276,262). These findings can be explained by a functional perspective on the information needs of the middle and upper classes, or by arguing the traditional point of view that there are more passive media consumers who tend to prefer content that is less difficult, less varied, and closer to their daily lives than that selected by more active media consumers.

Social class and stratification measures contribute significant results to the study of media behavior, not only suggesting clear demographic patterns that can reasonably explain volume, format, and content choices, but also linking easily into the uses and gratifications of research work to be discussed later. Social class variables are suggested as a true universal measure as well. Cross-national studies on media usage (163,262,285,350) find them both methodologically and theoretically powerful in validating U.S. results in other countries, especially in the more industrialized, media-rich societies. Although the list of demographics which *make up* social class (and other clustered profile measures) usually account for only about one-quarter of the total variance in media behavior (136), they are most useful as reliable benchmarks on which to build more complex psychological and sociological variables.

*Psychological Characteristics.* If there is any a priori set of variables that would be expected to contribute significantly to explaining media behavior, it is the set of individual psychological dimensions. Psychological variables that would affect both individuals' *motivation* to consume media and content and their *understanding* and *use* of the information for their own purposes are included in this set.

Some of the psychological influences studied can be easily related to an individual's social class standing and the personality traits that would correspond to his or her relative power within the social community.

For instance, a number of studies note the positive relationship between high degrees of media consumption and leadership and self-confidence (168,120), innovativeness and risk-taking (168,144), and other-directedness (349,36,46). Other researchers question this, noting that:

> the social character of an individual may possibly affect perception of a medium or . . . vehicle but not to any degree in which there will be a significant or meaningful variation in the extent of exposure or preferential feeling. . . . No one medium or . . . vehicle is singularly oriented to the interests and values of one social character type that differential patterns of mass media selection could occur.[d]

There are also measurable differences in the types of content preferred by varying personality types (6). For example:

> Inner-directed subjects appeared to prefer and be exposed to classical . . . music . . . more often read *Time* magazine and the editorial, syndicated columns. . . . Other-directed students . . . tended to prefer the sports sections and local news . . . rock and roll and popular music . . . and (TV) dramatic fare.[e]

Differences in preference for different types of content (in radio) can be attributed to the individual's "mental set," which is shaped by both psychological and demographic elements. Content preference is also related to anxiety (26), anomie or rootlessness (44), and a host of other, less-specific psychological states, such as perceptions of modernity, creativity, and social expectations (230,149).

Other workers in this area describe psychological characteristics of heavy and light TV viewers. Heavy TV viewers, for instance, not only seem to have lower self-esteem, but also have more conservative values. Light TV viewers had a significantly higher self-esteem, and values that were more oriented to "imagination" and "true friendship" (57). Often, the heavy TV viewer (more than thirty hours a week) is characterized as passive (19), with stimulation coming from the TV set, with the viewer contributing little.

> Often these types of people watch for hours on end. They expect immediate gratification in terms of entertainment value. Hence the immediate and obvious are most appreciated. Those who adopt this viewpoint are often people with few inner resources that would lead them to cultivate other "outside" interests and activities.[f]

Finally there is research that finds a relationship between media usage and psychological traits of community membership, similar to and corroborating the demographically defined community link. These studies link media use to an individual's degree of socialization (152,155,100) and extent of political activity (22,61).

These and other studies that investigate the relationships between media behavior and learning ability, social adjustment, or personality development open a complex arena for study and speculation. No theory is yet conclusive; it remains to be determined whether any of these psychological states are the cause for, the effect of, or simply coincidental with differing media behaviors.

*Life-Style.* Just as social class was described as a combination of salient demographic variables, the concept of life-style defines an individual's particular manner of living by combining and clustering his or her psychological, demographic, and behavioral traits. "Lifestyle" offers the communications researcher a powerful (though more complex) predictor of media behavior, because it is a relatively consistent and predictable measure of social behavior (66). Also, because media are so closely linked not only to an individual's self-image, but his projected "social self," life-style studies have proved a fruitful method of investigating media choices and use since the early 1970s.

Life-style patterns distinguish audience segments both for individual media (305,247,299,88,300,284,295,260) and for the heaviness or lightness of media use in general (102,284,98,75,221,72). Such studies fall into two general categories: those attempting to use lifestyle measures to segment the audience of a specific medium, and those seeking overall dimensions of life-style's effectiveness as a predictor of media use.

The first of these two research objectives is somewhat successful. The audiences of particular magazines, newspapers, and some television shows are found to be characterized by between three to nine life-style segments—often, but not always, differentiated by their content or media preferences. For the purposes of this chapter, the latter objective (to isolate overall dimensions) is more interesting, since the findings of these studies are generalizable across the complex of interrelated media "mix" decisions that individuals make.

In general, these studies conclude that (1) life-style is a telling and useful variable for predicting media preference and use; (2) life-style not only can measure differences between users and nonusers, but suggests a system of reasons for use or nonuse; (3) the previously discussed active/passive and inner-directed/other- (or community) directed dichotomies are valid; and (4) life-style is the best link for the explanation of how media use affects media perception and behavior. In addition, cross-national tests of the methodology and perspective of life-style analysis suggest that it could be used to study media behaviors in a "culture-free" manner.

Although life-style measures include demographic variables in some applications, they have significant independent power for prediction (182). Separately the nondemographic variables either outperform or equal the ability of the demographic variables to predict media behavior (126,72).

The most important of the life-style research conclusions concerns the cluster of traits that influences heavy and light media use among individuals. Research suggests that heavy media users, for instance, differ from light users in their shopping behavior—shopping more often beyond the local retail area, using more convenience outlets (97,75)—and their orientation, being more home-oriented (284), and conservative in their values and expressed attitudes (284,98). These characteristics tend to be predictive of an individual's volume of media use, rather than his or her choice of content. Also, because life-style is a behavioral concept that is most intimately related to the present environment, it is most important to distinguish between life-style influences on media behavior that are dependent on external conditions (e.g., the availability of cheap energy for heavy media-users' extended shopping), and those life-style influences that are more stable because they are grounded in basic demographic or social realities (e.g., the greater media use by outgoing, community-oriented life-style segments).

*Information-Seeking.* An important outgrowth of both demographic and life-style studies on media consumption levels is that which defines the "information seekers," a cosmopolitan elite that transcends national boundaries. This is not a large group (estimates range between 3 and 5 percent of the populations), but it is an influential one. The information seeker is described as an upper class individual who makes a greater use of print media than the average individual, who relies more on broadcast media (342). The information sought is either personal (for the fulfillment of self-defined needs and desires) or social (for the maintenance of social place or status as an opinion leader). In subsequent cross-cultural studies

(348,63,287,258), researchers conclude that the information seeker is a more rational and critical consumer of goods and services, has a strong interest in public affairs, and is a conservative individual who thinks that his or her purchases and actions have elements of social risk connected to them, perhaps because they would be used by others to evaluate the individual.

Among studies done in the 1960s on the relation of media usage to information seeking (205,346), some show differences between the information-seeking group and others with regard to the perceptions of innovation. In one study not substantiated by other work (63), a high degree of innovativeness is associated with information seekers. The original definition of the "cosmopolitan" is integrated with direct measures of this segment's social and physical mobility, finding that the information seekers are cosmopolites who sought new information and experiences through travel as well as through the media (292).

There are strong similarities between a number of these information-seeker characteristics and the characteristics attributed to the heavy-consumption "media imperative" groups defined by a study for the Magazine Publishers Association (322,324). The media imperative groups are defined by their relatively higher usage of one medium over another (television over magazines, for instance), and the study suggests that these groups not only behave toward the available media formats differently, but that they are demographically different as well. One could conclude that the information seekers are not only predisposed toward heavy media consumption, but would probably use the media for both financial and consummatory purposes. (This distinction is discussed in detail in the section on uses and gratifications research.)

Overall, then, the individual influences on media behavior range from the easily measured demographic variables through the more complex but richer life-style measures. Although variable sets that describe individual predispositions are somewhat arbitrarily differentiated, this stream of research suggests that these basic measures are both meaningful and relevant keys to the understanding of media behavior.

## Interpersonal Influences on Media Behavior

Because media are social, as well as individual products, use is influenced by both individual and social factors. A person's use of media (or information in general) is motivated to some degree by what he or she has learned or been told about their quality, their social acceptability, and their cost (in time, money, energy, or required attention). Another important aspect of interpersonal influence is the shared experience of certain types of media (such as television or cinema), which encourages people to talk about the content they have shared. Both the socialization and shared experience factors are considered to be highly predictive influences on present and future media consumption patterns but are also difficult to measure.

Another type of interpersonal influence, however, is well researched and flows directly from the individual influences previously discussed. Just as there is hypothesized to be an information-seeking segment, researchers also suggest an information-mediating segment of society, opinion leaders having influence over the choices (media-related and otherwise) of others. Because it is a key interpersonal effect on media behavior, this concept is explored in more detail.

*Opinion Leadership.*   The original work in this area hypothesized that opinion leaders share a set of characteristics, including "the personification of values (who one is), . . . competence (what one knows), . . . [and] strategic social location (whom one knows), . . . divid[ed] into whom one knows within a group and 'outside'."[g] These elements, in addition to the interest, experience, intent, and accessibility to information that reinforces the opinion leader's knowledge, are necessary conditions before the opinion leader can "legitimize" (74) and transmit information to his or her peer group or information dependents.

Opinion leaders mediate the individual's selection and use of the mass media by being

> more generally exposed to the mass media, and more specifically exposed to the content most closely associated with their leadership. Presumably, this increased exposure then becomes a component—witting or unwitting—of the influence which such influentials transmit to others.[h]

Just as the mass media fulfill individual needs for social prestige (32,208) and information, so opinion leaders seem to use the mass media to maintain their own status, and to support their own opinions with the weight of the derived information. Because opinion leaders also seem to exhibit a greater propensity to communicate than the average individual, this process of information transfer is conceptualized in the two-step flow of information—from media sources through opinion leaders to the rest of the public.

Other studies of opinion leaders suggest that they have a strong network of personal contacts and acquaintances (208), a tendency toward either local opinion leadership or cosmopolitan opinion leadership, differing in the scope and complexity of their role (161, 208,26) "specialty" defined by social context or topic of interest (216), and a willingness to communicate their knowledge (26). Of course, the opinion leader's media usage and selections are quite specific within his or her speciality.

In addition, one survey of the literature on opinion leadership reports that most studies show opinion leaders and innovators having a higher than average level of exposure to the mass media. Other research (161) again validates these findings, although one study found that opinion leaders were more likely to have greater exposure only in media that related to their areas of influence. Cross-national studies in a similar vein seem to bear out this distinction (258,287).

Although the groups of innovators and opinion leaders are observed to coincide on occasion (the "dual-role change agent") (74), they are most often not the same group of individuals. Likewise, the characteristics that define opinion leaders are not often the generalized traits that identify innovators. The opinion leader as an interpersonal influence on others' media behavior is far more important in mediating people's choices among the present media formats and types of content; the innovator would be a more significant influence in their decisions to buy or use new media formats or types of contents.

### Situational Influences on Media Behavior

Media consumption draws not only on people's monetary budgets, but also on their time budget. The traditional media are also very time-sensitive products—dependent on both absolute numbers of minutes and hours available for media use and on the appropriate allocation of these minutes and hours between the fixed-time format media (such as broadcast) and those that allow consumers to control the time of use, such as print.

Studies in the recently developed field of consumer time-budgeting are a key to the understanding of situational influences on media behavior. This research area contains two types of work: research on the meaning and perceptions of time, and empirical studies on patterns of individuals' time allocation. Although concentrating on media usage only as one part of the broader agenda of activities for an individual or household, the work contains strong suggestions that the situational elements in which media are consumed—the physical surroundings, social surroundings, temporal perspective, and task definition—can explain a significant proportion of the variance in behavior (78). This situational context can be defined as

> all those factors particular to a time and place of observation which do not follow from a knowledge of personal (intra-individual) and stimulus (choice alternative) attributes, and which have a demonstrable and systematic effect on current behavior.[i]

The first step in studying the situational effects on any behavior is to appreciate the consumer's point of view: how he or she defines these elements (especially time) and which of them are controllable. Perceptions of time seem to affect not only the perceived time supply and the pressure for accomplishment within a time period but the willingness to delay gratification in making relative activity choices (303). A highly active person who perceives time to be a commodity in short supply would be less likely to simply goof off in his or her leisure time and more likely to plan leisure activities that will begin and end on a certain schedule. Conversely, a similarly active individual who sees time as more of a flow from one activity into another is less likely to schedule or plan his time, but will adapt to its availability and make decisions as they are demanded. These differences in the perceptions of time may be related to differences between life-style groups (304).

Gratifications are also important in directing time decisions (47). The use of time is not just an individual tool, but an indicator of social change (347a,293). Time is finite. It cannot be stored and is always spent or traded; thus it can provide a clearly measurable touchstone on which to evaluate individual and social behavior (153).

In examining overall patterns of time-budgeting, most researchers make their first clear distinction between leisure and nonleisure time. (Nonleisure time is usually, but not always, defined as working, sleeping, commuting, and self-care.) Leisure has been defined as consisting of

> relatively self-determined active experience that falls into one's economically free-time roles, that is seen as leisure by the participants, that is

psychologically pleasant in anticipation and recollection, that potentially covers the whole range of commitment and intensity, that contains characteristic norms and constraints and that provides opportunity for recreation, personal growth and service to others.[j]

More focused definitions and codifications of leisure are found in other studies (23,147,27). The common factor in all seems to be the definition of leisure as unstructured, discretionary time as opposed to the biologically or socially determined allocations for sleep, work, and personal care.

There is a remarkable similarity in the overall measures that a variety of studies make regarding this basic time distinction: Almost all report that leisure-time activities (as traditionally defined) consume about five hours a day, with some differences noted between men and women (37,290,291,340).

A number of studies concentrate some part of their investigation on outlining the gross time allocations to the media as a whole or to specific media, often categorizing watching television as a separate activity, but lumping newspaper, magazine, and book reading into a total measure of "reading." As such, not only do these data overlook differing motivations, but print media findings are difficult to disaggregate. In most of these studies, media usage is defined as a leisure-time activity. Although the previously cited definition is broad enough to include many of the uses and gratifications attributed to the media, it must be remembered that the existing literature all but ignores media use that is nondiscretionary either because it is work-related or because it is "demanded" by the individual's social position.

Most studies find a surprisingly similar amount of television watching by individuals each day. With a variety of methods, different researchers at different times find an average of 128 minutes per day spent watching television (291,192,231). (Nielsen [309] summarizes the television numbers as 360 minutes per day spent in the average household.)

Time spent with print media ranges in these studies between three and eight hours a week (or 25 to 68 minutes per day). As a proportion of total available leisure time, then, television watching accounts for approximately 43 percent of leisure time per day, and the print media consume between 8 percent and 22 percent of available time. No attempt is made in these studies to calculate the difference in the *amount* of information that can be consumed per minute in reading versus watching or listening.

An important underlying perspective in much of this research holds that media use, especially of radio and television, is a physically and mentally passive activity. This assumption could be accepted, especially when the results of one study note that, when asked what they would do with an extra two hours per day, over 30 percent of the respondents noted that they would spend them in indoor activities, rest, or media use (290). This self-defined passive set of activities lends credence to the traditional "broadcast as passive medium" and "print as active medium" point of view, but it must be remembered that work on individual influences on media behavior and uses and gratifications of media use has offered a more complex categorization than this simple dichotomy. Individual differences may invalidate these generalizations. Some individuals may feel, for instance, that reading is a relatively passive, relaxing activity. Different contents promote or require different levels of activity, and the very volume of media consumption can affect changes in the stability, intensity, and involvement of the individual's media behavior (294).

Media not only consume time, but they can also economize it. A different type of media behavior uses the mass media as a way to purchase either more leisure time or to improve monetary effectiveness.

Besides time, there are other situational variables that influence media behavior: the presence or absence of other people (121), the place of consumption—in home or out of home (330)—the day, week, or season of the year as a frame for the individual's perception of time spent with the media (especially broadcast) versus all of the related competitors for the time (122,9,113). These and other factors, either socially or individually defined, create the environment in which the mass media are chosen and used. There are problems in the current state of research on situational variables, including questions regarding the reliability and validity of analytic procedures (294,47,257) used in previous research. Also at question is whether time and situation are truly independent factors or are highly correlated with life-style or product attributes (29). In any case the research on situational factors that influence media behavior seems to be moving in the right direction—exploring some of the basic patterns and motivations for time spent on the media. Future research in this area should concentrate on empirical and theoretical work that defines the relative worth of media behavior (worth measured as time spent, time saved, substitution for other information-seeking activities), and how that worth translates into direction for behavior and choice.

## Media-Related Influences
## on Media Behavior

A still-undefined part of the equation is an understanding of how much time and money the media earn through the quality of their contents and formats. These media-related influences include not only content but also people's attitudes toward the content, especially its usefulness and credibility, and their patterns of selecting and using the media.

These media influences are not left to chance (156). Decision-makers at mass-media firms make choices regarding the content and format delivered, and often these decisions are made in light of the need for a bigger or better quality audience for their advertisers. By altering the controllable elements of content, format, price, or distribution (265), managers attempt to influence audience selection among available media. A key uncontrollable, however, is the mix of media that individuals assemble to satisfy their own social and psychological needs. Because researchers have suggested that people consume different types and amounts of media based on their individual characteristics or interpersonal influences, we can assume that these are not, for the most part, random. It would also seem logical to suggest that instead of making independent decisions about each and every new television program or magazine, an individual evaluates media comparatively, judging the benefits of one format over another efficiently and, most often, correctly for his or her own needs.

How individuals make these judgments and assemble their media mix is directly affected by media-related factors. Some research finds that media selection (or the substitution of one medium for another) differs between the heavy and the light media user (82,93,79,76). More insight into this decisionmaking process, however, is gained when the research concentrates on media-related variables rather than on audience characteristics. Audiences for different media overlap, the media tend to complement, rather than compete with each other (181). The consumer's perception and use of these symbiotic relationships is discussed, by anecdote, in an article on the effects of the newspaper strike in New York City during the week of August 19, 1978 (210). It is suggested that, because households using television (HUT) levels declined during the newspaper strike, people withdrew from both media.

Without newspapers, they not only did not know what happened, but they ceased to ask. Any complementary roles among the media, then, not only serve its business aspects, but also influence the public's expectations and involvement with the media as a whole.

*Media Content.*    One of the most universally accepted influences on media consumption is the content of the media, whether a specific program or article on a topic of interest to the media consumer or a consistent editorial point of view expressed in a cluster of articles or programs. Most researchers recognize the impact of individuals' assessment of media content in making their media decisions; few have been able to isolate its effect.

In general, research defines three modes of media content preference: (1) the group of individuals who use only certain media formats; (2) those who use alternatives that are closely related to their preferences; and (3) those who use any available common denominator rather than not watch, listen, or read at all. (The last of these three groups is discussed in the section on the influence of media formats.)

Media content is influential in guiding media selection not only because it can provide specific, needed information in an appropriate format, but because it profoundly affects the individual's attitudes toward the medium itself. Content preference is sometimes, but not always, associated with interest.

> Television reaches the largest and most heterogeneous audience of any form of communication in human history. Because it is more visual than cerebral, television can be comprehended (and easily assimilated) by [all]. . . . It therefore attracts millions of viewers who are not interested in *reading* comparable material, or *thinking* about comparable content.[k]

Recent research, sponsored by the American Association of Advertising Agencies, notes that the vast majority of TV viewers misunderstand some part (between one-quarter and one-third) of what they see, regardless of the type of content. In addition they suggest that viewers misunderstand facts as often as they misunderstand inferences (313a).

When an individual has need for a specific piece of information, however, he or she will seek out sources for that information. One study notes that interpersonal sources of information (personal experience, friends, neighbors) account for the predominant sources of information. Less than half of the respondents report that they would search for information in a newspaper, magazine, or book as their first source (340a). Other results of this study intimate that certain types of individuals are more prone to search for information in certain sources; this supports, to some degree, the previously discussed influence of individual and interpersonal characteristics on media usage.

Content preferences and choices of individuals are found to relate to the psychological and life-style traits of the individual in the audience (193,248,182). People choose programs as "product categories"—perceiving attributes that they expect to fill particular informational or entertainment needs. The researchers who outline the functions of the media (166,176,138,106,318,332) all conclude with a "matching" of the person's content needs and the medium's ability to gratify those needs. These studies reinforce the power of personal content preferences as an influence on reading and viewing behavior.

Researchers relating audience loyalty to particular content types also conclude that it is not only the program or article that is evaluated by the consumer, but its relative strength (or attractiveness) compared to competing types of content available at that time (100, 236,274,64).

Supporting the general view that individuals do not make singular, individual content decisions is a body of research that investigates the "patterning effect," especially of television show viewership. By correlating and reducing voluminous television program measures, researchers have been able to find different clusters of programs or viewers (169,269,212). Unfortunately, most of these findings characterize the viewer groups simply by the types of programs they choose (calling certain viewers "soap opera addicts," for example), thus explaining little about the process of choice. These studies are flawed in that they overlook the important situational elements of scheduling, time, and the "network effect" (reflective of the network's strategy of scheduling shows to discourage channel-switching).

*Media Format.*   The supposed dichotomy between active and passive media use is as important an element in examining media-related influences as it is in examining situational influences. For example:

> Magazine readers are active in the sense that they must subscribe to or physically purchase the magazines in which they are interested. In addition . . . many [publishers] attempt to target relatively small segments of the population. . . . Consequently, the audiences of many magazines are

not only identifiable, but in many cases, unique. Television programs, on the other hand, especially those aired during prime time, usually attempt to reach large segments of the population. In addition, since TV requires little active commitment on the part of the viewer, audiences of the programs are not easily differentiated.[1]

Although this point of view is an overgeneralization, it does suggest that one of the reasons that magazines have become increasingly specialized is that it is economically feasible with regard to how they are consumed. A consumer making an active choice of a magazine is presumed to be less subject to situational factors; a passive consumer is more dependent on the broad-based, generalized format and structure such as is built into a passively consumed medium. Indeed it is even suggested that special interest magazines are those in which the reader actively engages in the subjects written about or depicted in advertisements (photography, skiing, coin collecting), while general interest magazines, such as *Life* or *Readers Digest,* tend toward passive editorial material and advertising. Other studies support this assumption by noting that network schedules (344,227), the quality of competition based on content, and even the popularity of the highest rated programs (129,113) influence individuals' media choice and use. A key proponent of the network-effect and channel-loyalty arguments finds that "the percentage of the audience of any TV program who watch a given TV program on another day of the week is approximately equal to the rating of the latter program times a constant."[m] Although this finding suggests that audience duplication is a significant factor, it is admitted that the pull of the box only works when the set is on: it dissipates once the individual leaves the room. A general programming guideline from this perspective would be McPhee's Law of Double Jeopardy: "Things which are liked by relatively few people are not all that much liked by even people who do like them" (113). Although the validity of this "law" is debatable, it is difficult to overlook empirical evidence that consistently reaffirms that it is the situation (time of broadcast, network scheduling, magazine availability on the newsstand) that is as significant as content preference in a media selection decision.

In summary, we can hypothesize that consumer media behavior appears to be a function of situational and individual factors, as well as the content and format of the media. If an individual watches television, his or her behavior seems more likely to be passive and guided by situational factors than if he or she had selected among the magazines on a newsstand. In the latter situation, content and individual factors would seem to be more powerful influences (and predictors) of that media decision. Therefore, to further our understanding of that most desirable (to the supplier) of consumer reactions to a medium—loyalty—research must concentrate on the media-related influence that most closely matches the consumer's perceptions and behavior toward that medium, whether format or content.

*Attitudes toward the Media.*    Another media-related influence is the set of expectations and perceptions that individuals have of different media formats. Some researchers find groups of people who have clear preferences for particular media formats (2), and others note that "heavy" media consumers are very often reading, viewing, and listening to a number of different ones (23). Sometimes use of one medium influences another; in a study of library usage, 28 percent of the respondents reported reading a book because of what they saw on TV (313b).

Even people's most general categorizations, their perceptions of media versus broadcast media, can influence their overall behavior. Attitudes toward the media are affected not only by the people's perceptions (based in experience or not), and the social character of the medium, but also by the complementary behaviors and skills necessary to use the medium efficiently and enjoyably. An element of skill is necessary to use the print media to learn the news, whereas less skill is necessary to learn the news from television.

Is this why attitudes toward television have changed? Since its inception, TV has gained steadily in hours spent being used, with median viewing hours increasing from 2.17 hours per day in 1961 to 3.08 hours per day in 1978 (336,337). With increased exposure, attitudes changed. A study in 1959 noted that newspapers and magazines were perceived as informative, while television and radio were seen as show business (334). By the early 1970s, however, not only did people perceive TV's dual role as provider of entertainment and information (215,195), but television began to surpass the printed media on preference dimensions such as "the most entertaining medium" (53,218, 336), the medium with the most favorable "associations"—translated into "impact measures" (93), and even as an indispensable and reliable source of news (336,337). Even though newspapers were still perceived as the basic news medium (337), television's audiovisual realism had changed people's attitudes toward its reportage of the news.

Many changes in TV, of course, have occurred in the past twenty years. Even with an improvement in transmission, a broader menu of programming, and a greater number of stations, one could suggest that it was really television's becoming more and more a part of daily life that accounts for increasingly higher measures of positive perception. This, in addition to a self-acknowledged dependence on television for relaxation and as an opportunity to be with the family (53), may parallel television's improvements in content and format and its increased acceptance.

All of these findings suggest that television's ubiquity within the home is the key factor that gradually fostered more positive attitudes of individuals about the medium and therefore changed their behavior toward it. Given the concurrent trend indicating that television has become the major, if not the sole source for most people's news (336,337), it would appear that television will contribute to changes in definitions of acceptable delivery, "quality," and topics of news interest. "Attitudes toward the mass media seem to transcend the specific context: they grow at least in part out of the physical and social demands the media impose upon the audience."[n]

*Credibility.*  For news consumption especially, a central element of an individual's perceptions and attitudes toward the media is credibility. Credibility of the medium is paramount, not only for the establishment of purchase pattern, but for stimulation of the all-important loyalty pattern. A 1979 Television Information Office publication (337) summarizing the findings of selected studies from 1959 to 1978 noted that in 1959, 29 percent of the people sampled said that television was the most believable medium, whereas in 1978, 47 percent of persons sampled said television was the most believable medium. Newspapers dropped from 32 percent to 23 percent, radio from 12 percent to 9 percent, and magazines from 10 percent to 9 percent. Despite some natural questioning of any individual research study's findings, it would appear that TV today has attained a news credibility unknown ten to twenty years ago.

There seems to be little agreement on an overall measure of media credibility, however. Researchers find that not only do different groups rate media differently (consonant with their goals), but furthermore that they react to a message independent of their assessment of the source (274). Some research (345) found the same, and it examines the facets of credibility including: authenticity, objectivity, and dynamism (with additional measures of bias, accuracy, and other subdimensions). Other studies expand this segmentation of the concept of credibility by suggesting that it depends also on the content being reported, or by suggesting that credibility is a relational term representing a broad judgment by users of the media source and its operational characteristics in the form of receiver perceptions (90,271). Credibility as well as other media-related variables has to be combined with and related to the individual and social influence variables in order for them to have meaning. The integration of these different consumer influences and judgments is discussed below.

*Selective Exposure.*   Selective exposure (the tendency of individuals to limit their exposures to communications that are consistent with already held interests and beliefs) and selective perception (the tendency to screen out of consciousness portions of all stimuli, including communications) are often cited as important mediating variables in the behavior of individuals toward communications. These audience predispositions are studied in the broadest context—in order to explore the conditions of effectiveness for mass communications—as well as in the narrowest sense—to determine how the "indexing process" (255) within media content can affect an individual's judgment of the medium. Selective exposure, selective perception, and their relative, selective retention, are described as the three concepts of audience control of the mass media communications process (8). Other researchers (285,243) suggest that these controls are more important than functional or public ones.

Selective exposure is, of course, related to individual influences on media consumption such as social class, time-budgeting, and psychological or cognitive style. These systematic biases in audience composition are similarly correlated with the uses and gratifications that audiences expect from the media (243). It is not enough, however, to believe that individuals will limit their exposure only to nondissonant or immediately useful source of information. For instance, accepting the selective *exposure* hypotheses does not imply that a selective *avoidance* hypothesis is operational (203). People will not, as a general rule, avoid information sources that are novel. It is more likely that when consuming these kinds of media, they will moderate their *attention* to individual elements of the content, rather than rule out contact with the medium entirely.

*Selective Perception.*    Selective perception translates the concept of selective exposure to the content of a particular medium. After the individual perceives and understands the overriding style (or "paradigm") of the medium, he or she attempts to maintain cognitive consistency by being selective in the choice of reading or viewing material (171). A study designed to determine the media characteristics that influence perception noted that receptiveness of an individual to a message "is directly and positively correlated with the number of types of media to which message recipients are exposed, the impact these media have, and the overt behavior induced by media exposure and contact."[o] As such, selective perception becomes an important consideration in judging ratings and audience response to programs or editorial content (306,110).

Selective perception may be viewed as a type of communications barrier (158), and it certainly is one that could influence the use of a medium, if not the choice of that medium itself. Selective perception is also linked to the types of rewards that can be expected from the media. These rewards "may be either the immediate pleasure reward of drive reduction or vicarious experience, or the delayed reality reward of . . . general preparedness and information."[p] Just as research identifies a link between the media people choose and the gratifications they expect from them, it also points out that there is a less objective influence at work. Individuals, whether expecting immediate or delayed rewards, look for content with which they can personally identify because "the ease of self-identification is powerfully influential on the probability that a reader will select the story."[q]

Other studies define "media personalities" as a key factor in developing this identification with the medium (51). That is, the human personalities portrayed within the editorial or advertising content provide a bond that increases not only the interest in but the relevance of the medium to its reader or viewer. For instance, people choose media personalities based on either actual or ideal self-perception (225); such figures have been termed "symbolic leaders" (170). Instead of typifying selective perception as avoidance or reduction of cognitive dissonance, then, it might be more useful to consider the positive effects of selective perception as individuals attempt to become more effective and involved media consumers, searching for relevant media personalities, information of immediate concern, or other stimulation from media content.

*Involvement.* The involvement of individuals with the media has been of significant concern to the advertising community and to media firms because it addresses such areas of interest as (1) the regularity or frequency of reading patterns (85); (2) the effects of time on recall of advertising messages (201,236); or (3) the differences (in involvement, commitment) between a magazine's original purchasers and its secondary readers (323). Some studies attempt to rank the different media by general involvement measures, which are defined as the degree of identification and imaginary interaction with the "persona" of the media (233). In these studies the ranks seem to be influenced not only by the individual's perceptions and behavior, but by the power of the medium to impinge on the situational and individual elements and force the reader or viewer to suspend disbelief for the time of the encounter. In this light one can see why movies are usually ranked as first on a scale of participation or intercourse with the individual, followed by television, radio, newspapers, magazines, and books (89). These findings seem reasonable in light of studies finding that it is not only the editorial environment but the general situational environment that influences attention and comprehension of a TV commercial (266).

Other studies are more specific in explicating the nature of media involvement. Experiments in Japan test the difference in the emotional impact and usefulness of information received through different modes of transmission. Not surprisingly, the researchers find that motion pictures with sound had more impact on these two measured dimensions than the writing alone, sound alone, or writing plus sound modes (347b).

Perhaps the most nontraditional work done on media involvement entails a variety of research methods, including a measure of involvement that asks respondents to list or number the outside thoughts or "connections" that come to mind while reading or viewing the test material. This work concludes that involvement is independent of the "noting" behavior measured by Starch scores (174) and of the amount of exposure time. Hypothesizing that the left side of the brain "reads" and the right side "scans" images (173,174), the researcher asserts that there are not only audience characteristic and content influences operating in the process of involving people with a medium, but that the media themselves may differ in the inherent levels of audience involvement that they can elicit.

Studies sponsored by the Magazine Publishers Association (324, 319) have continued to explore specific facets of media involvement, finding that it is influenced by the individual's receptivity (the mental set of past experience), the "engagement of mind" (the attention demanded by the particular media format), the editorial or program environment, and the actions that result from the communication. They conclude, not surprisingly given the source of the research, that print media are higher involvement media overall than are broadcast.

These findings on media involvement are key to this survey of the factors influencing media consumption, because they directly measure psychological, situational, and media-related variables, and implicitly account for demographic, social, and process variables—all of which have been discussed as significant factors that influence an individual's propensity toward media consumption and his or her choice patterns and behavior. An important caveat, however, is that these studies on involvement depend very heavily on the current definitions of print and broadcast format and content. As these elements change, the expected levels of involvement will also change, and not necessarily in the patterns that might be expected from an extrapolation of previous results. What we now know about audience involvement with print media as opposed to broadcast media, for instance, does not provide much useful information as the key elements of each of the present systems become intertwined. If text is no longer restricted to a printed format, will it be any more or less "involving" on a video screen? Without understanding whether the presentation portion of the media's format (the text) or the physical portion of the media's format (the paper or screen) contributes most significantly to higher involvement, we can easily under- or overestimate the impact of the new media technologies on consumers and their probable behavior patterns.

In order to understand the influences on media behavior, then, it is important to examine not only the prior influences, but the behavior itself: What are people looking for in the media, and how do they use them once the media and content choices have been made?

## RESEARCH ON THE USES AND GRATIFICATIONS OF THE MEDIA

The study of the "uses and gratifications" of mass communications . . . proceeds from the assumption that the social and psychological attributes of individuals shape their use of the mass media rather than vice versa. This is the approach that asks the question, not "What do the media do to people?" but, rather, "What do people do with the media?"[s]

## Perspectives on the Research

Media research today still concentrates a good deal of attention on defining the kinds of reading, listening, and viewing behaviors people exhibit. But the field goes further: It studies not only the patterns of behavior, but also the *value* of the media behavior to the individual. Published research is replete with references to a broad range of consumer motivations for media consumption, from the profound ("to search for meaning") to the pragmatic ("to kill time").

The earliest hints of interest in the *purposes* of media consumption were seen in communications research of the late 1940s and early 1950s, when there was a shift away from a concentration on message effects (early 1930s) and the social role of the—at the time, new—broadcast media. The focus shifted to audience members, who were highlighted both as a group and as individuals with particular social and psychological attributes, and therefore, needs.

By the 1960s media research had met quantitative analysis. For the first time, differential patterns of media consumption could be efficiently analyzed, correlating newly categorized hierarchies of uses and gratifications with both the individual's and the medium's characteristics. Research in the 1970s not only expanded the methodology for gratifications measurement, but began to link quantitative findings to theories of the communications process.

## Uses and Gratifications
## for the Individual

One of the earliest models in uses and gratifications research notes that the social and psychological origin of needs within the individual motivates media behavior and leads to an expectation of gratifications from the media (56). This approach assumes that the audience is active and goal-directed (seeking information and content to satisfy felt needs) and therefore assumes that communications must be a social system that satisfies the audience's intentional search for information (242).

Many researchers have attempted to list and codify these functions. Most operated from the viewpoint that "media-related needs . . . predate the emergence of the media and, properly, ought to be viewed within the wider range of human needs. As such, they have always been, and remain, satisfied in a variety of ways, most quite unrelated to the mass media."[t] This highlights the basic position of functional uses and gratifications research. It hypothesizes that all or most of mass media use is functional in character, presupposing that the media's main purpose is to help the individual fulfill his social needs and adjust to a social role (206). This "instrumentality" of the media (289) may be further divided into "specific instrumentality," which helps the individual in current decisionmaking by providing information, and "general instrumentality," which helps the individual collect information to be used in future social relations or decisionmaking.

In any case the functional approach places the dominant responsibility on the receiver. Because the act of communication is regarded as directed toward some goal and meaningful activity, the receiver is assumed to bring a priori expectations and knowledge to the event, and also to select and process actively the information he or she sought.

A prime example of this kind of research is a study of Israeli audiences that sets out a multifunctional analysis of audience needs (164). Aiming to study the gratifications that attracted and held individuals to both their media format and content choices, the reseachers classified thirty-five needs into five groups:

1. Cognitive needs—information, knowledge, and understanding.
2. Affective needs—positive emotional and aesthetic experiences.
3. Personal integrative needs—credibility, stability, and status.
4. Group integrative needs—strengthened contacts with others and with the world.
5. Tension-release needs—to "weaken" contact with daily life or with oneself.

In addition, the major media formats (video and print) were matched to specific needs, with TV and radio fulfilling mainly integration and release, and newspapers and magazines the others. Media were individually ranked with regard to their perceived helpfulness in satisfying these clusters of needs.

The key finding in this study, however, is that personal sources (friends, relatives), were more fulfilling than *any* media source for these needs. This conclusion was subsequently corroborated in other research (56). These researchers conclude that use of the media must be seen within the wider range of human needs and that the media are not only interchangeable solutions to a person's search for need-fulfillment, but also can be substitutes for a more gratifying, personal solution. At this historical point in the development of research on uses and gratifications, the stage was set for a series of detailed studies that explored the range of human needs that the media could satisfy.

*Functional Studies.*    Studies that take the functionalist perspective on media consumption assume that individuals are using media to fulfill some a priori social or personal needs. The media are cast as instruments, or facilitators, of individuals' search for information that aid in decisionmaking, define what is important ("agenda-setting") (70), maintain social contacts and contracts, and provide prestige. In this functional sense the media are considered truly extensions of man that substitute for the more laborious or difficult interpersonal communications they complement or preempt.

Studies of a single medium most often provide useful and valid findings. In general a number of these studies concentrating on largely advertiser-supported print media (265,177,204,188) and broadcast media (35,15,207,114,134,278) find that the functions discovered either reinforce or slightly restructure the basic five categories of needs previously described. Most often these studies more finely differentiate the powers of the media to fulfill these needs. Print media, for instance, seem to excel at gratifying needs for current information and important events, for social "belonging," and for conversational topic development. Television not only provides information and membership in a social group, it additionally gives pleasure and escape from the day-to-day realities. Radio fulfills the same general needs and is sometimes personified by the listener as a companion. It was only after these findings were well validated that the research focus turned from continued redefinitions of the needs to an exploration of the media as functional equivalents of one another.

Throughout all of the functionalist studies, the codification of needs has fallen into three basic categories (which collapse the original five):

1.    Media are sought after to provide information (or education).
2.    Media are used for escape from daily reality.
3.    Media fulfill people's needs to "belong" and "connect" to the social group.

Because these three gratifications are well validated and basic to the research, we will explore each in more detail.

*Media Gratification 1: Information.*    Information-oriented functions of the mass media are commonly cited, and easily understood. All media, and in particular current news-carrying media, offer the individual an opportunity for what has been termed "surveillance," a way to be immediately informed when crisis (wars, natural disasters) is imminent, as well as to be kept informed about "what's going on." These informational functions not only help in daily decisionmaking, but promote the development or reinforcement of useful attitudes and knowledge (204).

Other refinements in this area include work that details specific media functions (such as the use of magazines to promote discussion), the definition of areas of importance (e.g., the isolation and subsequent social emphasis placed on education after the *New York Times* highlighted it in a special section), and the enlargement of areas of interest for the individual (e.g., the multifeature presentation of a TV show such as "60 Minutes") (237,163). In addition, one theory of multi-image communications holds that media are used simultaneously for the information "density" on topics of especial interest to an individual (20).

An important link between the functionalist work in uses and gratifications and the previously discussed work on factors influencing media consumption is the use of the media by information and opinion leaders. A few studies intimate that the role of the opinion leader depends, to a great extent, on his or her use of the mass media to reinforce that self-definition. This hypothesis distinguishes between an individual's personal consumption of information to extend his own conception of the world, and the opinion leader's consumption of information as "a commodity for exchange, to be traded for further increments of prestige, by enabling him to act as an interpreter of national and international affairs."[u] The hypothesis is a key contribution to the study of media uses and gratifications. For the first time this research begins to differentiate between the use of the media to fulfill an existing need and the opinion leader's use of the media themselves—as a means to help him or her maintain a social role. Although not violating the functional perspective, this research opens the door to alternative theories that allow for the consumption of media for its own sake, rather than to fulfill any functional need.

*Media-Seeking versus Content-Seeking.*    One important distinction is between media behavior that is determined by format choice and that which is determined by message choice (154). The former is called "media-seeking" behavior—the individual choosing to consume the medium without regard to its content—and the latter "content-seeking," typified by the individual searching for particular content (as in the strict functionalist perspective). This difference may become crucial in attempting to anticipate market acceptance of distribution of content via alternative channels or media.

It has been suggested that the concept of media-seeking behavior can be expanded to see how individuals create a "communications repertoire" (276) that not only facilitates social interaction and role creation within the the group, but actually helps to define it. Reading the "right" magazine or expressing knowledge about the "right" television shows, then, can be construed to be a strong social motivator, a gratification unrelated to content-seeking. Media-seeking, as opposed to content-seeking, is a subtler and yet powerful gratification as the individual seeks to reinforce and build his "social self."

*Media Gratification 2: Escape.*    Media are also hypothesized to offer psychological and social escape, a retreat from personal interaction (163). The media are here considered as a form of "substitute gratification," which people seek when depressed or alienated. Various studies support this contention (222,49), although alienation was later defined as a dysfunctional aspect of media use. Much of the work on media's escape use centers on the types of people who are prone to alienation and the need for escape (163). Researchers note, however, that a simple theory of replacement is inadequate to explain the higher escape use of the media.

*Media Gratification 3: Social Connection.*    Much research finds that media usage patterns differ according to the social groups with whom individuals associate themselves, particularly when the content of the media gives audiences information about where the people with whom they identify are going, and what they are doing, buying, or thinking (344,229). The selective nature of media choice makes this a reasonable conclusion, since the behavior, aspirations, and evaluations of these social reference groups are significant to the individual. If, for instance, an individual wishes to perceive himself or herself as a member of the jet set, it would be important to keep up with the purchases and travels of those leaders by reading *Town & Country* or similar magazines that depict people and settings associated with that group. Similarly, depending on their reference groups, individuals are expected to be familiar with essential conversational and group-reinforcing information, whether this information consists of up-to-the-minute knowledge of a sports star's free-agent status, the latest exploits of a television series character, or the current writings of certain syndicated columnists.

Group pressure and guidance influences media selection (122), and because the media used within a social group reinforce the values and discourse of that group (28,170), the individual recognizes and selects media that confirm and reinforce his or her membership.

Even excluding the professional and job-related group pressures on the individual's information acquisition, it appears that membership in most social groups depends on at least a minimally adequate familiarity with topics that are of interest to, or even *define,* that group.

Because people must have use of the media to gather information that they can internalize and share with their social groups, the individual's social role influences not only each media decision, but the total amount of media consumed (98,183), and the frame of reference and the norms according to which messages are interpreted and evaluated (40).

What is noteworthy about the media's well-documented ability to gratify these "social integration" needs, however, is that media behavior can be motivated by absent others. For instance, some public television viewing may be motivated by a wish to be associated with the higher class of people who are believed to watch public television (36). Watching can reinforce a membership in this social group whom the individual will never meet face-to-face. Similarly, newspaper readership is not only rational, providing news and information, but nonrational, providing social contacts and prestige.

> We have hypothesized that reading has value *per se* in our society, value in which the newspaper shares as the most convenient suppliers of reading matter. In addition, the . . . reading of the newspaper has become a ceremonial or ritualistic or near compulsive act for many people.[v]

Besides the role that the media play as a reinforcing device in social group membership, then, the media behavior may take on a life and meaning of its own. Moreover, the functions of media are essentially the same as the functions of reference groups (information, social utility, and value expression) (185). Thus we approach a definition of the media as referents themselves, rather than solely as vehicles for communication. Simply watching, listening, or reading certain material is sufficient to establish an individual's self-perception as a member of some group. There is no need to physically contact other group members to share or reinforce the content received; being a member of a particular *audience* is enough. This may be a transient group (such as a visitor to a city who picks up a copy of a "What's Happening" magazine in his or her hotel room), as well as a more stable group.

These three basic gratifications that can be fulfilled by media consumption all assume: (1) that the receiver plays an active role in media-seeking or content-seeking to gratify his or her needs and desires; (2) that the media are only one means available for this use; and (3) that the media are convenient, available, and diverse enough to provide the individual with a range of choice.

*Latent Functions and Dysfunctions.*   These very assumptions have prompted some research on the natural dysfunctions that arise from such a goal-oriented system (166,114,41). One dysfunction of the mass media of special interest in today's environment is that of information overload. Using the logic of functionalism, an increase in the total amount of information available would tend to cause a proportional increase in media consumption among goal-oriented individuals. The overload is, more precisely, a cause of dysfunction rather than a dysfunction itself. Researchers have suggested a number of potential hazards. Information overload may interfere with the ability of the receiver to understand the message (239,313a); it may "desensitize" or "narcotize" the individual (204,41,123); or even cause a retreat from mass communications and the physical surroundings that they mediate (the cities): "Whereas villagers thirst for gossip, city dwellers with more ample choices may crave privacy."[w]

This theoretical drugging would seem to be supported by empirical evidence of individuals' responses to the functions of advertising: advertising effectiveness is accelerated by the novelty factor, and heavy media users need twelve or more exposures to achieve only one-quarter the overall response rate that nonheavy users achieve after only six exposures (288). In addition the previously cited findings indicating that people misunderstand some proportions of both fact and implication in television programming may be attributable to overloading (313a).

Overall, this research stream argues not for a rejection of the functionalist viewpoint, but for the determination of an optimal level of communication, a question that has been studied and restudied in advertising research for many years. This leads to another facet of media use and gratifications work that counterpointed a strict functionalist approach: social gratifications. The functionalist perspective extends a little into this area, by arguing that communications is a systematic interaction in which individuals adjust their "receptivity" as they meet or fail to meet their information, escape or integrative needs. Further, it is only the interaction of the individual's disposition and the social experience that contributes to his or her capacity to function in a socially acceptable manner (206). Thus the door is opened by the functionalists for consideration of a two-way rather than a one-way theory of mass media uses and gratifications, where functional need-gratification is a part of, but does not completely determine, the use of mass media by individuals.

## Consummatory Media Behavior

The media can both *create* and then *supply* needs for quantities and particular types of entertainment and information. For example, consider this hypothesis on how television came to be successfully introduced in new societies:

> Television did not make its appearance because it was needed. It appeared because it was invented, and it was technically possible to produce it. It then developed because it appeared to answer needs that were not typical only of the society where it was invented.[x]

This position is a far cry from the early functionalist explanations of media consumption.

These new media-generated needs have been termed "consummatory media behavior":

> When content of the mass media does not have a functional relationship to situations which involve people, they passively *process* (consume) media content as a means of filling available time.[y]

This theory suggests that people consider the media inefficient sources of functional information, and is supported by empirical evidence that finds a relatively high degree of low-involvement, consummatory media behavior.

> There is no need to resort to theory of human needs other than perhaps to the pleasure principle which characterizes economic theory. There is also no need to use a latent function theory to explain media use, unless we also attempt to construct theories of the functions of golf, tennis, or drama to social systems. People use the mass media because they enjoy them.[z]

Like the "play theory" of communications (54)—which defines play as an activity self-sufficient and not necessarily functionally or gainfully undertaken—the consummatory media behavior theory admits the existence of functional motives but also includes nonmotivated media behavior as well. Other researchers supporting this approach discuss the simple desire for variety (novelty-seeking) that is often operational in media use (116), or they intimate that consumers may derive sufficient satisfaction simply from the ownership and/or physical use of the supporting hardware such as television sets or audio components (142). These and other modern research findings reject the seemingly automatic linkages made by earlier studies between preexisting needs and media satisfactions (60,253).

How do these conclusions regarding a consummatory type of media behavior relate to the media's social role as a change agent? At the most basic level, they attribute a self-directed power to the media that is quite different from previous theories, which assume that the media were either controlled by the individual (who would make his or her needs known), or by society (to transmit messages and value-statements). The consummatory theory logically depends on a view of the media as businesses—able to direct and focus their content in their own self-interest. For the first time, then, the media are not reflecting, reinforcing, or performing any passive role in information flow; they are active players in the process, with their own objectives and *capabilities* to act as a change agent.

The simplest example of media's role as a social change agent is the individual's increasing dependency on the media—especially as their number and network grows. The telephone is a prime example of this. Because it is used as an "extension of self" (198), the telephone changes people's perceptions and use of time, distance, and social relationships. Mayer points out that the power of such a system depends on its intelligibility, ease of access, and degree of privacy, but once these conditions are met, there is an almost irreversible attachment to and dependency on the instrument (199). Similar dependencies and changes of attitude could be probable as individuals grow accustomed to using videotex systems (instead of talking to a travel agent or reading the classifieds in a printed newspaper, for example), home financial centers (instead of going over the bank statement or checking stock listings), and other new technologies. The functionalist perspective places the responsibility for media format selection on the individual; the consummatory outlook places the responsibility for attracting audiences on the medium itself.

Whether socially directed or self-directed, the media have an important role to play as change agents. The fact that these theories have developed long after the original functionalist, one-way approach was established is not surprising. The newer, integrative theories demanded the foundation of empirical research and thought that functionalism had provided. In addition, researchers who worked prior to the middle 1950s could hardly foresee the proliferation of media or the pervasive nature of today's broadcasting system.

The field of uses and gratifications research provides a bridge between the functional theories of behavior in psychology and sociology and the then-developing study of popular culture and its effect on the individual (163). Although some would argue that there is no direct link between early work in uses and gratifications and the philosophical positions of functionalism (6), an examination of commonly held ideas about mass-media consumption in the 1940s versus those of the 1970s would suggest otherwise. From the individually determined, purposeful search for information to satisfy existing needs (165), it is a long way to the present systems theories of balance between the power of society, the individual, and the media to control information.

The increased complexity and quantification of present-day theories is no guarantee of increased correctness of the conclusions. For example, the original five-part description of the uses and gratifications to be found in the mass media is enriched but not necessarily made obsolete by subsequent research. What we can say for sure, however, is that the mass media do indeed provide uses and gratifications that satisfy a complex cluster of needs (societal, individual, or otherwise), and that the understanding of these uses and gratifications is essential for explaining both the existence of mass-media systems and their functions.

## SUMMARY AND CONCLUSIONS

This chapter has outlined the major findings of over fifty years of research on consumers' media use: how they behave and what influences that behavior. The questions this work answers are (1) What have we learned about media selection and use? (2) What clues can be found as to probable consumer reactions to new media formats? and (3) What hypotheses can be drawn for future research?

### Patterns of Media Behavior

The research makes clear that media behavior is a dynamic process involving individual, interpersonal, situational, and media-related factors. Attempting to determine the relative power of each of these influences on a particular media choice or behavior is a complex task, however.

In the most basic sense, both the individual and the medium contribute to the ultimate resolution of these decisions. The individual consumer brings a set of personal characteristics, perceptions, and preferences. The medium brings a particular content (or contents) and format, which are weighed by the consumer against competing media choices.

We have learned that demographic characteristics (such as age or social class) affect the volume of media consumed, as well as content and format preferences. Psychological and life-style factors (such as cosmopolitanism or community ties) motivate media use, as well as the eventual application of media in the individual's personal and social life. If the research were to stop here, one could believe that to predict media choice, all that would be necessary would be to specify who the person was, and what media contents and formats were available to him or her.

A more realistic assessment, however, understands that media are social products as well as individual ones. We must consider the interpersonal and situational factors that influence media use: how much time is available, how people share and negotiate their media experiences with others, and how media use connects an individual with opinion leaders or other socially important reference groups. All of these situational and interpersonal elements filter the pure effect of what the receiver and the medium bring. They affect individuals' perceptions of the media, their use of the media, and even their definition of the value of the media. Instead of a simple gratification of needs, then, we must examine a complex network of interactions complicated by the ever-changing needs of the individual, and the similarly dynamic ability of the media to try to fulfill those needs. Also, when we evaluate the situational and interpersonal element, we see a richer role for the media in an individual's life. Media choices are no longer simply "matched" to individual predispositions; the media are used as a social tool in an active, goal-directed sense.

The fourth and final category of influence on media behavior is composed of the media-related factors, including the range of contents, formats, and combinations of media from which an individual can choose. Selective perception, selective exposure, and the formation of media habits or loyalties aid the individual in dealing with the constantly available range of choices and consolidate the pattern of media behavior.

Taken together, all of these influences on consumer/media behavior generate a type of matrix that characterizes the individual-medium interaction. Both the individual and the medium bring *a priori* characteristics and needs, and the continuing interaction of these is patterned and molded by perception, choice, and use. No matter how complex this system or how accurate the measurements of each factor, however, media use cannot be predicted from these *a priori* elements. By itself, this part of the research literature offers explanations of the *what*, but not the *why*, of consumers' media use.

## Uses and Gratifications of the Media

The literature to this point also assumes a functionalist perspective: it assumes that the media are relatively passive purveyors of desired content and format, and that individuals actively seek among the choices available.

Fundamental research in the uses and gratifications of media agrees with this point of view. It too classifies the media as an instrument that individuals use to satisfy media needs: the need to gather useful information, to escape the daily grind, or to "connect" socially. Satisfaction of these needs is very dependent on the physical and social situation, the decisionmaking style of each individual, and his or her history of involvement with the media.

Uses and gratifications research begins with a relatively simple supply-and-demand view of media behavior and evolves into a more dynamic outlook that concentrates on the actions and reactions of all three members of the interaction: the individual, the medium, and society. Later research on uses and gratifications introduces an interactionist perspective; more attention is paid to viewing the media and society as active, involved parties in the communications process—using each other to represent, mediate, and reinforce existing cultural and social realities. In some of the later research, the media are even presented as an instrument that society can use as a change agent, which is very similar to their earlier presentation as an instrument by which an individual can fulfill personal goals.

This expansion of theoretical perspective allows us for the first time in the literature to consider the influence of decisions made by public policy officials and managers of media businesses. It also frees us from the narrow, functional definition of media needs and allows us to explore simple consummatory media use—an individual reading, watching, or listening not to meet some deep-felt need, but simply to enjoy the experience.

With today's widening diversity of available media contents and formats and with increasing pressure for guidelines on which to develop private and public policy decisions regarding the new media formats, the research's abandonment of strictly defined need-gratification of media use is propitious. To study the probable consumer reaction to new media formats, we need a theoretical framework that considers both individuals and the media as active, decisionmaking partners and that allows for a wide diversity in the reasons and rationale underlying those decisions.

## Drawbacks of the Existing Research

There are, of course, still some gaps and problems in applying findings from the reviewed research to new media projections. The most basic is scope: the existing research in this field uses traditional definitions of the media (television, radio, newspapers), the content, and fulfilled attributes of the communications interaction. These are not acceptable for extrapolation to the future media environment, because of the likely blurring of distinctions between print and video format, process, and even content elements. In addition, consumers will bring new skills and facilities to the new media formats, and a range of new expectations and demands.

The body of work tends, at most times, to be somewhat unidimensional. Initially studies were done at only one point in time—not examining the effects of changes over time, or the evolution of behavior patterns. As a result, no suggestions are given as to how to measure *change* in the media environment. Moreover, early studies tended to equate correlation with cause-and-effect relationships, not being sensitive to the complex interrelation of the individual and the media. Even though later studies were methodologically and analytically more accurate, few permit intensive, theoretical development.

The studies concentrate (for understandable reason) on media *users*, mostly ignoring the media *nonuser*, and the significant understanding that this behavior pattern could contribute. They also imply, in most cases, that a behavior is chosen, rather than "accepted." (Media behavior that is purely consummatory should be further explored.)

Few studies concentrate on empirically determining the overall salience of media behavior itself. Gratification studies, for example (which tend toward tautological arguments), need to be grounded in not only a listing of attributes, but a weighting of those attributes as well. It is not enough to compare only one media format with another in evaluating consumer choice behavior; the overall media consumption patterns must be examined vis-à-vis other types of functionally satisfying and purely consummatory behavior as well.

Most important for the application of empirical results to a study of the new media environment is the lack of attention given to research on the individual's source manipulation, or how people behave toward the media format itself. Research in this area should differentiate between behavior toward the input, the output, the process, the "editing" function, and the storage of information through different formats—how people perceive these functions and behave toward them. (It may be true that little has been done in this area because, up to this time, most media equipment has primarily been of singular purpose, but it still is possible to study what people do, and how they do it, regarding display and access and storage of information.)

In what format, for instance, is a particular type of message better in a given group of information consumers? Is the basic behavioral difference between media sets grounded in audio versus visual presentation, or print versus video? Is text on paper, for example, significantly different from text on a screen in influencing consumer choice or behavior? At what point does the media format bridge the gap between active and passive involvement? Finally, how important is the quality of transmission to the consumer and his or her selection of formats? Such questions on source selection and manipulation are essential to the understanding of media behavior and the projection of consumer reaction to changes in choice set and behavior given the new environment.

## Research on New Media Formats

Some work is underway on the consumer behavior toward new media formats, but this work is just beginning to affect our understanding of the future media environment. The research reviewed in this chapter can be used to generate hypotheses about consumers' acceptance of and behavior toward new media formats, but very few projections can be made. Presently held assumptions about the perception, selection, and use of the media are likely to be invalidated as consumer choices broaden and the nature of competition within the media shifts.

## Areas for Future Research

Research on the new media environment has begun, but there is much unknown. This area of investigation will benefit most from research designed to integrate consumers' behavior toward new media formats with their present media perceptions and behavior, and to establish benchmarks by which to measure the development of new products and services.

Four areas of investigation are crucial to any projections of consumer behavior. The technological capabilities of the new formats give us some clues about their potential application, but only a solid base of consumer research can help us understand their probable use.

*Functions of New Media Formats.*    Because the perceptions and expected gratifications of people's use of the present mass media are so closely interlinked, new formats will likely give rise to new functions and uses of media that should be examined in research on future behavior. Some of these questions include How will individuals perceive and define the new media? What attributes will they grant to (or retract from) the new formats? What values will they perceive? How will the very volume of media format choices affect people?

This last question is especially troubling, because although it is widely accepted that individuals will have more choice regarding information and entertainment sources, we cannot assume that they will use the same decisionmaking strategies they now employ. How will consumers respond to a broader spectrum of alternatives? People's capacities to absorb information are not limitless, and many of the new media formats may offer, in essence, "unedited" information—in which case the consumer will have to accept the editorial role in using the system.

Some of the roles and uses of the new media are predetermined by the specific content or format involved, but others are not. The important element, in this area of the new research, centers on choice patterns and decisionmaking: How will consumers perceive and then accept what the new media are offering? For example, some new media formats will allow (or demand) different personal or social behavior patterns. The market acceptability of these features should be questioned. How the new media formats are marketed will affect their use just as much as their inherent technical capabilities; this must be a central element of any investigation of this new media behavior. Research is needed, however, that concentrates on the quality of an individual's *interaction* with new media formats, not simply the *needs* they can or will fulfill.

*Future Changes in the Structure of the Media Environment.*    Previous research has shown that the media are not just neutral carriers of messages, but that they bring with them a powerful environment both individually and in the aggregate. What impact will the new media systems have on each other (on their market territories and competition, their acceptable and profitable degrees of penetration, their own risk-taking and creativity), and on the social environment that supports them (and its values of information community definition, the social group)? What will be the nature of competition for audience or advertisers? How will the role of the existing media formats change?

Especially in the short term, the introduction of the new media processes will begin to influence (either for good or ill) the future relationships of these media with society and with the individual.

(Even the simple definition of what is an audience for the new media is as yet undefined except in total relation to existing audience definitions and expectations.)

These two factors, the ubiquity and the social impact of the new media, are critical to explore. A third is perhaps even more crucial to any research on consumers' media behavior: the trend and facilitation of specialization.

The new media will offer more choices, which in general can be expected to fragment mass audiences into smaller groups that might be more demanding of their targeted media formats and messages. One question to ask is whether any or all of the traditional "mass" media can survive, and if so, what will happen to consumers' perceptions or behavior toward them? Another question relating to this regards the consumers' behavior toward the centralization of data, the specialization (and expanded choice) of messages and all of the other changes that would seem to be on the horizon accompanying the new media environment. Will the very role and importance of the media be altered if they become more fragmented in their audience constitution? Likewise, will media's role in society change as their structure and "critical mass" change? These are strategic questions which will have an impact not only on the long-term market introduction and success of new media formats, but on their development as an industry.

*Impacts of New Media Formats on the Individual and Society.*   Because the reinforcing and mediating role of media is so important, is it possible that with different media and different audiences, we would have a different society? It would definitely require changes in the use of mass media for political or cultural transmission, not to mention the psychological void that might come about as the individual is no longer a daily member of a national public.

The new media will be, as are the present media, social change agents. Research in this area must explore the dimensions of this role: Will the new media alter the definitions of what is a community? What is reasonable as communicable time and distance? The new media also speed up social trends (urbanization, illiteracy, cultural diffusion, economic alienation)—or, alternatively, slow them down. They may enlarge individual horizons or shut them. They may replace face-to-face communication, or increase its value. In any case it is clear that the new media formats will have a significant impact on the structure and operations of society.

One potential area of controversy within this question revolves around the use of information to reinforce social stratification. One side would argue that technology can bring all of "culture" to each individual, reducing the distance and knowledge gap between individuals and social classes. Others would contend that although many will have access to the data, they will not be able to process or use them as effectively as the "knowledge elite," and they will be restricted in their creative use of the information because of decayed skills in reading, writing, and conceptual thought, or potentially higher costs.

Although this potential impact of the new media is possible, it is not suggested as the primary direction of the first studies on consumers' acceptance and use of the new formats. It is important, however, to consider not only the advantages of the new media but their disadvantages—whether these are discussed in a societal context or in an individual context. One potential dysfunction, for example, arises *because* of the new network: Because the media report everything and keep all lines of communciation open, there is nowhere for the individual to hide. Will people, then, be expected to be aware of everything because they have access to it? Shared information that provides pervasive knowledge about others is a key characteristic of any village, "global" or otherwise.

For the individual, there are similarly striking redefinitions. The new media may change perceptions of time, of "sharing" information, and of shared experience within a community of individuals. Like a gigantic nervous system, each individual will not only be wired and interacting with the broad range of information sources, but will be expected to be sensitive to the priorities and costs of the information. A key area for analysis, then, is the consumer's ability (and willingness) to cope with the new capacities (1) to develop trust in the systems, (2) to alter or modify their cognitive styles to deal with the rate and amount of transmission, and (3) to coordinate their daily behaviors to fit their informational sensitivities or vice versa. These social and psychological impacts are essential for understanding not only short-term, but long-term future for new media behavior.

*Uses for New Media Formats.*    The aggregate effects of the new media on the individual are only one part of the equation. Consider also the key strategic business and public policy decisions that can directly affect consumer acceptance, purchase, and use of new media formats.

One of the key research areas to explore here is the question of consumer investment: Who will be likely to use new media formats? Are people willing or able to make the necessary investments (time, money, skill acquisition, higher involvement) to use the new media formats and at what rate? The answer depends on the value of the media to each individual. First, let us examine the value of expanded choice.

Consumers might have to learn to deal with content and format surplus, which implies two important behavioral changes: selection rules and cost. The first is not a simple expansion of the concept of selective exposure or perception. The new media carry with them a different expectation of receiver involvement and the need for new skills (physical and cognitive). Some of these might be acquired in school, some in the workplace, others as part of aculturation. Acceptable interaction with the new systems demands experience with the equipment, the software, and both the range and process of selection. A new set of heuristics for the consumer must develop, interrelating the costs (of learning, monetary payment, and time) and the decision rules that will operate.

A second value of the new media relates to content choice, and is directly tied to consumers' preconceptions of the volume and depth of both message and format availability. What content, for instance, will be accessed, stored, or retrieved? Which formats will be used for access, storage, and retrieval? With the potential for a larger and more refined appetite for both content and format choice, time use becomes important.

Media forms that demand high involvement or interaction require more consumer time. Unlike previous studies, which tend to relegate media use to leisure time, the behavior toward new media formats will overreach this definition, and they may in fact be used as "time goods" with their capabilities for archiving, time switching (e.g., videotaping a television program for later replay), and individual choice. Underlying these assumptions, however, is a hypothesis that people must plan their time in order to manage it. How they will handle these changes in expected decisionmaking rules, involvement skills, and time and household budget allocation is an important part of this research area. For example, while the technology may promote individual choices for video (rather than the family arguing over which TV show to watch), this can occur only if the household has several video tubes for connection to the cable videodisc or videocassette machines or remote data base.

Another part of the question must explore the individual's desires and abilities to edit the information he or she has accessed, stored, or retrieved. Because a good deal of the value of mass media content today lies in its packaging or editing (which selects important material for a particular audience, checks its accuracy and presentation, and interprets it for the reader or viewer), it is essential to determine if this value will be demanded of the new media. Although much has been made of the individual's projected freedom of choice, he or she may want less choice (information on demand) and more efficiency (information when expected). That consumers are willing to be their own editors, then, should not be taken for granted.

The new media formats will change people's relative sensitivities as well: The price/value relationship which affects their satisfactions, and the importance they place on price, availability, quality, and the other attributes of a considered purchase. How much behavioral change is it reasonable to expect of consumers, simply because new products will be available?

## Conclusion

It would seem important (if not the most important of the research questions posed here) to clearly and accurately research the consumers' developing *strategies* for dealing with the new media formats and contents. Degrees of involvement, identification, possession, time use, monetary cost, and choice may be very different than they are today. Will people grasp the opportunities, grow to enjoy them, or reject them? The answer seems to depend, at least in part, on the strategy that consumers will use to evaluate the new media. Based on their perceived risks and rewards of the new purchase or use, consumers may simplify, optimize, or maximize each of these dimensions (and others) in making their decisions. The literature would seem to suggest that individuals will try to maintain relative homeostasis—stability— and will make changes gradually. Although this type of optimizing approach makes the most intuitive sense, it is quite possible that the consummatory behavior of content could spill over into a consummatory posture of the consumer toward new gadgets and devices. Because it is essential to define the probable consumer strategies (and possible, given the theoretical and empirical literature summarized in this chapter that could generate the basis for a trade-off analysis), this last question is presented as the most important of the four suggested.

We are yet uncertain as to whether the changes from the media environment of today to that of tomorrow will be evolutionary or radical, paced, or discontinuous. Regardless of the rate of change, the market law of reciprocity will probably be in effect; for example, as the media demand more of people (more time, commitment, involvement), people will demand more of the media. For business strategists and public policymakers to avoid the myopia of either attempting to duplicate the present media marketplace or being totally reactive to the increasing demands of consumers, it would seem appropriate first to investigate the given market resources of present perceptions and behavior, and then chart the optimum course to the emerging environment based on reasonable expectations of probable, rather than possible, consumer acceptance.

## NOTES

a.   S. Levy, "Social Class and Consumer Behavior," in J. Newman, ed., *On Knowing the Consumer* (New York: John Wiley, 1966), p. 155.

b.   It is important to remember that there are a variety of kinds of communities; some individuals may belong to an international community of interest and involvement, which is defined not by geography but by a connectedness of the individual with that specific arena.

c.   F. Williams and H. Lindsay, "Introduction: Language, Communication and Social Differences," in Mortensen and Sorens, eds., *Advances in Communications Research* (New York: Harper & Row), p. 372.

d.   B. Belson and A. Barban, "Riesman's Social Character Theory and Magazine Preference," *Journalism Quarterly* 46 (Winter 1969):717.

e.   H. Kassarjian, "Social Character and Differential Preference for Mass Communication," *Journal of Marketing Research* 2 (May 1963):152.

f.   L. Glick and S. Levy, *Living with Television* (Chicago: Aldine, 1962), pp. 54–56.

g.   E. Katz and P.F. Lazarsfeld, *Personal Influence: The Part Played by People in the Flow of Mass Communications* (Glencoe, Ill.: The Free Press, 1955), p. 154.

h.   Ibid., p. 316.

i.   Russell Belk, "An Exploratory Assessment of Situational Effects in Buyer Behavior," *Journal of Marketing Research* 11 (May 1974):157.

j.   M. Kaplan, *Leisure: Theory and Policy* (New York: John Wiley and Sons, 1975), p. 15.

k.  L. Rosten, "A Disenchanted Look at the Audience," in A. and L. Kirschner, eds., *Radio and Television: Readings in the Mass Media* (New York: Odyssey Press, 1971), p. 137.

l.  A.V. Bruno, "The Network Factor in TV Viewing," *Journal of Advertising Research* 13 (October 1973):39.

m.  G.J. Goodhardt and A.S.C. Ehrenberg, "Duplication of Television Viewing between and within Channels," *Journal of Marketing Research* 6 (May 1969):177.

n.  B. Berelson and G. Steiner, *Human Behavior: An Inventory of Scientific Findings* (New York: Harcourt, Brace and World, 1964), p. 540.

o.  G. Fisk, "Media Influence Reconsidered," *Public Opinion Quarterly* 23 (Spring 1959):83.

p.  Wilbur Schramm, ed., *Mass Communications* (Urbana: University of Illinois Press, 1949), pp. 302–303.

q.  Ibid.

r.  Daniel Starch & Staff, Inc. uses one technique of measuring magazine advertisement readership by asking respondents if they can recall certain advertisements in magazines the respondents said they read. Depending on their degree of recall of the content of the advertisement, they will be rated as having just "noted," "associated" (remembering one or two ideas) or "read most" (recalling more than 50 percent of the ad).

s.  E. Katz and D. Foulkes, "On the Use of the Mass Media as Escape: Clarification of a Concept," *Public Opinion Quarterly* 26 (Fall 1962):378.

t.  Ibid., p. 180.

u.  R.K. Merton, "Patterns of Influence: A Study of Interpersonal Influence and of Communications Behavior in a Local Community," in Lazarsfeld and Stanton, eds., *Communication Research 1948–1949* (New York: Harper Bros., 1949), p. 186.

v.  B. Berelson, "What Missing the Newspaper Means," in Lazarsfeld and Stanton, eds., *Communication Research 1948–1949* (New York: Harper Bros., 1949), p. 124.

w.  K.W. Deutsch, "On Social Communication and the Metropolis," *Daedalus* 190 (1961):101.

x.  J. Cazeneuve, "Television as a Functional Alternative to Traditional Sources of Need Satisfaction," in E. Katz and J. Blumler, eds., *The Uses of Gratifications Research* (Beverly Hills, Calif.: Sage Publications, 1974), p. 215.

y.  J.E. Grunig, "Time-Budgets, Level of Involvement and Use of the Mass Media," *Journalism Quarterly* 56 (1979):251.

z.  Ibid., p. 261.

## REFERENCE BIBLIOGRAPHY

### Books and Monographs

1. T. Allen, " Mass Media Use Patterns and Functions in a Negro Ghetto," Unpublished Master's Thesis, University of West Virginia, 1967.
2. R.A. Bauer and S.A. Greyser, *Advertising in America: The Consumer View* (Boston: Harvard University, Division of Research, Graduate School of Business Administration, 1968).
3. B. Berelson and G. Steiner, *Human Behavior: An Inventory of Scientific Findings* (New York: Harcourt, Brace and World, 1964).
4. A. Berler, *Urbanization and Communication: Communication Systems and Their Impact on Sociocultural Urbanization in Israel* (Rehovet: Settlement Study Center, 1974).
5. D.K. Berlo, *The Process of Communication: An Introduction to Theory and Practice* (New York: Holt, Rinehart and Winston, 1960).
6. J.G. Blumler and E. Katz (eds.), *The Uses of Mass Communications: Current Perspectives on Gratifications Research* (Beverly Hills, Calif.: Sage Publications, 1974).
7. H. Cantril and G.W. Allport, *The Psychology of Radio* (New York: P. Smith, 1941).
8. M.E. Cassata and M.K. Asante, *Mass Communication: Principles and Practices* (New York: Macmillan, 1979).
9. M.N. Chappell and C.E. Hooper, *Radio Audience Measurement* (New York: Stephen Daye, 1944).
10. M.H. Cheng, *Media Use and Program Preference of the Elderly Television Viewer* (Columbus: Ohio State University, 1978).
11. G. Comstock, *Priorities for Action Oriented Psychological Studies of Television and Behavior* (Santa Monica, Calif.: Rand Corporation, 1977).
12. R.E. Davis, *Response to Innovation: A Study of Popular Argument About New Mass Media* (New York: Arno Press, 1976).
13. M.L. DeFleur and S. Ball-Rokeach, *Theories of Mass Communication*, 3rd ed. (New York: David McKay, 1970).
14. L.A. Dexter and D.M. White (eds.), *People, Society and Mass Communications* (Glencoe, Ill.: The Free Press, 1964).
15. S.T. Eastman, *Uses of Television Viewing and Consumer Life Styles: A Multivariate Analysis* (Bowling Green, Ohio: Bowling Green State University, 1977).
16. L.W. Flatt, *Television in the Lives of Older Adults* (Columbia: University of Missouri, 1978).
17. W.E. François, *Introduction to Mass Communications and Mass Media* (Columbus, Ohio: Grid 1977).

18. R. Glessing and W.P. White, *Mass Media: The Invisible Environment Revisited* (Chicago: Science Research Associates, 1976).
19. L.O. Glick and S.S. Levy, *Living with Television*. Chicago: Aldine Publishing, 1962.
20. C. Harkins, *The Multi-Image User: A Diffusion of Innovation Investigation into the Adoption and Use of Multi-Image Communication Techniques* (Troy, N.Y.: Rensselaer Polytechnic Institute, 1978).
21. S.W. Head, *Broadcasting in America* 2nd ed. (Boston: Houghton Mifflin, 1972).
22. M. Jackson-Beeck, *Mass Media Exposure and Individual Political Activity* (Philadelphia: University of Pennsylvania, 1979).
23. T.M. Kando, *Leisure and Popular Culture in Transition* (St. Louis: C.V. Mosby, 1975).
24. M. Kaplan, *Leisure: Theory and Policy* (New York: John Wiley and Sons, 1975).
25. H. Kato, *Japanese Research on Mass Communication: Selected Abstracts* (Honolulu: University Press of Hawaii, 1974).
26. E. Katz and P.F. Lazarsfeld, *Personal Influence: The Part Played by People in the Flow of Mass Communications* (Glencoe, Ill.: The Free Press, 1955).
27. E. Katz and M. Gurevitch, *The Secularization of Leisure: Culture and Communication in Israel* (Cambridge, Mass.: Harvard University Press, 1976).
28. J. Klapper, *The Effects of Mass Communication* (New York: The Free Press, 1960).
29. F.G. Kline, *Media Time Budgeting as a Function of Demographics and Life Style* (Minneapolis: University of Minnesota, 1969).
30. P. Lazarsfeld, B. Berelson, and H. Gaudet, *The People's Choice* (New York: Columbia University Press, 1948).
31. P. Lazarsfeld and F.N. Stanton (eds.), *Communications Research, 1948–1949* (New York: Harper, 1949).
32. _____ , *Radio Research 1941* (New York: Duell, Sloan, and Pearce, 1941).
33. _____ , *Radio Research 1942–43* (New York: Duell, Sloan, and Pearce, 1944).
34. S.H. Lee, *A Factor Analytic Study of the Credibility of Newspaper and TV News* (Kent State University, 1976).
35. M.R. Levy, *The Uses and Gratifications of Television News* (New York: Columbia University Press, 1977).
36. A. Lichtenstein, *The Perceived Social Class and Public Television Use: A Study of the Effect of Cultural Reference Groups on Audience Behavior* (Gainesville: The Florida State University, 1978).
37. G.A. Lundberg, M. Komarovsky, and M.A. McInerny, *Leisure: A Suburban Study* (New York: Columbia University Press, 1934).

38. H.M. McLuhan, *Understanding Media: The Extension of Man* (New York: Signet, McGraw-Hill, 1964).

39. H.M. McLuhan and Q. Fiore, *The Medium Is the Message* (New York: Bantam, 1967).

40. D. McQuail, *Towards a Sociology of Mass Communications* (London: Collier-Macmillan, 1969).

41. R.K. Merton, *Social Theory and Social Structure* (Glencoe, Ill.: Free Press, 1957).

42. J. Meyrowitz, *No Sense of Place: A Theory on the Impact of Electronic Media on Social Structure and Behavior* (New York: New York University, 1979).

43. H.L. Nieberg, *Culture Storm: Politics and the Ritual Order* (New York: St. Martin's Press, 1973).

44. J. Philport, *A Multivariate Field Study of Patterns of Television Program Exposure: Gross Consumption of the Mass Media, and Machiavellianism, Anomie, and Self-Esteem* (Bowling Green: Bowling Green State University, 1975).

45. W.E. Porter, *The Assault on the Media: The Nixon Years* (Ann Arbor: University of Michigan Press, 1976).

46. D. Riesman, N. Glazer, and R. Denney, *The Lonely Crowd* (Garden City, N.Y.: Doubleday, 1955).

47. J.P. Robinson, *How Americans Use Time: A Social Psychological Analysis of Everyday Behavior* (New York: Praeger, 1977).

48. E.V. Rogers, *Diffusion of Innovations* (New York: The Free Press, 1962).

49. F. Satzerzadeh Kermani, *The Place of Mass Media in the Life of the Aged: A Study of Mass Media Consumption and Life Satisfaction among the Members of Eleven Senior Citizen Clubs in Wood County, Ohio* (Bowling Green: Bowling Green State University, 1977).

50. W. Schramm (ed.), *Mass Communications* (Urbana: University of Illinois Press, 1949).

51. W. Schramm and D.F. Roberts (eds.), *The Process and Effects of Mass Communication* (Urbana: University of Illinois Press, 1972).

52. W. Schramm, J. Lyle, and E. Parker, *Television in the Lives of Our Children* (Stanford: Stanford University Press, 1961).

53. G.A. Steiner, *The People Look at Television: A Study of Audience Attitudes* (New York: A.A. Knopf, 1963).

54. W. Stephenson, *Play Theory of Communication* (Chicago: University of Chicago Press, 1967).

55. R.E. Summers, *Broadcasting and the Public* (Belmont, Calif.: Wadsworth, 1964).

56. C. Swank, *The Needs of the Elderly: Media and Non-Media Sources of Gratification* (Iowa City: The University of Iowa, 1977).

57.    L.R. Thornton, *A Correlation Study of the Relationship between Human Values and Broadcast Television* (East Lansing: Michigan State University, 1976).

58.    F. and L. Voelker (eds.), *Mass Media: Forces in our Society* (New York: Harcourt Brace Jovanovich, 1972).

59.    R. Williams, *Television: Technology and Cultural Form* (New York: Schocken Books, 1974).

## Articles

60.    D. Aitchison, "Extending the Limits of Influence," *European Research* (September 1974):204–222.

61.    W.S. Alper and T.R. Leidy, "The Impact of Information Transmission through Television," *Public Opinion Quarterly* 33 (Winter 1969–1970):556–562.

62.    A. Alvarez Villar, "Television's Influence on Young Minds," *Revista del Instituto de la Juventud* 56 (December 1974):93–104.

63.    R. Anderson and J. Engledow, "A Factor Analytic Comparison of U.S. and German Information Seekers," *Journal of Consumer Research* 3 (March 1977):185–189.

64.    F. Andison, "TV Violence and Viewer Aggression: A Cumulation of Study Results: 1956–1976," *Public Opinion Quarterly* 41 (Fall 1977): 314–331.

65.    V. Andreoli and S. Worchel, "Effects of Media, Communicator, and Message Position on Attitude Change," *Public Opinion Quarterly* (1978):59–70.

66.    H.L. Ansbacher, "Life-Style: A Historical and Systematic Review," *Journal of Individual Psychology* 23 (1967):191–212.

67.    G. Armstrong and L. Feldman, "Exposure and Sources of Opinion Leaders," *Journal of Advertising Research* (August 1976):21–30.

68.    G. Assmus, "An Empirical Investigation into the Perception of Vehicle Source Effects," *Journal of Advertising* 7 (Winter 1978):4–10.

69.    L. Bailyn, "Mass Media and Children: A Study of Exposure Habits and Cognitive Effects," *Psychological Monographs* 73 (1959):1–48.

70.    S.J. Balbroke, "Dependency Model of Mass-Media Effects," *Communications Research* 3 (1976):3–21.

71.    S.J. Ball-Rokeach and M.L. DeFleur, "A Dependency Model of Mass-Media Effects," *Communication Research* 3 (January 1976): 3–21.

72.    F.M. Bass, E.A. Pessemier, and D.J. Tigert, "A Taxonomy of Magazine Readership Applied to Problems in Marketing Strategy and Media Selection," *Journal of Business* 42 (July 1969):337–363.

73.  Z. Bauman, "Two Notes on Mass Culture," *Polish Sociological Bulletin* 2 (1966):58–74.

74.  S.A. Baumgarten, "The Innovative Communicator in the Diffusion Process," *Journal of Marketing Research* 12 (February 1975):12–18.

75.  W.O. Bearden, R.M. Darand, and J.E. Teel, Jr., "Media Usage, Psychographic, and Demographic Dimensions of Retail Shoppers," *Journal of Retailing* 54 (Spring 1978):31–42.

76.  J.C. Becknell, Jr., "The Influence of Newspaper Tune-In Advertising on the Size of a TV Show's Audience," *Journal of Advertising Research* 1 (March 1961):23–26.

77.  R.W. Belk, "An Exploratory Assessment of Situational Effects in Buyer Behavior," *Journal of Marketing Research* 11 (May 1974): 156–163.

78.  _____ , "Situational Variables and Consumer Behavior," *Journal of Consumer Research* 2 (December 1975):157.

79.  W.A. Belson, "The Effects of Television on the Reading and the Buying of Newspapers and Magazines," *Public Opinion Quarterly* 25 (Fall 1961):366–381.

80.  J.J. Belson and S.M. Barban, "Riesman's Social Character Theory and Magazine Preference," *Journalism Quarterly* 46 (Winter 1969): 713–720.

81.  B. Berelson, "What Missing the Newspaper Means," in P. Lazarsfeld and F.N. Stanton, eds., *Communication Research, 1948-1949* (New York: Harper Bros., 1949), pp. 111–129.

82.  L. Bogart, "Is It Time to Discard the Audience Concept?" *Journal of Marketing* 30 (January 1966):47–54.

83.  _____ , "Black Is Often White," *Media-Scope* (November 1968): 53.

84.  A. Booth, "The Recall of News Items," *Public Opinion Quarterly* 34 (Winter 1977–1978):604–610.

85.  S. Broadbent, "Regularity of Reading," *Journal of Marketing Research* 1 (August 1964):50–58.

86.  A.V. Bruno, "The Network Factor in T.V. Viewing," *Journal of Advertising Research* 13 (October 1973):33–39.

87.  A.V. Bruno, T.P. Hustad, and E.A. Pessemier, "Media Approaches to Segmentation," *Journal of Advertising Research* 13 (April 1973): 35–42.

88.  A.E. Bryant, F.P. Currier, and A.J. Morrison, "Relating Life-Style Factors of Person to His Choice of a Newspaper," *Journalism Quarterly* 53 (Spring 1976):74–79.

89.  H. Cantril and W.G. Allport, "Radio and Other Forms of Social Participation," in W. Schramm, ed., *Mass Communications*, 2nd ed. (Urbana: University of Illinois Press, 1949), pp. 321–331.

90.    J.M. Carter, "Perceptions of a Mass Audience," in Yu, ed., *Behavioral Sciences and the Mass Media* (New York: Russell Sage Foundation, 1968), pp. 202–205.

91.    R.F. Carter and B.S. Greenberg, "Newspapers and Television: Which Do You Believe?" *Journalism Quarterly* 42 (Winter 1965): 29–34.

92.    J. Cazaneuve, "Television as a Functional Alternative to Traditional Sources of Need Satisfaction," in E. Katz and J. Blumler, eds., *The Uses of Gratifications Research* (Beverly Hills, Calif.: Sage Publications, 1974), pp. 213–223.

93.    L. Cheskin, "Association Test: Attitudes Toward 5 Media," *Advertising Age* 32 (April 3, 1961):102.

94.    T.E. Coffin, "Television's Effects on Leisure-Time Activities," *Journal of Applied Psychology* 32 (1948):550–558.

94a.   B. Compaine, "The Magazine Industry: Developing the Special Interest Audience," *Journal of Communication* 30 (Spring 1980):98–103.

95.    W.G. Cushing and J.B. Lemot, "Has TV Altered Students' News Media Preferences?" *Journalism Quarterly* 50 (1974):138–141.

96.    J.E. Danes, J.E. Hunter, and J. Woelfel, "Mass Communication and Belief Change: A Test of Three Mathematical Models," *Human Communication Research* 4 (Spring 1978):243–252.

97.    W.R. Darden, J.K. Lennon, and D.K. Darden, "Communicating with Interurban Shoppers," *Journal of Retailing* 54 (Spring 1978): 51–64.

98.    W.R. Darden and W.D. Perreault, "A Multivariate Analysis of Media Exposure and Vacation Behavior with Life Style Covariates," *Journal of Consumer Research* 2 (September 1975):93–103.

99.    W.R. Darden and F.D. Reynolds, "Backward Profiles of Male Innovators," *Journal of Marketing Research* 11 (February 1974): 79–85.

100.   W. Darschin, "Changes in Children's Amount of Television Viewing: New Findings from Continual Viewer Research," *Fernsehen und Bildung* 11 (1977):210–222.

101.   M.L. DeFleur, "Mass Media as Social Systems," in W. Schramm, ed., *Mass Communications*, 2nd ed. (Chicago: University of Illinois Press, 1960), pp. 63–83.

102.   J. Demuth and J.N. Nerac, "Typologie Socio-Culturelle et Fréquentations Media-Supports," *Revue Française du Marketing* 62 (May-June 1976):99–105.

103.   K.W. Deutsch, "On Social Communication and the Metropolis," *Daedalus* 90 (1961):99–110.

104. N.K. Dhalla and W.H. Makatoo, "Expanding the Scope of Segmentation Research," *Journal of Marketing* 40 (April 1976):34-41.

105. E. Diener and D. DeFour, "Does Television Violence Enhance Program Popularity?" *Journal of Personality and Social Psychology* 36 (1978):33-41.

106. W. Divale, "Newspapers: Some Guidelines for Communicating Anthropology," *Human Organization* 35 (Summer 1976):183-191.

107. A.N. Doob and J.E. Macdonald, "Television Viewing and Fear of Victimization: Is the Relationship Casual?" *Journal of Personality and Social Psychology* 37 (1979):170-179.

108. S.P. Douglas, "Do Working Wives Read Different Magazines from Non-Working Wives?" *Journal of Advertising* 6 (Winter 1977):10-17.

109. M. Drexler, "In Praise of Older Women," *Broadcasting* (April 23, 1979):14.

110. F.J. Dudek, "Relations among TV Rating Indices," *Journal of Advertising Research* 4 (September 1964):29-32.

111. W.B. Eberhard, "Circulation and Population: Comparison of 1940 and 1970," *Journalism Quarterly* 19 (1974):498-507.

112. J.S. Edwards and D.D.A. Edwards, "Conjugate Reinforcement of Radio Listening," *Psychological Reports* 26 (1970):787-788.

113. A.S.C. Ehrenberg, "The Factor Analytic Search for Program Types: A Comparative Evaluation," *Journal of Advertising Research* 8 (March 1968):55-63.

114. P. Elliott, "Uses and Gratifications Research: A Critique and a Sociological Alternative," in E. Katz and J. Blumler, eds., *The Uses of Gratifications Research*, (Beverly Hills, Calif.: Sage Publications, 1974), pp. 249-268.

115. R. Escarpit, "The Concept of 'Mass'," *Journal of Communication* 27 (Spring 1977):44-47.

116. E.W. Faison, "The Neglected Variety Drive: A Useful Concept for Consumer Behavior," *Journal of Consumer Research* 4 (December 1977):172-175.

117. S. Ferber, "Magazines—The Medium of Enlightenment," *USA Today* 108 (July 1979):42-45.

118. G. Fisk, "Media Influence Reconsidered," *Public Opinion Quarterly* 23 (Spring 1959):88-91.

119. W.S. Fox and W.W. Philliber, "Television Viewing and the Perception of Affluence," *Sociological Quarterly* 19 (Winter 1978):103-112.

120. R.E. Frank, J.E. Becknell, and J.D. Clokey, "Television Program Types," *Journal of Marketing Research* 8 (May 1971):204-211.

121. E. Friedson, "The Relation of the Social Situation of Contact to the Media of Mass Communication," *Public Opinion Quarterly* 14 (Summer 1953):23–27.

122. _____ , "Communications Research and the Concept of the Mass," *American Sociological Review* 18 (June 1953):313–317.

123. G. Fuchman, "Mass Media Values," *Society* 14 (November 1976): 51–54.

124. M.S. Fuertes Garcia, "The Influence of Radio and Television on Youth," *Revista del Instituto de la Juventud* 57 (February 1975):71–82.

125. K. Geiger and R. Sokol, "Social Norms in Television Watching," *American Journal of Sociology* 65 (1975):174–181.

126. D.H. Gensch and B. Ranganathan, "Evaluation of TV Program Content for the Purpose of Promotional Segmentation," *Journal of Marketing Research* (November 1974):390–397.

127. G. Gerbner, "Communication and Social Environment," *Scientific American* 227 (September 1972):152–160.

128. E.D. Glynn, "Television and the American Character—A Psychiatrist Looks at Television," in Kirshner, ed., *Radio and Television* (New York: Odyssey Press, 1971), pp. 149–154.

129. G.J. Goodhardt and A.S.C. Ehrenberg, "Duplication of Television Viewing between and within Channels," *Journal of Marketing Research* 6 (May 1969):169–178.

130. J. Goodman, "A Broadcaster Looks at Broadcasting," *Electronic Age* 30 (Spring 1971):1–11.

131. N. Goluskin, "Every Man a Walter Mitty," *Sales Management* (July 7, 1975):45–46.

132. H.H. Gould et al., "Research in Communications," *Public Opinion Quarterly* 14 (Winter 1950–51):860–865.

133. R. Green and E. Langeard, "A Cross-National Comparison of Consumer Habits and Innovative Characteristics," *Journal of Marketing* 39 (July 1975):34–41.

134. Bradley S. Greenberg, "Gratifications of Television Viewing and Their Correlates for British Children," in E. Katz and J. Blumler, eds., *The Uses of Gratifications Research* (Beverly Hills, Calif.: Sage Publications, 1974), pp. 71–92.

135. Bradley S. Greenberg and B. Dervin, "Mass Communication among the Urban Poor," *Public Opinion Quarterly* 34 (Summer 1970):224–235.

136. Bradley S. Greenberg and H. Kumata, "National Sample Predictors of Mass Media Use," *Journalism Quarterly* 45 (1968):641–646.

137. A. Greenberg and N. Garfinkle, "Delayed Recall of Magazine Articles," *Journal of Advertising Research* 5 (March 1962):28–31.

138. G.L. Grotta, E.F. Larkin, and B. DePlois, "Hometown Daily Newspaper Means 'Local' to Readers," *Oklahoma Journalism Reports* 5 (Winter 1977):1–44.

139. J.E. Grunig, "Time-Budgets, Level of Involvement and Use of the Mass Media," *Journalism Quarterly* 56 (1979):248–261.

140. G. Gumpert, "The Rise of Mini-Communication," *Journal of Communication* 20 (September 1970):280–290.

141. J. Gutman, "Self-Concepts and Television Viewing among Women," *Public Opinion Quarterly* 37 (Fall 1973):388–397.

142. D.K. Hawes, "Satisfactions Derived from Leisure-Time Pursuits: An Exploratory Nationwide Survey," *Journal of Leisure Research* 10 (Winter 1978):247–264.

143. R.S. Headen, J.E. Klompmaker, and J.E. Teel, "Predicting Audience Exposure of Spot TV Advertising Schedules," *Journal of Marketing Research* ((February 1977):1–9.

144. L.B. Hendry and D.J. Thornton, "Games Theory, Television and Leisure: An Adolescent Study," *British Journal of Social & Clinical Psychology* 15 (November 1976):369–376.

145. W.A. Henry, III, "Television Comes of Age," *Boston Sunday Globe Magazine*, February 11, 1979, pp. 7–26.

146. Hoffman, R.M. "How Many Watch the Commercials?" *Media-Scope* 9 (March 1965):49–54.

147. P. Hollander, "Leisure as an American and Soviet Value," *Social Problems* 14 (1966):179–188.

148. M.I. Horn and W.J. McEwen, "The Effect of Program Content on Commercial Performance," *Journal of Advertising* 6 (Spring 1977): 23–27.

149. R.C. Hornik, "Mass Media Use and the Revolution of Rising Frustrations: A Reconsideration of the Theory," *Communication Research* 4 (October 1977):387–414.

150. C.I. Hovland, "Effect of the Mass Media of Communication," in Lindzey and Aronson, eds., *Handbook of Social Psychology: Special Fields and Applications* (Reading, Mass.: Addison-Wesley, 1954), p. 1062.

151. D. Howitt and R. Dembo, "A Subcultural Account of Media Effects," *Human Relations* 27 (January 1974):25–41.

152. H.H. Hyman, "Mass Communication and Socialization," *Public Opinion Quarterly* 37 (Winter 1973–74):524–540.

153. J. Jacoby, G.F. Szybillo, and C.K. Berning, "Time and Consumer Behavior: An Interdisciplinary Overview," *Journal of Consumer Research* 2 (March 1976):320–328.

154. L.W. Jeffres, "Functions of Media Behaviors," *Communication Research* 2 (April 1975):137–161.

155. S. Jeffries-Fox and G. Gerbner, "Television and the Family," *Fernsehen und Bilding* 11 (1977):222–234.

156. V.J. Jones and F.H. Siller, "Factor Analysis of Media Exposure Data Using Prior Knowledge of the Medium," *Journal of Marketing Research* 15 (February 1978):137–144.

157. H.H. Kassarjian, "Social Character and Differential Preference for Mass Communication," *Journal of Marketing Research* 2 (May 1965):146–153.

158. E. Katz, "Psychological Barriers to Communications," in W. Schramm, ed., *Mass Communications*, 2nd ed. (Urbana: University of Illinois Press, 1949), pp. 275–287.

159. _____ , "The Social Itinerary of Technical Change: Two Studies of the Diffusion of Innovation," in W. Schramm, ed., *Mass Communications*, 2nd ed. (Urbana: University of Illinois Press, 1949), pp. 761–797.

160. _____ , "Mass Communication Research and the Study of Culture," *Studies in Public Communication* 2 (1959):1–6.

161. _____ , "The Two-Step Flow of Communication: An Up-to-Date Report on an Hypothesis," *Public Opinion Quarterly* 21 (Spring 1957):61–78.

162. _____ , "Communication Research and the Image of Society— Convergence of Two Traditions," in Dexter and White, eds., *People, Society and Mass Communications* (New York: The Free Press of Glencoe, 1964), pp. 110–120.

163. E. Katz and D. Foulkes, "On the Use of the Mass Media as Escape: Clarification of a Concept," *Public Opinion Quarterly* 26 (Fall 1962):377–388.

164. E. Katz, M. Gurevitch, and H. Haas, "On the Use of the Mass Media for Important Things," *American Sociological Review*, 38 (April 1973):164–181.

165. E. Katz, J.G. Blumler, and M. Gurevitch, "Uses and Gratifications Research," *Public Opinion Quarterly* 37 (Winter 1973–74):509–523.

166. E. Katz, "Utilization of Mass Communication by the Individual," in Katz and J. Blumler, eds., *The Uses of Mass Communication* (Beverly Hills, Calif.: Sage Publications, 1974), pp. 19–32.

167. J.R. Kennedy, "How Program Environment Affects TV Commercials," *Journal of Advertising Research* 11 (February 1971):33–38.

168. C.W. King and J.O. Summers, "Attitudes and Media Exposure," *Journal of Advertising Research* 11 (February 1971):26–32.

169. A.D. Kirsch and S. Banks, "Program Types Defined by Factor Analysis," *Journal of Advertising Research* 2 (September 1962):85–91.

170. J.T. Klapper, "What We Know about the Effects of Mass Communication: The Brink of Hope," *Public Opinion Quarterly* 21 (Winter 1975–76):453–474.

171. D. Krech and R.S. Crutchfield, "Perceiving the World," in W. Schramm, ed., *Mass Communications*, 2nd ed. (Chicago: University of Illinois Press, 1960), pp. 235–264.
172. H. Krugman, "The Measurement of Advertising Involvement," *Public Opinion Quarterly* 30 (1967):349–356.
173. _____ , "Memory without Recall, Exposure without Perception," *Journal of Advertising Research* 17 (August 1977):14–25.
174. _____ , "The Impact of Television Advertising: Learning without Involvement," *Public Opinion Quarterly* 30 (Winter 1966):583–596.
175. J.A. Landon, "Attitudes toward Commercial and Educational Television," *Journal of Advertising Research* 2 (September 1962):33–36.
176. E.F. Larkin and G.L. Grotta, "Consumer Attitudes toward and Use of Advertising Content of a Small Daily Newspaper," *Journal of Advertising Research* 5 (Winter 1976):28–31.
177. H.D. Lasswell, "The Structure and Function of Communication in Society," in W. Schramm, ed., *Mass Communications*, 2nd ed. (Chicago: University of Illinois Press, 1960), pp. 84–99.
178. R.A. Layton, "A Stochastic Model of Radio Listening," *Journal of Marketing Research* 4 (August 1967):303–308.
179. P.F. Lazarsfeld, "The Daily Newspaper and Its Competitors," *The Annals of the American Academy of Political and Social Science* 219 (January 1942):32–43.
180. _____ , "The Effects of Radio," in Kirschner, ed., *Radio and Television* (New York: Odyssey Press, 1971), pp. 185–186.
181. P.F. Lazarsfeld and P. Kendall, "The Communications Behavior of the Average American," in W. Schramm, ed., *Mass Communications*, 2nd ed. (Urbana: University of Illinois Press, 1949), pp. 389–401.
182. D.R. Lehmann, "Television Show Preference: Application of a Choice Model," *Journal of Marketing Research* 8 (February 1971):47–55.
183. D. Lerner, "Toward a Communication Theory of Modernization: A Set of Considerations," in Schramm and Roberts, eds., *The Process and Effects of Mass Communication* (Urbana: University of Illinois Press, 1972), pp. 861–889.
184. P. Lesly, "Communicating with a Segmented Society," *Public Relations Journal* 24 (June 1968):10–11.
185. V.P. Lessig and C.W. Park, "Promotional Perspectives of Reference Group Influence: Advertising Implications," *Journal of Advertising* 7 (Spring 1978):41–47.
186. S. Levy, "Social Class and Consumer Behavior," in J. Newman, ed., *On Knowing the Consumer* (New York: Wiley, 1966), pp. 155–169.
187. S. Lieberman, "How and Why People Buy Magazines," *Marketing News* (December 31, 1976):15.

188. R.M. Liebert and N.S. Schwartzberg, "Effects of Mass Media," *Annual Review of Psychology* 28 (1977):141–173.
189. O.R. Lindsley, "A Behavioral Measure of Television Viewing," *Journal of Advertising Research* 2 (September 1962):2–12.
190. Lee Loevinger, "There Need Be No Apology, No Lament," *TV Guide Magazine* (April 6, 1968):5–9.
191. _____ , "The Ambiguous Mirror: The Reflective-Projective Theory of Broadcasting and Mass Communication," in Voelker, ed., *Mass Media: Forces in our Society* (New York: Harcourt Brace Jovanovich, 1972), pp. 24–40.
192. B.H. Long and E.H. Henderson, "Children's Use of Time: Some Personal and Social Correlates," *Elementary School Journal* 73 (January 1973):193–199.
193. J.A. Lowenhar and J.L. Stanton, "A Psychological Need-Product Attribute Approach for TV Programming," *Journal of Advertising* 5 (Spring 1976):19.
194. E.E. Maccoby, "Why Do Children Watch Television?" *Public Opinion Quarterly* 18 (1954):239–244.
195. M. Mannes, "The Lost Tube of Television," in Kirschner, eds., *Radio and Television* (New York: Odyssey Press, 1971), pp. 143–148.
196. M. Marc, "Using Reading Quality in Magazine Selection," *Journal of Advertising Research* (December 1966):9–13.
197. G.F. Mathewson, "Consumer Theory of Demand for the Media," *Journal of Business* 45 (April 1972):212–244.
198. M. Mayer, "How Television News Covers the World in 4,000 Words or Less," *Esquire*, January 1978, pp. 86–182.
199. _____ , "The Telephone and the Uses of Time," *Journal of Advertising Research* 19 (April 1979):9–19.
200. E.D. McCarthy et al., "Violence and Behavior Disorders," *Journal of Communication* 25 (August 1975):71–85.
201. D.G. McGlathery, "Claimed Frequency vs. Editorial-Interest Measures of Report Magazine Audiences," *Journal of Advertising Research* 7 (March 1967):7–15.
202. W.J. McGuire, "Psychological Motives and Communication Gratification," in E. Katz and J. Blumler, eds., *The Uses of Mass Communications* (Beverly Hills, Calif.: Sage Publications, 1974), pp. 167–196.
203. _____ , "Some Internal Psychological Factors Influencing Consumer Choice," *Journal of Consumer Research* 2 (March 1976):302–315.
204. J. McLeod, S. Ward, and K. Tancill, "Alienation and Uses of the Mass Media," *Public Opinion Quarterly* 29 (Winter 1965):583–594.

205. J.T. McNelly, R.R. Rush, and M.E. Bishop, "Cosmopolitan Media Usage in the Diffusion of International Affairs News," *Journalism Quarterly* 45 (1968):329–332.
206. D. McQuail and M. Gurevitch, "Explaining Audience Behavior: Three Approaches Considered," in Katz and Blumler, eds., *The Uses of Gratifications Research* (Beverly Hills, Calif.: Sage Publications, 1974), pp. 287–301.
207. H. Mendelsohn, "Listening to Radio," in Dexter and White, eds., *People, Society and Mass Communications* (Glencoe, Ill.: The Free Press, 1964), pp. 239–249.
208. R.K. Merton, "Patterns of Influence: A Study of Interpersonal Influence and of Communications Behavior in a Local Community," in P. Lazarsfeld and F.N. Stanton, eds., *Communications Research— 1948–1949* (New York: Harper Bros., 1949), pp. 180–219.
209. P. Messaris, "Biases of Self-Reported Functions and Gratifications of Mass Media Use," *Etc.* 34 (September 1977):316–329.
210. K.E. Meyer, "Hut of Darkness: Television Viewing during the New York Newspaper Strike," *Saturday Review* 5 (November 11, 1978): 56.
211. D.F. Midgeley and G.R. Dowling, "Innovativeness: The Concept and Its Measurement," *Journal of Consumer Research* 4 (March 1978):229.
212. R.R. Monaghan, J.T. Plummer, D.L. Rarick, and D.A. Williams, "Predicting Viewer Preferences for Newly-Created Television Program Concepts," *Journal of Broadcasting* (March 23, 1973):31–38.
213. H. Morgan, "What's Wrong with Radio? 'The Audience'," *New York Times Magazine*, March 21, 1946, pp. 12–16.
214. G.P. Moschis and G.A. Churchill, Jr., "Consumer Socialization: A Theoretical and Empirical Analysis," *Journal of Marketing Research* 15 (November 1978):50–59.
215. J.P. Murray and S. Kippax, "Television Diffusion and Social Behavior in Three Communities: A Field Experiment," *Australian Journal of Pathology* 29 (April 1977):31–43.
216. J.H. Myers and T.S. Robertson, "Dimensions of Opinion Leadership," *Journal of Marketing Research* 14 (February 1972):41–45.
217. R.O. Nafziger, M. MacLean, Jr., and W. Engstrom, "Who Reads What's in Newspapers?" *International Journal of Opinion and Attitude Research* 5 (Winter 1951–52):519–540.
218. W.R. Neumann, "Patterns of Recall among TV News Viewers," *Public Opinion Quarterly* 40 (Spring 1976):115–123.
219. J.E. Nordlund, "Media Interaction," *Communications Research* 5 (April 1978):150–175.

220. C.G.F. Nuttall, "TV Commercial Audiences in the United Kingdom," *Journal of Advertising Research* 2 (September 1962):19–28.

221. G.J. O'Keefe, Jr., and H.T. Spetnegel, "Patterns of College Undergraduate Use of Selected News Media," *Journalism Quarterly* 50 (Fall 1973):543–548.

222. L. Pearlin, "Social and Personal Stress and Escape Television Viewing," *Public Opinion Quarterly* 23 (1959):255–259.

223. J. Penrose, D.H. Weaver, R.R. Cole, and D.L. Shaw, "The Newspaper Non-Reader 10 Years Later: A Partial Replication of Westley-Severin," *Journalism Quarterly* 51 (1974):631–638.

224. R. Peterson, "Psychographics and Media Exposure," *Journal of Advertising Research* 12 (June 1972):17–20.

225. J.T. Plummer, "A Theory of Self-Perception in Preference for Public Figures," *Journal of Broadcasting* 12 (Summer 1969):285–292.

226. N.I. Quisenberry and C.B. Klasek, "Can TV be Good for Children?" *Audiovisual Instruction* 22 (March 1977):56–57.

227. V.R. Rao, "Taxonomy of Television Programs Based on Viewing Behavior," *Journal of Marketing Research* 12 (August 1975):355–358.

228. G. Rarick, "Differences between Daily Newspaper Subscribers and Non-Subscribers," *Journalism Quarterly* 50 (1973):265–270.

229. M.W. Riley and J.W. Riley, Jr., "A Sociological Approach to Communications Research," *Public Opinion Quarterly* 15 (1951):445–460.

230. M.C. Roberts, A. La Greca, and B.A. Raymond, "Facilitation of Adult Creativity through Television Programs," *Psychology* 15 (February 1978):3–7.

231. J.P. Robinson, "Television and Leisure Time: Yesterday, Today and (Maybe) Tomorrow," *Public Opinion Quarterly* 33 (1969):210–222.

232. B.W. Roper, "Trends in Attitudes toward Television and Other Media," in Voelker, eds., *Mass Media: Forces in Our Society* (New York: Harcourt Brace Jovanovich, 1972), p. 249.

233. K.F. Rosengren and S. Windahl, "Mass Media Use: Causes and Effects," *Communications* 3 (1977):336–352.

234. L. Rosten, "A Disenchanted Look at the Audience," in Kirschner, eds., *Radio and Television: Readings in the Mass Media* (New York: The Odyssey Press, 1971), pp. 135–141.

235. T.E. Ryan, "Heavy User Theory: Apply It to Magazines," *Media-Scope* 13 (May 1969):9.

236. D.J. Sabavola and D.G. Morison, "A Model of TV Show Loyalty," *Journal of Advertising Research* 17 (December 1977):35–43.

237. S. Salomon and A.A. Cohen, "On the Meaning and Validity of Television Viewing," *Human Communication Research* 4 (Spring 1978):265–270.

238. L.W. Sargent and S.H. Stempel, "Poverty, Alienation and Mass Media Use," *Journalism Quarterly* 45 (1968):324–326.

239. D.L. Scammon, "'Information Load' and Consumers," *Journal of Consumer Research* 4 (December 1977):148–158.

240. L. Schatzman and A. Strauss, "Social Class and Modes of Communication," *American Journal of Sociology* 54 (January 1955): 329–338.

241. W. Schramm, "The Nature of News," *Journalism Quarterly* 26 (1949):258–269.

242. R.L. Scott, "Communication as an Intentional, Social System," *Human Communication Research* 3 (Spring 1977):258–268.

243. D.O. Sears and J.L. Freedman, "Selective Exposure to Information: A Critical Review," in W. Schramm and Roberts, eds., *The Process and Effects of Mass Communication* (Urbana: University of Illinois Press, 1972), pp. 209–234.

244. M.W. Segal, "Selective Processes Operating in the Defense of Consonance," *Psychology* 7 (1970):14–37.

245. D. Shaw, "The Newspaper Must Be Fit to Survive," *Quill* (February 1977):10–14.

246. J.N. Shurkin, "Soap Operas: America's Stuff of Escapism," *Philadelphia Inquirer* (January 11, 1976):1K.

247. A.K. Sosanie and G.J. Szybillo, "Working Wives: Their General Television Viewing and Magazine Readership Behavior," *Journal of Advertising* 7 (Spring 1978):5–13.

248. J.L. Stanton and J.A. Lowenhar, "Perceptual Mapping of Consumer Products and Television Shows," *Journal of Advertising* 6 (Spring 1977):16–22.

249. G.C. Stone, "Community Commitment: A Predictive Theory of Daily Newspaper Circulation," *Journalism Quarterly* 54 (1977):509–519.

250. W. Strob, "Is TV Panic Based on False Assumptions?" *Advertising Age* (June 2, 1978):40.

251. J.O. Summers, "Media Exposure Patterns of Consumer Innovators," *Journal of Marketing* 36 (January 1972):43–49.

252. C.E. Swanson and R.L. Jones, "Television Owning and Its Correlates," *Journal of Applied Psychology* 35 (1951):325–357.

253. D.L. Swanson, "The Uses and Misuses of Uses and Gratifications," *Human Communication Research* 3 (1977):214–221.

254. G. Szybillo, S. Binstok, and L. Buchanan, "Measure Validation of Leisure Time Activities: Time Budgets and Psychographics," *Journal of Marketing Research* 16 (February 1979):74–79.

255. P.H. Tannenbaum, "The Indexing Process in Communication," *Public Opinion Quarterly* 21 (Fall 1955):292–302.

256. J.W. Taylor, "A Striking Characteristic of Innovators," *Journal of Marketing Research* 14 (February 1977):104–107.
257. J.E. Teel, W.O. Bearden, and R.M. Durand, "Psychographics of Radio and Television Audiences," *Journal of Advertising Research* 19 (April 1979):37–46.
258. H. Throelli, "Concentration of Information Power among Consumers," *Journal of Marketing Research* 8 (November 1971):427–432.
259. P.J. Tichenor, D.J. Donahue, and C.N. Olien, "Mass Media Flow and Differential Growth in Knowledge," *Public Opinion Quarterly* 34 (1970):159–170.
260. D.J. Tigert, "Life-style as a Basis for Media Selection," in Wells, ed., *Life-style and Psychographics* (Chicago: American Marketing Association, 1974), pp. 173–201.
261. R.J. Twery, "Detecting Patterns of Magazine Reading," *Journal of Marketing* 22 (January 1958):290–294.
262. C. Urban, "A Cross-National Comparison of Consumer Media Use Patterns," *Columbia Journal of World Business* 12 (Winter 1977): 53–69.
263. K.E.A. Villani, "Personality/Life-style and TV Viewing Behavior," *Journal of Marketing Research* 12 (November 1975):432–439.
264. S. Wade and W. Schramm, "The Mass Media as Sources of Public Affairs, Science, and Health Knowledge," *Public Opinion Quarterly* 33 (1969):197–209.
265. D. Waples, B. Berelson, and F.B. Bradshaw, "The Effects of Reading," in W. Schramm, ed., *Mass Communications* (Urbana: University of Illinois Press, 1949), pp. 454–458.
266. P.H. Webb, "Consumer Initial Processing in a Difficult Media Environment," *Journal of Consumer Research* 6 (December 1979): 225–228.
267. R.H. Weigel, "American Television and Conventionality," *Journal of Psychology* 94 (November 1976):253–255.
268. W. Weiss, "Effects of the Mass Media of Communication," in Lindzey and E. Aronson, eds., *Handbook of Social Psychology* (Reading, Mass.: Addison-Wesley, 1969), Ch. 5, pp. 77–196.
269. W.D. Wells, "Psychographics: A Critical Review," *Journal of Marketing Research* 12 (May 1975):196–213.
270. _____ , "The Rise and Fall of Television Program Types," *Journal of Advertising Research* 9 (September 1969):21–27.
271. B.H. Westley and W. Severin, "Some Correlates of Media Credibility," *Journalism Quarterly* 41 (Summer 1964):325–335.
272. _____ , "A Profile of the Daily Newspaper Non-Reader," *Journalism Quarterly* 41 (Spring 1964):45–150, 156.

272a.   D.M. White, "Mass Communication Research: A View in Perspective," in Dexter and White, eds., *People, Society and Mass Communications* (Glencoe, Ill.: The Free Press, 1964), pp. 521–546.

273.    S.D. Wiebe, "Two Psychological Factors in Media Audience Behavior," *Public Opinion Quarterly* 33 (Winter 1969–70):523–536.

274.    J. Wilding and R.A. Bauer, "Consumer Goals and Reactions to a Communications Source," *Journal of Marketing Research* 5 (February 1968):73–77.

275.    F. Williams, "Social Class Differences in How Children Talk about Television," *Journal of Broadcasting* 8 (Fall 1969):345–357.

276.    F. Williams and H. Lindsey, "Introduction: Language, Communication and Social Differences," in Mortenson and Sereno, eds., *Advances in Communications Research* (New York: Harper & Row, 1973), pp. 363–375.

277.    C.R. Wright, "Functional Analysis and Mass Communication," *Public Opinion Quarterly* 24 (1960):603–620.

278.    _____ , "Functional Analysis and Mass Communication," in Dexter and White, eds., *People, Society and Mass Communications* (Glencoe, Ill.: The Free Press, 1964), pp. 91–109.

279.    F.W. Wylie, "Attitudes toward the Media," *Public Relations Review* 31 (January 1975):6–7.

280.    D. Yankelovich, "New Criteria for Market Segmentation," *Harvard Business Review* 42 (September-October 1964):83–90.

281.    F.S. Zufryden, "Patterns of TV Program Solution," *Journal of Advertising Research* 18 (March 1976):43–47.

## Proceedings

282.    S. Banks, "Patterns of Daytime Viewing Behavior," *American Marketing Association Proceedings* (Chicago: June 1967), pp. 139–142.

283.    P.H. Benson, "Segmentation Analysis of Media Exposure: Towards a Theory of Learning Opportunity," *Proceedings of the Annual Convention of the American Psychological Association* 6 (1971), pp. 661–662.

284.    E.K. Bernay, "Life Style Analysis as a Basis for Media Selection," *Proceedings of the 2nd Attitude Research Conference* (Chicago: American Marketing Association, 1971), pp. 189–195.

285.    S.H. Chaffee and F. Izcaray, "Models of Mass Communication for a Media-Rich Developing Society," *ESOMAR Conference Proceedings* (Montreux: September 1975), pp. 27–57.

286. A.S.C. Ehrenberg, "Patterns of TV Viewing," *European Association for Advanced Research in Marketing Proceedings* (Fontaine-bleau: April 1976), pp. 51-79.

287. J. Engledow, H.B. Thorelli, and H. Becker, "The Information Seekers—A Cross-Cultural Consumer Elite," *Association for Consumer Research Proceedings* (Chicago: 1975), pp. 141-155.

288. S. Geiger and O. Ernst, "Advertising Pressure: Advertising Response Differentiation of Response Functions According to Target Groups and Media Consumption Groups," *ESOMAR Congress Proceedings* (Helsinki: August 1971), pp. 36-62.

289. F. Hansen, "Perceived Instrumentality and Value Importance of Newspaper Information," *Association for Consumer Research Proceedings* (Chicago: October 1975), pp. 307-320.

290. D.K. Hawes, "Time Budgets and Consumer Leisure-Time Behavior," *Association for Consumer Research Proceedings* (Atlanta: 1977), pp. 221-229.

291. D.K. Hawes, S. Gromo, and J. Arndt, "Shopping and Leisure Time: Some Preliminary Cross Cultural Comparisons of Time-Budget Expenditures," *Association for Consumer Research Proceedings* (Miami: 1978), pp. 151-159.

292. D. Hempel, W. McEwen, "Mobility, Social Integration and Information Seeking across Cultures," *Academy of International Business Proceedings* (San Francisco: 1974), pp. 18, 24.

293. P.E. Hendrix, T.C. Kinnear, and J.R. Taylor, "The Allocation of Time by Consumers," *Association for Consumer Research Proceedings* (San Francisco: 1979), pp. 38-44.

294. R.H. Holman and M. Venkatesan, "Overview of Time: The Fundamental Things Apply," *Association for Consumer Research Proceedings* (Miami: 1978), pp. 34-37.

295. G. Homan, R. Cecil, and W. Wells, "An Analysis of Moviegoers by Life Style Segments," *Association for Consumer Research Proceedings* (Chicago: 1975), pp. 217-229.

296. C. Leavitt and J. Walton, "Development of a Scale for Innovations," *Association for Consumer Research Proceedings* (Chicago: October 1975), pp. 545-569.

297. D.R. Lehmann, "Using Specific Attributes for Predicting Television Show Audience Share," *American Marketing Association Proceedings* (Chicago: 1972), pp. 319-327.

298. V. Liberanome and G. Valentini, "Magazine Contents and the Needs of Different Sociological Segments of Readers," *ESOMAR Congress Proceedings* (Venice: 1976), pp. 51-81.

299. M. Lovell and E. Nelson, "Using Life-Style and Social Trends to Shape the Future of Media," *ESOMAR Congress Proceedings* (Montreux: 1975), pp. 661-681.

300.  P.W. Michaels, "Life Style and Magazine Exposure," *American Marketing Association Proceedings* (Chicago: 1972), pp. 324–331.
301.  G. Moshis and G.A. Churchill, Jr. "Mass Media and Interpersonal Influences on Adolescent Consumer Learning," *American Marketing Association Proceedings* (Chicago: 1977), pp. 68–73.
302.  W.R. Neumann, "Political Knowledge: A Comparison of the Impact of Print and Broadcast News Media," Paper delivered at the 29th annual conference of the *American Association for Public Opinion Research* (Chicago: 1974).
303.  R.B. Settle and P.L. Alreck, "Time Orientation and Consumer Attitudes," *American Marketing Association Proceedings* (Chicago: 1977), pp. 520–529.
304.  R.B. Settle, P.L. Alreck, and J.W. Glasheen, "Individual Time Orientation and Consumer Life Style," *Association for Consumer Research Proceedings* (Miami: 1978), pp. 315–319.
305.  D.J. Tigert, "Are Television Audiences Really Different?" *American Marketing Association Proceedings* (San Francisco: April 1971), pp. 239–246.
306.  M. Vincent, "Experience of Qualitative Media Research in Spain: Findings, Actual and Potential Use," *ESOMAR Congress Proceedings* (Budapest: March 1976), pp. 169–188.
307.  S. Zinhham, "Personality Traits, Anxiety and Message Preference," *American Academy of Advertising Proceedings* (Columbia: April 1978), pp. 82–85.

### Trade Journals, Industry Publications, and Other

308.  *Advertising Age*, "Commercial TV Alienating Educated Viewer, Harris Poll Finds," March 22, 1966, p. 58.
309.  *Advertising Age*, "TV Viewing Is Still on the Increase, Nielson Reports," May 24, 1971, p. 14.
310.  *Advertising Age*, "Trends in Leisure Time," August 11, 1975, p. 49.
311.  L. Bogart, "How the Public Gets Its News," address to the Associated Press Managing Editors, New Orleans (New York: Newspaper Advertising Bureau, October 27, 1977).
312.  Columbia University Bureau of Applied Social Research, *Radio Listening in America: Report on a Survey Conducted by the National Opinion Research Center of the University of Chicago* (Englewood Cliffs, N.J.: Prentice-Hall, 1948).
313.  _____ , *The People Look at Radio: Report on a Survey by the National Opinion Research Center* (Chapel Hill: The University of North Carolina Press, 1946).

313a.   *Editor & Publisher*, "Study Shows Most Viewers Misunderstand TV Programs," May 24, 1980, p. 18.

313b.   The Gallup Organization, *Book Reading and Library Usage: A Study of Habits and Perceptions* (October 1978).

314.   McCall Corporation, *A Qualitative Study of Magazines: Who Reads Them and Why* (New York, 1941).

315.   M.E. McCombs, *Mass Media in the Marketplace* (Lexington, Ky.: Journalism Monographs #2, 1972).

316.   J.M. McLeod and S.Y. Choe, "An Analysis of Five Factors Affecting Newspaper Circulation," *ANPA News Research Report #10*, (Reston, Va., March 14, 1978).

*317.*   *Marketing News*, "Saturday between 12 a.m. and 3 p.m.," September 22, 1973, p. 2.

318.   Magazine Publishers Association, *Magazine Newsletter of Research #8*, May 1974.

319.   Magazine Publishers Association, *Magazine Newsletter of Research #11*, November 1974.

320.   _____ , *Magazine Newsletter of Research #7*, October 1975.

321.   _____ , *Magazine Newsletter of Research #18*, February 1977.

322.   _____ , *Magazine Newsletter of Research #22*, July 1977.

323.   _____ , *Magazine Newsletter of Research #23*, August 1977.

324.   _____ , *Magazine Newsletter of Research #24*, January 1978.

325.   _____ , *A Study of Media Involvement*, 1979.

326.   *Media Decisions*, "Don't Overlook the $200 Billion 55-plus Market," 12 (October 1977):59–122.

327.   Media and Program Analysis Department, "Radio—1977: A Status Report," Chicago: Leo Burnett Inc., October 1977.

328.   Newspaper Advertising Bureau, *Quantitative and Qualitative Aspects of Daily Newspaper Reading: A National Study* (New York, 1973).

329.   _____ , "Young Adults and the Newspaper" (January 1978).

330.   *Newsweek*, "'Magazines' Daily Audience Accumulation Patterns and Inter-Media Activity Patterns," 1977.

331.   Politz Research Inc., *A Study of Primary and Passalong Readers of Four Major Magazines* (New York: Reader's Digest, 1964).

332.   Radio Advertising Bureau, *Radio Facts* (New York, 1975).

333.   G. Rarick (ed.), *News Research for Better Newspapers*, (Vol. 7), Washington, D.C.: ANPA Foundation, 1975.

334.   Richmond Newspapers, Inc., *The Climate of Persuasion: A Study of the Public Image of Advertising Media* (Richmond, 1959).

335.   J.P. Robinson, "Daily News Habits of the American Public," *ANPA News Research Report #15* (Reston, Va., September 22, 1978).

336.  Roper Organization, Inc., *Emerging Profiles of Television and Other Mass Media: Public Attitudes, 1959–1967* (New York: Television Information Office, 1967).

337.  _____ , *Public Perceptions of Television and Other Mass Media: A Twenty-Year Review, 1959–1978* (New York: Television Information Office, 1979).

338.  R.L. Stevenson, "Newspaper Readership and Community Ties," Reston, Va.: *ANPA News Research Report #18* (March 9, 1979).

339.  *Time*, "Learning to Live with TV," May 28, 1979, pp. 69–70.

340.  U.S. Department of Commerce, Office of Management and Budget/ Statistical Policy Division, *Social Indicators*, Washington, D.C., 1973.

340a.  U.S. Office of Education, *Citizen Information Seeking Patterns: A New England Study* (November 1979).

### Unpublished Papers

341.  P. Baran, "On the Impact of the New Communications Media upon Social Values." Paper presented at the Institute for the Future, Middletown, Conn.

342.  H. Becker, "The Cosmopolitan Information Seeker: Implications for the Multinational Corporation." Unpublished working paper, 1974.

343.  D.K. Berlo, J.B. Lemert, and R. Mertz, "Dimensions for Evaluating the Acceptability of Message Sources." Unpublished paper, Michigan State University.

344.  D.K. Darden, "The Media as Reference Group Relationship." Paper presented to the Southern Sociological Society, 1976.

345.  H.L. Jacobsen, "Mass Media Believability: A Study of Receiver Judgments." Unpublished paper.

346.  M.B. Rees and W.J. Paisley, "Social and Psychological Predictors of Information Seeking and Media Use." Report of the Institute for Communication Research, Stanford University, 1967.

347a.  J.P. Robinson, "Time as an Indicator of Social Change and the Quality of Life." Unpublished paper, Survey Research Center, University of Michigan.

347b.  N. Takasaki and K. Mitamura, "Social Acceptability of New Video Systems in Japan." Unpublished paper, available in summary translation from the Research Institute of Telecommunications and Economics, Tokyo, 1980.

348.  H.B. Thorelli, E.W. Kelley, H. Becker, and J. Engledow, "The Information Seekers—A Comparative Study of German and American Consumers." Unpublished working paper, 1974.

349.    D.J. Tigert, "A Psychographic Profile of Magazine Audiences: An Investigation of Media Climate." Working paper presented at the American Marketing Association Consumer Workshop, Columbus, Ohio, August 1969.

350.    C. Urban, "Cross-national Patterns of Media Consumption: The Influence of Demographic and Media-Usage Variables." Paper presented to The European Academy for Advanced Research in Marketing, Stockholm, 1978.

# III STRATEGIC IMPLICATIONS

# 9 CHANGES IN THE INFORMATION INDUSTRIES: STRATEGIC IMPLICATIONS FOR NEWSPAPERS

*John C. LeGates*

Beginning in spring 1980, the American Newspaper Publisher's Association (ANPA) chose to intervene in the legislative process, not on a bill focused on the newspaper industry, but on one whose intended thrust was telephone deregulation. This was but one of a string of interactions and confrontations with parts of the information industry the ANPA never had to worry about before.

## WHY IS THE BOSTON WEATHER FORECAST NOW ANNOUNCED BY NEW ENGLAND TELEPHONE AND NOT THE NATIONAL WEATHER SERVICE?

We Bostonians are famous for talking about the weather. From my earliest childhood, I can remember dialing WE-6-1234 to get another forecast, usually erroneous, from the National Weather Service. This would provide grist for the discussion mill until the next weather change.

Imagine my surprise, one day this spring, when I dialed 936-1234. Instead of getting the national weather service forecast, I got this:

will be sunny and humid, with temperatures in the mid 80s. The 8:00 A.M. temperature was 71, the relative humidity 66, and the winds from

285

from the southwest at 11 miles per hour. This is Steve Thompson for New England Telephone. The next weather update will be before noon. Thank you for calling.

Why would New England Telephone, a Bell System Company, want to be in the business of announcing the weather? To begin answering this question, we should inquire how many people use services of this type.

The Time and Temperature number (formerly the Time number) is the most popular. In 1976 Atlanta got calls at the rate of 106,000 a day. In Dallas, where callers were charged a dime, there were 108,000 calls a day, generating gross revenues of $6,132,000. In Great Britain, all announcement services combined got 600 million calls in 1977. In New York, in 1979, the seven counties around Manhattan generated 271 million announcement service calls, producing a reported revenue of $16 million. Part of the secret now unfolds. Providers of information services can charge for them. This is not news to newspapers.

If we look at what is being announced, the picture becomes a bit more interesting. The top ten announcements worldwide include the weather forecast, time and temperature, and also tourist information (ski conditions, tides), motoring, recipes, sports scores, sports schedules, gardening tips, racing, and exchange rates. No one would buy a newspaper to find out the time or temperature, but the others have a different flavor. They are all items one finds in newspapers. Indeed many of them are the names of major sections in newspapers, and newspapers are the traditional source of this information. This looks like competition for the time, attention, and purse of the information consumer.

There is another wrinkle to announcement services: They can be sponsored. The format might go like this:

> Hi, this is Big Name Sports Star. I have a question for you. Where does an 800-pound gorilla sleep? While you're thinking about that, let me remind you that if *you* can't sleep at night ACME SLEEPING PILLS are the very best. Now about that gorilla, he sleeps any place he wants. Get it?

The call would be free, or cheap. Here we have a product that supplies news or entertainment to the individual, is priced less than it costs, and is paid for by the sponsor as a way to get his message to his potential customer. Those words also describe a newspaper.

Why is AT&T getting involved in 936-1234? It looks to us as though individual pieces of news or entertainment can be unbundled and delivered for a price or sold as an advertising medium. AT&T could use some of these pieces to get its nose under the tent of information services generally and begin to condition people to use the telephone when they want to know something. As the average residential phone is used only twenty minutes a day, this is good marginal revenue along the way.

## WHY MIGHT AMERICAN EXPRESS HAVE ACQUIRED AN INTEREST IN WARNER CABLE?

Not only are there some very disparate organizations getting into the provision of information, but they have some very disparate ways of funding their services, with important implications for the price at which they might someday compete. This section provides a whirlwind tour of a few possibilities.

Much has appeared in the trade press about American Express (Amex) and its growing share of the market for international monetary transactions. Beginning with the market in individual rather than corporate accounts, it has moved in the direction of becoming the major transfer agent for funds across borders.

With the Amex position in Warner Cable and with Warner's experiments in electronic banking and GIRO[1] systems in Columbus, Ohio, there is a new opportunity for vertical integration. Amex could offer, as a competitive edge, complete electronic services, both corporate and consumer, around the world. It might turn out that by realizing the profit from replacing the cost of paper banking with electronic banking, even without conventional cable revenues, the system could be paid for. If so, Amex would have a two-way video and data system in many households, onto which the provision of news and entertainment could be added at incremental prices. These would be much cheaper than if they had to pay for the installation of the system.

France has spent 200 billion francs between 1976 and 1981 to upgrade the telephone system. In doing so, they have created a cadre of 150,000 skilled workers and a vested budget item looking for the next thing to upgrade. The government has already announced part of what this will be. Each household will have a video terminal and a keyboard instead of the telephone book. This capital investment will be paid for from two sources: displacement of the cost of the telephone book, and a charge of about 50 centimes per search. A representative of the PTT[2] assures us that there are no plans to hook a printer onto this terminal, but that it would be cheap and easy to do. If completed, this program will install a two-way video and data system in most households, onto which the provision of news and entertainment could be added at incremental prices. The French newspaper industry is struggling both to kill the project and to gain access to it.

In several countries, videotex services, such as Prestel (Great Britain), Antiope (France), Bildschirmtext (Germany), and Telidon (Canada) are being developed and market-tested by the national telephone companies or government communication departments. If successful they will provide a two-way video and data system into many households onto which news and entertainment could be added at incremental prices.

Source Telecomputing Company, a household computerized information service, has been acquired by Reader's Digest, giving "The Source" new cash and a parent in the business of providing information on an international scale.

Cable TV systems are now available to 60 percent of American households and about 35 percent already subscribe.

There were approximately 6 million personal computers in homes and offices in 1983 and sales in 1983 were at an annual rate of more than 3 million. Many of these are being used to communicate with each other or with remote data bases.

The Lexis system paid for its development costs largely by displacing the budgets spent on researchers in law firms. That meant that the Nexis system did not have to pay those development costs.

What do all these developments add up to? It is much too early to call the race, but by now we can identify some of the horses. Several organizations are already at work with the following attributes:

- They are large and/or well heeled.
- They have an existing business that gives them serious credentials as providers of information.
- They aspire to place video/data systems in households or select businesses.
- They can pay for part or all of this by charging for sevices related to their customary business.

- If they succeed, they will have installed a system capable of providing news and entertainment and will price it on the margin.

The companies that make up the list come from a wide variety of traditional lines of business with differing internal structures, regulatory environments, and corporate personalities. In confronting one another, they can be expected to pose more complex problems, not only for themselves, but for governments, than the confrontations among traditional competitors. Because of these unfamiliar shadows looming on the horizon the interaction of the newspaper industry with AT&T, via the House Subcommittee on Telecommunications, was the beginning in a long series of new and diverse interactions.

## WHAT PROTECTION IS ENOUGH?

The issues raised in this case, therefore, may indicate the issues coming up in future cases. There are two watchwords in Washington these days. One is competition, with the presumption that more competition is somehow better for the economy; the other is deregulation, with the presumption that less regulation, or, conversely, more deregulation, is also better for the economy. The Congress has approached the so-called rewrite of the Communications Act of 1934 with intention to see how much of these two virtues it could impart to the communications industry.

Testimony before Congress by members of Harvard University's Program on Information Resources Policy pointed out that the two concepts, competition and deregulation, did not necessarily go together. In response to the prospects of deregulation of the telephone company, the largest company in the world in terms of installed plant and one of the largest in terms of gross revenues, a number of other companies intervened. They claimed that deregulation would not foster competition. It would stifle it by imposing an undue threat to themselves. Arguments, by and large, were not made against competition itself. Instead it was argued that competition against AT&T would be unfair, and in that sense, not properly competition. It would be unfair because AT&T's enormous size would provide an unfair advantage, allowing predatory pricing. Furthermore, AT&T would retain a hand in a monopolistic market and could subsidize its offerings in unregulated markets with the profits. Competition, they said, should be allowed, but only with adequate protection in order to make it work. The committee was therefore compelled to wrestle with concepts of protection.

Protection comes at different levels. The simplest level is separation of accounting systems: requiring a different set of books to be kept for different product lines. This entails a severe problem in the case of AT&T, however. Over 50 percent of the telephone company's costs are joint and common costs. Since these cannot be allocated on any universally accepted economic principle, it remains for them to be allocated some other way. This is done today by negotiation among a variety of corporations and governmental entities. It is political accommodation. Competitors fear that joint and common cost will be loaded excessively onto some other product, allowing an artificially low cost for the one with which they compete. As there is no satisfactory economic criterion for the word *excessive*, this problem can be intractible in the absence of political agreement.

An apparent solution would be the next level of protection: separation of corporate entity. Separate offerings have to be provided by separate corporate entities, each with its own executive structure, accounting system, and so forth. Different lengths-of-arm may be specified between the subsidiary and the parent. The difficulty with this solution is that many of the services provided by different corporate entities must still be provided by the same physical plant at least into the foreseeable future. For example, long distance and local services still require the same switch; corporate services and private services still require the same lines. As long as the same plant is providing services to two separate corporations, the entity that owns the plant, or its regulator, retains the discretion of assigning its joint and common costs among those offerings. So it is the same problem in different clothing. This might be called the myth of separate subsidiaries.

Two other forms of protection seem to solve the protection problem. One is prohibition of a company from entering a particular line of business. This certainly prevents unfair competition by that company in that business. It also eliminates competition altogether.

The other is complete separation of plant. In other words, companies offering local service must use completely different plant from those offering long-distance service. Those offering private line, WATS, corporate, and other forms of service must use completely separate plant from one another. This will provide adequate protection.

However, it also requires duplication of plant. In many cases the cost would escalate to the point where the service is no longer viable. In most cases costs for the totality of the services would equal or exceed costs with joint plant. This solution creates economic inefficiencies. Elimination of economic inefficiencies was the goal of competition in the first place and therefore this option can defeat the goal.

Congress does not have a clean solution to the problem of competition with adequate protection. Instead it must do a balancing act between the horns of the dilemma of protection versus efficiency. Accommodation rather than solution will be the outcome.

## ET TU, BRUTE?

By the time ANPA entered the discussions in the Committee, these issues had been heard many times. The newspaper industry's position was supported by two major arguments. One was that AT&T's size, perhaps including its monopoly power in other markets, distorted the market in such a way as to provide unfair competition with newspapers. This could damage the diversity of the press and therefore the freedom of the press. Its other argument was that vertical integration, provision of both the content of an information service and the conduit over which it is conveyed to its recipient, is a form of control regardless of the size of the provider. The first of these arguments had been used by a variety of interveners to support separation of AT&T as a form of protection for themselves. The vertical integration argument had been used by companies who wished to prohibit AT&T from getting into their business. The newspapers' solution was the prohibition of AT&T from a market—namely provision of content in any form over the network which it controlled. The industry's success with the Wirth Amendment[3] may well have depended upon its ability to invoke the First Amendment, an option not available to most of the others, rather than on the use of the economic arguments. Even so, critics of the Wirth Amendment have referred to it as pure and blatant protectionism.

Although these arguments may have worked before the House Subcommittee on Telecommunications, they may be considerably more ambiguous in other forums in the future. For example, the size argument can work for or against a firm depending on whether the competitor is bigger or smaller. The control argument works for a newspaper publisher when it controls the content and does not wish the conduit company to get into that business. It may work against the organization if it controls the content and is trying to acquire a different kind of conduit, such as a cable company. It is worth noting that the Times Mirror Company was initially ruled ineligible to own cable companies in the Hartford, Connecticut area by arguments very similar to these. Times Mirror were viewed as too dominating to foster diversity of sources within that market. It was also seen as threatening to own multiple conduits of information as well as the sources of that information.

An important element in whether these precedents are helpful or harmful may be the size of the competition. The list of unfamiliar competitors, cited earlier in this discussion, had mostly large organizations. There are also products supplied (or potentially supplied) by small organizations. Examples include cable TV, data-base services, cassettes, and videodiscs, direct broadcast satellite receivers, shoppers, libraries, and so forth. Each is coming at the market from a different angle, and each is competing for the time, attention, and pocketbook of the consumer who desires information.

## WHAT'S GOING ON HERE ANYWAY?

What is happening from the perspective of the customer? We think that the very nature of the consumer is changing. We are constantly being told of the declining literacy of the American public. On the other hand there are new capabilities that the public never had before. Almost every student graduating from high school has seen and used a hand-held calculator. Almost every child has played with an interactive electronic game. Many private motorists and almost every professional trucker uses a citizen's band radio. Many employees of airlines, insurance companies, banks, and, of course, newspapers, spend several hours a day in front of a video terminal interacting with a computer. These people will behave like a new and different kind of media customer. No longer satisfied with media that do not interact or with plain old telephone service, the new consumers can handle a more sophisticated kind of medium. They can interact with it and demand the information they want. Responding to (and partly causing) this change in the nature of the consumer are changes in all of the information industries. The nature of the products and services available is evolving, the nature of the corporations providing them is changing, new and uncertain government actions may appear, and the pie is being resliced.

## WHAT CAN NEWSPAPERS DO?

Newspapers must try a new way of thinking about themselves if they wish to remain competitive in the information marketplace. The word *newspaper* covers a variety of different, indeed disparate, items. A newspaper shares with any other communications medium three common building blocks. These are:

1.  Content, the information presented as news, editorials, advertisements, or feature stories
2.  Process, the gathering, storing, preparation, printing, and delivery of content items
3.  Format, the way in which material is displayed to its ultimate consumer—in the case of newspapers, as print on paper

Other media, such as television, differ in the nature of these three elements, but they all have them. Newspaper publishers, rather than thinking of their organization as a newspaper alone, need to think of themselves as a corporation possessing strengths and weaknesses in content, process, and format.

Process, in newspaper publishing, is the phase, invisible to the consumer, in which the content goes from the form in which it arrived into a fully composed page. Formerly done manually, this step is now done electronically. During this phase a machine-readable version of the newspaper is produced although it is not seen by the customer. Just as the process has changed, so are the content and format.

Concerning content, newspapers were once the standard source for information about exchange rates and stockmarket prices. Both of these, so far as the professional users are concerned, have been taken away from the newspaper by electronic services. On the other hand newspapers have been steadily increasing the number of pages devoted to so-called features. Many of these in turn are on the list of telephone announcement services.

As to process, the dramatic change from manual to electronic composition of the newspaper has positioned the newspaper for electronic delivery over wires. At the same time the traditional conduit for newspapers, namely transportation and newsboys, is becoming increasingly expensive and difficult to manage. Independent delivery services, including some owned and operated by ANPA members, have appeared as a new form both of profitable subsidiary and of ways to deliver the newspaper.

On the format side, very little is new in the newspaper industry, but there is new competition, such as cable TV, videodiscs, video cassettes, and the telephone. Newspaper companies appear to be strong on content and format relative to other companies. They are, however, possibly very weak on process. Let us look at each of these in a little more detail.

Content is a diverse bundle of types of information held together by the (now shifting) economics and technology of the process and format. Some kinds of content are under more direct threat than others. Many are amenable to quite different treatments than the others.

Part of newspapers' content is numerical data such as stockmarket reports and exchange rates. These have long since gone to the electronic competitors for use by the professionals. The question is whether the householder is next. These data are very easily carried on telephone call or announcement services or put in readable format over cable television.

Classified advertising is one of the mainstays of a newspaper's income stream. It is for all practical purposes a data-base service, albeit one offered on paper. Other companies could easily offer it by computer. The advantages of computer-readable classified advertising are quite convincing. It could be up-to-the-minute and contain no obsolete entries. Readers could search for the exact product they want, the location they want, the price they want, or other indexible properties. Certain big ticket items, such as real estate, are already listed on nationwide data bases. Obvious questions arise as to who will provide the data for these data bases, who will own the data bases, who will operate them, and who will provide access to them. Newspaper publishers should choose which of these roles they would like to play rather than leave them for some other type of industry to take over.

Display advertising is another major portion of newspapers' income stream. It was the combination of display and classified advertising that appeared to be threatened by AT&T's electronic Yellow Pages. There may be a less direct but equally significant threat. As has been suggested, consumers are able to get the information they want in new and different ways and more and more under their own direction. Consumers use pay-TV and cable TV in order to get the programming they want without the advertisements—and they pay for it. With increasing control of content by the user, services will appear in which the information is available without the advertising. One of the major challenges facing newspapers in the coming years will be to preserve the income stream from advertising or to replace it with income derived from selling the information (content) itself.

News, graphics, and opinion are the information associated with newspapers' greatest traditional strength, but are there new competitors? The TV networks are all upgrading the news at the moment. Wire services could offer competition at least in theory. In practice, wire services are available over household data-base services such as The Source and Compuserve working with Warner Amex in Columbus. Nonetheless, the overwhelming advantage in reputation, expertise, and investment in the preparation of news, graphics, and opinion rests with the newspaper industry.

Finally, it is clear that magazines can compete and have been competing with features, in fact increasingly so. It may also be that data-base services can compete as can announcement services via telephone. The timeliness and referencibility of the specific feature may determine how well it can be conveyed by a newspaper relative to some other medium.

Content appears to be a strong area for newspapers. Process, however, is a different story. The raw ingredients of the business—paper, ink, and labor—are among the largest and the fastest growing budget items. Delivery costs appears to be growing more rapidly than content gathering or preparation.

By contrast there are dramatic cost declines for computers and electronic switching and transmission equipment. They go down by a factor of 10 every two to six years depending upon whom you ask and which part of the business they are measuring. If we compare the two cost trends, we see printing and delivery of newspapers increasing by at least double every decade and electronic delivery and preparation declining by at least a factor of 10 every six years. We are more or less forced to a conclusion: electronic delivery of information will eventually become very appealing economically.

Once the question has been phrased in this manner some interesting possibilities emerge. In ANPA's dealings with AT&T and the House

Subcommittee, they appear to have perceived electronic communication as a threat to its members' mainstream business, used against them by a competitor. There is another possibility. Electronic communication may be the industry's alternative to the increasing costs of printing and delivering the news on paper. As such it would not be a threat but an opportunity. The newspaper business can be seen as weak in the area of conduit and open to opportunities for change.

Change, however, may not be forced upon newspapers too quickly because of its strengths in format. Imagine a room full of technicians. I come in and announce that I have a new technology. It will carry 30 million bits of information, weigh less than 3 pounds, handle both text and graphics, be completely portable, be accessible in any order, operate 24 hours a day, cost less than 25 cents a connect hour and be mostly paid for by someone else. I can assure you that the roomful of technicians would be amazed by this advanced capability. It is far ahead of anything currently available. The technology which I have described is the daily newspaper. It continues to be the most advanced format for the information you wish to display. With this strength, the daily newspaper will retain its technological lead for years. It is generations, not just minutes, ahead of the technological competition.

What, if any, messages can be distilled from the content, process, format scheme? It suggests that newspaper companies should stop thinking of themselves as companies in the newspaper business, but rather as companies which possess strengths and weaknesses in content, process and format. Their goal is to try to contract out the newspaper industry's weaknesses and leverage its strengths into the best position in the coming information order.

Consider the complexity of a newspaper publisher's relationship with the telephone companies. This relationship has more than one aspect. Newspapers are at present a customer—in fact a heavy user. Newspapers have historically taken very good advantage of certain practices called discriminatory by their critics, such as Hi-Lo Tariffs, Telpak-end-links, and WATS lines. In addition to being a customer, newspapers are a possible competitor, hence their lobbying effort. They are also a potential customer of a very different kind. Can publishers use the telephone companies as the alternative to newsboys? Can they capitalize on their installed billing plant for tailored services? Can they establish joint ventures to take advantage of the telephone companies' strong credit ratings for cheaper capital?

The world of the telephone companies is changing at least as fast as and perhaps even faster and more fundamentally than that of newspapers. Some alternatives have them worried, and the newspaper industry may be able to use them. Cable, videotex, data-base information sources, and other modern communications developments may be used to distribute content to segments of the newspaper's audience.

## CONCLUSIONS

The chairman of the board of an independent telephone company once took me aside and explained, "This used to be such a nice quiet business. We had our feuds, but we were able to keep them in the family. Now everything is changing and I don't like it." He retired the next year, and the year after that, his company began a diversified acquisitions program. They have done well. The newspaper world has also been a nice quiet business. It has had its feuds, but they have been within the family. The newspaper industry will soon find itself in a world populated by unfamiliar kinds of companies and governmental bodies. It will no longer be a nice quiet business, and it will no longer concern only the family.

Second, the newspaper business has enjoyed a kind of moral aloofness from lobbying or pressuring the government on its own behalf. This era is drawing to a close. Editorials supported the lobbying efforts against the Communications Act rewrite or favored the Wirth Amendment. Some of them admitted their paper's financial stake. It will become harder to stay detached.

Finally, the role of ANPA itself will become less easy to identify. As other information businesses are drawn into the newspapers' orbit or newspapers into theirs, ANPA members will respond differently. Some will perceive threats and others opportunities. The luxury of identifying a common enemy or a common friend will become scarcer. ANPA itself will begin an ongoing task of trying to identify the common interests of its members.

## NOTES

1. A procedure that directly debits an individual's checking account at the time of a purchase while simultaneously crediting the merchant's bank account. It is widely used in Europe today.

2. Postal, telephone, and telegraph agencies that are government-owned or controlled in most West European countries.

3. This refers to a proposal from Representative Tim Wirth (D., Colo.), the chairman of the House Subcommittee on Telecommunications, Consumer Protection, and Finance, which would have prohibited AT&T from entering the content business if it involved using its own lines.

# 10 THE FIRST AMENDMENT MEETS THE SECOND REVOLUTION

William H. Read

Contemporary case law reflects concepts born of the Gutenberg revolution. Leading illustrations are two cases decided by the U.S. Supreme Court: one on broadcasting, the other on newspapers. A reexamination of those decisions—*Red Lion Broadcasting Co. v. FCC* (hereafter cited as *Red Lion*) and *Miami Herald Publishing Co. v. Tornillo* (hereafter cited as *Miami Herald*) is offered here.[1] The purpose is twofold. The first is to argue that one of those cases would be decided differently today. The second is to suggest that, should the court revisit this area, any new holding ought to be conditioned by the fact that the Gutenberg revolution, which created the foundation for the "press clause" of the First Amendment, is giving way to a new revolution that is blurring boundaries between, on the one hand, broadcasting and the press, and between, on the other hand, the "institutional media" and other modern communicators.

The second revolution is not likely to compel a wholesale reappraisal of First Amendment law. True, the advent of new communications technologies like cable television, Xerox copiers, and teleprocessing have had a sweeping impact on the laws of copyright and privacy.[2] And other applications of electronic technology may coerce change elsewhere, too.[3] Electronic eavesdropping by foreign agents may, for instance, become intolerable and thereby give rise to passage of protective statutes or negotiated international conventions.[4] But just because there are more abundant and versatile means of communications now available does not necessarily mean that the courts will find it necessary to rethink all the rules.

The new era does put some once settled questions at issue again. Among them is the judicial notion that a greater scope of government regulation is permissible as to broadcasting than as to the press.[5] That notion is embedded in a two-track legal approach to mass media: one track for publishers, another for broadcasters.

For print the First Amendment stands behind the idea that no government, either federal or local, has authority to interfere with the right of a publisher to print whatever information that person cares to put on paper.[6] This is not to say that eighteenth-century images of a persecuted John Peter Zenger fighting to protect his press have inspired courts to insist on anything like a complete arm's-length relationship between press and government. Government can, and does, regulate publishers in much the same manner as it controls other business enterprises.[7] But even though antitrust, labor relations, and other business-oriented laws do present some limitations, reporters, writers, and editors carry out their publishing functions generally free from repressive or chilling governmental controls.[8] This is so because the press has come to assume a special place in this country. Its role is popularly thought of as the independent Fourth Estate, watchdog of the other three, and profit-making servant of an informed electorate.

While the basic law sanctioning freedom of the press is the two-centuries-old First Amendment, judicial interpretations of that constitutional provision are of more recent vintage. Only after the outbreak of World War I and the radical agitation that followed did the U.S. Supreme Court begin to search for coherent theories to explain either tolerance or suppression of expression in specific cases. The early judicial theorists of note were Justices Oliver Wendell Holmes and Louis Brandeis, who, in the absence of a "clear and present danger,"[9] favored "free trade in ideas."[10] The benefit of such a marketplace was later stated by Judge Learned Hand in these words: "[Right] conclusions are more likely to be gathered out of a multitude of tongues, than through any kind of authoritative selection."[11]

That government must keep its hands out of the editorial process of print media was made unequivocally clear a half-century after the Supreme Court first began to explore the contours of the First Amendment. At issue in *Miami Herald* was a Florida right-of-reply statute which provided that, if a candidate for office were attacked in a newspaper, the newspaper must offer rebuttal space to the offended candidate. A unanimous Supreme Court struck down the Florida statute in 1974 saying in part:

> The choice of material to go into a newspaper, and the decisions made as to limitations on the size of the paper, and content, and treatment of public issues and public officials—whether fair or unfair—constitutes the exercise of editorial control and judgment. It has yet to be demonstrated how governmental regulation of this crucial process can be exercised consistent with First Amendment guarantees of a free press as they have evolved to this time.[12]

This thumping endorsement for a free print press stands in sharp contrast to an earlier but still recent view of the court with regard to broadcasting. The judicial position there upholds the right of government to interfere in programming decisions of radio and television station operators. It is a position grounded in a tradition apart from that of print media. That tradition began in 1927 when it was established by statute that the electronic media (then only radio) have no right to exist without a federal license.[13]

The licensing requirement runs counter to a basic tenet of the First Amendment,[14] because this requirement mandates prior official approval before anyone can communicate by radio or television. Licenses are issued only to those persons whom federal regulators determine will best serve the "public interest."[15] Moreover, the licensing scheme sets into motion controls and influences on the content of broadcast programs that surely would be held unconstitutional if applied to newspapers, magazines, and books. The most striking of these is the so-called Fairness Doctrine, which commands broadcasters to put balance in their public affairs programming and to provide air time to persons or points of view that the licensee might otherwise ignore.[16] The Fairness Doctrine was upheld by the U.S. Supreme Court in 1969, in the *Red Lion* case. The Court offered this rationale:

> It is the purpose of the First Amendment to preserve an uninhibited marketplace of ideas in which truth will ultimately prevail, rather than to countenance monopolization of that market, whether it be by the Government itself or a private licensee.[17]

The premise upon which this statement rests was the Court's acceptance of the argument that broadcast media are fundamentally different from print media. Thus the Court reasoned, "Differences in the characteristics of news media justify differences in the First Amendment standards applied to them."[18]

What makes broadcast media different from print for constitutional purposes is the reliance of the former on the radio spectrum, or airwaves, for carrying information from senders to receivers. The spectrum is a natural and limited resource, something like navigable waterways, which generally are not considered to be suitable for private exploitation. When radio first took hold in this country there was chaotic competition to exploit this finite resource, until the federal government effectively stepped in to control the technology and allocate frequencies.

More than technical controls soon were to evolve, although these too were premised on the condition of spectrum scarcity. Because only a few could be licensed to broadcast, the idea developed that broadcasters were public trustees and therefore subject to governmental regulation.[19] That idea came to be bolstered on two counts: profits and power. As it turned out, the spectrum was a valuable resource government had "given away." So it seemed proper to many that broadcasters should "pay back" in kind, ergo with programming not merely of commercial value, but of public interest value too. Furthermore the supposed but never quite proven influence of the broadcast media, especially TV, over political and cultural attitudes was perceived by some as being too potent to be left wholly in the hands of media merchants. Thus by statute and regulation, held to be constitutional by federal courts, the legal scheme for broadcast media fits a different mold than that of print media.

From an intellectual, not to mention practical, standpoint the two-track legal system for mass media seems unsatisfactory. In effect we have an eighteenth-century standard for one medium, and a twentieth-century standard for another. While many commentators favor the older view for both, a substantial argument is on the record for unifying the law of mass communications under something like the Fairness Doctrine approach.[20] For proponents of either view, however, the Supreme Court erected a high barrier in *Red Lion,* with its "differences in characteristics . . . differences in . . . standards" approach.

Are the media—print and broadcasting—truly different? As yet the only difference of constitutional dimension is that one medium uses the finite natural resource known as the radio spectrum. But, as has been mentioned, economic and social reasons also are said to support a two-track approach. The validity of all these reasons has been questioned in the past. More challenges can be anticipated in the future. For the fact is that as a new communications era further unfolds, the divergent legal approach to mass media makes less and less sense. To explain why, we can look at each of the foregoing reasons in light of current realities and trends.

## SOCIAL PERSPECTIVE

The argument for government regulation of media from a social viewpoint is the belief that the media in general, and television in particular, exert a powerful influence over cultural and political attitudes. Some jurists have seen this as an acute problem. In the decision upholding the power of the Federal Communications Commission to regulate broadcast commercials for cigarettes, the U.S. Court of Appeals for the District of Columbia said:

> Written messages are not communicated unless they are read, and reading requires an affirmative act. Broadcast messages, in contrast, are "in the air." In an age of omnipresent radio, there scarcely breathes a citizen who does not know some part of a leading cigarette jingle by heart. Similarly, an ordinary habitual television watcher can avoid these commercials only by frequently leaving the room, changing the channel, or doing some other such affirmative act. It is difficult to calculate the subliminal impact of this pervasive propaganda, which may be heard even if not listened to, but it may reasonably be thought greater than the impact of the written word.[21]

Since the District of Columbia Appeals Court offered these comments in 1968, all cigarette advertising on radio and TV has been banned. A decade later, however, the consumption of cigarettes continued to pose a serious health hazard to the country, according to the U.S. Secretary of Health, Education, and Welfare.[22] Does this suggest that print media, which subsequently carried nearly all cigarette advertising, are more powerful than the Appellate Court had thought? Or, is there possibly another explanation? Could it be that smokers enjoy their cigarettes and light up for pleasure and not merely in response to "pervasive propaganda"? Countless millions of Chinese do that every day, even though they never have seen a cigarette advertisement, either in print or on television.

The evidence is equally ambiguous with respect to the impact of broadcasting on politics. A few years ago the idea spread that media were responsible for the expanded powers of the president.[23] Not only was it contended that the media helped to create an "imperial presidency" but that television caused such a shift to the national level of American politics that only Washington politicians could hope to reach the White House.[24] That supposed trend of course was broken by Jimmy Carter, who upon reaching the White House found that the pendulum of power had swung back toward the Congress, "presidential television" notwithstanding.

A proper, indeed sensible, answer to those who advance the notion that media exert so much influence on the public mind that government must control them came from Justice William O. Douglas.

> To say that the media have great decision-making powers without defined legal responsibilities or any formal duties of public accountability is both to overestimate their power and to put forth a meaningless formula for reform. How shall we make the *New York Times* "accountable" for its anti-Vietnam policy? Require it to print letters to the editor in support of the war? If the situation is as grave as stated, the remedy is fantastically inadequate. But the situation is not that grave. The *New York Times,* the *Chicago Tribune,* NBC, ABC, and CBS play a role in policy formation, but clearly they were not alone responsible, for example, for Johnson's decision not to run for re-election, Nixon's refusal to withdraw the troops from Vietnam, the rejection of the two billion dollar New York bond issue, the defeat of Carswell and Haynesworth, or the Supreme Court's segregation, reapportionment and prayer decisions. The implication that the people of this country—except the proponents of the theory—are mere unthinking automatons manipulated by the media, without interests, conflicts, or prejudices is an assumption which I find quite maddening. The development of constitutional doctrine should not be based on such hysterical overestimation of media power and underestimation of the good sense of the American public.[25]

## ECONOMIC PERSPECTIVE

Here too the evidence is at least ambiguous on the question of whether substantial and significant differences exist between print and broadcast media. Supporters of broadcast regulation make much of government's role in saying who shall operate a station. While this is true, it is also the case that newspapers do not exist solely as a result of free-market decisionmaking. As Justice Potter Stewart has pointed out, "Newspapers get government mail subsidies and a limited antitrust immunity." Because of this, Justice Stewart has written that "it would require no great ingenuity" to make the same argument for newspapers as has been made for broadcasting.[26]

Nor does it take much ingenuity to stand the scarcity argument on its head. While the Court in *Red Lion* relied on spectrum scarcity to distinguish between media, the crucial reality for both print and broadcast media is "economic scarcity." A clear indicator of this is the trend of recent years toward the one-newspaper town.[27] In broadcasting, too, there are constraints on the number of economically viable outlets. In an indirect but underemphasized manner, this was acknowledged in *Red Lion*. The court's words were these:

> We need not deal with the argument that even if there is no longer a technological scarcity of frequencies limiting the number of broadcasters, there nevertheless is an economic scarcity in the sense that the Commission could or does limit entry to the broadcasting market on economic grounds and license no more stations than the market will support.[28]

Another economic argument is based on the fact that entry to the broadcast market is denied to some. It is said, therefore, that the Fairness Doctrine is essential to satisfy the claims of those who are excluded from operating stations. This argument finds some support because there is, after all, an absolute time limit on the amount of material that can be broadcast. In a practical sense a similar sort of limitation exists for newspapers, too. And this too has been acknowledged by the Supreme Court.

> It is correct . . . that a newspaper is not subject to the finite technological limitations of time that confront a broadcaster but it is not correct to say that, as an economic reality, a newspaper can proceed to infinite expansion of its column space to accommodate the replies that a government agency determines or a statute commands the readers should have available.[29]

So when the economics of publishing and those of broadcasting are examined, what emerges is support for a conclusion reached by Justice William O. Douglas in *Columbia Broadcasting System, Inc. v. Democratic National Committee* (hereafter cited as *Columbia Broadcasting*):

the press in a realistic sense is likewise not available to all . . . the daily papers now established are unique in the sense that it would be virtually impossible for a competitor to enter the field due to financial exigencies of this era. The result is that in practical terms the newspapers and magazines, like TV and radio, are available to only a select few.[30]

But what about the idea that, absent government control, greedy broadcast executives would commercially exploit the medium, with minimal regard for public service? The trouble here is that newspaper executives are, in large measure, of the same breed. In so-called cross-ownership situations, top managers both publish newspapers and operate broadcast stations.[31] And even when this is not the case, commercial motivations apparently can be strong in either publishing or broadcasting. Again, Justice Douglas provides a useful insight:

> TV and radio broadcasters have mined millions by selling merchandise, not in selling ideas across the broad spectrum of the First Amendment. But some newspapers have done precisely the same, loading their pages with advertisements: they publish, not discussions of critical issues confronting our society, but stories about murders, scandal, and slanderous matter touching the lives of public servants.[32]

Finally, and most importantly, comes the question of monopoly. The Supreme Court in *Red Lion,* it may be recalled, spoke of a First Amendment that promotes "an uninhibited marketplace of ideas . . . rather than to countenance monopolization of that market . . . [by] a private licensee."[33] As a practical matter, there are far more broadcast stations on the air each day in this country than there are daily newspapers—three times as many, in fact.[34] But a more telling point comes from Professor Bruce Owen, a Duke University economist who has analyzed media industries.

In examining the changing structure of the newspaper industry—an industry in which the number of daily and weekly newspapers has steadily declined since 1900, while the number of one-newspaper towns has risen—Owen has concluded that restructuring has come about in part because of "the introduction of new competing advertising and consumption technologies—motion pictures, radio, and television."[35] In other words, from an economic perspective the mass media *compete* with each other. Indeed, according to a study produced by the Harvard Business School, "Competition [for newspapers] from the electronic media had become particularly strong in large metropolitan markets."[36] And this is so not just for advertising dollars. The Harvard study reported that:

Some industry analysts believe that VHF-TV stations with their network news programs had severely affected afternoon daily papers in some markets. Newspapermen claimed that TV could not provide in-depth coverage of the news, particularly local news. An one-hour television news show presented the equivalent of only a page or two from a newspaper. In the final analysis, the various media were competing for the time the consumer had to receive the information that she/he desired.[37]

If print and broadcasting do compete with each other, as Professor Owen says that they do, and if that competition is essentially for the time of "information consumers," as the Harvard Business School study found, then on economic grounds at least the legal line drawn between media is weak, perhaps even arbitrary.

## TECHNOLOGICAL PERSPECTIVE

At the heart of the distinction drawn by the U.S. Supreme Court between the press and broadcasting is the belief that "the broadcast media pose unique and special problems not present in the traditional free speech case." What the court finds to be "special" is the technological nature of the medium. Because broadcast frequencies are finite (and thus for reasons of efficient use must be allocated), the court came to conclude in *Red Lion* that "it is idle to posit an unabridgeable First Amendment right to broadcast comparable to the right of every individual to speak, write, or publish."[38]

The advent of cable television, over which the FCC has assumed jurisdiction[39] and regulates in a mold similar to that as over-the-air TV, gives rise to an obvious counter argument. "Economic scarcity," as opposed to "physical scarcity," is the inherent condition of cable. In other words the spread of cable depends, minus government regulations, entirely on market forces and not on an orderly allocation of spectrum. Cable is more like telephone technology in this regard, although the concept of regulating cable like a common carrier has been rejected. Nonetheless, as cable gains greater acceptance around the country, it adds to growing pressures for a unitary legal approach to mass media.[40]

Of greater significance, however, is the convergence of broadcast and print technologies. Yes, convergence. Professor Owen has a word for it: the print media, he says, are experiencing "electronification."[41]

Electronic technology, Owen points out, is gradually replacing mechanical technology in printing. "In the past 10 or 15 years," he writes, "the electronic revolution has finally begun to be applied to the technical process by which newspaper and magazine copy is printed."[42] Already reporters and editors are writing and processing news stories on television-like devices called video display terminals (VDT). And electronic transmission of even color pictures to distant printing plants has arrived. The *Wall Street Journal* and *Time,* in other words, are using the same basic technology to produce and nationally distribute their products as do the television networks. The technology includes the use of satellites, which, like over-the-air broadcasting, requires spectrum allocation and is therefore regulated by the FCC.

The convergence of print and broadcasting is perhaps best revealed by the advent of "teletext." These are systems that transmit computerized information that is electronically displayed on a television screen. That teletext systems technologically transcend media is evidenced by the fact that they are operated by all sorts of communications organizations. In Britain, for instance, there are three systems: one run by the British Post Office, another by the BBC, and a third by a consortium. Similar services are being tried in six other countries, including three systems here in the United States—two are broadcast types being tested by the Public Broadcasting Service, while the other is operated by Reuters News Agency over the Manhattan Cable TV Network. Teletext is a leading example of what has been called the "still poorly charted area of 'media convergence,' where newspaper publishers, broadcasters and Post Offices and PTT's [government operated telecommunications companies] find their interests overlapping and possibly conflicting."[43]

The convergence of print and broadcast technologies actually is just a part of a larger pattern. Harvard professor Anthony G. Oettinger has shown that the basic convergence is between communications technology on the one hand and computer technology on the other. That convergence, which Oettinger has labeled "compunications," already has blurred the boundaries between the once distinct telecommunications and computer industries.[44] This in turn has caused a major regulatory headache, since by law telecommunications has developed as a regulated monopoly, while the computer industry grew up in an intensely competitive marketplace.[45]

The impact of technological convergence makes for a rather interesting comparison. From a regulatory viewpoint, the computer and publishing industries have developed largely outside the ambit of direct governmental control. The contrary has been the case for telecommunications and broadcasting; both have been highly regulated, indeed by the same agency—the FCC. With convergence, the same basic technology is common to all these industries. The FCC, however, has statutory responsibility for two of those industries, not all four. Broadcasting and telecommunications are within the agency's jurisdiction; computers and print are outside.

This is not to suggest that all should be within, or all should be outside the FCC's jurisdiction. From a technological perspective, however, it seems clear that these industries are bound to become further entangled. Evidence of this goes beyond teletext. At a recent meeting of the American Newspaper Publishers Association, AT&T and IBM presented their versions of the technological outlook for the years ahead. Essentially publishers were told that digitizing information—putting pictures, data, news, graphics, and so on into computer form—and then communicating that information at lightning speeds within manageable costs are the two principal trends of great significance for everyone interested in the communication of information.

What do those trends mean? An answer came from Robert G. Marbut, chief executive officer of a major newspaper and broadcast chain:

> Regardless of the medium—television, CATV, newspapers, magazines—the technology to gather and process information and get it to a certain point along the distribution channel will be essentially the same for all. . . . Common equipment will be used by all media. Whether it be VDT's [video display terminals], computers or broad band communications, we can expect all information providers to take advantage of this new technology. What I'm saying is this: *the same technology is available to all information providers.*[46]

The upshot of all this is clear: The technological underpinnings of *Red Lion* are eroding as the technological distinctions among media blur. To cling to spectrum scarcity as a rationale for a divergent legal approach to broadcasting is no longer viable. Indeed it is risky. For as newspapers and magazines more and more come to rely on satellites and other regulated communications technologies the danger exists that they too will be drawn into the regulatory web. An argument can be made, of course, that this would be in the national interest. But if the national interest is otherwise then "in order to avoid regulating the content of print media," says Professor Owen, "we may have to start now to deregulate the electronic media."[47]

## CONCLUSIONS

The conclusion to be drawn from the foregoing is simply this: the rationale for a divergent, two-track legal approach for mass media has eroded. Once seemingly clear distinctions between print and broadcasting are no longer so clear; "blur" is fast becoming a more appropriate word. The question then is whether both media should be placed under the print or under the broadcast standard—or perhaps a standard yet to be developed.

The progression of case law would suggest the print standard. *Red Lion* fixed the broadcast standard in 1969. Then four years later the Supreme Court seemed to be having second thoughts, or at least a multiplicity of thoughts, for in *Columbia Broadcasting* the Supreme Court gave us more of a symposium than a clear decision. In over 100 pages of opinions, the justices revealed just how divisive the First Amendment can be. The case is notable for its range of views, not for any clear, concise judicial rulemaking. The issue in *Columbia Broadcasting* was whether a broadcast licensee could refuse to sell air time for political messages. The FCC had said the licensee could. A divided and overly opinionated Supreme Court agreed.[48] Then it its next term a unanimous Court in *Miami Herald* held that government may not intrude into the function of editors in choosing what materials go into a newspaper and in deciding on the size and content of the paper and the treatment of public issues and officials.[49]

Curiously, the court in *Miami Herald* never cited the *Red Lion* decision. Nor did the court give any indication of the reason for this omission. The court did, however, present a clear interpretation of the press clause of the First Amendment on the issue of right-of-reply. Since, as has been shown, press and broadcasting are converging, it seems logical to say that the *Miami Herald* rule ought to be extended to broadcast media, too.[50] That same conclusion has been reached earlier, on the grounds, by Justice Douglas in *Columbia Broadcasting*.

> TV and radio stand in the same protected position under the First Amendment as do newspapers and magazines. The philosophy of the First Amend-

ment requires that result, for the fear that Madison and Jefferson had of government intrusion is perhaps even more relevant to TV and radio than it is to newspapers and other like publications. . . . What kind of First Amendment would best serve our needs as we approach the 21st century may be an open question. But the old-fashioned First Amendment that we have is the Court's only guideline.[51]

## Future of First Amendment Rights

Aside from concluding that a single standard should be applied to both print and broadcasting, Douglas also put his finger on an important question, one that leads to a postscript in this constitutional inquiry. What kind of a First Amendment does this country need in the future? That is an uncomfortable question because the performance of the Supreme Court so far has been less than satisfying in this area of the law. As yet the court has not provided a solid sense of just what the free press clause means.

The problem of the past is that the court never has attempted to confront the communications process as a whole. At times its analysis has focused on who was communicating, as in cases dealing with the privilege of news reporters[52]; at times the focus has been on content, as in the obscenity cases[53]; and at times the focus was on individual's right to know, as in recent commercial speech cases.[54] By shifting the focus around, it is possible even when identical issues are before the court to have different outcomes. Both *Red Lion* and *Miami Herald* were, after all, right-of-reply cases. No right attached in *Miami Herald* under an analysis that emphasized freedom to communicate; a right did attach in *Red Lion,* where the emphasis was placed on the public's right to know. The once seemingly viable "different standards for different media" reasoning facilitated the contradictory results. With that reasoning now being technologically undermined, it seems prudent to recall that the communications process is exactly that, a process. For there to be completed or actual communications, as Claude E. Shannon demonstrated in his classic diagram of the process,[55] there must be a source of information, transmission, and reception. Absent any one, there is no communication.

It may be argued that the Constitution does not reach all these elements. Conceivably the "press clause" can be read as meaning that publishers have a right to print whatever they like and that right exists in a vacuum. Yet this is hardly realistic. Even Justice Stewart, who takes the position that "The publishing business is . . . the only organized private business that is given explicit constitutional protection,"[56] recognizes by implication that publishers do not exist in a void. What they print is meaningless unless read. Otherwise, for Stewart, the guarantee would not serve "to create a fourth institution outside the Government as an additional check on the three official branches."[57]

Stewart's view raises a point that deserves some consideration. A democracy that worries about abuse of power certainly is well served by an additional check. But the notion of a Fourth Estate is not altogether trouble free. For one thing, it is becoming more and more difficult to say who is entitled to constitutional protection under the press clause. From a legal viewpoint, a graduate of Columbia University's School of Journalism who goes to work for the *New York Times* certainly is a full member of the Fourth Estate. That same person's classmate who joins CBS is almost certainly not. Behind this segregation is an outmoded belief that broadcasting and the press have embodied a different set of values. It used to be said that the line between broadcast news and broadcast entertainment was a very fine one. Today the same can be said about newspapers. Like broadcast stations before them, newspapers now are realizing that their profitability, and in some cases their survival, depends on sound business judgment. As a consequence editors no longer merely try to supply a diet of information that they believe an informed electorate needs. Now they are more responsive to the fact that their business must be sensitive to the market. Even the venerable *New York Times* has created "Weekend," "Home," and other special sections that some critics say are more like "all the news that's fit to sell" than in the *Times'* tradition of publishing "all the news that's fit to print."[58]

For those who champion a Fourth Estate, "supermarketing" information is a troubling trend in American journalism.[59] It is a trend, however, consistent with realities that even the biggest communications company of all, AT&T, has found in the new era of communications. That corporation is striving to transform its "century-old business from a supply-oriented business to a demand-oriented one."[60]

What we are witnessing then is a new communications market, a market where suppliers no longer can afford to take consumers for granted. Whether it is the marketplace of ideas that Holmes and Brandeis thought of, or the technological market that AT&T long has dominated, the communications marketplace is changing. The old-fashioned arrogant editor who informed the public as he saw fit today faces the same profound problem of readjustment as does the giant telephone monopoly that now must learn how to compete for customers.

Meanwhile the thrust of applied technology is to put the ability to communicate into more and more hands. Any person today with access to a Xerox copier has as much, nay more, publishing power than did Benjamin Franklin and his fellow colonial printers, for whose benefit the press clause was written. Any political candidate today may, moreover, find a bank of telephones or a computerized mailing list to be a greater communications asset than the editorial endorsement of a newspaper.

From a legal point of view, then, the ultimate issue goes beyond whether we need a First Amendment that protects broadcasting as fully as it does the press. The larger question is whether each form of communications should judicially be considered in isolation[61] or as part of a collection of competing forms of communications.

The question is not idle. The ability to communicate to masses of people is spreading beyond the "institutional media." Already, this development presents new legal questions. For example, the U.S. Supreme Court recently had before it a case in which the question was "whether the First Amendment . . . is violated by an order of the Public Service Commission of the State of New York that prohibits the inclusion in monthly electric bills of inserts discussing controversial issues of public policy."[62] The court held the prohibition to be unconstitutional.

But to reach that conclusion, Justice Lewis Powell, writing for the majority, had to distinguish *Red Lion*. It was necessary to say legally that *Red Lion* did not apply to political messages in billing envelopes, since the New York Public Service Commission had argued that *Red Lion* stood for the proposition that government commissions can exercise unusual authority over the communications carried out by the corporations that they regulate.

In deciding that a governmental body cannot prohibit a utility company from including political messages in billing envelopes, the Supreme Court gave added meaning to a new concept that might be called "corporate free speech."[63] But in distinguishing *Red Lion*, the Court preserved the old notion that the media still are sufficiently different to justify different legal standards. In effect the law has moved forward by extending First Amendment guarantees to a new class of communicators (corporations), but at the same time the law still preserves the old notion that the media are different enough to justify different legal standards. This notwithstanding the fact that all the trends—social, economic, and above all technological—cut the other way.

In sum the First Amendment has yet to catch up with the "second revolution" in communications. It is the kind of situation that brings to mind a comment by Justice Oliver Wendell Holmes: "It cannot be helped, it is as it should be, that the law is behind the times."[64]

## NOTES

1. *Red Lion Broadcasting Co. v. FCC,* 395 U.S. 367, 1969; *Miami Herald Publishing Co. v. Tornillo,* 418 U.S. 241, 1974.
2. A survey of privacy laws, including the Federal Privacy Act of 1974, has been prepared by David Seipp, "Privacy and Disclosure, Regulation of Information Systems," Publication P-75-8, (Program on Information Resources Policy: Harvard University, 1975). An overview of how the Copyright Act of 1976 relates to mass media can be found in Harvey L. Zuckerman and Martin J. Gaynes, *Mass Communications Law,* West Nutshell Series (St. Paul, Minn.: West, 1977), pp. 262–283.
3. A distinction of importance is between pure and applied technology. Technology by itself does not create a revolution in communications. While the inventions of yesteryear and modern day research and development projects certainly have said what was possible, it is *applied technology* that says what is feasible. And applications, in turn, have depended on many factors. Consider the case of the first medium of mass communications, the printing press. Four hundred years elapsed between Gutenberg's invention and the institutionalization of the mass newspaper, or "penny press" as it was initially called here in the United States. Why did it take so long to apply this new technology? Sociologist Daniel Lerner has offered these thoughts: "The answer is that the West was transforming its social order completely in order to absorb the innovation of printed information available to all who wanted it. Consider that this transformation involved at least three basic dimensions of any social process: (1) *literacy:* enough people had to learn to read to make a penny press feasible; (2) *income:* enough readers had to earn "disposable income" (a very modern concept) to make the penny press a paying proposition; (3) *motivation:* enough readers with an extra penny had to want to spend it on information rather than on cakes and ale or beer and skittles."

(Daniel Lerner, *Communications, Development, World Order,* Occasional Papers of the Edward R. Murrow Center of Public Diplomacy, September 15, 1978, p. 4).

4.  Senator Daniel Patrick Moynihan (D., N.Y.) drafted a bill, "The Foreign Surveillance Prevention Act," aimed at curbing Soviet eavesdropping in the United States by electronic means and under diplomatic immunity. (Senator Moynihan, Press Release, July 27, 1977).

5.  That government could regulate broadcasting in ways that were forbidden with respect to the press is not a judicial, but an executive and legislative innovation. For historical treatments on broadcasting and broadcast regulation see Eric Barnouw, *A History of Broadcasting in the United States,* vol. 1 (New York: Oxford University Press, 1966), and R.H. Coase, "The Federal Communications Commission," *Journal of Law and Economics* 2 (1959):1–40.

6.  The First Amendment was applied to the states through the due process clause of the Fourteenth Amendment in *Gitlow v. New York,* 268 U.S. 652 (1925).

7.  *Associated Press v. United States,* 326 U.S. 1 (1945)—holding that the antitrust laws can be applied against a news agency.

8.  Depending on the issue the U.S. Supreme Court has tended to follow either an absolute approach (see *Saia v. New York,* 334 U.S. 558) or a balancing approach (see *Konigsberg v. State Bar of Cal.,* 366 U.S. 36 [1961]) in the First Amendment area.

9.  *Schenck v. United States,* 249 U.S. 47 (1919).

10. *Abrams v. United States,* 250 U.S. 616 (1919) (Holmes and Brandeis dissenting). *Whitney v. California,* 247 U.S. 357 (1927) (Holmes and Brandeis concurring).

11. *United States v. Associated Press,* 52 F. Supp. 362, at 372 (S.D.N.Y. 1943) *aff'd.* See note 14.

12. *Miami Herald,* p. 258.

13. The Radio Act of 1927 created the Federal Radio Commission with power to issue broadcast licenses if the "public convenience, interest, or necessity will be served thereby." 44 Stat. 1162 (1927). The legislation followed a period in which then Secretary of Commerce Herbert Hoover unsuccessfully tried to bring some order to the allocation and use of frequencies. His efforts were thwarted in part by federal courts. *Hoover v. Intercity Radio Co.,* 286 Fed. 1003 (D.C. Cir. 1923)—holding that the Commerce Secretary was without authority to withhold or renew a license. *United States v. Zenith Radio Corp.,* 12 F. 2d 614 (7th Cir. 1926)—denying the secretary power to put restrictions on use of frequencies.

14. Historical roots of the "press clause" of the First Amendment are found in adverse reaction to the press licensing system that existed in England until Parliament refused to renew the Printing Act in 1695.

15.  48 Stat. 1064 (1934), as amended 47 U.S.C. 151 et seq. (1970).
16.  The Fairness Doctrine evolved out of a series of decisions by the FCC and subsequently was endorsed by the U.S. Congress in its 1959 Amendments to Section 315 (a) of the Communications Act (see note 6) P.L. 86–274, 73 Stat. 557. The doctrine amplifies on the "public interest" standard by providing that broadcasters "afford reasonable opportunity for the discussion of conflicting views on issues of public importance."
17.  *Red Lion,* p. 390.
18.  Ibid., p. 386.
19.  A trustee is not a true owner of property, but rather has duties and obligations to administer property for the benefit of others. The "property" in question here, the radio spectrum, is said to be an "inalienable possession of the people of the United States and their Government." S. 2930, 65 *Congressional Record* 5735 (1924).
20.  Jerome Barron, "Access to the Press—A New First Amendment Right," *Harvard Law Review* 80 (1967):1641. It is worth noting that although print and broadcasting are treating differently by the law in some respects, they do in fact share much in common. Private ownership is perhaps the most striking feature. Few countries in the world, even democracies, have placed broadcasting, as well as print, in the private sector.
21.  *Banzhaf v. FCC,* 132 U.S. App. D.C. 14, at 32–33, 405 F. 2 ed 1082, at 1100–1101 (1968), cert. denied, 396 U.S. 842 (1969).
22.  The *New York Times,* January 12, 1979, p. A1.
23.  See, e.g., Douglass Cater, "Toward a Public Philosophy of Government Media," in William L. Rivers and Michael J. Nyhan, eds., *Aspen Notebook on Government and the Media* (New York: Praeger, 1973), p. 6.
24.  Michael J. Robinson, "American Political Legitimacy in an Era of Electronic Journalism," in Douglass Cater and Richard Adler, eds., *Television as a Social Force: New Approaches to TV Criticism* (New York: Praeger, 1975), p. 97.
25.  *Columbia Broadcasting System Inc. v. Democractic National Committee* 412 U.S. 94, at N. 3, 152 (1973) (Douglas concurring).
26.  Ibid., p. 94.
27.  Bruce Owen, "The Role of Print in an Electronic Society, in Glen O. Robinson, ed., *Communications for Tomorrow: Policy Perspectives for the 1980s (New York: Praeger, 1978), p. 232.*
28.  *Red Lion,* p. 416.
29.  *Miami Herald,* pp. 256–257.
30.  *Columbia Broadcasting,* p. 159.
31.  "Cross-ownership" refers to common ownership of a newspaper(s)

and broadcast station(s) in the same market. Some 150 media combinations exist in 44 states. UPI, "News Media Oppose Court Order to Ban Cross-Ownerships," *New York Times,* November 22, 1977, p. 23.

32. *Columbia Broadcasting,* p. 161.
33. Robinson, "American Political Legitimacy in an Era of Electronic Journalism," p. 97.
34. *Columbia Broadcasting,* p. 93.
35. Owen, "The Role of Print in an Electronic Society," p. 233.
36. *Note on the Newspaper Industry,* Case No. 4-376-082 (Cambridge, Mass.: Harvard Graduate School of Business Administration, 1975), p. 4.
37. Ibid.
38. *Red Lion,* p. 388.
39. *United States v. Southwestern Cable Co.,* 392 U.S. 157 (1968).
40. Benno C. Schmidt, Jr., "Programming and Regulation of Mass Media," in Glen O. Robinson, ed., *Communications for Tomorrow: Policy Perspectives for the 1980s* (New York: Praeger, 1978), p. 213.
41. Owen, "The Role of Print in an Electronic Society," p. 242.
42. Ibid., p. 237.
43. Rex Winsbury, "Newspapers' Tactics for Teletext," *Intermedia* 6, (no. 1, February 1978):10. See also in the same issue: "A Chart of Teletext Systems," p. 12; "How the Post Office Wants to Use Viewdata," p. 13; and Edward W. Ploman, "Teletext Arrives—but What is Teletext?" p. 32.
44. Anthony Oettinger, Paul Berman, and William Read, *High and Low Politics: Information Resources for the 80s* (Cambridge, Mass.: Ballinger, 1977), pp. 1-146.
45. For an in-depth treatment of what has been called reformulation of telecommunications regulation, see G. Hamilton Loeb, "The Communications Act Policy Toward Competition: A Failure to Communicate," *Duke Law Journal* 30 (March 1978):1.
46. Robert G. Marbut is president and chief executive officer of Harte-Hanks Communications. The quotation is from Marbut, "The Future of Newspapers," Presentation to the 50th Production Management Conference of the American Newspaper Publishers Association Research Institute, St. Louis, Mo., June 8, 1978.
47. Owen, "The Role of Print in an Electronic Society," p. 242.
48. Narrowly read, *Columbia Broadcasting* is consistent with *Red Lion* since the holdings in both cases affirmed decisions made by the FCC. For his part, Chief Justice Warren E. Burger viewed the FCC's rule-making process as a dynamic one and he cautioned his colleagues against freezing that process with a constitutional holding. *Columbia*

Broadcasting, p. 132. In effect Burger reinforced a line of reasoning taken in *Red Lion,* where the Court put heavy emphasis on the fact that the Congress had chosen to regulate broadcasting through a federal commission.

49.  *Miami Herald,* p. 258.

50.  Absent recognition of convergence, the courts are likely to continue to perpetuate the two-track approach in the mistaken belief that meaningful distinctions between the two media are still to be found. See Judge Quinn Tamm's comments in *National Broadcasting Company, Inc. v. FCC,* 516 F. 2d 1101 (1974), p. 1193.

51.  *Columbia Broadcasting,* pp. 148, 160.

52.  See *Branzburg v. Hayes,* 408 U.S. 665 (1972).

53.  See *Roth v. United States,* 354 U.S. 476 (1957).

54.  See *Bigelow v. Virginia,* 421 U.S. 809 (1975).

55.  Shannon's diagram is reproduced in John R. Pierce, "Communication," *Scientific American* 227 (no. 3, September 1972):32.

56.  Justice Stewart spoke a few months after *Miami Herald* at Yale where he commented on the role of the press in American society. The excerpt is contained in Benno C. Schmidt, Jr., *Freedom of the Press vs. Public Access* (New York: Praeger, 1976), p. 32.

57.  Ibid., p. 239.

58.  For a good discussion of why the *New York Times* has been altering its traditional product, see "The *New New York Times,*" *Newsweek,* April 25, 1977, p. 84.

59.  Fergus M. Bordewich, "Supermarketing the Newspaper," *Columbia Journalism Review* 16 (no. 3, September/October 1977):30.

60.  Speech by Charles L. Brown, then chairman-elect of AT&T, *Telecommunications Reports* 44 (no. 47, November 27, 1978):8.

61.  Lee C. Bollinger, Jr., "Freedom of the Press and Public Access: Toward a Theory of Partial Regulation of the Mass Media," *Michigan Law Review* 75 (November 1976):1–42.

62.  *Consolidated Edison Company of New York, Inc. v. Public Service Commission of New York,* 40 CCH S. Ct. Bull. B3239, 1980.

63.  The basis of the "corporate free speech" concept is found in *First National Bank of Boston v. Bellotti,* 435 U.S. 765 (1978). In this case, the U.S. Supreme Court held that "the inherent worth of the speech in terms of its capacity for informing the public does not depend upon the identity of its source, whether corporation, association, union, or individual." (Ibid., p. 777.)

64.  Oliver Wendell Holmes, *Collected Legal Papers* (New York: Harcourt, Brace, 1921), p. 231.

# 11 VIDEOTEX AND THE NEWSPAPER INDUSTRY: THREAT OR OPPORTUNITY?

*Benjamin M. Compaine*

There are at least two approaches by which one could introduce a discussion on newspapers and videotex. The first option begins:

Newspaper publishers beware. The era of the electronic newspaper is upon us. Soon, consumers at home will be reading their news, getting their classified ads, checking the weather, and ordering merchandise from local department stores via their television sets. Soon, that monster printing press in your plant will be fit only for an exhibit in the Smithsonian.

A second alternative starts:

Those blue sky futurists predicting the demise of newspapers clearly do not understand the nature of the print medium. A newspaper on the television screen will never replace the ink-on-newsprint product. That is because, unlike the television set, the newspaper is portable. You can clip out articles. It is easy to use. It is cheap. People will not find it very comfortable to spend much time reading text off a television screen—it hurts the eyes. And the graphics necessary for display advertising are very primitive compared to print.

319

As with many controversial issues, the future of the newspaper is not so clear cut as either of these scenarios would have us believe. Newspaper publishers and others would be wrong to ignore the threats posed by electronic delivery of content to consumers, and by doing so might also preclude themselves from taking advantage of real opportunities. At the same time, those entrepreneurs who see electronic newspapers as the key to pay private college tuition for their 18-year-olds had better be looking for scholarships.

## VIDEOTEX TODAY

The label that has been applied to the "thing" that may be the electronic replacement of or supplement to the traditional newspaper is *videotex.* For some reason there is no final "t." Some use the term *viewdata* instead. There is also something that looks the same on the screen, called *teletext* (note the final "t"). The latter is essentially a one-way transmission, in which the viewer "grabs" the desired page next time it comes around the loop. In videotex, the data stays in the computer until it is specifically requested by the user. It is possible to create a teletext system that has most of the features of a videotex system.

The current state of thinking about videotex is that it must do more than merely parrot the pages of newspapers. Besides news, weather, sports, and so on, all the systems tested include interactive transactional services. This means combining some advertisements with advantage provided by the telephone or cable link, making every home a potential place for "point-of-sale" purchase decisions. Thus users interested in a product or service advertised on the videotex system can order them immediately on-line. This is not really revolutionary: the use of toll-free telephone numbers and other mail-order devices is old hat. Most systems also include the participation of one or more banks to provide on-line banking for almost any banking service other than taking deposits and dishing out cash. The latter still requires taking a trip somewhere.

Videotex got its real start in England in 1979 with a system called Prestel. Developed by the British telephone authority, it was seen as a way to get greater volume on the vastly underutilized British residential telephone wire. The Prestel people predicted 100,000 residential subscribers by the end of 1980. By the end of 1982, they still could count home subscribers in four figures. Business users, such as travel agents who could view train and plane schedules on-line, found greater applications. As is often the case when selling information, business is willing to pay its own way, while consumers are used to having their information content subsidized by advertisers. (Of consumer mass media, only books are typically totally user supported.)

The French and Canadians were also ahead of the United States in playing around with videotex systems. For the most part they concentrated on developing the technology for storage, manipulation, and display of the images. The French version is called Antiope, and the Canadian package is Telidon. A lively debate over which system is best fills up thick volumes of newsletters and reports from standards committees. The French government is way out in front in pushing its videotex system as a matter of national policy.

United States companies have, wisely it seems, taken a far more deliberate approach to jumping into videotex. In the fray longest and deepest is Knight-Ridder Newspapers, by some measures the largest newspaper chain in the country. Using a system developed largely by American Telephone & Telegraph (AT&T), they have field tested a system they have dubbed Viewtron. They expected to start selling this commercially in Southern Florida in late 1983. Initially consumers will be asked to pay $25 or $30 monthly. Viewtron reportedly will have 75,000 "pages"—read "screensful"—of content available on day one.

Knight-Ridder is selling franchises for Viewtron. Among those who have bought in are *The Boston Globe* and Capital Cities Communications. In exchange for a six-figure fee, Viewtron partners get to see the research data from the trials. If they start their own local service, Knight-Ridder will get 25 percent of the take for providing the system and some of the nationally based content. Looking for advertiser support, Viewtron issued its first rate card early in 1983. Fees are based on the number of pages of advertising created, plus a monthly storage fee per page and other charges. Viewtron also takes a 1 percent commission on goods ordered through the system.

Also in the game is Times Mirror Company, publisher of *The Los Angeles Times* and *Newsday*, among other newspapers. It has run trials in South California, trying out both telephone and cable-connected versions. Times Mirror is also signing up other newspaper publishers, including *The Washington Post*, to buy into its "gateway" service. Newspaper companies have made more limited excursions into the videotex waters. A.H. Belo, publisher of the *Dallas Morning News* and Capital Cities' *Fort Worth Star-Telegram* tried simple text-only services in 1981 and 1982 for short periods before finding them not financially viable. Eleven newspapers, including *The Washington Post* and the *Middlesex* (Mass.) *News* (a Harte-Hanks newspaper) contributed some content to CompuServe, a time-sharing service that made portions of the text of these papers available to people with personal computers. By videotex standards, these were primitive efforts.

As with the British experience, electronically delivered newspaper-like services have been most successful when aimed at the business market. Dow Jones' News Retrieval Service, reportedly at 60,000 subscribers and growing, provides the requisite financial data, supplemented by a growing base of sports, weather, movie reviews, shopping services, and other consumer features. It is text only, no color—a much ballyhooed feature of the other videotex services—and is fairly expensive (usage fees start at $0.15 per minute and go up, depending on time of day and information needed). Advertising has not been sought, nor have there been any announcements that it will be.

The most advanced and expensive electronic newspaper comes not from a publisher but from a supplier of raw material, Mead, the paper manufacturer. Its Nexis service has a full text service that goes back as far as 1978 for *The Washington Post, Newsweek, U.S. News & World Report, The Economist*, AP, and UPI, and, since mid-1983, *The New York Times*, among dozens of other print publications. Nexis, however, has been designed as a research tool, so it never includes the most current issue of the publications. And it also costs about $1.00 per minute or more to use, plus rental of a special terminal.

CBS and AT&T are other nonnewspaper publishers engaged in videotex. They are conducting a trial called Venture One in Ridgewood, New Jersey, which entered its second phase in 1983. High on the list of objectives is finding a legitimate way to involve advertisers. At least fifteen clients of the J. Walter Thompson agency are involved. According to Thompson senior vice president Norman Varney, "The trick . . . is to give consumers real information that can lead to a purchase of [its] product." CBS expects the service to sell for between $15 and $30, plus the cost of the terminal.

Cox Cable Communications, a large cable system operator, has a videotex system called Index, which it expects to provide over a channel on some of its cable franchises.

Clearly, there is activity. Some is motivated by fear, some by a sense of opportunity. Some participants may make it if they hold on long enough or if their services have been designed to operate at relatively low cost. It is not cheap to be a pioneer. One publicly quoted account reports that Knight-Ridder spent $20 million on its Viewtron trial. That is probably a low figure for its total investment to date.

## CRUCIAL FORCES AND TRENDS

There are at least a baker's half dozen major forces that will interact and shape the outcome of electronic information services. They are identified below, with only minimal elaboration.

*Regulation and Methods of Transmission.*    Videotex was initially designed to use the telephone network. Its advantage is that it is already in place, it is a two-way system, it is switched (that is, any terminal is capable of addressing any other terminal), and it is reliable. Its current drawbacks are that it handles data at relatively slow transmission speeds, which is a problem for improved graphics. It is also in the midst of a massive structural change, mandated by both court and FCC rulings, which may produce uncertainty in the immediate future over the pricing of its components and the ability of each region to offer consistent quality and services.

Cable, on the other hand, is a possible alternative. Its strength is its high transmission rate, which allows fast creation of text and graphics. It is also untariffed, so cable operators can bundle the cost of the content with the price of the transmission channel. However, only the newest cable systems were installed for two-way service, and few systems were built to the technological standard necessary for the transmission of accurate and reliable data. Cable operators also may have to look over their shoulders at state utility commissioners. These regulators may find the notion of regulating charges for telephone company data transmission, while having no say in charges for doing the same thing over cable wires, a discrepancy that will require adjustment.

*Standardization and Compatibility.*  So far, just about every videotex trial has used its own proprietary system. That means, for example, a Knight-Ridder customer could not use the same equipment for the Times Mirror service. There are both software and hardware problems. There has been talk of a "North American Standard" for videotex, but it remains more promise than reality. There are ways to build "smarts" into computers, either at the user's end or in a central location, to make nonstandard systems compatible. But this has a price, either in the cost of equipment, in time for access, or in technical glitches. Lack of easy connection from system to system confuses consumers and delays widespread acceptance.

*Physical Delivery.*   Much of the smart money is saying that videotex will be driven in large measure by the transactional service. We can look at trends such as increases in both spouses working and the strength of catalog sales for background. But the delivery of goods ordered via a videotex system, much as with an order form or telephone call to a catalog seller, requires a reliable parcel delivery service. This might be United Parcel Service, or the U.S. Postal Service, or others. But factors that affect the price of physical delivery, including energy cost and labor contracts, may play a role in the feasibility of mass appeal transaction services. (There is also the problem of accepting delivery of parcels if both spouses are working.)

*Cost of Paper, Energy, Digital Storage and Transmission.* Paper manufacturing is one of the most energy intensive operations. This accounts in large part for the rapid escalation of paper prices in the last decade. The physical delivery of printed materials is also energy intensive. In the short term, the cost of oil at least has been down from its recent historic highs. Nonetheless the long-term outlook is for continued increases in energy cost, compared to a decline in computer storage costs (they have declined at a compound rate of 25 percent annually for more than thirty years). The cost of telecommunication will be partly the function of political decisions at state public utility commissions and other government jurisdictions.

*Degree of Advertiser Support.*   As noted, most consumer media are largely or completely advertiser supported. A daily newspaper costs the reader under $10 per month as a result. It is likely that it will take some time for advertisers to figure out how to use videotex in a way different from existing media. One limitation, for example, is the relatively crude graphics of even the best systems. There are some technological fixes possible, although they remain to be proven. Warner-Amex Cable has a prototype version of a system that combines full motion video using videodisc players with videotex. Use of this system, however, demands at this point a cable or other broadband transmission into the home.

*Technological Developments.* It would be a mistake to presume that we have reached the state of the art of videotex. It is more likely that we are at the Model-T stage. Today's display screens for the consumer market do not produce text images suited to long use. Moreover, the cathode ray tube is inappropriate for portability. Many people cannot type, so depending on a keyboard for data entry is a problem for a potential mass medium. But work is being done to produce higher resolution screens, at least to the standard of a printed newspaper page. Flat screens with low power consumption are in the laboratories, and over the next decade or two we should expect to see them improve and decline in price. Methods besides keyboards are used for certain types of input. Inexpensive computer chips that can recognize the instructions of the human voice are among the most promising.

*Development of Cultural Pulls and Resistance.* Use of print has developed into a culturally familiar habit over centuries. We are comfortable with it. It is quite "user friendly." On the other hand, we see the phenomenon of children playing video games today. The same children are becoming increasingly familiar with microcomputers in school and at home. Unlike the older television generation, which has used television as a passive entertainment medium, today's youngsters look at a video screen as a display format that is theirs to manipulate, with joystick, keypad, or whatever else comes along. By the time today's ten-year-olds reach adulthood, they may find that the use of video-output information of all sorts will be quite natural. Already millions of adults working as travel agents, billing clerks, and secretaries use computer-connected video display terminals. How will they react to the prospect of using a similar device in their homes for their own information and entertainment purposes?

## One Scenario

One possible scenario for the future is based on technology that already exists but is still impractical because of its cost at this time.

The newspaper may be produced just as it is today, up to the point of the press. Pages are laid out on a computer terminal. But instead of making plates, rolling the press, and loading papers on trucks for delivery, a command is given to send the complete newspaper, via telephone lines, to memory modules in subscribers' homes. This could be done at night. In the morning, subscribers plug the module into their battery-powered flat-screen monitor. They can then read the paper, full page, complete with graphics and ads, at the breakfast table, on the train, or by the fireside in the evening. Those who demand the printed version may also be able to buy that, but at a premium price.

### CHOOSE YOUR CONCLUSION

There are elements of truth in the first option at the start of this chapter. There is reason to believe that some of us will have the option of receiving much of the content of today's newspapers—and books, magazines, direct mail circulars, and more—via systems that use a television screen for display. Among the major unknowns, however, are when they will be available to a mass audience, at what price, how easy they will be to use, and why consumers would want to use them in place of the familiar newspapers. The answers will determine the extent and rate of market adoption.

Those who proclaim the robustness of print, on the other hand, do have a substantial body of history to support their view. Thomas Edison predicted that film and records would make textbooks obsolete. Others ballyhooed television from its earliest days as a revolutionary force in education and high culture. They were wrong and print has thrived. Nonetheless, the latter-day Luddites may be shortsighted.

One thing is certain, however. We will not wake up one morning and find print newspapers gone and electronic newspapers in their place. Change is likely to come piecemeal. Technology, economic shifts, and cultural adaptation cast a long shadow. Fortunately we have innovators who will take financial risks, with the hope of being the first in a growing market. But there is room for many others to join in as developments sort themselves out. Only those who ignore the signs of change will be left behind.

# IV LOOKING AHEAD

# 12 THE NEW LITERACY: Or How I Stopped Worrying and Learned to Love Pac-Man

*Benjamin M. Compaine*

I believe books will never disappear. It is impossible for it to happen. Of all of mankind's diverse tools, undoubtedly the most astonishing are his books. . . . If books were to disappear, history would disappear. So would men.—*Jorge Luis Borges*[1]

Reading and writing will become obsolete skills.—*Sol Cornberg*[2]

On any given workday, perhaps 7 million employed people get paid to spend their time in front of a television screen. They are not part of a Nielsen survey, but rather are reading from these terminals material produced by a computer. These people are airline reservation clerks and travel agents, stockbrokers, newspaper reporters and editors, catalog showroom order takers, and customer service representatives at telephone, utility, and other sorts of firms. Among the 7 million there are secretaries and, to a small but increasing extent, there are executives. They clearly have many different jobs and levels of responsibility, but all share one trait: To an increasing degree they are using the computer for some portion of their information storage and retrieval. And instead of using a computer information specialist as an intermediary, as they would have done only a few years ago, they are interacting directly with the computer. That means that much of what they read appears on a video display terminal—VDT— instead of in the ink-on-paper format.

This chapter is about the implications of the skills these workers are developing. It is about the possible significance of the $8 billion spent on video games in 1981, more than what was spent on movie theater admissions and record purchases combined. It is about the phenomenon of using microcomputers in elementary and secondary schools, often at the insistence of children and their parents before the curriculum supervisors know what is happening. It is about computer summer camps for kids. It concerns the "wired" university.

Our objective here is to describe several of the forces and trends at work in society, only in part a function of technology, and the implications of these for traditional concepts of literacy. Central to this discussion is the role of the engine of this change, the computer.

This chapter does *not* predict the future. Nor does it advocate a course of action; it neither salutes nor denigrates the idea of a new literacy. But there is evidence that change is clearly in the wind. This chapter, then, suggests that factors may impinge on future developments in reading and literacy and that those who consider themselves to be educated and, above all, literate, will want to take heed.

## THE OLD LITERACY

We cannot talk about the future of reading or the book without reference to their fellow traveler, literacy. Each generation tends to assume literacy is static, petrified, as it were, in their moment of time. Literacy, however, is dynamic, a bundle of culturally relevant skills. The appropriate skills for literacy, moreover, have changed over time. Before the written record came into wide use (in England starting in the last half of the eleventh century), the oral tradition predominated. To be literate meant to be able to compose and recite orally. In the twelfth century, to make a "record" of something meant to bear oral witness, not produce a document for others to read. For example, even if a treaty was in the form of sealed letters, "both parties also named witnesses who were to make legal record . . . in court if necessary." Despite the existence of written documents, "the spoken word was the legally valid record."[3]

Furthermore, at that time to be *litteratus* meant to know Latin, rather than having the specific ability to read and write. To be sure, the vernacular replaced Latin for discourse. But even then, because of the difficulty of writing with a quill on parchment or a stylus on wax-coated tablets, writing was considered a special skill that "was not automatically coupled with the ability to read."[4] The most common way of committing words to writing in twelfth-century England was by dictating to a scribe, who was a craftsman, and not necessarily himself able to compose. Thus reading and dictating were typically paired, rather than reading and writing.

Although the basic skills of modern literacy—reading and writing—had become relatively widespread in England by the mid-nineteenth century, the literati of the period seemed to impose a greater barrier for admission to full-fledged literacy. It was not merely the ability to read, they said, for example, but the reading of the "right" materials that separated the truly literate from the great unwashed. How, if at all, they asked, did the spread of the printed word contribute to the spiritual enrichment and intellectual enlightenment of the English nation? "More people were reading than ever before; but in the opinion of most commentators, they were reading the wrong things, for the wrong reasons, and in the wrong way."[5]

All this is grist for the notion that today's standards of literacy are rooted in the past, yet at the same time should not be presumed to be the standards for the future. For example, at a meeting of "experts" convened to discuss the status of books and reading in 1982, several participants indicated that when they referred to the status of "the book," they had in mind great literature and intellectual enrichment. They were not referring to the 38,000 other titles (out of about 40,000 published annually) that range from cookbooks and how-to books to Harlequin romances. Thus they were carrying on the tradition of the nineteenth-century literati, who idealized their own past. They felt that things were far different—and infinitely better—in the old days.

Similarly, the library, today's bastion of the book and reading, has not always been held in such high regard by the literati. Free libraries for the common people in England were viciously criticized by the reading elite. Instead of encouraging "habits of study and self-improvement, they catered to the popular passion for light reading—above all, for fiction."[6] Indeed, one librarian told a meeting in 1879 that "schoolboys or students who took to novel reading to any great extent never made much progress in after life."[7] The irony of attitudes such as this should not be lost to the critics of video games as a corrupting influence on today's schoolboys or students.

## THE NEW LITERACY

"To describe our business as one that traffics in paper, ink, and type is to miss the point entirely. Our real enterprise is ideas and information." A quote from a futurist? Perhaps. This is the strategic outlook of W. Bradford Wiley, chairman of John Wiley & Sons, one of the oldest publishing houses in New York. It was the publisher of Herman Melville, Nathaniel Hawthorne, and Edgar Allen Poe and most of the first American editions of English art historian and critic John Ruskin. Wiley adds, "Until now, our medium has been the bound book; tomorrow our medium will expand to include [computer-stored] data banks and video discs."[8]

What evidence is there that Wiley is onto something? First, he has at least implicitly recognized that Marshall McLuhan was off base. The medium, by and large, is *not* the message. The message is the content and the medium is the way it is conveyed and displayed. *Content*— ideas, knowledge, story, information—is the work of an author, a producer, a photographer. Technology, history, and even politics play a role in how this content is processed and the format in which it is ultimately displayed. *Process* incorporates the gathering, handling, storage, and transmission of the content; it may involve typewriters, computers, file cabinets; telephone lines, broadcasting towers, printing presses; and trucks and retail stores. *Format* is the manner of display—such as ink-on-paper, sound from a vibrating speaker cone, images on a cathode ray tube, light projected through a film, and so on.[9] Thus the content may be quite independent of process and format—the medium.

This chapter, for example, was written at a standard typewriter keyboard. But instead of paper as the format, the letters appeared on a green television screen. Although you are now reading this in a conventional ink-on-paper format, the process for creating this bound version may be quite different from that used only ten or twenty years ago. Computerized phototypesetting equipment has substantially replaced all the old Linotype machines that used to produce lead slugs for galleys. Moreover, there is no technological, or perhaps even economic reason, to keep subscribers to a journal from reading articles like this chapter the same way this was written—on a video screen. The major barrier at this may be cultural: Most of us have been brought up with print on paper. Many adults would today recoil at the thought of losing the feel and portability of printed volumes. But, as Wiley indicated, print is no longer the only rooster in the barnyard.

Solid trends support Wiley's view. One is the pervasive and perhaps long run impact of video games. In short order, these have gone from barroom novelties to a worldwide phenomenon. In 1976 Atari's sales were $39 million; in 1982 they were about $2.0 billion. Americans spent about 1 billion in 1982 on cartridges for home video games, and they dropped more than 30 billion quarters into video game machines. That money is coming from somewhere, most likely from the implicit budget people have for other media and entertainment. This includes movie admissions, records, and to some extent, books.

Even if the video game craze itself is a fad, it nonetheless may have considerable culture significance, much as the dime novel or penny press had in earlier eras. For the first time, it has made the video tube into something other than a passive format for the masses. Heretofore, only a handful of specialists, mostly computer programmers and some designers, used VDTs as an interactive medium. The rest of the world sat back and watched on their television tube what others provided.

Moreover, while critics of video games decry the presumed ill effects of the video game parlors, much as their nineteenth-century counterparts lamented the coming of literacy for the common reader, they may well prove to be myopic regarding the nature of the games themselves. As with much great literature, which can be appreciated on several levels of understanding, video games can be viewed on one level as simply entertainment. But in his book *How to Master Home Video Games*, Harvard undergraduate Tom Hirschfeld described these games as presenting players with a challenge. He notes that those who become the best at it are those who figure out the pattern programmed into the computer. The game players are becoming, almost painlessly, computer literate. Without becoming computer experts, they may be intuitively learning the strengths and limitations of computer logic. The U.S. Army, which must train large numbers of youngsters fresh from the video game rooms, has quickly understood the implication of the games. They have already contracted for training exercises using video-game-like lessons played on microcomputers. The schools will no doubt follow.

The home video games are actually specialized personal computers. They have made consumers familiar with the concept of a computerized console that plugs into a video tube. All that a computer adds is a keyboard. There were about 1.5 million personal desktop computers in place by the end of 1981, with about 500,000 of these in homes. The retail price for a real, programmable computer has fallen to under $100 with the Timex/Sinclair 1000. As a result, estimates indicate that the number of home computers tripled by the end of 1982. Thus, unlike the miserable failure of computerized education in the 1960s, when expensive computers were imposed from the top, the current era has seen the development of grass-roots interest in having microcomputers in the schools. It is the children and their parents who are often in the forefront of this effort, with local PTAs holding bake sales and the like to raise the money when school districts are pinched for funds. (In the past, some of that effort went to buying books for the school library.)

Thus, although educators are still concerned primarily with how students learn from print, today's young people spend more time (about twenty-eight hours weekly by one study) using electronic devices, like television and electronic games, than with print (about twenty-five hours). Moreover, most of the discretionary time is spent with the electronic medium, while most of the time spent with printed material is involuntary.[10] Together with the video game trend, this suggests that the school children of today are developing a new set of skills that may lead to a different standard for literacy.

But while much of the focus is on the kids, what of the 7 million or more adults working with VDTs as part of their daily routine? Already using a keyboard and terminal in the workplace, how will they approach the prospect of adopting similar tools at home to retrieve and manipulate content? Besides home computers, there are a few such opportunities already to retrieve and manipulate content, with a great many more in prospect. Services such as those offered by CompuServe Information Service and Source Telecomputing have already offered portions of newspapers such as *The New York Times* and *The Los Angeles Times* via computer to home terminals, in addition to a wide range of other types of information. Book publisher Houghton Mifflin has produced an interactive videodisc version of Roger Tory Peterson's venerable bird identification books.

Three videotex services, Oracle, Ceefax, and Prestel, have been commercially available in Great Britain since 1980.[11] Prestel, the most ambitious, has been slow to achieve much popular interest, perhaps because of its cost, its strangeness, and the method required for users to get access to its voluminous information stores. Nonetheless, several videotex services, in the prototype stage in the United States so far in the 1980s, may well be made available commercially by traditional publishing firms. These include the Times Mirror Company (publisher of newspapers, books, and magazines), Knight-Ridder Newspapers (publisher of newspapers and books), and CBS, Inc. (which in addition to being the largest television network also owns Holt, Rinehart, & Winston publishers and many well-known magazines). While the services offered by these firms are likely to tie together home terminals with large computers by telephone lines, the country's largest book and magazine publisher, Time Inc., has also tested a text-on-the-video-screen service to be delivered via cable.

Not lost on the traditional publishers is the fact that nonpublishers are getting into the act as well. Mead Corporation, one of the largest paper manufacturers, is also one of the most successful electronic publishers. On its Nexis service, it offers the full text of articles from *The Washington Post; Newsweek; U.S. News & World Report; Business Week*; UPI, Associated Press, and Reuters news services; the *Encyclopaedia Brittanica*, and scores of other publications. The company's Lexis service is known by most lawyers and used by many. It provides nearly unlimited access to tens of thousands of laws and cases, at the federal, state, and international levels, research that often required days of work using books in the library. These services can be accessed by users who have received very little special training. Although the cost today restricts Nexis and Lexis to use in institutions, over time, similar services may become as inexpensive as today's mainstream media.

The interest in electronic publishing is motivated by more than a mere fascination with technological toys. Some significant economic trends are involved. The price of the paper used in book and magazine publishing has jumped substantially since the early 1970s, following years of little increase. The cost of newsprint, used by newspaper publishers, jumped 200 percent between 1970 and 1981, well over twice the rate of the increase for all commodities. In large measure these huge increases reflect the high energy component in the manufacture of paper. Moreover, the physical distribution of printed material, especially newspapers, is highly energy intensive. These cost trends contrast dramatically with the costs for computer-stored information, which have been declining at about 25 percent annually for the last thirty years. (The magnitude of this is illustrated by the rough calculation that if the price of a Rolls Royce had decreased in proportion to that of computer storage, a Rolls Royce would cost about $2.50 today.) The outlook for the foreseeable future is for continued similar decreases in cost.

As a preliminary indicator of the changing demand for new information skills in the workplace, Carolyn Frankel, a researcher with Harvard's Program on Information Resources Policy, surveyed the help wanted ads in *The New York Times* for the same June day for every year from 1977 through 1982. She counted all jobs or skills in those ads that mentioned some "computer literacy" skill, such as word processing, programming, or data entry. In 1977, 5.8 percent of the want ads specified those skills. The percentage increased regularly to 1982, when 10.3 percent of the jobs listed required such skills. Perhaps of equal significance is the way these jobs were described. Earlier in the period the ads were for specific jobs that implied a computer skill, such as "Wang operator" or "word processor." By 1982 conventional job titles such as secretary specified the required skills as "experience with word processing" or "knowledge of Sabre" (a computer system for travel agents). From this apparent trend we might conclude that as the new technology becomes more commonplace and the skills in it more widespread, the skills become incorporated into traditional jobs. For one analogy, when the power saw was a novelty, a building contractor might have sought out power saw operators. But by the time most carpenters were expected to have some familiarity with this tool, builders again began to seek out carpenters who had, among other skills, knowledge of the power saw.

In 1977 none of the help wanted advertisements for travel agents in *The New York Times* on the day surveyed mentioned any sort of computer skill; in 1980, one-fifth mentioned a computer-related skill. By 1982, 71 percent required familiarity with such skills, paralleling the implementation of computer reservations services by the industry. Similarly, though less dramatically, the number of bookkeeper jobs requiring computer-related skills doubled to 24 percent from 1977 to 1982. And the proportion of secretary/typist want ads that required word processing skills went from zero in 1977 to 15 percent by 1982. The number of jobs that were labeled "word processing" or requested word processing ability increased eightfold in that period, despite the recession in 1982 and a lower level of help wanted ads overall.

The impact of all this in the workplace will be visible, if not profound. Whereas there is about $25,000 of capital invested for every worker in a manufacturing setting, until recently there has been only about $4,000 in capital for every office—or knowledge—worker. But that may change soon. In 1980 even an information-intensive company such as Aetna Life & Casualty had only one video terminal for each six employees. By 1985 they expect to have one terminal for every two employees. The ubiquity of these terminals and the increased familiarity workers will have with them may result in expanded application, such as electronically transmitted and stored "mail" both within an office and from remote office sites, including overseas offices.

There are other indications that suggest that we are in the midst of a fundamental change in the way we receive and process information. In Ottawa, Canada a taxi service has eliminated the crackling radio heretofore used to dispatch taxis, replacing it with a video screen in the cab on which the messages flash. When the driver is called, a buzzer sounds and a fare's location is printed on the screen. Since no other driver gets that message, no one can beat him or her to the fare. The head of one cab company using the system likes it because he complained that voice dispatching caused noise and confusion.

Department stores and toy stores now carry computers, taking them out of the realm of hobbyist devices. This means that consumers do not have to go into the threatening territory of a specialty store. This has coincided with the computer manufacturers' taking prime time television commercials, featuring celebrities such as Bill Cosby and Dick Cavett, to further demystify their product.

Meanwhile, centers of higher learning have been using computers in the liberal arts. Classics scholars at Princeton are using a computer to help study Virgil. The program quickly scans the text to pick out passages that contain the same word used in different context. Users claim this reduces the drudgery and allows them more time to study the meaning. Similar analytical techniques have been applied to the Bible and Shakespeare at Dartmouth College. Apparently, students are integrating this technology into their academic lives as easily as they did the simpler calculator in the last decade.[12]

## COMBINING THE OLD AND THE NEW

Historically, the development of a literacy has gone through a series of identifiable stages. Starting with specialists, literacy then begins to have a wider impact on institutions as it becomes the preferred medium of business, culture, and politics. Finally it becomes so pervasive that even the masses are considered handicapped without it. Thus we could trace modern notions of literacy from eleventh-century England in the movement from reliance on spoken words to written records, first in the Church and then in political institutions; to the introduction of the printing press in the fifteenth century; and finally to the development of the newspaper and mass-consumed book along with popular education in the nineteenth century.

History also provides suggestions that one does not have to be fully literate to participate in literacy. For example, one measure of changing literacy in the twelfth and thirteenth centuries in England was possession of a seal. In the reign of Edward the Confessor, only the king possessed a seal to authenticate documents. By the reign of Edward I (1307), even serfs were required by statute to have one.[13] In colonial times in the United States, signing one's name was skill enough to be called literate.

In the thirty-five or so years since the development of modern computers, we might identify trends similar to the much slower advance of traditional literacy. At first computers were strictly for a priestly class that could read and write in the tongue of computer machine language. All users of computers had to depend on this group of initiates. As computers became more widespread and their application more pervasive, they began to have a greater impact on business and social institutions. The languages (COBOL, FORTRAN, BASIC) evolved into something closer to the vernacular, so that more people were able to learn to read and write computer language.

Today we are perhaps at the threshold of an era where the computer is becoming simple and inexpensive enough that the masses can use it without having to understand how it works. They can thus participate in computer literacy without necessarily being computer literate. That may come in time, as the computer becomes as commonplace as the book. Yet if we look at the computer as a tool, it may be no more necessary for the mass of people to understand how a computer works than one needs to understand the mechanics of the internal combustion engine to be able to drive a car. (This suggests a nice parallel. In the 1950s, when the automobile was king, many boys were born with a "wrench in their hand." Today, we see kids barely teenagers playing around with RAM chips in much the say way.)

## IMPLICATIONS FOR READING AND THE BOOK

It would be foolish, though perhaps fun, to speculate on the long-term societal impacts that may grow out of the trends identified here.

As some guru may have once said, "Predicting is a hazardous occupation, especially when it deals with the future." Moreover, while this paper has tried to identify some forces and trends relative to literacy and reading, there are other cultural, political, and technological trends that have not been included or even recognized as yet.

In the long term it is possible, even probable, that the computer, combined with modern communications facilities, will be named by historians of the future as a fundamental milestone for civilization, out of which many changes will be traced. What those changes will be cannot be foretold. It is difficult enough to understand the implications of our own historical antecedents. As explained by Elizabeth Eisenstein, for example, "It is one thing to describe how methods of book production changed after the mid-15th century. . . . It is another thing to decide how access to a greater abundance or variety of written records affected ways of learning, thinking, and perceiving among literate elites."[14]

In the near term, we might profitably think about the implications of computer skills as additional proficiencies to the bundle we call literacy. Note that the reference is to computer skills being added to, not replacements for, existing skills. Reading and writing will continue to be essential. Computer memory may replace some paper and file drawers. But we will still have to compose sentences for a documentary format. And although the text may appear on screen, it must still be read, and, of course, understood. Thus the written word must be taught and learned. Later, however, writing, meaning physically composing with pen in hand or fingers on keyboard, may become less necessary. Although still far from perfected, work on voice recognition by computers is proceeding rapidly. Already today an increasing number (based on sales of dictating machines) of busy people dictate their letters, memos, and even books onto audio tape for later transcription by someone else. Ironically this harkens back to the medieval era when the educated composed orally and scribes made the written record. With reliable voice recognition computers, we could return to such an era of oral literacy.

There is even a greater likelihood of computer-generated voice synthesis. Thus instead of the output from a computer coming as text on a screen or a printer, it could be by voice. It is unlikely that this form would totally replace reading, in that we can assimilate information much faster with our eyes than with our ears.

Even that assertion is subject to question, however. The current adult generation, raised on print and the book, have a close cultural identity with it. We have *learned* how to use it: how to skim, to rapidly use an index. We associate certain pleasant emotions with the tactile sensation of the book. As one skeptic put it, could we imagine curling up in front of a fire with a Tolstoi novel on the video screen?

But these are largely cultural biases. They are learned. The kids today playing Pac-Man are learning to assimilate great amounts of information rapidly from a video screen. They are learning to manipulate the information on that screen at an intuitive level, using keyboards or joysticks. If technology can produce a video screen with about twice the resolution of today's video screens (it can be done now, but not at a very affordable cost), combined with electronic storage costs' continuing to come down rapidly (perhaps using a videodisc), it may not be all that farfetched to expect tomorrow's generation to bring their thin, high-resolution video screen with them onto the train or in front of the fireplace to read Tolstoi. And, conceivably, an oral generation may also absorb content from speech at a faster rate and with greater skill—or literacy—than we can reading words from a book and with equal enjoyment.

Such speculation (as opposed to prediction) should not obscure the robustness of older formats in the face of new ones. Audio records, then film, radio, and television have each been prospectively feared as threatening print. Yet each has survived and thrived, though sometimes having to fill somewhat different functions. General interest mass audiences magazines like *Look* and *Life* lost their national audiences to television, and as a result generally became largely a special interest medium. Books on the other hand have shown a remarkable resilience in the face of additional information and cultural formats. Indeed, new processes and formats frequently create new opportunities for the older ones. Television has spawned magazines like *TV Guide* and is widely credited with sparking interest in sports magazines and expanded newspaper sports pages. Theatrical and television films based on books have resulted in increased sales of those books. In some cases original scripts for films were later published as books. Examples range from *Star Wars* to *The Ascent of Man*. Computer magazines are thriving. And there are now books and magazines for video game enthusiasts.

There are few fears evoked today about the new information technology that were not previously heard during the Victorian era. Today the enemy of reading is television. But those who have faith in the habit of reading may take comfort in that the doom of reading has been falsely prophesized ever since the invention of the pneumatic tire (when the forecasters of the era believed the bicycle would put the whole family on wheels and thus spell the end of fireside reading).[15] On the other hand there is a certain face validity to the pessimism of Samuel Johnson, who could have had in mind Atari's Pac-Man when he wrote, "People in general do not willingly read if they can have anything else to amuse them."[16]

In the last analysis it is likely we are on the verge of yet another step in the evolution of literacy. Yet we can feel confident that whatever comes about will not replace existing skills, but supplement them. Neither the printing press nor the typewriter replaced either speech or handwriting. The electronic hand calculator has not replaced the need to understand mathematics (though it may reduce the need to memorize multiplication tables). The new literacy will likely involve a greater emphasis on the visual, but only as a continuation of a trend that has involved the improvement in photography, printing techniques, and television.

Above all, the new literacy, whatever it looks like, is not to be feared. First, it will come about regardless of what we think about it. Second, for any threat to some existing institution or relationship, the new literacy could be shown to provide some equal or greater opportunity. Finally, because change brought about in part by technology casts a long shadow, it takes place incrementally, and adjustments by society and individuals will evolve naturally.

We may be haunted, however, by how a 16-year-old reporter for the *Children's Express,* a newspaper published entirely by schoolchildren, characterized the Fourth Assembly of the World Future Society in July 1982, whose theme was the new world of telecommunications: "I think the message was clear that it's really our [young people's] world. I was kind of laughing at the people here. This technology, all they talked about, they really couldn't grasp. This belongs to us."[17]

## NOTES

1.    From *Horizon* magazine, about the importance of books in an era of mass communication. Quoted on the editorial page of *The Wall Street Journal,* February 6, 1982.

2.    Quoted in Alvin Toffler in *Future Shock* (New York: Random House, 1970), p. 144. Cornberg is identified as a communications systems designer.

3.    M.T. Clanchy, *From Memory to Written Record, England, 1066–1307* (Cambridge, Mass.: Harvard University Press, 1979), p. 56.

4.    Ibid., p. 88.

5.    Richard D. Altick, *The English Common Reader: A Social History of the Mass Reading Public, 1800–1900* (Chicago: University of Chicago Press, 1974), p. 368.

6.    Ibid., p. 231.

7.    Ibid., p. 233.

8.    Jack Egan, "Publishing for the Future," *New York,* August 16, 1982, p. 10.

9.    Benjamin M. Compaine, *A New Framework for the Media Arena: Resources Content, Process and Format* (Cambridge, Mass.: Program on Information Policy, Harvard University, 1980), pp. 6–17.

10.    Fred M. Hechinger, "About Eduction," *The New York Times,* December 15, 1982, p. C–5.

11.    *Videotex* (sometimes *videotext*) is a term being used to describe any service that provides text and graphics on a video screen in a "page" format. That is, each screenful of material is identified like a print page and can be viewed in its entirety by the user. Videotex (in a version sometimes called "viewdata") may be transmitted from a computer to the user by a telephone connection, by cable, or conceivably by other electronic transmission techniques. It is considered "interactive" because each user determines which "pages" should be sent by some type of controlling mechanism, such as a numerical keypad or a full typewriter-like keyboard. Videotex may also provide opportunity for ordering goods that are featured or advertised on the system, or even for certain financial functions, such as checking banking account balances or transferring funds. Teletext refers to systems that appear similar, but involve transmission of the video pages by cable or broadcasting in a continuous stream. The user has a numerical keypad to identify a particular page to view. The next time that page is transmitted (probably no longer than thirty seconds), it will be "grabbed" and held on the video screen until another page is requested. It is therefore not a truly interactive service, as the user never has access to the computer itself.

12.    "The Wired University is on the Way," *Busines Week,* April 26, 1982, p. 68.

13.    Clanchy, *From Memory to Written Record,* p. 2.

14.    Elizabeth L. Eisenstein, *The Printing Press as an Agent of Change,* (Cambridge, England: Cambridge University Press, 1979), p. 8.

15.    Altick, *The English Common Reader,* p. 374.

16.    Ibid., p. 373.

17.    "Time Tripping at a Convention of World Futurists," *The Boston Globe,* August 4, 1982, p. 55.

# 13 FINAL THOUGHTS

*Benjamin M. Compaine*

> "Would you tell me, please, which
> way I ought to go from here?" asked Alice.
> "That depends a good deal on where you
> want to get to," said the Cat.
> "I don't much care where," said Alice.
> "Then it doesn't matter much which way
> you go," said the Cat.
>
> —Lewis Carroll, *Alice's Adventures in Wonderland*

A few years ago, as the traditional media industry began to feel the presence of newer technologies, the prevailing attitude among both corporate and governmental policymakers may have been summed up in this hypothetical dialogue:

Chief executive officer (or commissioner or congressman): "We've got to do something."

Vice president for strategic planning (or bureau chief or top staff aide): "What should we do?"

CEO. (etc.): "I don't know, but we've got to do something."

Hence we saw a flurry in the early 1980s (much of which is continuing) of joint ventures, acquisitions, announcements of new services, experimental services, mergers, and a general flailing about. In the public sector a new piece of legislation seemed to be introduced every nine seconds, and the regulatory agencies at the federal level were deregulating or reregulating or holding hearings with such determination that even a related weekly newsletter, fearing that it was falling behind, started a daily newsletter.

The result of this blur of activity through 1983 has been, as might be expected, a mixed bag. Moreover, some of the apparently successful developments may have been flukes, while some of the failures may have come about despite solid analysis and careful planning. Yet it is likely that we have before us, at least for the remainder of this decade, if not longer, a period in which change and greater than usual uncertainty are likely to be the rule. This means that for policymakers in the traditional media industry, as well as in adjacent territories, threats, and opportunities will continue to present themselves, sometimes in surprising places. Perhaps the biggest unknown, especially for those who have been in the relatively protected print media business, is the extent to which their plans and expectations for new technology-driven ventures may be hostage to regulatory developments either out of their control or in which they are merely one interested party among many in the political process.

For example, providers of electronic information services that rely on the telephone network are dependent on the decisions of fifty state regulatory commissions for the rates that may eventually be charged for data transport by local telephone companies. Their ability to use cable systems as an alternative may be limited not only by the technical capabilities of the thousands of cable systems, but also by differing local regulations on rates and services offered by cable operators. It remains to be seen how crucial these factors will be. Magazine publishers, faced with the phasing out of postal subsidies for second class mail, found that they could indeed pass the additional cost to subscribers with little difficulty. Will that be the case for less-established media products?

In general the lessons of *Understanding New Media* may be categorized into three related slots: considerations for strategic planning, for marketing, and for regulation. Marketing may be a subset of strategic planning but is discussed here separately.

## STRATEGIC PLANNING CONSIDERATIONS

Managements have a tendency to respond in one of two ways to change. One is defensive. They seek foremost to protect their existing business. If they do move into new areas, it is often more with a sense of protecting their turf than with a true commitment to the new business. This strategy has its successes. Many newspaper publishers moved into radio and then television and more recently cable as defensive postures. In many cases this approach has turned out quite profitably.

The second basic strategy, not surprisingly, is to take the offensive. The forces seen as a threat to the defensive players are interpreted as opportunities by the offensive ones. From an outsider's perspective, for example, Ted Turner's initiatives in first making his local independent Atlanta station, WTBS, into the first television superstation for cable operators and then starting an all-news cable network are instances of recognizing opportunity.

To be sure, firms are most likely to be using an offensive strategy when they are moving into new territory. But we could ask why one of the existing television networks, with their strong news operations, did not initiate a cable news channel before Turner. Again as outsiders, we could speculate that they did not want to take any measures that would further the development of cable, which they have long seen as threatening to their dominance in television. Why didn't the motion picture studios move before Time Inc. to establish their own pay cable network for their films? Why have so few major newspaper publishers established a substantial interest in cable systems?

In developing a strategic plan, firms that are in or wish to enter media arena activities need to balance several sometimes contradictory considerations. These include questions such as the following:

1. What business are they in now and what business do they want to be in? A newspaper publisher could view itself as being a manufacturer, a publisher of printed products, a distribution service, an information compiler, and perhaps other self-descriptions. Viewing oneself as an information compiler may lead to making different strategic choices than as a publisher of printed products. On the other hand, having experience in creating, gathering, and processing content for a newspaper does not necessarily translate into the experi-

ence needed for performing similar functions for making video tapes for the home market. The two processes—print and video production—may be so dissimilar that simply saying both are part of the information business would lead to some ill-conceived decisions.

2. Which alternatives present a short-term window and which are ripe for long-term opportunities? There are times when an organization thinks it can take advantage of a venture that may have little long-term viability but can be started quickly and be profitable. Such ventures can be worthwhile if the payback period is short and the move is made knowing its limited lifespan. Time Inc. and some others thought that pay-television using UHF (ultra high frequency) or microwave television stations, could be a viable business in cities that did not yet have cable. Although the financial results seem to be mostly disappointing, the concept was appropriate. More recent plans of CBS and Microband Corporation to use multichannel microwave systems in large, noncabled cities employ a similar strategy. In the telephone business, a host of firms have taken advantage of what may be a brief anomaly in the tariff structure to lease lines wholesale from AT&T and resell use of them to business and residential customers at a discount from AT&T's own long-distance rates.

Long-term opportunities on the other hand tend to produce lower initial returns and require more substantial capital investment. This would include cable programming networks, direct broadcast satellite (DBS) systems, and cable systems. Firms interested in providing mass audience videotex and teletext systems have not only to create the physical system itself, but also to educate and develop the market for a service that has no familiar analogies (unlike DBS, for example, which can still be sold as a form of familiar television). Whether short-term windows or long-term development, the strategic decision is tied closely to the next consideration: rate of financial return.

3. What is the payback period, return on investment, or other appropriate measure of return on invested capital? This of course is a standard criterion for investment decisions. It is worth asking in the context of this discussion because of the uncertainty of the ultimate cost of so many of the investment opportunities. Videotex, for example, may indeed be a profitable business some time in the future. But how much should one be willing to invest today? How is the investor to predict, with any reliability, what the ultimate cost of getting into this business will be and when, if at all, it will provide a return better than other, less risky investment alternatives? Here the

lure of short-term, quick-payback ventures meets the challenge of long-term but capital-intensive development. Who would not like to get in now on the next Home Box Office–like success? But at what expense, uncertainty, and risk?

4. Who is the likely competition? As work with the information business map suggests, determining who the competition is or may be for any piece of turf is getting more difficult. Reliance on peripheral vision is of greater importance than ever. Was Sears an obvious candidate for competing in financial services? Did IBM ever expect to be upstaged in the personal computer business by start-ups such as Apple? And should Warner Communication's Atari have been able to anticipate a challenge from Coleco, a manufacturer of above-ground swimming pools? The newspaper industry was certainly surprised when AT&T suddenly loomed as a competitor for its lucrative classified advertising business. And bankers found that less-regulated money-market mutual funds and others were successful poachers in what they had long considered their own preserve for time deposits.

5. Is it necessary to be first in, or is there room for "me, too"? The difficulty that competitors have had in catching up with Time Inc.'s Home Box Office has apparently sent a message that in many areas there may only be room for one or a small number of players. Here it may be useful to distinguish the system-operating business from the content-providing business. Whether in television networks, pay cable networks, and perhaps in videotex networks, there may indeed be opportunity for only a handful of players. On the other hand all of these have a voracious appetite for "product," so there is plenty of opportunity for those who want to be in the content providing business. Whether the two or three players who operate the relevant systems can exercise oligopoly-like economic power to extract a disproportionate share of the revenue and profit is a topic for consideration as part of the planning process. Still, providers of content, by being able to sit back and wait for proven markets to develop, presumably face less risk.

6. Which technologies will win and which will lose? This is a question that is at the heart of the uncertainty of much strategic planning. Will DBS be able to make substantial inroads on cable? Will videotex be best delivered by cable systems or via telephone lines? Is the videodisc going to surpass cassettes? Is cable teletext better than videotex? Will electronic information services replace the newspaper, magazines, or books? In addressing this issue the stakes can be high. Betting

on a particular technology as a winner might be likened to betting on an "exacta" at the race track, where the wager, to collect, must pick the winner of several races. The odds are long, but the return, if successful, is great.

A different strategy is to be technology neutral. Information providers for data-base services can provide materials for systems that distribute by cable, telephone, or even over-the-air teletext. Filmmakers can distribute their material via any video outlet, including incompatible forms of videotape, such as Beta and VHS.

A third strategy is to help a particular technology develop by using its unique advantages. For example, the optical videodisc combined with a microprocessor has versatility that is not available with other video processes. Thus some firms are providing programming designed for this technology's specific strengths. One use is for fully animated video games, such as the initial venture of Cinematronics with "Dragon's Lair." Demonstrating this capability may in turn help the optical videodisc manufacturers sell more machines and further the success of that technology.

Yet another approach might be termed a "portfolio strategy." Here, planners invest in a variety of ventures that are based on different technologies or delivery mechanisms, perhaps aimed at different market segments.

## MARKETING CONSIDERATIONS

The questions that best summarize the dilemmas of those responsible for selling the products and services of the new media are not very different from the questions that should be asked for any offering. But when the products or services being offered are so new that there is little historical evidence or traditional market research to rely on, the answers—riddled with uncertainty in predicting market success even in the best circumstances—are softer than ever. The questions, then, are Who will want it? At what price? When?

Is there a market for videotex? For television programming delivered directly to the home via satellite? For cookbooks on floppy disks? For electronic banking? For a television channel devoted to macramé, health, science fiction movies, weather, high-brow music? For a financial data base? For a legal data base?

The "who" question encompasses not only intended users but also those who have been counted on to finance much consumer media—advertisers. Consumer media other than books have been largely paid for by advertiser dollars. If advertisers do not think they need the audience that would tune into a cable show for macramé lessons, that changes the chance of survival of such a service.

The price question seems to have been ignored by some of the creators of futurist scenarios and market predictors. Does the new service offer users value greater than that currently available, even if the existing methods are less than state-of-the-art? For example, what will three or six channels of television provide that would make it competitive with cable television in the same market at the same price or less?

Finally, "when" acknowledges that providers of new services and products have a timing problem. This is especially evident in areas where technological change comes quickly. In the case of home computers, improvements in performance and price were so rapid in 1982 and 1983 that the market moved much more quickly than most of the players expected, catching Texas Instruments and Atari, among others, in a crunch. In other cases we may see markets developing too slowly to generate the revenues players need to stay in the game.

The marketing equation in new media, then, requires the weighing of the price of the product (or service) with the substitutability of this product for existing products that impart similar information or function. For example, does the ability to check airplane schedules and prices, then make an airline reservation using a consumer videotex system, offer any advantage, in convenience or price, over picking up the telephone and having a travel agent make the arrangements? What would have to change to make the videotex approach attractive to the user?

The elements in this marketing equation can be analyzed in terms of the content, process, and format framework presented in Chapter 3. That is, in determining the market for a product or service, the potential supplier asks if this offering is providing content or substance that in itself is fundamentally new or different from that which is currently available. Wire service news stories delivered by a videotex system, for example, are essentially the same content as is provided in the print newspaper or read on many news broadcasts. Travel schedules, classified advertisements, or stock quotations would be a similar case of old content. Motion pictures, whether shown via cable television, videocassettes, videodiscs, DBS, or in theaters would also be a case of familiar content. Video games, on the other hand, are an example of new content (although the extent of their substance may be subject to debate).

In most cases the analysis will find that most new media are not yet providing new content. Rather, their presumed newness is in their process. Thus, users are being asked to pay for the value—convenience, timeliness, or other utility—of the manner or form in which the content is made available. The value of real-time stock quotations is low for the occasional investor, but high for a professional financial manager. First-run movies via pay-TV in the home (by whatever distribution mechanisms) may save families money over a trip to the theater or may just be more convenient. Thus the marketing strategy for process asks what groups will find value in providing content using a gathering, storing, or delivery mechanism that some newly developed technology makes feasible. The pitfall here is that often simpler, cheaper, or proven methods may be more attractive to consumers than the bells and whistles of high tech. For example, getting the latest weather via some electronic data-base service may be possible. But punching seven buttons on the telephone to reach a Time and Temperature service may be quicker, easier, cheaper, and just as effective.

Format is the third component for assessment. Format itself can help create a market for some processes. For example, for most of the short history of the computer, the primary form of output for on-line users was hard copy printers, usually teletype-like printers. These were relatively slow and cumbersome. Their use for functions such as text editing resulted in the need for procedures that restricted their use to a few specialists. It was the general adoption of video display terminals, a different format, that expanded the range of uses for on-line computer use. It is not likely that widespread word processing or personal computers would have come about were it not for marrying high-resolution VDTs to computers.

For the most part consumers buy a package of content and format. Process is of concern primarily to suppliers of information and services. For example, consumers have never been very aware or concerned about the development of cold type and offset presses and electronic editing systems adopted in the 1970s by newspaper and magazine publishers. These processes may help in selling a better product or one less expensive to produce, but it is not the process that the consumer buys. Similarly, given equivalent quality and price, telephone customers really do not care whether their call is switched electronically, if the call is routed over optical fiber or satellite lines instead of terrestrial modes.

## REGULATORY CONSIDERATIONS

Telephone companies have operated in a highly regulated environment for decades. Broadcasters have had fewer regulatory constraints, and the trend is to a lessening of what remains, especially in radio. The cable television industry has gone from being highly regulated at the federal level to having varying, mostly minor, regulation from state and local jurisdictions. The print segment, however, has traditionally faced only the barest forms of regulation, those that apply to all business in general. The financial community also exists under an umbrella of federal and state restrictions. Commercial banks claim to have been put at a disadvantage to nonbank financial institutions such as American Express.

With this mixed bag of regulation is the uncertainty of the shape of the regulatory future for telecommunications. For the immediate future it appears that there will be a lessening of regulation at the federal level. But fifty state regulatory commissions will likely be regulating local telephone operating companies as much as ever and perhaps more closely than ever. And as Robert Pepper noted in Chapter 6, as the cable television industry expands its horizon as an alternative carrier for local telephone transmission of data, we may expect to see more contention between cable and telephone interests at the state level. The hodge-podge of outcomes in the states may result in pressure for Congress to create a national policy. Who will benefit most from such legislation will likely depend on the currently unknown mood of the lawmakers some time in the future.

Thus the degree and manner of regulation must remain a concern and major source of risk. Creation of regulation is largely a political process; rulemaking or rate setting by agencies have substantial political components, especially at the state level. One senator, facing a constant procession of competing interests lobbying him for favorable treatment in legislation, reportedly claimed, "All everyone wants here is a fair advantage."[1]

Players in the media must therefore assess the degree to which their business plan depends on services from regulated industries or ventures that will require direct regulatory approval, oversight, or rate setting. Prognosticators of implementation of new media similarly need to factor in assumptions of what regulatory responses will be to specific developments. And regulators themselves will be called on to balance competing interests that could result in hindering or furthering the adoption of one piece of technology over another. One of the most complex problems involves the telephone network. On the one hand those who wish to provide electronic data services would benefit from a telephone network that utilizes digital rather than analog technology. They would benefit from a system that could routinely carry data at 5.600 or more bits per second (compared to the 300 to 1,200 bits per second that can be pumped over regular dial-up lines today). They would be better off with a system that offered cheap multiplexing services to households (so that a single telephone line could carry data without interfering with normal voice service).

However, instituting these upgrades has a cost. In some cases, facilities that have a depreciable life of up to forty years would have to be replaced sooner, resulting in huge bookkeeping write-downs. This in turn would require substantial increases in some or all telephone rates to maintain a reasonable rate of return to telephone companies. Political forces being what they are, this may not be popular among regulatory commissioners. Should the potential suppliers turn to cable or other technologies to get around telephone industry regulation, the telephone companies themselves may cry foul and exert their own pressure to bring these competing technologies into the regulatory fold (or argue to unleash themselves)—the "level playing field" argument.

The rate of adoption of many technologies may therefore depend on the following regulatory factors:

- The degree of stability of the regulatory regime. Deregulation at one level of government may trip greater regulation at another level. Areas of regulation below the federal level may result in a crazy quilt of differing state and local restrictions and opportunities.
- The assumptions made about the price of regulated services. As every business knows, price is not always a direct function of cost. In highly regulated industries, such as telephone, this is particularly true, as disputes continue as to what costs should be attributed to local calls and how much to long-distance service.

- The number and nature of alternatives to a particular technology. That is, if one avenue of distribution becomes too expensive or inaccessible or too constrained by regulation, are there other avenues? Examples include substituting cable or floppy disks for telephone, using DBS instead of terrestrial broadcasting, and so on.

- Finally, the pros and cons of entering regulated businesses directly, especially by those who have had little experience in this area. One of the information business maps in Chapter 2 showed IBM's activities overlayed with the FCC's jurisdiction. It appears that IBM carefully skirted involvement in businesses that would have directly involved it in telecommunications regulation. The decision is not a trivial one, as some newspaper firms found out when they plunged into the telecommunications waters with applications for cellular mobile telephone franchises, given out by the FCC starting in 1982, or when the Times Mirror Company ran into a lengthy legal cross-ownership dispute with the state of Connecticut over the company's ownership of both the newspaper and some cable systems in the Hartford area.

## IN THE LAST ANALYSIS

Whether the evolving media processes and formats are revolutionary or evolutionary, we are certainly in the midst of change. However, even when it seems to come rapidly, for those living through it the change happens incrementally. Futurists who paint pictures of how we will live at some future date do not leave us with the working drawings of how we will get from here to there. A Rip Van Winkle who falls asleep today and wakes up in twenty-five years may find some major differences in life. But when one lives minute by minute through those years, there may be far less future shock.

Consider for example the strides made in transportation in this century. Essentially, within the span of a human lifetime we went from Kitty Hawk to the Concorde. The time to cross the continent was cut from days to hours, to cross the oceans from weeks to hours. We think nothing of taking a day trip between Boston and Washington or Los Angeles and San Francisco. The impact of air travel—and of the automobile as well—has been profound and, in the context of history, quite rapid. Changes in transportation have had their social as well as economic impact. They have created new businesses and opportunities and eliminated others. And society has adjusted because the change in human terms came incrementally.

In general the pace of the adoption of innovation is inversely related to reliance on institutions. That is, stand-alone applications, such as hand-held calculators or personal computers, can move into the mainstream at a rate based on their merits. Services that require cooperation of major institutions—or for whom existing institutions can erect barriers to cause delay—require far more time to achieve widespread availability. The resistance of broadcasters to cable is an example of an institutional barrier. The reliance of electronic information providers on the technology and tariffs of the highly regulated local telephone industry is an example of the need for cooperation of parties (the telecommunications companies and their regulators) over which there may be little control by those who wish to offer the videotex service.

Despite the seeming acceleration in the rate of technological change these days, we would be well advised to recall Richard Rosenbloom's reminder, that technology does indeed cast a long shadow. For those who scan the horizon and remain aware of developments, there remains a substantial lead time between the creation of some new or improved technology and its commercial adoption. This means that industry has time to react without panic; that government need not respond immediately to every scenario of what "could happen," and that society as a whole will likely be able to determine, as well as ever, its direction without being stampeded by technological determinism.

## NOTE

1.    Attributed to the former senator from Washington, Warren Magnuson.

# APPENDIX A: PROGRAM ON INFORMATION RESOURCES POLICY

**Harvard University**          **Center for Information Policy Research**

## Contributors

Action for Children's Television
American Broadcasting Companies, Inc.
American District Telegraph Co.
American Telephone & Telegraph Co.
Arthur D. Little, Inc.
Auerbach Publishers Inc.
Automated Marketing Systems
Bell Telephone Company of Pennsylvania
The Boston Globe
Booz-Allen Hamilton
Canada Post
CBS Inc.
Channel Four Television Co. (Ltd.) (United Kingdom)
Citibank N.A.
Codex Corp.
Communications Workers of America
Computer & Communications Industry Assoc.
COMSAT
Continental Cablevision, Inc.
Continental Telephone Corp.
Coopers & Lybrand
Copley Newspapers
Cowles Media Co.
Cox Enterprises, Inc.

Des Moines Register and Tribune Co.
Dialog Information Services, Inc.
Digital Equipment Corp.
Direction Generale des Telecommunications (France)
Diversified Communications, Inc.
Doubleday, Inc.
Dow Jones & Co., Inc.
Drexel Burnham Lambert Inc.
Dun & Bradstreet
Economics and Technology, Inc.
Federal Reserve Bank of Boston
France Telecom (France)
Frost & Sullivan, Inc.
Gannett Co., Inc.
Gartner Group, Inc.
General Electric Co.
General Telephone & Electronics
Hallmark Cards, Inc.
Hambrecht & Quist
Harte-Hanks Communications, Inc.
Hazel Associates
Hitachi Research Institute (Japan)
Honeywell, Inc.
Hughes Communication Services, Inc.
E.F. Hutton and Co., Inc.
Illinois Bell
IBM Corp.

Information Gatekeepers, Inc.
International Data Corp.
International Resource Development,
  Inc.
Invoco AB Gunnar Bergvall (Sweden)
Irving Trust Co.
Knowledge Industry Publications, Inc.
Kokusai Denshin Denwa Co., Ltd.
  (Japan)
Lee Enterprises, Inc.
John and Mary R. Markle Foundation
MCI Telecommunications, Inc.
McKinsey & Co., Inc.
Mead Data Central
MITRE Corp.
Motorola, Inc.
National Association of Letter Carriers
NCR Corp.
National Telephone Cooperative Assoc.
New Jersey Bell
New York Times Co.
NEC Corp. (Japan)
Nippon Telegraph & Telephone Public
  Corp. (Japan)
Norfolk & Southern Corporation
Northern Telecom Ltd. (Canada)
Ohio Bell
The Overseas Telecommunications
  Commission (Australia)
Pearson Longman Ltd.
  (United Kingdom)
Pitney Bowes, Inc.
Public Agenda Foundation
Reader's Digest Association, Inc.
Research Institute of Telecommunica-
  tions and Economics (Japan)
St. Regis Paper Co.
Salomon Brothers
Satellite Business Systems

Scaife Family Charitable Trusts
Scott & Fetzer Co.
Seiden & de Cuevas, Inc.
Southern Pacific Communications Co.
Telecommunications Research
  Action Center (TRAC)
Time Inc.
Times Mirror Co.
Times Publishing Co.
United Parcel Service
United States Government:
  Central Intelligence Agency
  Department of Commerce:
    National Telecommunications and
      Information Administration
  Department of Defense:
    Office of the Under Secretary of
      Defense for Policy
  Department of Energy
  Federal Communications Com-
    mission
  Internal Revenue Service
  National Aeronautics and Space
    Admin.
  National Communications System
  National Security Agency
  United States Information Agency
  United States Postal Rate Com-
    mission
  United States Postal Service
U.S.-Japan Foundation
U.S. West
United Telecommunications, Inc.
Warner Amex Cable Communications
  Inc.
Warner Communications, Inc.
The Washington Post Co.
Western Union
Wolters Samson Group (Holland)

# APPENDIX B:
# DEFINITION OF TERMS

In this book, *information* is used in a broad sense, to include all types of media content, including segments commonly called news, advertising, entertainment, literature, propaganda, graphic design elements, data, bits. It does *not* include such highly subjective and even controversial conduits as body language or similar interpretive symbols.

The *mass media* includes the traditional products and conduits such as newspapers, magazines, books, periodicals, broadcasting, cable. These terms are used for convenience only and with some hesitation, since the point of much of the proposed research is to highlight the difference between, for example, the newspaper as a physical product and as a collection of information that can be distributed in formats other than ink on paper.

*Content* is the information provided by the supplier and received by the user. It is composed of words, paragraphs, photographs, graphics. *Process* includes conduits—the highways over which information travels—as well as the gathering, creation, and storage of information. *Format* is the form in which the information is handled as well as type of display of the content (on a video screen, on paper, as sound).

Among the terms that have appeared in the popular or professional literature to describe some of the newer processes, *videotex* is a

357

generic term for all the various processes that involve sending textual material for display on a video display screen, often the home television receiver. *Viewdata* has been used as a generic name for videotex that involves interaction between the user, who requests specific information, and a usually vast computer-stored data base, with transmission both ways generally coming over conventional voice-grade telephone lines through the switched telephone network. Some proprietary viewdata systems are Prestel in Great Britain; Viewtron, Knight-Ridder's version; Gateway, the system marketed by Times Mirror Company, and various Canadian services using their Telidon system. *Teletext*, on the other hand, is a videotex system that is transmitted in the vertical blanking interval within a conventional televised broadcast signal or using a full cable channel. In general, teletext offers less information capability than viewdata and tends to be one-way rather than interactive, although individual screenfuls of desired data can be "captured" when sent and stay on the screen as long as the user desires.

*Electronic data-base services* include videotex services. The latter tends to be used for services directed to residential users (although there is no reason that it must be so) and in many installations to date they rely on an operationally simple retrieval protocol involving a simple numeric keypad for the user and a tree-structure system that gets users to desired information by a process of elimination. More sophisticated services, used by institutions at first, allow the user to search data bases using key words typed on a full alphanumeric keyboard. Firms such as Source Telecomputing Company (subsidiary of Reader's Digest Association), CompuServe (subsidiary of H. and R. Block), and Dow Jones are marketing this type of data-base service to residential as well as institutional customers.

*Videocassette recorders* (VCRs) or videotape recorders (VTRs) became a consumer item in 1975 with the introduction of a ½-inch tape model from Sony. They can play prerecorded videotape through a conventional television set or record programs received by the set. *Videodisc players* today can play only prerecorded discs over the television set, but the discs are generally less expensive than identical taped prerecorded programs.

*Cable* refers to the use of coaxial cable to deliver broadband video programming to the television set. It can also be used for sending signals from the subscriber back to the origination point (called the "headend") of the cable operator. Initial cable installations carried twelve channels and mostly retransmitted broadcast signals. Newer systems are specifying as many as 108 channels and most carry special programming not available by broadcast. *Basic* cable service includes the channels subscribers get for the minimum monthly fee. *Pay-TV* refers to premium programming, often theatrical films, for which subscribers must pay an additional fee. Most systems charge a flat rate for premium service, but a few charge on a per-program watched basis. *Qube* is Warner-Amex Cable Communications' proprietary name for a two-way cable service that enables subscribers to respond to questions or other "action information" on certain channels.

*Subscription television* (STV) is essentially pay-TV sent usually over-the-air via a normal UHF signal. It is encoded so that it comes out scrambled when it is tuned in by anyone but subscribers who pay a monthly fee for a decoder.

*Multipoint distribution* services (MDS) is a low-power broadcast signal, using microwave frequencies. It is being used to a limited extent for pay-TV services. Here, the subscriber needs a special receiver.

The *switched telephone network* refers to the common telephone service that allows, through a series of switches (or equivalents using digital technology) for any telephone in the world to reach any other telephone.

*Direct broadcast satellite* (DBS) is a service that would permit individual homes (or apartment complexes, hotels), to receive broadcast signals directly from earth satellite orbiting 22,900 miles above the earth. Currently, these satellites are used to transmit signals from program originators to cable operators (or conceivably local broadcast stations), for retransmission to conventional antenna and receivers.

# SELECTED BIBLIOGRAPHY

Compaine, Benjamin M., et al. *Anatomy of the Communications Industry: Who Owns the Media?* White Plains, N.Y.: Knowledge Industry Publications, 1983.

Dizard, Wilson P., Jr. *The Coming Information Age: An Overview of Technology, Economics and Politics.* New York: Longman, 1982.

Ganley, Oswald H., and Gladys D. Ganley. *To Inform or To Control? The New Communications Networks.* New York: McGraw-Hill, 1982.

Haigh, Robert W., George Gerbner, and Richard B. Byrne, eds. *Communications in the Twenty-First Century.* New York: John Wiley and Sons, 1981.

Lewin, Leonard, ed. *Telecommunications in the U.S.: Trends and Policies.* Dedham, Mass.: Artech House, 1981.

Martin, James. *The Wired Society: A Challenge for Tomorrow.* Englewood Cliffs, N.J.: Prentice-Hall, 1978.

NAB Committee on Science and Technology. *New Technologies Affecting Radio and Television Broadcasting.* Washington, D.C.: National Association of Broadcasters, November 1981.

Neustadt, Richard M. *The Birth of Electronic Publishing: Legal and Economic Issues in Telephone, Cable, and Over-the-Air Teletext and Videotext.* White Plains, N.Y.: Knowledge Industry Publications, 1982.

Oettinger, Anthony, and Carol L. Weinhaus. *The Telecommunications Industry: An Eye to the Future.* Cambridge, Mass.: Program on Information Resources Policy, Harvard University, 1983.

Pool, Ithiel de Sola. *Forecasting the Telephone: A Retrospective Technology Assessment of the Telephone.* Norwood, N.J.: Ablex, 1983.

———. *Technologies of Freedom.* Cambridge, Mass.: Belknap Press of Harvard University Press, 1983.

Robinson, Glen O., ed. *Communications for Tomorrow: Policy Perspectives for the 1980s.* New York: Praeger Publishers, 1978.

Sigel, Efrem, et al. "The Future of Videotext." In *Worldwide Prospects or Home/Office Electronic Information Services.* White Plains, N.Y.: Knowledge Industry Publications, 1983.

Smith, Anthony. *Goodbye Gutenberg: The Newspaper Revolution of the 1980s.* New York: Oxford University Press, 1980.

Tydeman, J., et al. *Teletext and Videotex in the United States. Market Potential, Technology, Public Policy Issues.* New York: McGraw-Hill, 1982.

U.S. Congress. House. Subcommittee on Telecommunications, Consumer Protection, and Finance, of the Committee on Energy and Commerce. *Hearings on the Status of Competition and Deregulation in the Telecommunications Industry.* Serial no. 97–29, 97th Cong., 1st sess., May 20, 27, and 28, 1981.

# INDEX

# ABOUT THE EDITOR

Benjamin M. Compaine, executive director at the Program on Information Resources Policy, specializes in issues of concern to the media industry. Prior to joining the Program, he directed economic and marketing studies of mass media industries and library automation and technology at Knowledge Industry Publications. He has taught marketing, management, and journalism; has been a consultant; and has published, edited, or managed several newspapers. Among his other publications are: *Who Owns the Media: Concentration of Ownership in the Mass Communications Industry* (2nd ed., 1982), *The Business of Consumer Magazines* (1982), *The Newspaper Industry in the 1980's: An Assessment of Economics and Technology* (1980), and *The Book Industry in Transition* (1978). He is also co-author of a textbook, *Business: An Introduction* (1984). A graduate of Dickinson College, he received an M.B.A. degree from Harvard and a Ph.D. from Temple University.

# ABOUT THE
# CONTRIBUTORS

Robert Pepper is a communications policy analyst with the National Telecommunications and Information Administration, U.S. Department of Commerce, and with the National Science Foundation. He wrote *Competition in Local Distribution: The Cable Television Industry* at the Program on Information Resources Policy while on leave from the University of Iowa where he is an associate professor of communication. He has written widely on cable television and broadcast policy issues and has served as a consultant and advisor on cable communication to industry, state, government, cities, universities, and advertising agencies.

John F. McLaughlin, executive director, Program on Information Resources Policy, brings sixteen years of federal government experience to his work in the postal; command, control, and intelligence; and national security arenas. He has served with the Federal Aviation Agency's Research and Development Service and then with the U.S. Post Office Department and Postal Service headquarters. He founded and directed the Postal Service's Office of Strategic Planning. He is the primary author of *Necessity for Change* (USPS Staff Study) and *Telephone Letter Mail Competition*.

John C. LeGates, managing director, Program on Information Resources Policy, directs research on the effects of information on organizations and institutions. Previously, as executive director of the Educational Information Network at EDUCOM, he directed the development of nationwide computer communications networks. As vice president of Cambridge Information Systems, Inc., he was project director for the Massachusetts General Hospital Integrated Information System. He was in charge of exploring the use of computers in education at Bolt, Beranek, and Newman, Inc.

William H. Read, a former fellow of the Harvard Program on Information Resources Policy, is communications counsel in the Bureau of Programs, U.S. Information Agency. His previously published works include *America's Mass Media Merchants,* a study of multinational media.

Richard Selig Rosenbloom, the David Sarnoff Professor of Business Administration at Harvard Business School, is director of the Business School's doctoral program and an authority on the management implications of social and technological change. He is the author of several books and essays on technology transfer and information flow, including *Technology and Information Transfer* (1970).

Christine D. Urban is president of Urban and Associates, a firm that specializes in market research and consulting for newspapers and other media companies. She also conducts seminars for such groups as the American Press Institute and the American Newspaper Publishers Association. Among her articles and papers are "Life-Style Analysis for the Evaluation of Newspaper Audiences" and "A Cross-National Comparison of Consumer Media Use Patterns." Before starting her consulting firm, she was an assistant professor in the marketing area at Harvard Business School.